FROM ROCHESTER TO WINCHESTER

The Regimental History
of the
22nd New York Cavalry

1864-1865

Michael G. Burns

HERITAGE BOOKS
2007

HERITAGE BOOKS
AN IMPRINT OF HERITAGE BOOKS, INC.

Books, CDs, and more—Worldwide

For our listing of thousands of titles see our website
at
www.HeritageBooks.com

Published 2007 by
HERITAGE BOOKS, INC.
Publishing Division
65 East Main Street
Westminster, Maryland 21157-5026

Copyright © 2000 Michael G. Burns

All rights reserved. No part of this book may be reproduced or transmitted in any form or by any means, electronic or mechanical, including photocopying, recording or by any information storage and retrieval system without written permission from the author, except for the inclusion of brief quotations in a review.

International Standard Book Number: 978-1-58549-586-7

TABLE OF CONTENTS

Introduction..i

Chapter 1. Recruiting the Regiment......................................1

Chapter 2. Organization of the Regiment............................3

Chapter 3. On to the Wilderness..5

Chapter 4. The Wilson Railroad Raid...................................9

Chapter 5. Rebuilding the Regiment...................................13

Chapter 6. The Shenandoah Valley Campaign..................15

Chapter 7. The Battle of Waynesboro.................................21

Chapter 8. The Regiment is Dismissed...............................25

Chapter 9. The Fate of Colonel Crooks..............................29

Appendix A. Regimental Casualties....................................31

Appendix B. The Diary of Seth M. Hall.............................35

Appendix C. Medals of Honor..41

Appendix D. Register of Officers and Enlisted Men........43

Appendix E. My Civil War Ancestor................................222

Endnotes...223

Index...227

Sgt. Romaine B. Hart, Co. H, 22nd N.Y. Cavalry
[Chris Jordan Collection, U.S. Army Military History Institute]

Introduction

Rochester, New York, February 1864. A new regiment of cavalry was being formed to fight the Rebel forces and help restore the Union. An eighteen year old boy named James Herald, my great grandfather, like so many other young men, eagerly signed up for service. Some joined because they were eager to fight; others for the bounty money. Many signed up, but deserted long before the regiment left the state. Politics and egos nearly destroyed the morale of the regiment before it was organized. The incompetence of several different commanders nearly led to disaster on more than one occasion. But finally, when George Armstrong Custer took command of the 3rd Cavalry Division, the true bravery and ability of the men shone through.

All the exploits of these men came to light only after my wife, Cindy, a genealogical researcher, discovered that my ancestor was a part of this regiment. Her find promoted my casual interest in the Civil War into a thirst for knowledge about these men and where they served. To my dismay, I quickly learned that this regiment, like so many regiments that were formed later in the war, when interest and fanfare were beginning to wane, had no compiled information regarding them published. I found that even the city where the regiment was formed, Rochester, New York, had little information of the exploits of these men.

I felt a great disservice was being done to this regiment, who as green troops, were to serve in their first engagement at the Battle of the Wilderness. Great many of the soldiers in this regiment would be captured, including James Herald, at Stony Creek, Virginia, during the Wilson railroad raids. Finally, they served with distinction and valor at the battles of Waynesboro, Virginia and Cedar Creek, Virginia. I felt obligated to the memory of my Great Grandfather, as well as to the other brave men of the regiment, to tell their story.

Pvt. Henry C. Noble, Co. M, 22nd N.Y. Cavalry
[Div. Military-Naval Affairs, N.Y. State Adjt. Gen. Office, Albany, N.Y.]

Chapter 1

Recruiting the Regiment[1]

On September 24, 1863, Colonel Samuel Crooks was authorized to form a regiment of cavalry. This regiment was organized in Rochester for a service of three years. The companies were recruited principally as follows:

> Company A: Rochester, Penn Yan, Perrington, Penfield and Jerusalem. Mustered into service December 20, 1863.
>
> Company B: Syracuse, Rochester and Utica. Mustered into service January 5, 1864.
>
> Company C: Brockport, Riga, Rome, Churchville, Sweden and Rochester. Mustered into service January 5, 1864.
>
> Company D: Rochester, Lyons, Cuba and Lindon. Mustered into service January 10, 1864.
>
> Company E: Cazenovia, Madison, Manilius, Syracuse and Smithfield. Mustered into service January 10, 1864.
>
> Company F: Rochester, Albion, Barre and Dunkirk. Mustered into service January 10, 1864.
>
> Company G: Bath, Avon, Urbana, Plattsburgh and Rochester. Mustered into service February 2, 1864.
>
> Company H: Syracuse, Arcadia, Sodus, Huron, Lyons and Palmyra. Mustered into service February 2, 1864.
>
> Company I: Rochester, Auburn, Syracuse and Seneca Falls. Mustered into service February 2, 1864.
>
> Company K: Rochester, Portland, Pomfret, Lenox, Smithfield and Dunkirk. Mustered into service February 6, 1864.
>
> Company L: Plymouth, Norwich, Otsego, Oxford, Middlefield, Greene, Unadilla, and German. Mustered into service February 12, 1863.
>
> Company M: Rochester, Oneida, Bath, Auburn and Utica. Mustered into service February 23, 1864.

2nd Lt. Henry P. Starr, Co. K, 22nd N.Y. Cavalry
[Martin Schoenfield Collection, U.S. Army Military History Institute]

The Colors of the 22nd New York Cavalry

The colors of the 22nd New York Cavalry consists of a red silk banner mounted on a staff with a spearhead and tassels. Embroidered upon the banner appear crossed sabers with the inscription, "22nd Cavalry New York Vols." On the staff, on an engraved plate is the inscription, "presented to the 22nd N.Y.C. by Mrs. H.B. Reed Feb. 22, 1865."

HEADQUARTERS STATE NEW YORK.
Adjutant General's Office.
Albany Sept 24th 1863

Special Orders
No. 707

(Copy)

In accordance with a communication from the Provost Marshal General dated Washington September 16th 1863, a Regiment of Volunteer Cavalry is hereby authorized to be raised in this State to be known as the 22nd Regiment of Cavalry New York State Volunteers to serve in the Army of the United States for three years unless sooner discharged.

Samuel J. Crooks is hereby appointed Colonel of this Regiment who will establish his Head-Quarters at the City of Rochester in the County of Monroe and proceed in its organization in conformity with the provisions of General Orders No. 110 War Department, current series, and such orders as have been or may be issued from this Office governing the recruiting service.

Forty (40) days will be allowed for the organization of this Regiment and if not completed in that time will be liable to be consolidated.

By order of the Commander-in-Chief
(Signed) John T. Sprague
Adjutant General

Albany October 26th 1863.
A true copy
J. B. Stonehouse
Assistant Adjutant General

Chapter 2

Organization of the Regiment

In September 1863, Colonel Samuel J. Crooks, formerly of the 8th New York Cavalry was authorized to raise a new cavalry regiment in the state of New York. Colonel Crooks promised the recruits that the new regiment would not be treated like the 8th was by the government, being left for months without horses and suitable equipment for the service. The designation of the new regiment would be the 22nd New York Cavalry.[1]

On October 7, 1863, a meeting presided over by Rochester Mayor Bradstreet was held, designed to promote interest in the new regiment. The Mayor made an address appealing to the patriotism of the people of Rochester and Monroe County to assist in the work of adding a new regiment to the army to aid in the Union cause. Colonel Crooks addressed the meeting, stating what he had designed to do and he assured the attendees that his new regiment would perform as well as the 8th New York, which was conceded to be one of the best in the army. The meeting resolved that Colonel Crooks would receive Rochester and Monroe County's united support in his efforts.[2]

In November of 1863, as recruitment continued, Colonel Crooks obtained possession of the Monroe County Fair Grounds for rendezvous of his regiment. The camp became known as Camp Crooks. Not a better place could have been selected for this purpose, with the men, both officers and privates being provided with very comfortable quarters. Things were going well for the regiment. Recruitment was filling relatively quickly and good officers were being assigned to fill companies. However, in February of 1864 problems began to emerge. Orders came down to Colonel Crooks to organize the regiment and prepare to leave for Washington. However, days turned into weeks and the regiment did not leave. Speculation surfaced that the regiment was destined for Texas, but these rumors proved false. As time passed and the men saw no action, they started to desert the regiment.[3]

By March, problems of command emerged out of a bad state of feelings among some of the field officers. Colonel Crooks had not yet been mustered and had no real authority to command the regiment. Lieutenant Colonel Johnson B. Brown who had been mustered was the senior officer and wanted to assume command. Morale and discipline in the camp was non-existent as every man did as he pleased. Subsequently an order came down that only a portion of the companies be sent away, which was designed to prevent Colonel Crooks from taking command as he could not be mustered until the regiment was full. This order made Colonel Crooks indignant. He assigned command of the camp to Major Peter McLennan, then disappeared. However, Lieutenant Colonel Brown did not recognize the right of an inferior officer to assume command over him. This caused a question of jurisdiction to arise, which further demoralized the troops.[4] An order then came from the U.S. Mustering and Disbursing Officer, that Colonel Crooks would not be mustered in and that Lieutenant Colonel Brown should take command and prepare to get under way. Major McLennan yielded command and the regiment prepared to move out.

Almost a week passed and the regiment was still camped at the fair grounds, and again disputes abounded over who was in command, Crooks or Brown.

3

Finally Governor Seymour decided that when a man has the ability to get a regiment together, he ought to be permitted to take that regiment to Washington. If the authorities there believed he was not competent to command, then they could easily remove him.[5] Colonel Crooks assumed command of the regiment.

Sunday morning, March 6, 1864, the 22nd New York Cavalry, accompanied by a marching band, marched from their camp at the Monroe County Fair Grounds to the Genesee Valley railroad depot. There were 12 companies numbering about 800 men.[6] The soldiers boarded the emigrant train cars about 11 o'clock a.m. and headed for Elmira, New York, singing and shouting and in fact making all the noise they possibly could. They arrived in Elmira, that evening and changed cars, and what a change it was. They were moved from the elegant emigrant cars, to freight and cattle cars, which they traveled in until they arrived in Baltimore, Maryland on March 8th. The next day they arrived in Washington, D.C. and were marched to Capitol Hill where the regiment remained in camp until March 12th when they broke camp and moved to the cavalry depot at Giesboro Point, D.C.[7]

Camp life consisted of reveille at 5 a.m. when every soldier answered roll call in full uniform. At 6 a.m., breakfast, 7 a.m. police call, 9 to noon, company drill, then dinner. From 2 to 4, more drill, and at 5 p.m., dress parade. At 6 p.m. supper was served. Last roll call was at 8 p.m., then fifteen minutes later was lights out. This monotony was not to change until about the 29th of March, when two transports loaded with horses arrived. The officers selected their horses first as to rank, followed by the non-commissioned officers. The enlisted men were obliged to select their mounts according to how their names appeared on the company roll. Those with names starting with A, B and C, had first choice, while those beginning with U, W and Y had to take the last of the lot. Those men, who were disappointed with their mount, would try to trade, hoping that they could better themselves. Some perhaps did, while others found they wished they had kept their first choice.[8] There were reports that the mounts assigned to the regiment were an awful lot. Some horses were lame, saddle sore and full of vermin. Poor horses, however, would prove to be the least of the regiment's problems.

On April 24, 1864, Major General Henry Halleck pronounced the 22nd New York Cavalry undisciplined and unfit for the field and ordered the regiment dismounted and armed as infantry. This order much depressed the men of the regiment, but Colonel Crooks went to the War Office and got the order countermanded. Major General Ambrose Burnside, decreed that while the 22nd New York was attached to the 9th Corps, they could to keep their horses. He then ordered the regiment to proceed directly to Fairfax Court House with five days rations and 150 rounds of ammunition for each man. This however, was not the last problem the 22nd would face over keeping their mounts.[9]

Chapter 3

On to the Wilderness

On April 29th, the regiment broke camp at Giesboro Point and headed out to join the Grand Army of the Potomac.[1] In early May, however, the controversy continued on whether the horses of the 22nd would better serve a veteran cavalry unit. Halleck pressed Grant to order General Burnside to dismount the 22nd. However, Grant did not give a peremptory order for dismounting the regiment.[2] Burnside was satisfied that General Meade would make better use of the horses, but fear of being short of cavalry eventually lead to the decision to keep the regiment mounted, and they were assigned to the 4th Division.[3]

The 22nd New York made Fairfax Court House on the evening of May 3rd, with rumors that the Rebels were in their immediate front. The rumors succeeded in making some of the members of the regiment a little nervous, but they kept to their saddles while they formed a line of battle. The rumors proved to be unfounded as they soon learned that no Rebels had been seen there in quite some time. The regiment then proceeded through Warrenton Junction, then over a portion of the Bull Run battlefield.

The morning of May 4th, the regiment broke camp and started down the Warrenton Pike towards Brandy Station and once again rumors abounded that Rebs were in their front. About noon they reached the station, but again, no Rebels were found. Instead they found forage for the horses and stores of rations for the men. After the rations were issued to the regiment, a detail was assembled to remain at the station until the command was away, and then ordered to burn the remaining stores and anything else that could be used by the enemy. About 2 p.m. the regiment left Brandy Station headed toward Germanna Ford, and after a short time, looking back to the rear, the thick black rising smoke from the direction of the station indicated that the details mission was accomplished. At 5 p.m. that night, the regiment crossed the Rapidan River at Germanna Ford and entered a thick, dense forest, which was so difficult to traverse, the regiment had to march in double file. Soon the regiment made camp, while hearing the distinct firings of a nearby battle.

Early morning brought the order to mount-up and once more the 22nd New York Cavalry was riding toward the Confederate lines and the battle of the Wilderness. The regiment left the woods and came out on a broad sandy road. Off in the distance appeared a large swiftly moving white cloud. It was the army wagon train of General Burnside's Ninth Corps, which had crossed the Rapidan at Ely's Ford. The infantry of the Fourth Division guarded the wagon train. After a short march, the regiment went into camp. Cannons could be heard in the distance, signifying that the Union Army had finally found the Army of Northern Virginia. The Battle of the Wilderness had begun.

Orders were given for every man to prepare for battle and be ready to march at daybreak. At dawn, accompanied by the booming sound of artillery, the regiment took to the march. Following volley after volley of cannon, they went on and on, until 11 a.m. when they halted in an orchard under the brow of a hill. Over this hill was a section of woods assumed to be controlled by Confederate troops. The 22nd, then joined by the 3rd New Jersey Cavalry, set up pickets and proceeded to build small fires for coffee and preparing the noon time meal. While quietly preparing their meals, shots rang out, and bullets came whizzing over their heads smashing into the trees behind them. Shortly after, the pickets began running back towards the camp shouting, "The Rebs are coming!" The order was given to mount-up and a line of battle was formed. Colonel Crooks sent dispatches to Major General John Sedgwick, reporting that he believed there were enemy cavalry pickets on the plank road at Ely's Ford. Meanwhile, the Rebels of Ewell's Corps, charged the Yankee line, met by volley after volley of carbine from the 22nd, but soon the order was given for the New York regiment to fall back. They fell back with a vengeance. Disorder and confusion reigned! Each man tried to beat the other to the cover of the trees. Down the plank road they stampeded, chased by the screech of artillery shells, which the Rebels were pouring down on the terrified Union column as they retreated. The dust was so thick it made visibility impossible. A short distance into the woods, a retreating horse and rider went down and over him many more horses and riders fell, causing a serious blockade. Fortunately, because of the denseness of the woods, the shells of the enemy fell harmless, and the victims of the pile up were able to recover, re-organize, and work their way into back into the union lines.[4]

    This inept performance did not set well with the command of the Army of the Potomac. General Meade, believed that Colonel Crooks overreacted to the situation and reported false information in relation to the enemy. Reports from Colonel George Chapman's brigade disputed Crook's claims, Chapman's men finding no enemy in that area. Meade placed Colonel Crooks under arrest and ordered him to turn over command of the 22nd New York to the next ranking officer, which was Major Peter McLennan. Major McLennan was to report to Colonel Hammond commander of the 5th New York Cavalry for orders.[5]

    On May 8, 1864, the regiment was ordered to report to the Second Corps of the Army of the Potomac, under the command of General Winfield Scott Hancock. They were assigned as rear guard to the 2nd Corps on its march south on the Rockville road. About three miles south of Fredericksburg, the enemy using trees and entrenchment's as cover fired upon the regiment. Major McLennan, dismounted a portion of the command and deployed them in front of the entrenchments as skirmishers, while the rest of the regiment continued to cover the rear of the column. The Rochester troopers were then ordered forward, but for some unexplained reason several companies did not follow. Scouting parties were sent out, 6 men the first time, then 10 more additional. The searchers returned and reported that they could not locate the lost companies. The search was soon abandoned, as Major McLennan assumed that the lost companies had taken some other path back into the Union lines. McLennan moved the remainder his men forward to Todd's Tavern to await further orders from General Hancock.

    The result of these two days marching and skirmishing, was a reported loss of 3 men killed, 8 wounded, one officer missing, one officer captured and 97 men missing. The regiment also had 27 horses killed and 4 more dead due to fatigue and lack of food, and reported 241 mounts missing.

    Hancock, who was extremely unhappy with the new commander of the 22nd New York, later reporting that he "appeared stupid." He ordered McLennan to join the remainder of his command who were serving as escorts for the ambulance train from Piney Branch Church to Fredericksburg, Va. Details of the regiment were stationed as pickets on every road leading into Fredericksburg. For a dreary 19 days, among the moans and groans of the wounded and dying brought there from the

Wilderness battlefield, the 22nd served as escorts of every supply train and ambulance from Fredericksburg to Belle Plain, and as defenders of the town from the threat of Rebel guerrillas.[6]

On May 29, the 22nd New York was assigned to the 2nd Brigade, 3rd Division of the Cavalry Corps, under the command of Colonel George H. Chapman. The other regiments in the Brigade were the 3rd Indiana, 1st New Hampshire, 8th New York and 1st Vermont. The Brigade marched to Totopotomy, Va., where they once again encountered the Confederate army. On June 3rd, the regiment moved to White House Landing, then on to Hanover Court House, where they were held in reserve line of battle, listening to shot and shell as they passed over. On the 6th of June, the 22nd New York was camped near Bottom's Bridge near the Chickahomony then ordered to advance the lines the following evening. On the 12th of June, they reached the Chickahominy River at Long Bridge, Virginia. Colonel Chapman expected to find a bridge ready for them to cross. What he found however, was the officer in charge of the pontoons too incompetent for the task. Colonel Chapman was compelled to take matters into his own hands. He dismounted the 22nd New York along with the 3rd Indiana, then had the New York boys wade the stream by means of fallen trees and overhanging limbs. After much difficulty, they finally succeeded in pushing their way across. The 3rd Indiana then launched a pontoon and pushed their way across the river under heavy fire from the Rebels who were posted in pits on the opposing bank. The Indiana troopers charged the Rebel line, driving the enemy from the rifle pits. The 22nd joined in the charge after working their way out of the swamp. The Union troopers skirmished with the enemy all night long. General James H. Wilson, the commander on the 3rd Division Cavalry Corps, impressed by the courage of the troopers, complimented the units by reporting, "Nothing could have been more steady and dashing than the conduct of these two regiments."[7]

On the 13th of June the 22nd New York was held in support of an artillery battery at White Oak Swamp on the Chickahominy, while the rest of the brigade skirmished with a brigade of Rebel cavalry. At 2 p.m. the regiment was ordered to take the front of the brigade. They crossed the river, a great part of the regiment swimming their horses, while the others crossed by pontoon bridge. They had barely made it to shore, when the enemy, from the cover of heavy brush, opened fire. The New York boys rallied and formed a line of battle. They skirmished, at times hot and heavy for almost 5 hours. At dusk, the enemy troops advanced from the cover of the trees in an ominous line of infantry. The Rebel advance forced the right of the Union line to give way. The left of the line soon followed in good order. At about 11 p.m., Chapman was directed to withdraw and proceed down the Charles Court-House road in the direction of Saint Mary's Church, and ordered to place pickets on the road to White Oak Swamp. They arrived at Nancy's Shop' near the church at 2 a.m. and bivouacked. At first light on the 14th, the regiment moved out, continuing the march to the Westover Church where they received supplies. That afternoon, Rebel cavalry troops attacked the pickets, stationed on the road but the New York boys rallied and drove off the gray clad invaders.[8]

The men of the 22nd were sent in to relieve the 3rd New Jersey Cavalry after their lines gave way and were forced to fall back. The regiment passed through the lines of the 3rd New Jersey and formed a line of battle. The enemy did not engage the regiment to any great extent and soon fell back. The 22nd then continued to advance the line, skirmishing for several days at Malvern Hill until they reached the James River. On the 15th, while performing reconnaissance duty with the 1st Vermont near Malvern Hill, they encountered the Rebels in several skirmishes. The 16th of June, they moved by way of Charles City Court House to the James River and encamped until morning. They crossed the James at Jone's Landing over pontoon bridges on the 17th of June, and camped near Prince George Court House. On the 18th of June the 22nd New York was in camp at Mount Zion Church, where they enjoyed a well-deserved 3 days rest before heading out on that historic 7 days journey known as the Wilson Raid.[9]

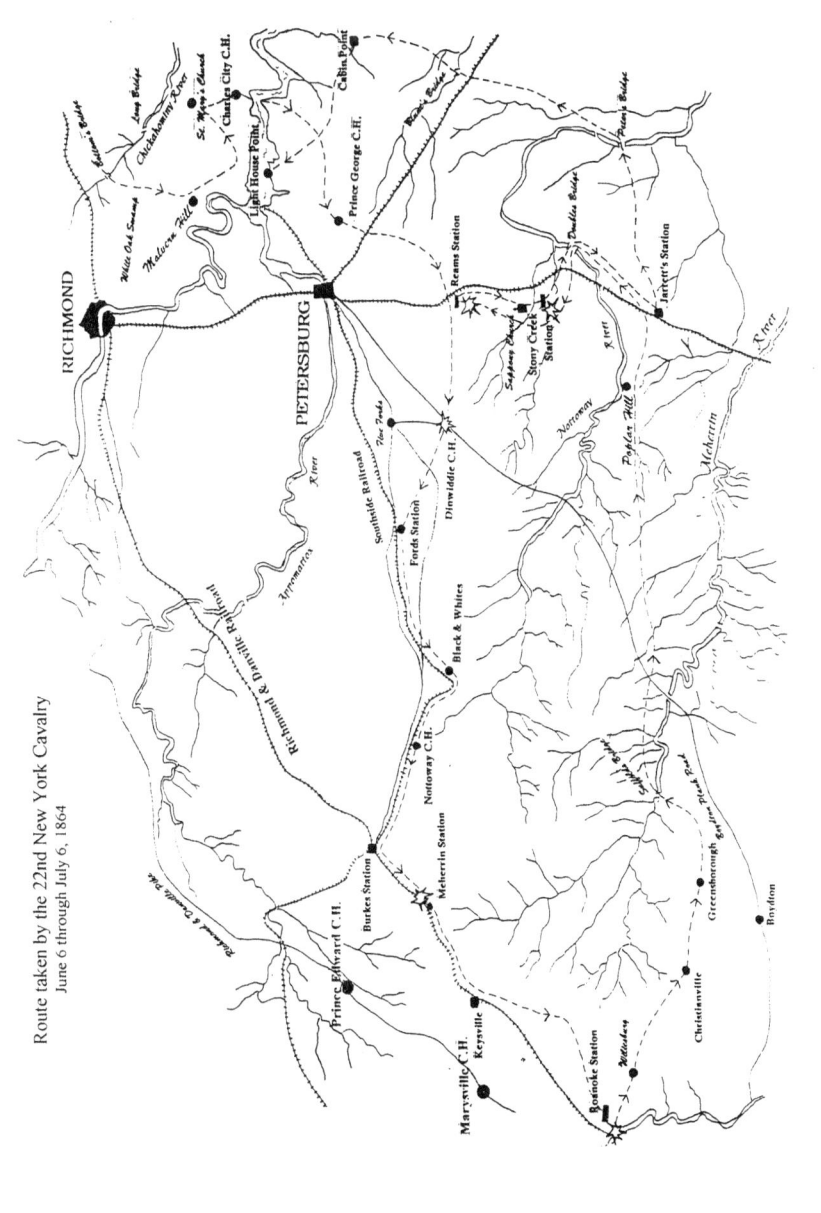

Route taken by the 22nd New York Cavalry
June 6 through July 6, 1864

POSITION NEAR REAMS' STATION, JUNE 29, 1864

Chapter 4

The Wilson Railroad Raid

General Grant was in the midst of planning an operation designed to disrupt the trains supplying Petersburg. His hope was that in the Federal cavalry could destroy enough railroad track, the Confederates would be forced to abandon Petersburg and head west in search of food and supplies. Of the 4 rail lines that entered Petersburg, the Rebels controlled two, the Weldon and the Southside. General Grant decided that a cavalry strike on these lines would be a feasible and desirable operation.

On June 20th, he organized his plans for the raid, and assigned the mission to the 3d Division of the Cavalry Corps. The burden of command rested on 27-year-old Brigadier General James Harrison Wilson. Wilson requested two days to rest and refit his regiments. On the 22nd of June at 2 a.m. the bugle sounded, and before dawn the Division was mounted up with 5000 troopers and headed out on its fateful mission.[1]

The 2nd Brigade broke camp, and was assigned to the rear of the column. They reached the Weldon Railroad at Reams Station, 10 miles south of Petersburg by midmorning, without any opposition. The soldiers stopped briefly to tear up several hundred yards of track and burn the railroad depot and water tank. As they pushed on from this point toward the Southside Railroad however, the enemy cavalry division of William Henry Fitzhugh Lee, son of Robert E. Lee, followed the rear of the column and continually skirmishing with the Federals until a few of hours after sundown. The 22nd was ordered to relieve an exhausted 1st Vermont who was covering the columns rear. The Vermont troops retired back through the Federal line with the enemy in hot pursuit. The Rebels were met with volley of carbine, which checked their advance. The New Yorkers held their position for about an hour but without support and with their ammunition supplies running low they withdrew and followed the main column, still protecting the rear. While passing through a dense forest, the Rebels made another attack, driving back the Federal horsemen. Major McLennan was ordered to retreat. When the enemy heard the command, they let out a cheer and charged the Union troops. The Confederates continued to press McLennan's men until they were halted by the soldiers of the 3rd Division. The regiment then was allowed to withdraw and join the main column. The regiment bivouacked that night, near Ford's Station on the Southside Railroad.[2]

The following morning the brigade moved out before daylight and followed the railroad, detaching regiments at different points to tear up track. Using railroad ties, they built fires and heated the rails red-hot, twisting the rails out of shape and rendering them useless. They continued this process until they arrived at Black and White Station, where the column halted for about an hour. The raiders located a store of 150 bales of cotton, which they destroyed before resuming the march. The head of the column reached a point near Nottoway Court House, where they came in contact with the Confederate cavalry. It was soon discovered that the enemy engaged, was the same force of Rebels that had harassed the rear of the column the previous day. The four squads of the 22nd New York regiment were placed on each side of the road. The troopers had barely taken position when the enemy forces made a charge. When the Confederates were in easy carbine range, the

New York boys opened fire, which halted the onset of the gray troops. The Rebel advance was checked for a time, but soon they were able to bring up reinforcements. The Union regiments were forced to fall back to their original positions along the railroad and they held strong, in spite of numerous efforts of the enemy to dislodge them. They remained in line of battle until near dawn, then quietly withdrew and proceeded along the Hungarytown road toward the Meherrin Station on the Danville Railroad, with Rebel forces in dogged pursuit. They then moved on to Keysville where they set-up camp for the night.[3]

    Early in the morning of the 25th of June, the brigade was once again on the march, still assigned to the rear of the column. They slowly moved along the Danville road, assigning several details for the purpose of destroying the rails. Troopers complained that they had no time to do the job right, with Lee's cavalry skirmishing at their rear. They could simply overturn the rails and ties, which could be done quickly, but would prove not to be a permanent form of destruction.[4] The brigade continued their assault on the rails until the enemy once again assaulted the rear of the column, near the crossing of the Little Roanoke River. Only light skirmishing occurred, with the Rebels contented with long-range artillery barrages. The Union forces held their positions until 2 a.m. on the 26th, when Chapman's troops re-assembled and headed along the railroad to Roanoke Station. A superior force of the Rebel army at their front interrupted the march. The Federal troops were forced to backtrack, and at this point the direction of the march changed. General Wilson led the division eastward back towards Petersburg over wild and unbroken terrain, through Christianville and Greensborough, finally making camp at Buckhorn Creek.

    On the 27th of June, the brigade, now leading the advance of the column, crossed the Meherrin River at Saffolds Bridge and proceeded across the countryside to the Boydton plank road. They bivouacked for the night on Great Creek. Early on the morning of the 28th, they arrived at the Doubles Bridge and crossed over the Nottoway River. The brigade halted here to rest. Colonel Chapman dispatched the 3rd Indiana down the road in the direction of Stony Creek Depot. Union scouts reported that there was a picket of about fifty Rebels stationed at Sappony Baptist Church. The Indiana troops drove the pickets back, but soon the enemy was re-enforced and the Indiana boys were forced to retreat.

    Colonel John McIntosh's 1st brigade was brought up and engaged the Rebel forces. Chapman's brigade was ordered to support McIntosh's efforts. Wilson hoped his troops could skirt the horsemen of General Chambliss' Rebel cavalry, and make their way towards Prince-George Court House. The brigade formed a line of battle, and the 22nd was placed in the reserve line along with the 8th New York.[5] The fighting at Stony Creek consisted of charge and counter charge, the savage fighting continuing well into the night.

    June 29th 1864 would turn out to be the one of the most eventful days in the regiment's history. Just before daylight, the brigade was positioned at the crossing of the Stony Creek Station and Dinwiddie Court House road, near Sappony Baptist Church. The 22nd New York, along with the 1st Vermont, 8th New York and 3rd Indiana, were dismounted and formed in line of battle. They were stationed behind hastily thrown-up breastworks made mostly of rails. Just before dawn, Wilson received word that the road to Ream's Station was clear. He ordered his troops to disengage the enemy and march north. After receiving the order, Colonel

John McIntosh, asked Chapman to hold his troops in position until the men of the 1st brigade had retired, and then move the 2nd brigade in behind. The 1st brigade's withdrawal was difficult at best, and the exhausted men stumbling though the dense woods in the darkness was enough to alert the Rebel troops to the situation. At full daylight, Wade Hampton's Rebels attacked in force on the Federal line near the Sappony Church. The gallant New York boys stood their ground until the line was flanked on the left and gave way under the force of Generals Butler and Rosser's superior numbers.

The retreat had become a rout as the troops scattered in all directions, every man for himself. The great "skedaddle" had begun. The Union troops had fallen back into the trees south of Stony Creek, many of them cut off from their horses, while the commanders tried to rally the men and reform their lines. In their attempt to cover the rear of the Union column, a great many of the guard were cut off and captured. Colonel Chapman was able to assemble a portion of his command, and headed north about ten miles to Reams Station where they were reunited with the main body of the division. The 3rd division was in full retreat and Chapman's brigade was assigned the lead. To avoid complete disaster, Wilson had to stay one step ahead of Lee and Hampton's pursuing troops, so the Federals kept up the march. In an effort to lighten the column, Wilson ordered his men to fill their ammunition pouches, burn the supply wagons, spike the cannons, abandon the ambulances and 200 wounded, and proceed back across the Doubles Bridge over the Nottoway River and head for Jarratts Station. About two miles from the station, the men exhausted from the fight, halted for a few hours rest.

The retreat turned into a grueling, merciless march on both men and beast. Many of the soldiers were asleep in the saddle as they rode. Just after daylight on the 30th, they crossed the railroad and moved along the plantation roads to Peter's Bridge on the Nottoway River. When they reached the river around noon, they found the bridge destroyed, and were forced to ford the river. After the crossing was completed, the brigade came to a halt for a much-needed rest. The time was 6 p.m. when they resumed the march passing through Waverly to Blunt's Bridge on the Blackwater River, arriving there at about midnight. Again, to their dismay, they found the bridge had been burned and only charred portions of the structure remained. Within an hour the bridge was partially repaired. The men were well aware of the threat of an attack from a trailing enemy. Unfortunately before a complete squadron was across the bridge, it collapsed, sending several horses and riders falling fifteen feet and crashing into the stream. The exhausted soldiers again took to the task and rebuilt the bridge, and within 30 minutes it was once again repaired. By daylight the entire command was across the river. Soon after the last man was clear of the crossing, the enemy made an appearance. General Wilson personally set fire to a pile of dried leaves and pine fence rails, which he previously had ordered, stacked under the bridge. The bridge quickly caught fire and was fully engulfed in flames when a Rebel officer trotted up to the shore and shouted "Good-bye boys, I am sorry to see you safely over." General Wilson, realizing that his men were out of danger, cheerfully waved back.

On Friday, July 1st they finally reached the Federal lines, and went into camp near Cabin Point, twenty miles east of Petersburg. For the first time in ten days, the men unsaddled their mounts, set pickets, and went to sleep. On the 2nd of

July they moved into camp near Light House Point on the James River and remained there until July 6th. The raid on the railroad was finally over.

During the campaign, the brigade marched over 335 miles and lost a total of 705 men both officers and enlisted. Many of the missing men managed to straggle back into the camp in the days following the expedition. Colonel Samuel Crooks, the man who organized the regiment, was captured in the action, along with Major McLennan. Lt. Colonel J.B.Brown took command after McLennan was captured, but was relieved for incompetence and the regiment was assigned to Major Caleb Brown of the 8th New York.[6]

Chapter 5

Rebuilding the Regiment

The 3rd division remained in camp at Light House Point, Va. recuperating. On the 29th of July, they marched to Westbrook House near the Jerusalem plank road and took position as pickets on the left and rear of the army.[1]

The men, who had lost or disabled their horses, were labeled the "dismounted men of the regiment" and they received orders to board the *John A. Harder* Government Transport. The ship sailed down the James River to Fortress Monroe and then up the Chesapeake Bay to Baltimore where they boarded awaiting trains, and headed for Washington. They arrived at 8 p.m. on the July 10th, and by the 11th were mounted up and moved to the city to face the Rebel army.

Confederate General Jubal Early and his veteran soldiers were in sight of the National Capitol. The 22nd New York, along with other troops from the Remount camp, formed a skirmish line across Rock Creek where they remained under fire from the Confederate troops. They held the line against the infantry division of General Rhodes, from noon until 4 p.m. when they were relieved by General Wright, and the veterans of the 6th Corps.

The following day the regiment was sent back to Washington and to relieve the 8th Illinois Cavalry. They spent a week doing practically nothing, the men joking that they were the cheapest Provost Guard that the city of Washington ever had. They were not asked to do any work, so consequently they did none. After a week of this light duty, the regiment was sent after the Union Army and caught up with them near Snickers Gap. On the afternoon of July 18th the brigade, now called the "Provisional", under the command of Colonel Young, numbering nearly 1000 men was assigned the right of the line at Island Ford about a mile below Snickers Gap. The pickets were engaged by Early's Rebels and were driven back. Soon, the entire command broke and made tracks for the river, leaving the dead and wounded behind in the hands of the enemy. The next day they crossed the river again and took back the ground that they had "skedaddled" from the day before. The regiment pushed on until they reached Leesburg and then returned to Washington, successfully thwarting the advance of the Rebels.[2]

The companies of the regiment that were not in need of re-mounting remained with General Wilson and the Third Division at Lee's Mill. They performed picket duty on the left of the Union line from the 31st of July until the 4th of August, when Wilson received orders to move the division to the Shenandoah Valley. At daylight on the 5th, the division marched to City Point where they boarded steam transports destined for Giesboro Point, near Washington. After several days, they arrived at their destination and began the march towards the Shenandoah Valley.[3]

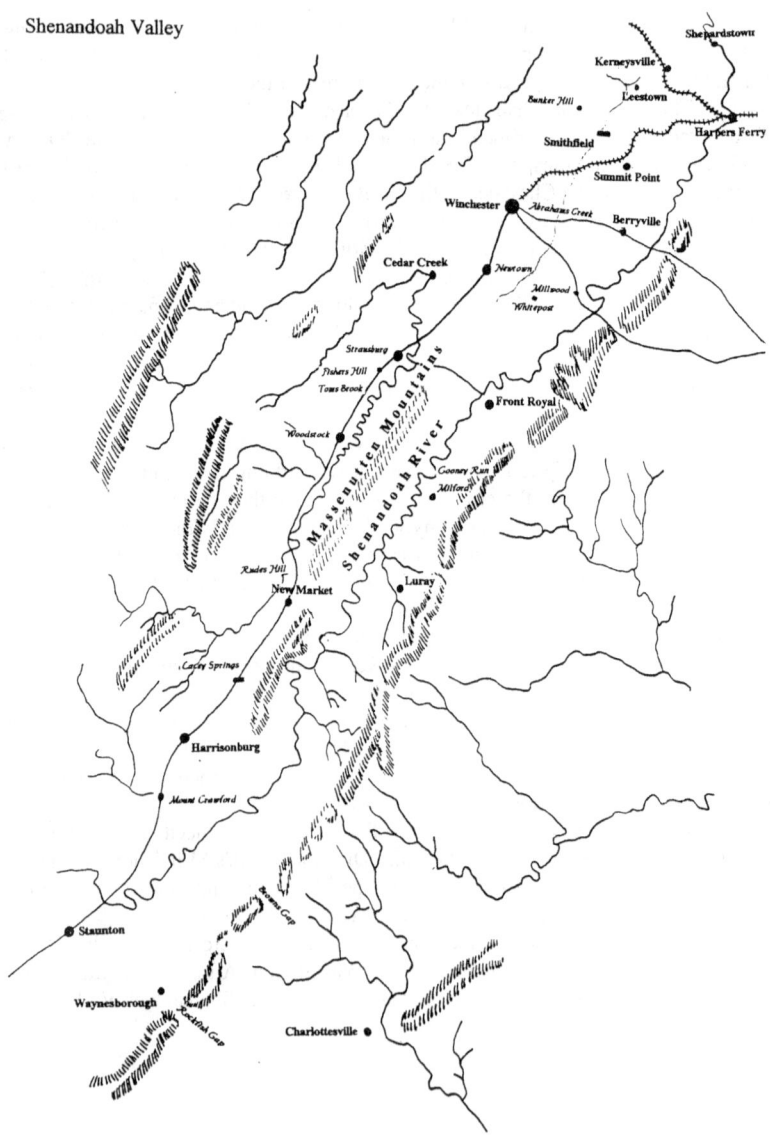

Chapter 6

Shendoah Valley Campaign

From the 1st day of August, through the 5th, the "dismounted men of the regiment" temporarily part of the "Provisional" regiment was on the march. They headed for Frederick Md. then to Harpers Ferry, Va., then two miles south to Sandy Hook, up to Boonsboro and Harpers Ferry once again. Their mission was to keep Early's Rebels out of Pennsylvania. On the 7th of August the regiment was deployed to Hall Town and remained there on the 8th and 9th. They moved to Summit Point on the 10th, and on to Winchester on the 11th. August 12th, was a feverishly hot day as the Union troops marched to Fisher's Hill, a steep bluff on the outskirts of Strausburg, where they once again met the forces of General Early who were in possession of strong positions, and re-enforced by corps of infantry and a cavalry division under the command of General W.H.F. Lee. For two days the Yankee troops held their position within gunshot range of the Rebels, and watched and waited. The regiment then withdrew from the enemy's front, without engaging. On August 17th, they marched back to Winchester, where they were reunited with the other companies of the 22nd New York Cavalry, whom they left over a month earlier at Light House Point.[1]

General Sheridan had received information that Early had strengthened his force to about 40,000 men, much too large a force for his Federals to attack.. His strategy was to move the army to an area in the valley where he could establish a defensive line. This would enable his smaller number of troops to repel a force of superior numbers. He decided to retreat to Halltown.[2]

The army had fallen back from Cedar Creek on August 18th, and was retiring from Winchester. The reunited 22nd New York was posted on the pike leading to Harper's Ferry to cover the retreat of the army. On the 20th the regiment bivouacked at Smithfield. At 7 a.m., the 21st of August, the enemy crossed the Opequon in force and attacked the 22nd in their camp. The Rebels drove the New York boys back about two miles, before the advance was checked and the regiment was withdrawn from line of battle and moved to Summit Point.

On August 25th, the regiment was on the road headed toward Leetown, on orders to locate the position of the enemy. They had barely crossed the Baltimore and Ohio Railroad at Kerneysville, when they encountered Rebel skirmishers of Rhode's Division. The gallant Rochester boys formed a line of battle taking cover behind rail fences. After briefly engaging the enemy, they were ordered to fall back after Major Theodore Schlick, who was in command of the attack, was killed.[3]

The regiment was soon on the move again, this time crossing the Potomac near Sheperdstown and continuing to Boonsboro, Md. Their mission was to ride picket along the passes of South Mountain and the fords of Antietam Creek. The high command expected Early to once again invade Maryland. The intuition of the Union leaders was incorrect however, as Union scouts reported that Early had fallen back to Bunker Hill, waiting for the return of the blue troopers. The New York troopers re-crossed the Potomac on August 29th, and moved to Berryville on August 30th, and made camp.

On September 2nd, they were in the saddle once again. They left Berryville and moved along the Front Royal road to Millwood then Whitepost. From

15

the 5th of September to the 19th the regiment was assigned scouting detail from Berryville to Winchester and from Winchester to the foot of the Massanutten Mountains.

The regiment was assigned to patrol the roads of Virginia. They traveled from Harper's Ferry to Berryville to Winchester to Stephenson Station to Summit Point and on and on. They made this trip so often, they had been nicknamed the "Harpers Weekly." September 19th, however, would end this tedious duty of the regiment. At daylight, the New Yorkers were formed up and crossed the Opequon while under heavy fire. They reached the open fields two miles outside of Winchester at about 7 a.m., and remained in line of battle until 9 a.m. At noon of this day, while the 2nd brigade engaged the enemies pickets and gained ground on the south bank of the Opequon, the soldiers of the 22nd were moved to the extreme left flank and attacked the Rebel cavalry. They succeeded in driving the enemy off the field and back to Abraham's Creek, and vigorously pursued them until dark. General Chapman was wounded in the action, and Colonel William Wells assumed command of the brigade.[4]

On September 20th the brigade was mounted-up, and headed for Front Royal, Va. They met no Rebel troops on the advance and reached their destination that night. At daylight, the 21st of September, the brigade crossed the Shenandoah River behind the 2nd Ohio. Blanketed by a dense fog, Major Caleb Moore sent Companies D and I into the woods on a charge. Those fifty men, accompanied by the cheers of the whole regiment, drove the enemy in force from their position on the south bank of the Shenandoah River back to Gooney Manor. At daylight on September 22nd, the Federal troops marched on country roads headed for Milford. At noon, they encountered Rebel troops on the outskirts of Milford. The 22nd New York and the 1st New Hampshire dismounted and made a vigorous attack on the enemy's right flank but the rebels held their position. After dark, the Union troopers withdrew, and moved on to Bentonville where they bivouacked.

On September 23rd and 24th the brigade marched through Milford to the Luray Court House but this time they met no Rebel resistance. They crossed over the Shenandoah River and camped near Massanutten Mountain. The next day they crossed over the mountain and came to a halt at New Market. At 5 p.m. the regiment mounted up and marched on to Harrisonburg where they bivouacked. They moved to Staunton, on September 26th, and then on to Waynesborough the following day. On September 28th, while the regiment attempted to pass through Brown's Gap in the Blue Ridge Mountains, the 22nd found themselves hemmed in by a superior force of infantry and cavalry. They managed to elude a major engagement with the enemy, and joined up with General Wesley Merritt's Cavalry Division at Piedmont and rode with them until they reached Mount Crawford on September 30th.[5]

September 30th, Major General George Armstrong Custer took command of the 3d Division Cavalry Corps, which so far under General Wilson had held its reputation with respectability. The following day General Wilson bid a fond farewell to the men who had served with him so gallantly. By October 5th, Custer had his horsemen back in the saddle, this time accompanied by Merritt's Cavalry Division. The destination was Winchester, and the regiment was assigned to the rear of the column, with orders to burn hay, grain, mills and anything else that could be useful to the enemy. As the division traveled through the Shenandoah Valley, they were constantly harassed by Rebel skirmishers from Brigadier General Thomas Rossar's

Division. This action continued until October 9th, when Custer received an order from Sheridan by way of Corps Commander General Alfred Torbert which said," whip Rossar or get whipped yourself."[6]

The movement against Rossar's Rebels began by backtracking about two miles to a little creek called Tom's Brook. Battle lines were formed and the New Yorkers were placed on the right of the Union line. Shells and shot were flying all around as the regiment passed along the flank by fours, until they reached the road where they met General Custer and staff. As the lead of the column turned up the road, a great cheer rose from the ranks and every horse broke into a sprint. Off in the distance on the road lay the destination of the charge, Rossar's supply and wagon train. The road they approached had everything expected to be found at the rear of an army. There were wagons, ambulances, forges, and men, lots of men, both mounted and dismounted. The realization that they were outnumbered however, did not slow the charge. Major Moore and his command reached the head of the train, and gathered up the teams of about 50 wagons and made their escape.

For over two hours, enemy clashed, lines charging and counter charging. Custer's men finally managed to turn the left flank of Rosser. This maneuver, accompanied with a smashing blow by Merritt's cavalrymen to the Confederate center, resulted in the crumbling of the Rebel line. The rest of the day, and into the night, the division harassed the columns of retreating Rebels, and pursued the beaten enemy for 26 miles, halting when they came up against Jubal Early's infantry at Rude's Hill, just north of New Market. When the contest was concluded, the Federals had driven the enemy 30 miles, relieved them of all of their artillery and wagons and captured nearly 100 prisoners.[7]

Custer returned with the regiment to the Shenandoah Valley on October 13th, and was placed on the right of the Union line at Cedar Creek, where they remained until the 19th. At 5 a.m., still positioned on the right of the line, they were attacked by Rosser's cavalrymen. Rosser's plan was to catch the Union off guard, but the Federals were awake under standing orders to be up before dawn when located close to the enemy lines. The Federal troops discovered the Rebel approach and stopped the attack cold. They continued to skirmish with enemy pickets for most of the day. The brigade held the gray troops at bay as they attempted to turn the flank. Rossar was hesitant to launch an attack on the Federal line, after the whipping he previously received at the hands of Custer's horsemen. The ease of checking Rosser's advance on the right line prompted Torbert to move Custer's cavalrymen over to help support the faltering Union left, where they stayed the course of Early's advance. At 2 p.m., when Sheridan arrived on the field however, he sent Custer back to the Federal right, where they again managed to check the advances of Rosser's troops. As the enemy crossed infantry and cavalry over Cedar Creek, Custer led his cavalry in a charge, which drove the Rebels back over a mile, until they reached the cover of their infantry. At 4 p.m. Sheridan launched his attack, with an entire division of cavalry turning each flank of the Confederates. A tremendous fear of the Union cavalry spread throughout the gray troops, as they retreated back towards Fisher's Hill and New Market. The Union horsemen rode furiously though the open fields in an attempt to intercept the retreating Rebel troops before they crossed Cedar Creek. Many of the enemy troops were cut off and captured. The Federals continued their pursuit in an attempt to reach the enemy artillery reserve and supply trains. The command halted near the foot of Fishers Hill, about four miles from

Cedar Creek. They had succeeded in capturing 45 artillery pieces, 32 caissons, 184 horses, 156 mules, 46 army wagons, 5 battle flags and 672 prisoners. The following day the regiment followed the Rebel retreat picking up stragglers and keeping Rosser's Rebels on the run.[8]

On October 21st the regiment returned to Cedar Creek, and made camp. They were assigned scouting detail day after day until November 9th. when they headed back down into the Shenandoah Valley and bivouacked on the outskirts of Newtown. The regiment encountered General Early's Confederates on November 12th, at Ninevah, Va. near Mulberry Run, north of Cedar Creek. The 22nd was positioned on the flank of the Union line, when Major Brown ordered the New York troopers to charge. Up the hill the men went shouting and shooting until they reached the top, and engaged the Rebels in close quarters. Soon the command was given to fall back, as a gray line of troops were closing in rapidly on the left and rear. One squadron retreated slowly in the face of the Rebel line, while the remainder of the regiment turned to the left to hold the oncoming flanking Confederate troops. Luck was on the side of the regiment, as they succeeded in retreating fairly unscathed.[9]

Very little action was seen until the November 20th, when the 22nd New York once again mounted-up and headed up the Pike to Mount Jackson where the troops of General Early had made winter quarters. The blue troopers skirmished briefly with Early's men with no major consequence on either side. The regiment retired to Winchester and remained there for about a month. Lieutenant Colonel Horatio B. Reed assumed command of the regiment November 26th.[10]

Monday morning, December 19th, the division was mounted-up and headed up the icy roads toward Lacey Springs. The following day it rained and rained, all day and all night. The regiment made camp that night at Lacey Springs. A force of Rebels made a charge into the camp just before dawn, and fierce fighting commenced mostly hand to hand. When daylight broke, and the troops could be distinguished friend from foe, a squadron from the regiment under the command of Lieutenant William Brown, broke loose and headed north up the Pike, where they ran head long into another band of gray clad soldiers. They were about 2 rods from each other when the recognition was made, and the New York boys opened up on the Rebels with carbine and revolver. The enemy troops quickly scattered and the Federals rapidly pursued them through the fields to the left of the road and up the hill where they ran smack into a line of Confederate infantry. The Union horseman found themselves outgunned and out manned, a situation that forced them to fall back to the road and attempt to rejoin the rest of the command. With the Rebels in hot pursuit, the Federals were in a race to reach the bridge that crossed the north fork of the Shenandoah River. The road was a sheet of ice, and the horses were smooth shod. On and on the New York troops rode, with the Rebels attacking their front and rear. They traveled almost 12 miles, their horses slipping and sliding all the way, until the bridge was in sight. The crossing was covered with only a few dismounted Union soldiers, who opened fire on every unfortunate Rebel in sight. These gallant troopers held the enemy at bay, forcing the Confederate troopers to give up the chase and allow the Union horsemen safe passage across the Shenandoah.[11]

The regiment made winter quarters at Camp Russell, located between Newtown and Kernstown. They remained there from January 26th, until February 26th, 1865, without incident. February 27th, the regiment was saddled up and started up the Shenandoah Valley towards Staunton. At Mount Crawford, the Federals confronted a small band of Rebels from General Rosser's command who had barricaded a bridge and with the intention of burning it. The Union boys plunged into the icy water and made a crossing upstream of the bridge, flanked the Rebel troops and saved the bridge. In the contest, 30 prisoners and one gun were seized.[12]

On March 2nd the regiment was about four miles from Staunton. The weather was dismal, with rain, sleet and hail. These conditions made the troopers uncomfortable and the roads almost impassable. When they arrived at Staunton they were disappointed to find that Early's army had vacated the town and moved east first to Fisherville and then on to Waynesborough.[13]

John R. Hanyon, Co. I, 22nd N.Y. Cavalry
[Chris Nelson Collection, U.S. Army Military History Institute]

Chapter 7

The Battle of Waynesboro

Custer received orders to immediately move his division to Waynesboro to reconnoiter the position of Early's army and the estimate its size. Over mud soaked roads and through rain and ice storms, the cavalrymen pushed on. About three miles from Staunton, a squadron from the 22nd New York under Captain Lycurgus Lusk attacked the rear guard of Early's Confederate army. A sharp skirmish ensued until the Rebels finally broke off from the contest and retired to Fisherville. The column pressed on until they came in sight of the Confederate position at Waynesboro. The Rebels had seized the heights west of the town and had erected earth work fortifications. They had positioned the artillery to concentrate their fire on the only road leading toward the Rebel line. The open fields were so soaked from the heavy rains that they seemed impassable for cavalry. The New York troops were immediately deployed as skirmishers and assaulted the gray troops, driving them back to their breastworks. They were then ordered to hold this position until the remainder of the brigade could be assembled in support.[1]

General Custer ordered a regiment to be sent in to support the 22nd New York on the skirmish line, while the 1st and 3rd Brigades were massed in columns of squadrons in the woods just beyond the range of the Rebel artillery. Between the barrage of shot and shell and the fields of mud, the regiment bogged down, almost unable to advance or retreat. General Custer, in a quick reconnaissance, discovered that the Rebel left flank was vulnerable and devised a plan for attack. He dismounted 3 regiments of the 1st brigade and dispatched them toward the left of the Rebel line under the cover of dense woods. This movement was followed by a simultaneous attack of that position along with the Confederate front. The 22nd New York and the 8th New York, in columns of fours, followed by the 1st Connecticut, charged up the road along the woods at full gallop, with bugles sounding "Charge!" This movement caught the immediate attention of the Rebel artillery, attracting their concentrated fire on the narrow road on which the Union horsemen were traveling. With shot and shell tearing through the ranks, the Federal horsemen galloped on. They reached the Confederate breastworks, sabers in hand, and overwhelmed the Rebel gunners. Breaking through the lines of Rebel infantry, the Union boys headed into town with hopes of capturing General Early at his headquarters.[2]

General Early, along with several staff officers had fled the town, crossed the South River east of Waynesboro, and headed up the road to Rock Fish Gap. The Federal troopers formed a line on the east bank of the river to cut off any further Rebel escape in that direction. Captain Lusk, along with six men of his regiment and several men from the 8th New York set out in pursuit of Early and his staff. The road was cluttered by the wagons of the Rebel army on their way to Greenwood Station in an effort to avoid capture by Custer's troops. A few mounted soldiers were spotted down the road galloping their horses toward Rock Fish gap. The Union troopers took off in hot pursuit of the fleeing Rebel horsemen. Confident that one of these retreating Rebels was General Early, they pressed on, and finally overtook the gray clad horsemen. To the New Yorkers disappointment however, General Early was not among them.[3]

21

After a short halt, the Union troopers regrouped and moved forward down the rocky road, capturing men, horses and supplies as they went. After reaching and securing Rock Fish Gap, the regiment continued on to Brookville and Greenwood Station. The spoils of the charge consisted of four captured battle flags credited to the 22nd New York Cavalry, and five captured flags to the 8th New York. The flags captured by the 22nd were credited to Captain Christopher Bruton, Company C, Harry Harvey, Michael Crowley of Company A and George Ladd of Company H.[4]

The 22nd New York remained at Waynesboro to assemble the prisoners and escort them to Winchester. There were nearly thirteen hundred prisoners, eleven artillery pieces, and a train of more than one hundred wagons, including General Early's headquarters wagon with all of his official books. They encamped at Fishersville on the night of March 3rd, and proceeded through Staunton the following day. Colonel John Thompson of the 1st New Hampshire, the commander of the escort, had learned that General Rosser was attempting to re-assemble his command. Rosser had sent dispatches out to all surrounding areas directing soldiers and citizens to rendezvous at Mount Jackson and prevent the Federals from crossing the North Fork of the Shenandoah. Rosser would then follow with his troops and capture the Union horsemen and take back the prisoners. When the Federal troops arrived at Mount Jackson, they found the river impassable except for a ford near the pike. Unfortunately, a force of about 200 Rebels held the area. At daylight on March 7th, the 22nd New York, under the command of Major Charles Brown and accompanied by the 1st Rhode Island was ordered to take the ford above the pike and drive the Rebels out of the main ford. The New York horsemen viciously attacked the enemy. In approximately ten minutes the contest was complete, and the Rebels were scattered throughout the mountainside. Meanwhile, another force of Rebels attacked the column's rear guard near Rudes Hill, but the assault was repulsed. The command was ordered to cross the rapidly moving, chest high waters of the Shenandoah. Almost every men in the command, even though not an hour before were beating back an enemy that were trying to kill them, took the prisoners on their horses to save them from having to wade those icy waters. The crossing was nearly complete, when once again the Rebels made a vigorous assault on the rear guard. This offensive was once again repulsed, with a Confederate loss of at least 10 killed and several more wounded. The Federals moved across Cedar Creek and encamped in the earth works that night, then continued the march until arriving at Winchester at about noon on the 8th.[5]

The 22nd New York was again saddled up and rode out of Winchester on the morning of March 17th. They moved up the back road toward Cedar Creek, with the intention of crossing at either Fawcett's or Mount Hope Gap. When they arrived at Cedar Creek they found the water so high it was impossible to cross. Instead the regiment headed up the Morefield Pike moving up through Cedar Valley and crossed Cedar Creek at Rudolph's Pass. They then proceeded along a back road to the Woodstock Road where they camped for the night. Upon reaching Woodstock, the scouts dashed into the town followed by the advance guard and captured two Confederate cavalrymen in the assault. Major Brown received information from the citizens that General Rosser had assembled a force of about 800 men and was falling back toward Richmond. Certain that there was no active Rebel force in the area, and with the regiment running short on rations, on March 19, Major Brown decided to return his troops to Winchester where they would remain for several weeks.[6]

Even though General Lee surrendered at Appomatox Court House on April 9th, 1865, the conflict in the Shenandoah Valley would continue. On April 26, the 22nd New York along with the 8th Pennsylvania moved out of Winchester, and rode to Cedar Creek were they encamped for the night. The following day they marched to Mount Jackson. While setting up camp, Colonel Reed noticed several men on an adjacent hill apparently on patrol. A small force of Federal troops was deployed to determine if these men were connected with a larger force of Rebels. As the Confederates disappeared into the woods however, Colonel Reed was convinced that the Rebels were just a small band of guerrillas. Friday April 28, the regiment moved on toward Harrisonburg and made camp. On Saturday April 29, they marched on to Staunton.

Colonel Reed received information that General Rosser had been there for several days previous, attempting to raise a force, but had left earlier that morning after the citizens refused to join him. Sunday, April 30, Colonel W.P. Thompson, the commander of Jackson's Cavalry Brigade requested surrender terms from Colonel Reed. The Rebel commander declined the offer, apparently not satisfied with the terms, which were the same as General Grant gave General Lee. Reed sent out scouts in an effort to ascertain the enemy's strength and position. The scouts reported that the Confederate force consisted of about 100 men, but were widely scattered throughout the mountains. Believing that it would take more time than was justifiable to capture these stragglers, and because he was under orders to return in 10 days, Colonel Reed decided to leave the rogue Rebels behind. Tuesday morning, May 2nd, the regiment left Staunton and made the return trip to Winchester where they arrived on May 5th.[7]

Lt. Col. Horatio Reed
[Karl Sodstrom Collection, U.S. Army Military History Institute]

Chapter 8

The Regiment is Dimissed

The regiment completed the remainder of its duty in Winchester, stationed with the 5th New York and the 12th Pennsylvania. The 22nd New York cavalry was officially mustered out of service on August 1st, at Winchester, Virginia. However detachments of the regiment were also discharged on May 6th, 1865 at Hart's Island, New York, and on June 6th, 1865 at Washington, D.C.[1] The men were sent by train to Baltimore, then on to Rochester.

They arrived at 6 a.m. on August 4th, and proceeded directly to the fairgrounds. There was no formal reception for the remaining seven hundred men, but Mayor Bradstreet greeted them at 8 o'clock that morning. There was little delay in paying the men and discharges were rapidly completed. The men who had served so gallantly in the 22nd New York Volunteer Cavalry were finally allowed to go home.[2]

On July 30, 1865, Colonel Horatio B. Reed delivered this address to the regiment:

> Comrades of the 22nd Cavalry:
>
> The time has arrived when we are to separate and return to our homes. The cruel and fratricidal war that our brothers waged against us has ended, and God has decided in favor of a Free Government and a Free People.
> Our services can now be dispensed with, and in a few days, the 22nd Cavalry as a military organization will cease to exist.
> I came among you, from the army proper, a stranger, and it affords me great pleasure in saying that I have received the kindest and most generous treatment from both officers and men. My commands have been obeyed with alacrity and good faith.
> My orders may have at times appeared hard and perhaps severe, but when such have emanated from me, the good of our regiment was my only desire. The discipline, which, I am aware, has at times appeared rigid, has resulted in our regiment being considered "Second to none in the Cavalry Service." I do not take credit to myself for this, but gladly award it to your intelligence, patriotism, and your desire to discharge your duties as becomes good and faithful soldiers. As to your gallantry in the face of the enemy you are known as "The bravest of the Brave."

I said we are soon to be disbanded. Accept, then, my heartfelt thanks and gratitude for your kindness to me, both officers and men, and my sincere wishes for your future happiness and prosperity through life. May God bless each and every one of you.[3]

Horatio B. Reed
Colonel 22nd New York Cavalry

Unfortunately the controversy with this regiment was not yet over. On August 9, 1865, a portion of the regiment assembled at the court house to voice their discontentment with the command of Colonel Horatio B. Reed. The non-commissioned offers and enlisted men claimed that Colonel Reed misused and ill-treated them, and they suffered the most degrading punishment for the most trivial offenses. They claimed that worthy men were refused Reed's influence in obtaining commissions while incompetent men could buy the same. The men resolved to disclaim the rights of Colonel Reed to take credit for the regiments accomplishments, but give credit to Major Caleb Moore and the other officers who did not retire to the rear when the regiment went into battle, but bravely lead them though the smoke and fire of many conflicts. For those officers they men professed their utmost respect.[4]

CUSTERS FAREWELL ADDRESS TO THE DIVISION

Headquarters Third Cavalry Division
Appomattox C.H., Va.
April 9, 1865

Soldiers of the 3rd Cavalry Division:
With profound gratitude toward the God of battles, by whose blessings our enemies have been humbled and our arms rendered triumphant, your commanding general avails himself to this, his first opportunity, to express to you his admiration f the heroic manner in which you have passed through the series of battles which today resulted in the surrender of the enemies entire army.

The record established by your indomitable courage is unparalleled in the annals of war. Your prowess has won for you even the respect and admiration of your enemies. During the past 6 months, although in most instances confronted by superior numbers, you have captured from the enemy, in open battle, one hundred and eleven pieces of field artillery, sixty five battle flags, and upwards of ten thousand prisoners of war, including seven general officers. Within the past ten days, and included in the above, you have captured forty-six pieces of field artillery and thirty-seven battle flags. You have never lost a gun, never lost a color, and have never been defeated, and not withstanding the numerous engagements in which you borne a prominent part, including those memorable battles of the Shenandoah, you have captured every piece of artillery which the enemy has dared to open on you.

The near approach of peace renders it improbable that you will again be called upon to undergo the fatigues of the toilsome march or the exposure or the battle field; but should the assistance of keen blades, wielded by your steady arms, be required to hasten the coming of that glorious peace, for which we have been so long contending, the general commanding will meet with hearty and willing response.

Let us hope that our work is done, and that, blessed with comforts of peace, we may be permitted to enjoy the pleasures of home and friends. For our comrades who have fallen, let us ever cherish a grateful remembrance. To the wounded and those who languish in Southern prisons, let our heartfelt sympathy be tendered.

And now speaking for myself alone, when war is ended and the task of the historian begins-when those deeds of daring, which have rendered the name and fame of the Third Cavalry Division imperishable, are inscribed upon the bright pages of our country's history-I only ask that my name may be written as that of the Commander of the Third Cavalry Division.[5]

G. A. Custer
Brevet Major General Commanding

Appl

Charge and Specification against Colonel Samuel J. Crooks, 22d New York Cavalry

Charge: Occasioning a false alarm in the army. (49th Article of War)

Specification — In this that Colonel Samuel J. Crooks, 22d New York Cavalry, being in command of his regiment and sent out to watch and protect the right flank of the Army of the Potomac, did repeatedly send reports to the Commanding General of that Army that the enemy was appearing in force and turning the right flank, which reports were not well grounded — This in the Wilderness Va, on or about May 7, 1864.

(signed) E. R. Platt
Judge Advocate A.P.

Witnesses
Maj. Genl. Meade
"   "   Humphreys
"   "   Wright
Officer of the Staff
of Maj. Gen. Wright

(Official despatches)   (Over)

Chapter 9

The Fate of Colonel Crooks

Colonel Samuel Crooks, the man selected to organize the 22nd New York Cavalry regiment, was put under arrest on May 7, 1864 by order of General George G. Meade. He charged Crooks with violating the 49th Article of War, "*in occasioning a false alarm in the army in which he is serving*". A directive from the President stated that as of July 22, 1864, Colonel Crooks was to be mustered out of the service.

Crooks however, was accompanying his regiment on the Wilson Railroad Raid, and on June 30, 1864, was taken prisoner at Ream's Station. He was sent to Richmond, Va. on July 3rd, and on to Macon, Ga. on July 16th. While confined in Macon, Colonel Crooks was ordered to be placed in irons and held in close confinement in retaliation for similar treatment practiced on Confederate Colonel Angus McDonald, who was captured by Crooks' command. Crooks was able to delay the punishment for a time by convincing the prison physician that he was ill, but after a failed escape attempt from the hospital, the punishment was invoked. He finally ended up confined at Richland Jail in Columbia, South Carolina.[1]

Colonel Crooks was paroled on December 10, 1864 and reported to Camp Parole on December 15th, where he received 30 days leave. By order of the Secretary of War, Edward Townsend, Colonel Crooks' dishonorable discharge was revoked, and on March 21, 1865, he received an honorable discharge from the Union Army.[2]

1st Lt. Daniel Layton, Co. G, 22nd N.Y. Cavalry
[Div. Military-Naval Affairs, N.Y. State Adjt. Gen. Office, Albany, N.Y.]

Appendix A

Regimental Casualties[1]

Killed in Action

Major Theodore Schlick, Killed August 25, 1864 in action at Kearnsville, Va.
Second Lieutenant Patrick Glennan, Company D. Killed June 22, 1864 at Dinwiddie Court House.
1st Lieutenant, Daniel Layton, Company G. Killed June 14, 1864 of wounds received in action at White Oak Swamp.
1st Lieutenant Squire M. Yates, Company K. Died in action April 7, 1865 near Winchester, Va.
1st Sergeant Florence McCarthy, Company D. Killed in action September 22, 1864 at Luray Valley, Va.
Sergeant William Stormont, Company M, died of wounds, date and place not stated.
Corporal Hiram W. Goodrich, Company B. Died June 14, 1864 from wounds received in action at Harrison's Landing.
Corporal William G. Peck, Company E, died of wounds December 9, 1864.
Corporal Wallace M. Preston, Company H. Killed September 19, 1864 at Winchester, Va.
Private Frederick Eaves, Company A. Killed, June 13, 1864 at White Oak Swamp.
Private Milo D. Eldridge, Company L. Died October 10, 1864 of wounds received in action.
Private Milton Freeman, Company E. Killed, August 21, 1864 at Smithfield, Va.
Private William R. Larcom, Company B. Died September 19, 1864 of wounds received at the Battle of Winchester.
Private James G. Skinner, Company L. Died in hospital at City Point Va. on June 20, 1864 from wounds received in action.
Private George Vice, Company E. Died of wounds, February 20, 1864 at Jarvis Hospital, Baltimore, Md.
Private Israel H. Ward, Company E. Died of wounds May 7, 1864 at Fredericksburg, Va.
Private Edward Wellman, Company K. Died from wounds June 20, 1864 at Hampton Va.

There were 2 officers were reported missing in action, 2nd Lieutenant Israel B. Taylor, since May 12, 1865, and Surgeon James D. Jones since December 21, 1863.

Died as Prisoners of War

Quartermaster Sergeant Robert H Osborn, Company E, died no date at Andersonville, Ga.
Commissary Sergeant Henry Gartsee, Company L, died August 29, 1864 at Andersonville, Ga.
Sergeant William Allen, Company E, died no date given at Andersonville, Ga.
Sergeant Thomas Dewer, Company F, died June 19, 1864 at Andersonville, Ga.
Sergeant Henry Gartsee, Company L, died August 29, 1864 at Andersonville, Ga.
Sergeant Perry V. Sisson, Company M, died July, 1864 at Andersonville, Ga.
Sergeant Robert Southworth, Company E, died date not stated at Andersonville, Ga.
Sergeant Fayette York, Company L, died, date not stated at Andersonville, Ga.
Corporal Samuel Dalton, Company K, died, date not stated at Florence, S.C.
Corporal John Hopper, Company K, died, date not stated at Andersonville, Ga.
Corporal Irving Merriam, Company L, died August 23, 1864 at Andersonville, Ga.
Corporal John Moochler, Company E, died, date not stated at Andersonville, Ga.
Corporal William Robinson, Company M, died September 15, 1864 at Andersonville, Ga.
Corporal Lorenzo Shepardson, Company E, died date not stated at Andersonville, Ga.
Corporal William V. Walker, Company E, died date not stated at Andersonville, Ga.
Corporal Henry Webster, Company M, died August 15, 1864 at Andersonville, Ga.
Trumpeter Ara Moore, Company E, died date not stated at Andersonville, Ga.
Farrier Nicholas Cooper, Company L, died December 13, 1864 at Andersonville, Ga.
Farrier John W. Hulbert, died September 10, 1864 at Andersonville, Ga.
Farrier James B. Jones, Company F, died July, 1864 at Andersonville, Ga.
Farrier Gardiner Milliman, Company B, died September 7, 1864 at Andersonville, Ga.
Farrier Patrick O'Neil, Company E, died date not stated at Andersonville, Ga.
Saddler Nelson C. Main, Company L, died date not known at Andersonville, Ga.
Wagoner James G. Peck, Company F, died June 9, 1864 at Andersonville, Ga.
Private William Attridge. Company A, died on April 28,1865 at Andersonville, Ga.
Private Calvin Bentley, Company L, died on August 16,1864 at Andersonville, Ga.
Private John Baum, Company A, died on April 28, 1865 in Rebel Prison.
Private Llewellyn Weaver Baxter, Company A, died October 18, 1864 at Andersonville, Ga.
Private James H. Bliss, Company I, died on August 6, 1865 at Andersonville, Ga.
Private Augustus Bohlman, Company F, died October, 1864 at Florence, S.C.
Private Jasper A. Bolles, Company I, died on December 10, 1864 at Andersonville, Ga.
Private Frederick Bopp, Company F, died on December 10, 1864 at Andersonville, Ga.
Private Lamont Burdick, Company L, died date not stated at Andersonville, Ga.
Private Alfred Butler, Company E, died date not stated at Andersonville, Ga.
Private Thomas Condon, Company F, died on July 18, 1864 at Andersonville, Ga.
Private Edward Crawford, Company A, died October 29, 1864 at Andersonville, Ga.
Private Birdsall Cummings, Company L, died, date not stated at Andersonville, Ga.

Private Jonah Dakins, Company F, died February 5, 1865 at Salisbury, S.C.
Private William E. De Clercq, Company E, died, date not known at Andersonville, Ga.
Private David Dikeman, Company F, died July 19, 1864, at Andersonville, Ga.
Private Henry Finch, Company L, died August 23, 184 at Andersonville, Ga.
Private Jonas Finch, Company L, died September 14, 1864 at Andersonville, Ga.
Private Orville Flanders, Company F, died November 9, 1864 at Florence S.C.
Private Peter Fleming, Company I, died date not stated, at Andersonville, Ga.
Private Edward Flynn, Company F, died October 1864, at Charleston, S.C.
Private Ira Franklin, Company L, died July 28, 1864 at Andersonville, Ga.
Private Myron H.Gibbs, Company E, died, no date stated at Andersonville, Ga.
Private Charles Gilbert, Company B, died September 20, 1864 at Andersonville, Ga.
Private Frank Gustin, Company M, died, date not stated, at Andersonville, Ga.
Private Seth M. Hall, Company M, died December 30, 1864, at Salisbury, N.C.
Private Ferdinand Hawkings, Company C, died, date and place not stated.
Private George F. Hawkins, Company F, died, date and place not stated.
Private Jacob Hodge, Company A, died of wounds, August 23, 1864, at Andersonville, Ga.
Private William W. Horton, Company I, died January 22, 1865, at Salisbury, N.C.
Private Myron H. Hoyt, Company A, died July 30, 1864 at Andersonville, Ga.
Private Samuel Hoyt, Company M, died September 30, 1864 at Andersonville, Ga.
Private Adelbert Hues, Company E, died, date not stated at Andersonville, Ga.
Private William H. Hulet, Company L, died June 27, 1864 at Andersonville, Ga.
Private W. Hullt, Company L, died on June 27, 1865 at Andersonville, Ga.
Private David Johnson, Company A, died of wounds September 1, 1864 at Charleston.
Private Thomas Joice, Company C, died, date unknown at Andersonville, Ga.
Private Alanson Ladd, Company F, died September, 1864 at Andersonville, Ga.
Private J. March, Company C, died on July 4, 1865 at Andersonville, Ga.
Private Jerome D. Marsh, Company E, died date not known at Andersonville.
Private Andrew McLennan, Company M, died September 1864 at Andersonville, Ga.
Private Jason Moore, Company E, died date not stated at Andersonville, Ga.
Private Ira S. Morrison, Company B, died September 25, 1864 at Andersonville, Ga.
Private Porter H. Northrup, Company L, died date unknown at Andersonville, Ga.
Private Henry H. Olmstead, Company A, died August 25, 1864 at Andersonville, Ga.
Private J.G. Peck, Company F, died on June 19, 1865 at Andersonville, Ga.
Private Robert Reed, Company E, died date not stated at Andersonville, Ga.
Private William H. Rignor, Company M, died October 20, 1864 at Charleston, S.C.
Private Henry H. Rose, Company H, died date not stated, at Andersonville, Ga.
Private John W. Russ, Company E, died date not stated at Andersonville, Ga.
Private James Ryan, Company E, died date not stated at Andersonville, Ga.
Private William Sager, Company C, died date not known at Florence, S.C.
Private Elmer Sawyer, Company M, died November 25, 1864 at Florence, S.C.
Private Albert G. Sayles, Company F, died date not stated at Andersonville, Ga.
Private William Scholl, Company M, died October 20, 1864 at Charleston, S.C.
Private Benjamin N. Shaver, Company E, died date not stated at Andersonville, Ga.

Private Theodore Smith, Company F, died October, 1864 at Florence, S.C.
Private Hiram M. Stanton, Company K, died July 12, 1864 at Richmond, Va.
Private David Stellrecht, Company L, died August 16, 1864 at Andersonville, Ga.
Private Charles Stevens, Company F, died November 5, 1864 at Florence S.C.
Private Miles T. Terrill, Company A, died October 8, 1864 at Florence, S.C.
Private Ernest Trumpp, Company F, died August 30, 1864 at Andersonville, Ga.
Private John Turner, Company M, died September, 1864 at Andersonville, Ga.
Private George Vibbori, Company E, died date not stated at Andersonville, Ga.
Private Decalyus Wescott, Company F, died February 2, 1865 at Salisbury, N.C.
Private George L. White, Company E, died date not stated at Salisbury, N.C.

Appendix B

Diary of Seth M. Hall
Twenty Second New York Cavalry[1]

On the person of Mason M. Sutherland, who died in Naval School Hospital, March 17th, 1865, from cruel treatment while a prisoner for five months, was found the following diary given him by the writer, who died in prison, December 30th, 1864, to carry to his young wife:

Title page

"Owner of this book, Seth M. Hall, Lieghton, Allegan County, Michigan. If I die here in prison, some friend please to send this to my wife, Emma F. Hall, Lieghton, Allegan County, Michigan".

Diary

Maryland Heights, sitting on a big rock on the edge of the precipice, which is so steep here that a man can hardly go down. It is nothing but rocks here, with a few bushes growing out of the crevices. The side of the mountain further down is covered with chestnut. *** Sergeant Ferris***

September 16th, 1864.- Enlisted at Avon Springs, New York.

September 17th - Mustered into the Twenty-Second New York Cavalry, and went home to Leighton, Allegan Co., Michigan, on furlough. Met Emma at Kalamazoo. Stayed to the fair, and then went home.

October 1st - Reported at headquarters.

October 4th- Went to Elmira; went into barracks No.1, and stayed there until the 15th.

October 15th- Left Elmira and went to Baltimore, Fort Federal Hill. Rode Saturday night, Sunday and all Sunday night in an old freight car and among a set of thieves-hundred days' men of the New York State Militia, Fifty-Sixth regiment.

October 17th- Arrived at Baltimore; met Henry F. Chase, of New York First Dragoon's. Got acquainted with William H. Smith, brother of Laura Smith, Muir, Michigan; his address, William H. Smith, Company K, One Hundred and Eighty-fourth New York State Volunteers.

October 20th- Left Baltimore for Harper's Ferry--rode in a freight car. Heard that Mosby had just captured and robbed the express train; did not know but he would attack us.

October 21st- Arrived at the Ferry all safe. Cavalry sent to Remount Camp at

Pleasant Valley, one mile east of Harper's Ferry. Met G. Willard; found it a pleasant place to stop.

October 25th- Mounted and equipped, and left Remount Camp at 5 o'clock p.m.; marched to Martinsburg, and encamped for the night. Mosby captured General Duffee.

October 26th- Ordered to saddle horses at 4 o'clock a.m., to be ready to repel an attack in case Mosby attacks the town; did not have a chance to fight him. Ordered to pitch tents.

October 27th- Saddled horses at daylight. Left Martinsburg; went as advance guard to a wagon train to Winchester; arrived at 4 o'clock; pitches tents; rained all night; expected an attack from Mosby on the road here, but were disappointed; had our suspicions aroused once by seeing men crossing and recrossing the road ahead, but they proved to be all right. Camp at the front, near Middletown, Virginia.

October 28th- Struck tents and left Winchester at 8 o'clock a.m.; escorted General Seymour to the front; got here at noon; met Iky Wade; our regiment on picket; Iky and I are sitting by our camp fire, with our carbines loaded and ready to sling; our camp is pleasantly situated with but one exception; it is an open field surrounded by a few cedars and plenty of rails; the exception, it is rather close to the rebel lines.

October 29th- Relieved of picket duty at 3 o'clock, and returned to camp and pitched tents. Stood on picket last night for the first time. Wrote a letter to Emma. Heard that Hank Webster is a prisoner at Andersonville.

October 30th- Saddled horses for inspection at 10 a.m. Iky and I took a ride about camp. Iky wrote to mother and I to my wife Emma.

October 31st- Our regiment are out on picket. Harvey Hall and I stood on one post together. Nothing occurred of importance.

November 1st- Relieved of picket duty about 3 o'clock.

November 2nd- Stood guard at the barn with Harvey Hall. Wrote to Emma.

November 3d- Stayed in camp. Rained all day

November 4th- Regiment detailed as escort to Gen. Sheridan. Went up beyond Winchester to look, as I suppose, for winter quarters. Return to Winchester. General Sheridan poisoned.

November 5th- Iky and I slept in a log stable last night. Ordered to saddle up; ordered to unsaddle. General Sheridan recovering. Lay in Winchester all day. A few flakes of snow fell.

November 6th- Returned to camp weary and sick. Received two letters from Emma. Baldwin and Reading got wounded while foraging. Olton missing.

November 7th- Lying in camp

November 8th- Inspection at 8 o'clock. Regiment set out on picket.

November 9th Regiment on picket. I am excused from duty.

November 10th- Ordered to break camp. Marched to near Winchester. Camped on the hill-side in the woods.

November 11th- Moved camp about one mile. Wrote to my wife Emma. Regiment went on reconnaissance [sic].

November 12th- Ordered to saddle up for reconnaissance (sic). Went out and met the Jonnies, and fought them for a while. I was captured in the afternoon by a soldier of the Second Virginia Cavalry. Taken to Strausburg.

November 13th- Lodged in an old house last night. Marched to near Mount Jackson. Lay in the woods over night. Drew our rations regularly.

November 14th- Marched to New Market. Lay in the cold wind all night.

November 15th- Marched to Harrisonburg. Camped in the woods three miles south.

November 16th- Marched to Staunton. Drew rations. Robbed of most all of my clothing.

November 17th- Lay in an old log jail, nasty as a hog-pen.

November 18th- Lying in jail and thinking of my dear wife. Oh how her heart will ache when she hears that I am a prisoner.

November 19th- The same thing as yesterday.

November 20th- Lying in jail at Staunton- a miserable place.

November 21st- Started for Richmond.

November 2nd- Arrived at Richmond in Libby.

November 23d- Removed from Libby across the street to a worse place.

November 24th- Lying in Pemberton prison.

November 25th- Nothing new.

November 26th- Began to draw rations of rice.

November 27th Made some good resolves to serve my God.

November 28th- Prison life is a monotony. Sleep on a hard floor as best you can, without any bedding or blanket; draw rations twice a day; scanty at that, and no news to read, but the sweet angel of hope is ever near.

November 29th- A fellow stole my shirt; but I detected him, and he has been court-martialed and will be punished.

November 30th- Nothing new.

December 1st- Prison life wears heavily.

December 2d- Hoping and talking about exchange of prisoners every day.

December 3d- Moved to third story, east end.

December 4th- Started for Salisbury, North Carolina.

December 5th- Started for Dansville.

December 6th- Arrived at Salisbury. Found a camp of eight thousand prisoners, some of them in tents, and some of them "denned" up in the ground, living on very coarse bread, made of meal and bran, rice once a day, and meat once in three or four.

December 7th- Hard prison life. My thoughts are now reverting to home and the loved ones, those whose thoughts are ever about me.

December 8th- The guard shot five of our men for going to the privy after dark.

December 9th- A hard snow storm. Oh! How my heart aches for suffering humanity in this camp. Many of the boys are without shoes and without any shelter. Oh! Dear Emma, the chances of life here are small. Seventy-seven died today.

December 10th- Cold weather, snow on the ground. Dear Emma, I may never see you more, but still the bright angel of hope keeps my heart whole. My trust is I God. Oh, that you would learn to pray. I pray for you.

December 11th- Weather warmer. All slop under foot. Read a chapter to the boys from the Testament and sung two hymns.

December 12th- One month today since I was taken prisoner. I met Sergeant Ferris, an old acquaintance and friend; he took me into his tent. I am digging a cave in the ground for four of us to live in; one is Friend Hindman, of Company I, Twenty-Second, another Sergeant Cameron, and Pratt.

December 13th- Darling Emma, I many times think I shall never see you more, for the chances of life are small. Three thousand men have died here, out of eight thousand, in two months and a half.

December 14th- I know that many prayers are going up to God for my safety. My trust is in God who is able to deliver.

December 15th- This place of great, great suffering. We live in the mud and filth, with about half enough to eat.

December 16th- The guards shot a negro boy without any provocation.

December 17th- Good news from General Sherman.

December 18th- Oh! Dear ones at home, I know your prayers are ascending to my God for me. You are going to the place of worship. All I have and am is laid on my country's altar. Sergeant Ferris has written home. God bless you, Emma.

December 19th- Pleasant weather. Oh, how my heart aches for the suffering and misery here.

December 20th- Rainy weather. I have got the diarrhea.

December 21st- Sick somewhat. Very cold night. I laid in the hospital over night. My diarrhea worse.

December 22d- Weather keeps cold. A good many have frozen their feet.

December 23d- The Southern Confederacy don't give us half wood enough to keep anywhere near comfortable.

December 24th- Very sick in hospital.
December 25th- Dear mother and father, and Emma; how I wish I was in your society, you could soon nurse me up. I expect you will get this book, if I never return.

December 26th- I am going to write my will. I want this book sent to Emma. I want Emma to have all my property after all my debts are paid. I owe Cheeney $31, with interest. I owe Daniel $161, with interest for one year. Once more; there is a man in Saugatuck, by the name of Jim. Williams, whom I owe a watch; interest and all ought to be about $30. Emory, one dollar.

S.M.HALL

December 27th- I feel a little better today that I have, so that I have wrote my will, how I wish my property disposed of. I pray for deliverance. My thoughts are much on home. You handed me a bowl of bread and milk last night, Emma.

December 30th- I am in hospital very sick, a skeleton, so poor. I hardly expect to ever see sweet home again. Darling Emma, meet me in Heaven. Christmas-day, one year ago, I was at home. I die here- give this to my---

Appendix C

Medals of Honor Recipients

There were four individuals in the 22nd New York Cavalry, who distinguished themselves and earned a Medal of Honor, awarded by the President.[1]

~ Captain Christopher Burton, of Company C, for the capture of General Jubal Early's headquarters flag, the Confederate National Standard, at Waynesboro, Va., on March 2, 1865.

~ Corporal Harry Harvey, of Company A, for the capture of a flag, & bearers at Waynesboro, Va., on March 2, 1865.

~ Private Michael Crowley, of Company A, for the capture of a flag at Waynesboro, Va., on March 2, 1865.

~ Private George Ladd, of Company H, for the capture of a standard bearer, his flag, horse & equipment at Waynesboro, Va. on March 2, 1865.

Capt. Truman H. Allen, Co. K, 22nd N.Y. Cavalry
[Div. of Military Affairs, N.Y. State Adjt. Gen. Office, Albany, N.Y.]

Appendix D

Register of Officers and Men of the Regiment

The officers register of the Twenty Second New York Cavalry reads as follows:[1]

COLONELS:

SAMUEL J. CROOKS, from September 24, 1863, to March 21, 1865
Late Colonel, 8th Cavalry. Appointed Colonel, this regiment September 24, 1863. Mustered in as such March 4, 1864. Discharged March 21, 1865. Commissioned Colonel, May 4, 1864, with rank from January 29, 1864, original.

HORATIO BLAKE REED, from April 14 to August 1, 1865.
2d Lieutenant, 5th U.S. Cavalry; Mustered in at Kearnstown, Va. as Lieutenant-Colonel, this regiment, November 26, 1864; as Colonel, April 14, 1865. Mustered out with regiment on August 1, 1865 at Winchester, Va. Commissioned Lieutenant-Colonel, September 14, 1864, with rank from September 13, 1864, vice Brown, discharged; Colonel, commissioned recalled, not mustered, January 25, 1865, with rank from January 24, 1865, vice Cram, not mustered; Recommissioned Colonel March 10, 1865, with rank from January 24, 1865, vice himself, not mustered.

LIEUTENANT-COLONELS:

JOHNSON BUTLER BROWN, from October 5, 1863 to July 20, 1864
Late Lieutenant-Colonel 101st Infantry: enrolled at Yates to serve three years and appointed this regiment October 5, 1863. Mustered in as such February 17, 1864. Discharged July 20, 1864, Commissioned Lieutenant-Colonel March 30, 1864, with rank from January 10, 1864, original.

HORATIO BLAKE REED, from November 26, 1864, to April 14, 1865.
See Colonel this regiment.

PETER McLENNAN, from May 5 to August 1, 1865
Late Captain 101st Infantry. Mustered in as Major, this regiment on February 4, 1864; Captured in action and paroled, no date. Mustered in as Lieutenant Colonel, May 5, 1865. Mustered out with regiment on August 1, 1865 at Winchester, Va.; Colonel U.S. Volunteers by brevet, from March 13, 1865; commissioned major, March 30, 1864, with rank from January 10, 1864, original; Lieutenant Colonel, March 21, 1865, vice Reed, promoted.

MAJORS:

PETER McLENNAN, from February 4, 1864, to May 5, 1865.
See Lieutenant Colonels this regiment.

CHARLES C. BROWN, from February 23, 1864, to August 1, 1865
Late Captain 13th Infantry. Mustered in as Captain, Company A, this regiment

December 31, 1863, as Major, February 23, 1864, Mustered out with regiment August 1, 1865 at Winchester, Va. Lieutenant-Colonel N.Y. Volunteers, by brevet, not commissioned Captain: commissioned Major, March 30, 1864, with rank from January 29, 1864, original.

THEODORE SCHLICK, from March 4 to August 25, 1864.
Late Captain, 23d Infantry; mustered in as Major, this regiment, March 4, 1864. Killed in action, August 25, 1864, at Kearnsville, Va.; commissioned Major, March 30, 1864, with rank from January 29, 1864, original.

GEORGE R. FRENCH, from September 13, 1864, to August 1, 1865.
Age 20 years. Enrolled at Syracuse to serve three Years and mustered in as a Captain in Company B, January 5, 1864: as Major, to date September 13, 1864. Mustered out with regiment on August 1, 1865 at Winchester, Va. See 101st Infantry. Commissioned Captain, March 30, 1864, with rank from January 5,1864, original. Major, September 13, 1864, with rank from August 25, 1864, vice Schlick, killed in action.

BENJAMIN BENNETT, from April 14 to August 1, 1865.
Late First Lieutenant, 23d Infantry. Enrolled November 9, 1863 at Urbans to serve three years. Mustered in as a Captain in Company G, this regiment. January 29, 1864. Captured in action and paroled, no date given. Mustered in as Major, April 14, 1865 at Winchester, Va. Lieutenant Colonel, U.S. Volunteers, by brevet from March 13, 1865. Commissioned Captain, March 30, 1864, with rank from January 29, 1864, original. Major, March 21, 1865, with rank from January 24, 1865, vice McLennan, promoted.

ADJUTANTS:

JOSEPH H. SUGGETT, from September 26, 1863, to July 25, 1864.
First Lieutenant, 140th Infantry; mustered in as a First Lieutenant and Adjutant, this regiment, September 26, 1863. Dismissed, July 25, 1864. Commissioned First Lieutenant and Adjutant, March 30, 1864, with rank from September 26, 1863, original.

CHARLES H. CLARK, from January 18 to August 1, 1865
Late Lieutenant-Colonel 121st Infantry. Mustered in as First Lieutenant and Adjutant in this regiment January 18, 1865. Mustered out with regiment August 1, 1865 at Winchester, Va. Commissioned First Lieutenant and Adjutant, December 24, 1864, with rank from December 20, 1864, vice Suggett, dismissed.

QUARTERMASTERS:

GEORGE B. BRAND, from September 28, 1863 to March 4, 1864
Age 32 years. Enrolled at Rochester to serve three years. Mustered in as First Lieutenant and Quartermaster, September 28, 1863. Resigned March 4, 1864; see 90th Infantry. Commissioned First Lieutenant and Quartermaster March 30, 1864, with rank from September 26, 1863, original.

JAMES H. NELLIS, from March 7, 1864, to May 15, 1865.
Age__ years. Enrolled to serve three years and mustered in as First Lieutenant and Quartermaster at Giesboro Point, D.C., March 7, 1864. Captured in action and paroled, no date. Mustered out may 15, 1865; Major N.Y. Volunteers, by brevet; commissioned First Lieutenant and Quartermaster, March 7, 1864, vice Brand, resigned.

SURGEONS:

JAMES D. JONES, from _____, to December 19, 1863.
Age 35 years. Reported to the War Department as surgeon, no date of entry into service; accepted appointment as Surgeon, in 25th Cavalry, December 19, 1863; not commissioned.

DAVID B. VAN SLYCK, from November 7, 1863, to August 1, 1865.
Late surgeon 101st Infantry. Enrolled at Rochester to serve three years. Mustered in as a Surgeon this regiment November 7, 1863. Mustered out with regiment, August 1, 1865 at Winchester, Va. Commissioned Surgeon, March 30, 1864 with rank from October 24, 1863, original.

ASSISTANT SURGEONS:

PATRICK McSHANE, from January 20 to June 12, 1864.
Age 43 years. Enrolled at Sparta to serve three years, and mustered in as Assistant Surgeon, January 20, 1864; Discharged for disability, June 12, 1864; remustered in the same grade, September 2, 1864. Discharged for disability, December 2, 1864; commissioned Assistant Surgeon, March 30, 1864, with rank from January 4, 1864, original. Recommissioned, August 22, 1864, with rank from August 9, 1864, vice himself, discharged.

JESSE B. LOSEY, from February 2 to July 6, 1864.
Age 35 years. Enrolled at Sparta to serve three years and mustered in as Assistant Surgeon, February 2, 1864. Discharged for disability on July 6, 1864. Mustered in with same grade on January 1, 1865. Mustered out with regiment on August 1, 1865 at Winchester, Va. Commissioned Assistant Surgeon on March 30, 1864, with rank from January 23, 1864, original. Recommissioned on November 30, 1864, vice McShane, resigned

DWIGHT M. LEE, from May 5, to August 1, 1865.
Age 22 years. Enrolled April 11, 1865 at Rochester to serve three years. Mustered in as Assistant Surgeon, May 5, 1865. Mustered out with regiment on August 1, 1865 at Winchester, Va. Commissioned Assistant Surgeon April 22, 1865 with rank from April 11, 1865, vice Losey, discharged.

Co. A

CAPTAINS:

CHARLES C. BROWN, from December 31, 1863, to February 23, 1864
See Majors this regiment.

JOHN WRENN, from February 23 to July 13, 1864.
Age 23 years. Enrolled October 9, 1863 at Rochester to serve three years. Mustered in as First Lieutenant, Company A, December 31, 1863; as Captain, February 23, 1864; resigned, July 13, 1864, at City Point, Va. Subsequent service in 1st Independent Battalion Light Cavalry, Militia; not commissioned First Lieutenant; commissioned Captain, March 30, 1864, with rank from January 5, 1864, original.

HARLAN P. LLOYD, from July 23, 1864, to August 1, 1865
Age 24 years. Enrolled August 29, 1862 at Perry to serve three years. Mustered in as a Private in the 24th Battery on August 30, 1862; promoted Sergeant, November 1, 1862; First Sergeant, January 6, 1863; transferred to this regiment on March 23, 1864. Mustered in as a First Lieutenant in Company A on April 7, 1864; as Captain July 23, 1864. Mustered out with company on August 1, 1865 at Winchester, Va.; Major U.S. Volunteers by brevet from March 13, 1865; commissioned First Lieutenant, March 26, 1864, original; with rank from January 5, 1864, original; Captain, August 12, 1864 with rank from July 23, 1864, vice Wrenn, resigned.

1st LIEUTENANTS:

JOHN WRENN, from December 31, 1863, to February 23, 1864.
See Captains, this regiment.

HARLAN P. LLOYD, from April 7 to July 23, 1864.
See Captains this regiment.

GEORGE SPERRY, from_____, to April 29, 1865.
See Captains Co. F.

2nd LIEUTENANTS:

HENRY P. STARR, from December 20, 1863, to November 2, 1864.
Age 21 years. Enrolled August 12, 1862 at Rochester to serve three years. Mustered in as a Private, Company M, 3d Cavalry, September 10, 1862; as Second Lieutenant, Company A, this regiment, December 20, 1863. Captured in action and paroled, no dates. Transferred to Company K, November 2, 1864; to Company E, no date. Mustered out with company, August 1, 1865 at Winchester, Va. Commissioned Second Lieutenant, March 30, 1864, with rank from January 5, 1864, original.

ORAN EMMETT, from January 28 to June 28, 1865.
See First Lieutenants Co.B.

DWIGHT W. HAZELTON, from January 4, to April 9, 1865.
Age 18 years. Enrolled December 12, 1863 at Smithfield to serve three years. Mustered in as a private in Company G, February 2, 1864; as Second Lieutenant, March 4, 1864. Captured in action and paroled, no date. Transferred to Company M, no date, to Company A, January 4, 1865; to Company G, April 9, 1865; to Company D, May 27, 1865. Mustered out with company on August 1, 1865 at Winchester, Va. Commissioned Second Lieutenant, March 30, 1864, with rank from January 29, 1864, original. Commissioned First Lieutenant, not mustered, July 15, 1865, with rank from June 22, 1865, vice Davidson, not mustered.

LEWIS MOORE, from April 23 to August 1, 1865.
Age 26 years. Enrolled November 10, 1863 at Rochester to serve three years. Mustered in as Sergeant in Company A on December 30, 1863, as Second Lieutenant to date April 23, 1865. Mustered out with company on August 1, 1865 at Winchester, Va.; commissioned Second Lieutenant on April 22, 1865, with rank from April 14, 1865, vice Conover, promoted ; First Lieutenant, not mustered, July 15, 1865, with rank from July 11, 1865, vice Smyth, discharged

Co. B

CAPTAINS:

GEORGE R. FRENCH, from January 5 to September 13, 1864.
See Majors, this regiment.

LUCIEN B. CADWELL, from September 27, 1864, to August 1, 1865
Late First Lieutenant 61st Infantry . Mustered in as a First Lieutenant in Company B of this regiment January 5,1864. As Captain, September 27, 1864. Mustered out with company August 1, 1865 at Winchester, Va. Major, U.S. Volunteers, by brevet from March 13, 1865, commissioned First Lieutenant March 30, 1864, with rank for January 16, 1864. Commissioned Captain September 16, 1864 with rank from July 27, 1864, vice Provost, discharged.

1st LIEUTENANTS:

LUCIEN B. CADWELL, from January 5 to September 27, 1864
See Captains Co. B

CHARLES W. PATRICK, from October 26, 1864, to July 5, 1865.
Age 19 years. Enrolled August 26, 1862 at Rome, to serve three years. Mustered in as a Private in Company I, 81st Infantry, September 9, 1862; promoted Corporal, September 23, 1863, discharged for promotion, September 30, 1864. Mustered in as First Lieutenant, Company B, this regiment, October 26, 1864; discharged for disability, July 5, 1865. Major, N.Y. Volunteers, by brevet; commissioned First Lieutenant August 15, 1864 with rank from same date, vice Lloyd promoted; Captain, not mustered, declined, May 31, 1865, with rank from May 15, 1865, vice Wisner, discharged.

REUBEN L. FOX, from November 26. 1864, to March 29, 1865
Age 20 years. Enrolled August 1, 1862 at Munnsville to serve three years. Mustered in as a private in Battery A 1st Light Artillery, August 13, 1862. Promoted Sergeant, no date given. Discharged April 1, 1863 at Utica, N.Y. Again enrolled at Fabius to serve three years and mustered in as a private in Company B, January 5, 1864; as Second Lieutenant, January 15, 1864; as First Lieutenant, November 26, 1864. Discharged for disability March 29, 1865. Commissioned Second Lieutenant March 30, 1864 with rank from January 5, 1964, original; First Lieutenant, December 19, 1864 with rank from November 23, 1864, vice Newman, promoted.

HERBERT D. PECK, from May 5 to June 22, 1865.
See Captains, Company I.

ORAN EMMETT, from July 7, to August 1, 1865.
Age 20 years. Enrolled May 22, 1861 at Hammondsport to serve two years. Mustered in as a sergeant, Company I, 34th Infantry, June 15, 1861. Promoted Sergeant-Major, March 16, 1863. Mustered out with regiment June 30, 1863 at Albany N.Y. Again enrolled January 1, 1864 at Urbana to serve three years. Mustered in as a Sergeant, Company G, this regiment February 2, 1864. Promoted Sergeant-Major, no date given. Mustered in as a second Lieutenant in Company A, January 28, 1865, transferred to Company F, June 28, 1865. Mustered in as a First Lieutenant, Company B, July 7, 1865. Mustered out with company August 1, 1865 at Winchester, Va. Commissioned Second Lieutenant January 20,1865 with rank from January 3,1865, vice Cornes, commission revoked. First Lieutenant May 31, 1865, with rank from May 15, 1865, vice Patrick, discharged.

2nd LIEUTENANTS:

REUBEN L. FOX, from January 15 to November 26, 1864
See First Lieutenant Co. B.

GEORGE B. CORKINS, from January 7 to August 1, 1865
Age 31 years. Enrolled November 18, 1864 at Syracuse to serve three years. Mustered in as a First Sergeant in Company B, January 5, 1864, as Second Lieutenant January 7, 1865. Mustered out with the company on August 1, 1865 at Winchester, Va. Prior service in the 5th U.S. Cavalry. Commissioned Second Lieutenant December 19, 1864 with rank from December 1, 1864, vice Arnd, declined.

Co.C

CAPTAINS:

FRANKLIN EDWARDS, from January 16, 1864, to March 29, 1865
Age 25 years. Enrolled at Rochester to serve three years. Mustered in as a Captain in Company C, January 16, 1864. Discharged for disability, March 29, 1865. Commissioned Captain March 30, 1864 with rank from January 5, 1864, original.
CHRISTOPHER C. BRUTON, from November 4, 1864, to August 1, 1865

Age 22 years. Enrolled January 6, 1864 at Rochester to serve three years. Mustered in as a First Lieutenant, Company C, January 16, 1864, as Captain, November 4, 1864. Mustered out with company August 1, 1865 at Winchester, Va. Major U.S. Volunteers, by brevet from March 13, 1865. Medal of Honor awarded. Commissioned First Lieutenant, March 30, 1864 with rank from January 5, 1864 original. Captain, October 4, 1864, vice T.H. Allen, discharged.

1st LIEUTENANTS:

CHRISTOPHER C. BRUTON, from January16 to November 4, 1864
See Captains Co.C.

GEORGE SPERRY, from January 4 to ___,1865.
See Captains Co. F

FRANKLIN A. COLLISTER, from January 12 to June 26, 1865
Age 28 years. Enrolled November 10, 1863 at Riga to serve three years. Mustered in as a First Sergeant in Company C, January 5, 1864, as Second Lieutenant, February 24, 1864. Discharged for disability, September 8, 1864. Mustered in as a First Lieutenant in Company C to date January 12, 1865. Transferred to Company D June 26, 1865. Mustered out with company August 1, 1864 at Winchester, Va. Commissioned Second Lieutenant March 30, 1864 with rank from January 1864, original. First Lieutenant, November 19, 1864 with rank of same date, vice Bruton, promoted.

WILLIAM H. CONOVER, from April 23 to August 1, 1865
Age 19 years. Enrolled January 4, 1864 at Norwich to serve three years. Mustered in as a private in Company L February 12, 1864, as Second Lieutenant February 15, 1864. Captured in action and paroled, no date given. Mustered in as First Lieutenant in Company C, April 23, 1865. Mustered out with company August 1, 1865 at Winchester, Va. Commissioned Second Lieutenant, March 30, 1864 with rank from January 29, 1864, original. First Lieutenant, April 22, 1865 with rank from April 14, 1865, vice Fox, discharged.

2nd LIEUTENANTS:

FRANKLIN A. COLLISTER, from February 24 to September 8, 1864
See First Lieutenants Co.C.

EDWARD W. NEWMAN, from June 6 to August 1, 1865.
Late Second Lieutenant, 111th Infantry, not mustered; Mustered in as a Second Lieutenant, Company C, this regiment, June 6, 1865. Mustered out with company, August 1, 1865at Winchester, Va. Commissioned Second Lieutenant, April 22, 1986, with rank from April 14, 1865, vice Beeby, promoted.

Co.D

CAPTAINS:

MICHAEL McMULLEN, from January 30, 1864, to March 8, 1865.
Late First Lieutenant, 105th Infantry ; enrolled November 10, 1863 at Fenner, to serve three years. Mustered in as a Captain in Company D this regiment, January 30, 1864; wounded in action, November 12, 1864. Discharged for disability from wounds, March 8, 1865; commissioned Captain, March 30, 1864, with rank from January 10, 1864, original.

JOHN SPREADBURY, from March 28 to august 1, 1865
Age 43 years. Enrolled to serve three years and mustered in at Kearnstown, Va. as First Lieutenant, Company D, November 19, 1864; as Captain, March 28, 1865; mustered out with company, August 1, 1865 at Winchester, Va.; Major, U.S. Volunteers, by brevet, from April 2, 1865; commissioned First Lieutenant, September 17, 1864, with rank from same date, vice Cadwell, promoted; Captain, March 21, 1865, with rank from same date, vice McMullen, discharged.

1st LIEUTENANTS:

JACOB FISHER, from January 30, to November 29, 1864.
See Captains Co. G.

JOHN SPREADBURY, from November 19, 1864, to March 28, 1865.
See Captain this regiment.

WILLIAM P. BROWN, from January to May, 1865.
See First Lieutenants Co.H.

FRANKLIN A. COLLISTER, from June 26 to August 1, 1865
See First Lieutenants Co.C.

2nd LIEUTENANTS:

PATRICK R. GLENNAN, from January 30 to June 22, 1864.
Age 22 years. Enrolled April 25, 1864 at Rochester to serve two years. Mustered in as a private in Company I 13th Infantry on may 14, 1862; transferred Company H, October 29, 1861; Promoted to first Sergeant, no date. Returned to ranks on November 1, 1861, promoted Sergeant, January 1, 1862. First Sergeant, may 1, 1862; returned to ranks and captured in action, June 27, 1862 at Meadow Bridge,Va. ;paroled August 5, 1862; transferred to Company D October 31, 1862 and mustered out with company may 14, 1863 at Rochester N.Y. Enrolled again November 30, 1863 at Hamilton to serve three years; mustered in as a First Sergeant in Company D, this regiment on January 10, 1864; as Second Lieutenant, January 30, 1864. was killed in action June 22, 1864 at Dinwiddie Court House, Va. Commissioned Second Lieutenant, March 30, 1864, with rank from January 10, 1864, original.

DWIGHT W. HAZELTON, from May 27 to August 1, 1865.
See Second Lieutenant Co. A.

Co. E

CAPTAINS:

FRANKLIN R. PERKINS, from January 30 to November 23, 1864.
Age 22 years. Enrolled January 10, 1864 at Cazenovia to serve three years. Mustered in as Captain, Company E, January 30, 1864; discharged for disability, November 23, 1864. Commissioned Captain March 30, 1864, with rank from January 10, 1864, original.

GEORGE W. NEWMAN, from January 4 to August 1, 1865
Age 21 years. Enrolled June 13, 1861, at Rochester to serve three years. Mustered in as a Private in Company A, 3d Cavalry, July 17, 1861. Re-enlisted as a veteran, January 5, 1864. Mustered in as a Second Lieutenant, Company G, this regiment, February 6, 1864; as First Lieutenant, Company E, January 1, 1865; as Captain, January 4, 1865. Mustered out with company, August 1, 1865 at Winchester, Va. Major, N.Y. Volunteers, by brevet, from March 13, 1864, original; First Lieutenant, June 29, 1864, with rank from June 14, 184, vice Layton. Died of wounds received in action; Captain, December 19, 1864, with rank from November 23, 1864, vice Perkins, discharged.

1st LIEUTENANTS:

ALONZO B. ALLEN, from February 1 to July 27, 1864
Age 20 years. enrolled January 10, 1864 at Cazenovia to serve three years. Mustered in as a First Lieutenant in Company E, February 1, 1864. Discharged for disability July 27, 1864. Commissioned first Lieutenant March 30, 1864 with rank from January 10, 1864, original.

GEORGE W. NEWMAN, from January 1 to January 4, 1865.
See Captain this Regiment.

JAMES STEVENSON VAN CORTLANDT, from October 31, 1864 to August 1, 1865.
Second Lieutenant 15th Infantry; appointed First Lieutenant, this regiment, October 31, 1864. Mustered in as such in Company E, at Winchester, Va., January 1, 1865. Mustered out with company August 1, 1865 at Winchester, Va. Commissioned First Lieutenant, August 25, 1864, with rank from August 23, 1864, vice Lusk, promoted; Captain, not mustered, September 18, 1865, with rank from August 31, 1865, vice Vaughan, discharged.

2nd LIEUTENANTS:

HERBERT D. PECK, from January 10, 1864, to May 5, 1865.
See Captain, Company I.

HENRY P. STARR, from ____ to August 1, 1865.
See Second Lieutenant Co. A.

Co. F

CAPTAINS:

ISADORE E. PROVOST, from January 30 to July 27, 1864.
Age 46 years. Enrolled at Rochester to serve three years and mustered in as Captain, Company F, January 30, 1864. Discharged for disability, July 27, 1864. Commissioned Captain March 30, 1864 with rank from January 10,1864, original.

GEORGE SPERRY, from April 29 to August 1, 1865
Age 38 years. Enrolled At Homer, Ill, to serve three years, and mustered in as a Private, Company C, 100th Ill. Volunteers, August 30, 1862; as First Lieutenant, this regiment, June 25, 1864, Commanding Company F, from September 1864. Transferred to Company C, January 4, 1864, to Company A, no date. Mustered in as a Captain, Company F to date April 29, 1865. Mustered out with company, August 1, 1865 at Winchester, Va.; Major U.S. Volunteers, by brevet, from March 13, 1865; Commissioned First Lieutenant, March 30, 1864, with rank from January 10, 1864, original; Captain, April 22, 1865, with rank from March 29, 1865, vice Edwards, discharged

1st LIEUTENANTS:

GEORGE SPERRY, from September, 1864 to January 4, 1865
See Captain, this regiment.

MARVIN R. SHERWOOD, from March 31 to May 5, 1865.
See Captains Co.M.

HENRY E. BEEBY, from May 5 to August 1, 1865
Age 24 years. Enrolled June 13, 1861 at Syracuse to serve three years. Assigned to Company B, 3d Cavalry, no date. Promoted Sergeant July 30, 1861. Re-enlisted as a veteran January 5, 1864. Mustered in as a Second Lieutenant in Company F this regiment January 30, 1864. Captured in action and paroled, no date given. Mustered in as First Lieutenant to date May 5, 1865. Mustered out with company, August 1, 1865 at Winchester, Va. Captain U.S. Volunteers, by brevet from March 13, 1865. Commissioned Second Lieutenant, March 30, 1864 with rank from January 10, 1864. First Lieutenant, April 22, 1865 with rank from April 14, 1865, vice Yates. Accidentally killed.

2nd LIEUTENANTS:

HENRY E. BEEBY, from January 30, 1864, to May 5, 1865
See First Lieutenants this regiment.

ISRAEL B. TAYLOR, from May 16 to May 24, 1865.
Age 40 years. Enrolled December 8, 1863 at Rochester to serve three years. Mustered in as Commissary-Sergeant, Company I, February 2, 1864. Promoted Second Lieutenant Company F, May 16, 1865. Resigned, May 24, 1865; commissioned Second Lieutenant, December 7, 1864, with rank from September 26, 1864, vice Redington, dismissed.

ORAN EMMET, from June 28 to July 7, 1865.
See First Lieutenant Co. B.

GEORGE F. WOODWARD, from July 30 to August 1, 1865.
Age 30 years. Enrolled to serve three years and mustered in at Giesboro Point, D.C., as Private in Company F, March 23, 1864. Promoted Sergeant, no date, Sergeant-Major, no date. Mustered in as Second Lieutenant, Company F, July 30, 1865. Mustered out with company, August 1, 1865 at Winchester, Va. Commissioned Second Lieutenant, commission revoked, not mustered, November, 10, 1864, with rank from September 10, 1864, vice Collister, discharged. Recommissioned Second Lieutenant, May 31, 1865, with rank from May 22, 1865, vice Taylor, resigned.

Co. G

CAPTAINS:

BENJAMIN BENNETT, from January 29, 1864 to April 14, 1865
See Majors, this regiment.

JACOB FISHER, from December 1, 1964, to April 30, 1865.
Age 25 years. Enrolled November 10, 1863 at Fenner to serve three years. Mustered in as a First Lieutenant in Company D, January 30, 1864; as Captain, Company M, November 29, 1864, commanding Company G from December 1, 1864, to April 30, 1865: Company M from May, 1865. Transferred to Company K May 31, 1865. Mustered out with company August 1, 1865 at Winchester, Va. Major, U.S. Volunteers by brevet, from March 13, 1865, commissioned First Lieutenant March 30, 1864, with rank from January 10, 1864, original; Captain, November 11, 1864, with rank from August 25, 1864, vice French, promoted.

1st LIEUTENANTS:

DANIEL LAYTON, from February 24 to June 14, 1864.
Age 28 years. Enrolled January 21, 1864 at Utica to serve three years. Mustered in as a First Lieutenant in Company G, February 24, 1864. Died June 14, 1864 of wounds received in action on June 13, 1864 at White Oak Swamp, Va. Commissioned First Lieutenant, March 30, 1864, with rank from January 29, 1864, original..

JAMES AUSTIN, from April 23 to August 1, 1865
Age 31 years. Enrolled at Winchester, Va. to serve three years. Mustered in as First Lieutenant in Company G, April 23, 1865. Mustered out with company August 1, 1865 at Winchester, Va. Prior service in the 5th U.S. Artillery. Commissioned, not mustered Second Lieutenant January 25, 1865 with rank from January 15, 1865, vice Woodward, commission revoked. First lieutenant, February 18, 1865 with rank from February 1, 1865, vice Cooney, not mustered

2nd LIEUTENANTS:

GEORGE W. NEWMAN, from February 6, 1864 to January 1, 1865.
See Captain Co. E.

DWIGHT W. HAZELTON, from March 4, 1864 to ____
See Second Lieutenant Co. A.

FREDERICK ARND, from July 12, 1864 to June 28, 1865
Age 31 years. Enrolled April 30, 1861 at Bath to serve three years. Mustered in as a sergeant in Company A, 23d infantry, May 16, 1861. Transferred to Company L, 1st Cavalry, September 21, 1861. Discharged to date May 22, 1863 at Elmira, NY. Enrolled January 4, 1864 to serve three years. Mustered in as a First Sergeant in Company G, 22d New York Cavalry February 2, 1864. Captured June 29, 1864, paroled November 30, 1864. Mustered in as a Second lieutenant to date July 12, 1864. Discharged June 28, 1865. at Winchester Va. Commissioned Second Lieutenant June 29, 1864, vice Newman, promoted. Recommisioned, not mustered, declined, Second Lieutenant, May 15, 1865, vice Emmett, promoted.

DWIGHT W. HAZELTON, from April 9 to May 27, 1865
See Second Lieutenant Co. A.

Co. H

CAPTAINS:

JAMES G. VAN MARTER, from January 29, 1864 to July 26, 1864.
Age 28 years. Enrolled at Lyons to serve three years and mustered in as Captain, Company H, January 29, 1864; dismissed July 26, 1864. Commissioned Captain, March 30, 1864 with rank from January 29, 1864, original.

LYCURGUS D. LUSK, from July 29, 1864 to August 1, 1865.
Late Second Lieutenant, 17th Infantry. Mustered in as a First Lieutenant in Company H of this regiment on February 6, 1864; as Captain, July 27, 1864. Mustered out with company on August 1, 1865 at Winchester, Va.; Major, U.S. Volunteers, by brevet, from March 13, 1865; commissioned First Lieutenant, March 30, 1864, with rank from January 29, 1864, vice Van Marter, dismissed.

1st LIEUTENANTS:

LYCURGUS D. LUSK, from February 6 to July 27, 1864.
See Captain Co. H.

WILLIAM P. BROWN, from January 4 to January 27, 1865
Age 26 years. Enrolled January 18, 1864 at Syracuse to serve three years. Mustered in as a First Sergeant, Company H, February 2, 1864, as Second Lieutenant January 4, 1865, as First Lieutenant January 27, 1865 commanding Company D, from January to May, 1865, inclusive, Mustered out with company, August 1, 1865 at Winchester Va. Prior service in 2d U.S. Cavalry, commissioned Second Lieutenant, December 19, 1864 with rank from November 23, 1864, vice Fox, promoted ; First Lieutenant, January 20, 1865, with rank from December 21, 1864, vice Whitfield, discharged.

2nd LIEUTENANTS:

HERMAN R. DUNNING, from February 8 to August 9, 1864
Age 27 years. Enrolled at Lyons to serve three years and mustered in as second Lieutenant in Co. H, February 8, 1864. Discharged for disability from wounds, August 9 1864. Commissioned Second Lieutenant March 30, 1864 with rank from January 29, 1864, original.

WILLIAM P. BROWN, from January 4 to January 27, 1865
See 1st Lieutenants Co. H.

HERBERT LORD, from March 24 to August 1, 1865.
Age 20 years. Enrolled December 24, 1863 at Manilas to serve three years. Mustered in as a Sergeant in Company E January 10, 1864; as Second Lieutenant in Company H, March 24, 1865 commanding Company I, in the month of April, 1865. Mustered out with company August 1, 1865 at Winchester, Va. Prior service in the 1st Wisconsin Cavalry. Commissioned Second Lieutenant, March 21, 1865 with rank from January 24, 1865, vice Peck, promoted.

Co. I

CAPTAINS:

OSCAR F. WISNER, from February 10, 1864, to May 15, 1865.
Age 38 years. Enrolled February 2, 1864 at Sparta, to serve three years. Mustered in as Captain this regiment, February 10,1864. Discharged, May 15, 1865. Commissioned Captain, March 30, 1864, with rank from January, 29, 1864, original.

HERBERT D. PECK, from June 22 to August 1, 1865.
Age 21 years. Enrolled at Dewitt to serve three years, and mustered in as Second Lieutenant, Company E, January 10, 1864; Captured in action and paroled, no dates. Mustered in as First Lieutenant, Company B, May 5, 1865; as Captain, Company I, June 22, 1865. Mustered out with company August 1, 1865 at Winchester, Va.

Commissioned Second Lieutenant, March 30, 1864, with rank from January 10, 1864, original. ;First Lieutenant, March 21, 1865, with rank from January 24, 1865, vice Sherwood, promoted; Captain, June 29, 1865, with rank from June 22, 1865, vice Patrick, declined.

1st LIEUTENANTS:

EBEN WHITFIELD, from April 16 to December 19, 1864.
Age 28 years. Enrolled to serve three years and mustered in at Camp Stoneman, D.C. as First Lieutenant, Company I, April 16, 1864. Discharged for disability, December 19, 1864. Commissioned First Lieutenant, March 30, 1864 with rank from January 29, 1864, original.

2nd LIEUTENANTS:

WARREN W. LAMB, from February 12, to September 8, 1864.
Late Second Lieutenant, 50th Engineers. Enrolled December 9, 1863 at Rochester to serve three years. Mustered in as a Second Lieutenant in Company I, February 12, 1864; commissioned Second Lieutenant, March 30, 1864, with rank from January 29, 1864, original.

HERBERT LORD, in April 1865.
See Second Lieutenant Co. H.

Co. K

CAPTAINS:

TRUMAN H. ALLEN, from February 9 to July 27, 1864
Age 32 years. Enrolled at Pomfret to serve three years. Mustered in as a Captain in Company K February 9, 1864. Discharged for disability July 27, 1864. Commissioned Captain March 30,1864 with rank from January 29, 1864, original.

ROBERT E. ELLERBECK, from April 9 to May 15, 1865.
See Captains Co. M.

JACOB FISHER, from May 31 to August 1, 1865.
See Captain Co. G.

1st LIEUTENANTS:

SQUIRE M. YATES, from February 17, 1864 to April 9, 1865.
Age 21 years. Enrolled November 15, 1861 at Smyrna to serve three years. Mustered in as a Private in Company I, 8th Cavalry, November 28, 1861. Promoted Regimental Quartermaster-Sergeant, April 14, 1862. Re-enlisted as a veteran, December 1, 1863. Mustered in as a First Lieutenant, Company K, this regiment, February 17, 1864. Accidentally killed, April 9, 1865. Commissioned First Lieutenant, March 30, 1864, with rank from January 29, 1864, original.

ARTHUR T. TILESTON, from May 10 to August 1,1865.
See First Lieutenants Co. L.

2nd LIEUTENANTS:

CHARLES F. REDDINGTON, from February 16 to September 26, 1864.
Age 19 years. Enrolled January 29, 1864 at Pomfret to serve three years. Mustered in as Second Lieutenant in Company K, February 16, 1864; dismissed, September 26, 1864; commissioned Second Lieutenant, March 30, 1864 with rank from January 29, 1864, original.

HENRY P. STARR, from November 2, 1864 to _____
See Second Lieutenant Co. A.

JAMES P. CORNES, from May 19 to August 1, 1865
Age 18 years. Enrolled January 22, 1864 at Brockport to serve three years. Mustered in as Commissary-Sergeant, Company K February 6, 1864. Transferred to Company C, March 25, 1864, mustered in as a Second Lieutenant in Company K May 19, 1865. Mustered out with company August 1, 1865 at Winchester, Va. Commissioned, not mustered, Second Lieutenant December 22, 1864, with rank from December 2, 1864, vice Dayton, not mustered. Recommissioned Second Lieutenant, February 25, 1865 with rank from February 1, 1865, vice Austin, promoted.

Co. L

CAPTAINS:

HENRY S. VAUGHAN, from February 15, 1864 to August 31, 1865.
Late Second Lieutenant 101st Infantry. Enrolled December 30, 1863 at Pitcher to serve three years. Mustered in as Captain, Company L, this regiment, February 15, 1864. Discharged August 31, 1865; Commissioned Captain March 30, 1864, with rank from January 29, 1864, original

1st LIEUTENANTS:

MARVIN R. SHERWOOD, from February 15, 1864 to March 31, 1865.
See Captain Co. M.

GEORGE SPERRY, from June 25, 1864 to January 4, 1865.
See Captain, Co. F

ARTHUR T. TILESTON, from September 29, 1864 to May 10, 1865.
Age 19 years. Enrolled September 10 1861 at New York to serve three years. Mustered in as a Private Company C, 5th Cavalry, September 13, 1861; re-enlisted as a veteran, January 1, 1864; promoted and First Sergeant, no dates; discharged April 10, 1864, for promotion; mustered in as First Lieutenant, Company L, this regiment, September 29, 1864. Transferred to Company K, May 10, 1865;

commanding Company L, June and July 1865; mustered out with Company K, August 1, 1865 at Winchester, Va. Commissioned First Lieutenant, September 17, 1864 with rank from same date, vice A.B. Allen, discharged.

JAMES MONTRESSOR SMYTH, from May 27 to July 6, 1865.
Age 37 years. Enrolled at Jamaica to serve one year. Mustered in as a Private 79th Infantry, September 19, 1864. Mustered out May 8, 1865 at Hart's Island, New York Harbor. Mustered in at Winchester, Va. as First Lieutenant, Company L, this regiment, May 27, 1865; discharged, July 6, 1865, commissioned, not mustered, Second Lieutenant, January 20, 1865, with rank from January 3, 1865, vice Brown, promoted; First Lieutenant, March 21, 1865, with rank from same date, vice Weeks, discharged.

2nd LIEUTENANTS:

MARVIN R. SHERWOOD, from February 12 to February 15, 1864.
See Captain Co. M.

WILLIAM H. CONOVER, from February 15, 1864 to April 23, 1865.
See First Lieutenant Co. C.

GEORGE W. MOXCEY, from May 5 to August 1, 1865.
Age 17 years. Enrolled November 30, 1863 at Rochester to serve three years. mustered in as a Private in Company A, December 20, 1863; promoted to Corporal, no date. Mustered in as Second Lieutenant in Company L, May 5, 1865. Mustered out with company on August 1, 1865 at Winchester, Va. Commissioned Second Lieutenant, April 22, 1865, with rank from April 14, 1865, vice Smyth, promoted.

Co. M

CAPTAINS:

ROBERT E. ELLERBECK, from February 23, 1864 to April 9, 1865.
Late Captain 6th Cavalry. Enrolled December 26, 1863 at Rochester to serve three years. Mustered in as Captain in Company M this regiment February 23, 1864. Transferred to Company K, April 9, 1865. Discharged for disability, to date May 15, 1865. Major U.S. Volunteers, by brevet from March 13, 1865. Commissioned Captain March 30, 1864, with rank from January 29, 1864, original.

JACOB FISHER, from November 29 to December 1 1864, and in May,1865.
See Captain Co. G.

MARVIN R. SHERWOOD, from May 5 to August 1, 1865.
Age 28 years. Enrolled at Pitcher to serve three years and mustered in as Second Lieutenant in Company L, February 12, 1864; as First Lieutenant, February 15, 1864. Transferred to Company F, March 31, 1865; mustered as Captain, Company M, May 5, 1865, Mustered out with company, August 1, 1865 at Winchester, Va. Not commissioned Second Lieutenant; commissioned First Lieutenant, March 30,

1864, with rank from January 29, 1864, original. Captain, March 21, 1865, with rank from January 24, 1865, vice Bennett, promoted.

1st LIEUTENANTS:

JAMES E. WEEKS, from March 4 to October 31, 1864.
Age 26 years. Enrolled January 29, 1864 at Rochester to serve three years. Mustered in as First Lieutenant, Company M, March 4, 1864. Discharged for disability, October 31, 1864 at Washington, D.C. Commissioned First Lieutenant, March 30, 1864, with rank from January 29, 1864, original.

FREDERICK LEAKE, from April 11 to August 1, 1865.
Age 18 years. Enrolled to serve three years, and mustered in at Winchester, Va., as First Lieutenant, company M, April 11, 1865. Mustered out with company, August 1, 1865 at Winchester, Va. See 14th Artillery. Commissioned First Lieutenant, March 21, 1865, with rank from that date, vice Spreadbury, promoted.

2nd LIEUTENANTS:

DWIGHT W. HAZELTON, from _____ to January 4, 1865.
See Second Lieutenant Co. A.

BYRON TALLMAN, from August 10, 1864 to August 1, 1865.
Age 25 years. Enrolled October 12, 1863 at Perrinton to serve three years. Mustered in as First Sergeant, Company A, December 20, 1863; as Second Lieutenant, Company M, August 1, 1864. Mustered out with company August 1, 1865 at Winchester, Va. Captain U.S. Volunteers by brevet, from March 13, 1865; commissioned Second Lieutenant, August 18, 1864 with rank from August 9, 1864, vice Dunning, discharged.

Pvt. Jon R. Babcock, Co. E, 22nd N.Y. Cavalry
[Col. Tom Clements Collection, U.S. Army Military History Institute]

The Men of the 22nd New York Cavalry

ABBOTT, CHARLES— Age 22 years. Enlisted December 7, 1863 at Cazenovia as Private, Co. E to serve three years. Rejected.

ABER, GEORGE G.— Age 34 years. Enlisted January 5, 1863 at Bath as Private, Co. G, to serve three years. Rejected.

ABLE, CHRISTOPHER— Age 18 years. Enlisted December 21, 1863 at Rochester; mustered in as Private, Co. A, December 21, 1863 to serve three years. Mustered out with company on August 1, 1865 at Winchester, Virginia.

ABLE, FREDERICK— Age 35 years. Enlisted February 22, 1863 at New York. Mustered in as Private in Co. H, February 22, 1863 to serve three years. Mustered out with company on August 1, 1865 at Winchester, Virginia. Also borne as Abell.

ACKERMAN, FREDERICK— Age 34 years. Enlisted April 13, 1865 at New York. Mustered in as Private "unassigned," April 13, 1863, to serve one year. Mustered out with detachment on May 6, 1865, at Hart's Island, New York Harbor.

ACKERMAN, FRED R.— Age 18 years. Enlisted December 18,1863 at Utica. Mustered in as a Private, Co. B, January 10, 1864 to serve three years. Mustered out with company on August 1, 1865, at Winchester, Virginia.

ACKLEY, JOHN— Age 18 years. Enlisted on November 23, 1863 at Albion. Mustered in as a Private, Co. F, January 10, 1864, to serve three years. Deserted from camp near Rochester, February, 1864.

ACTIVE, JAMES— Age 22 years. Enlisted on April 1, 1865 at Kingston. Mustered in as a Private "unassigned," April 1, 1865, to serve three years. Mustered out with detachment on May 6, 1865 at Hart's Island, New York Harbor.

ADAMS, EDWIN C.— Age 21 years. Enlisted on January 4, 1864 at Greene. Mustered in as Trumpeter, Co. L, February 12, 1864 to serve three years. Mustered out with detachment, June 21, 1865 at Washington, D.C.

ADAMS, FREDERICK— Age 30 years. Enlisted on February 20, 1865 at New York. Mustered in as Private Co. H, February 20, 1865 to serve one year. Mustered out with company on August 1, 1865 at Winchester, Virginia.

ADAMS, JOHN— Age 24 years. Enlisted on April 15, 1864 at Greene. Mustered in as Private, Co. M, April 15, 1864, to serve three years. Appointed Corporal, April 10, 1865. Mustered out with company on August 1, 1865 at Winchester, Virginia.

ADAMS, JOHN— Age 21 years. Enlisted on December 12, 1863 at Rochester. Mustered in as Private, Co. F, January 10, 1864 to serve three years. Deserted from camp near Rochester, February 1864.

ADISON, JOHN— Age 21 years. Enlisted on January 4, 1864 at Cammillus. Mustered in as Private, Co. E, January 10, 1864 to serve three years. Deserted at Rochester, January 13, 1864.

ALBRIDGE, EDWIN R.— Age 34 years. Enlisted on December 8, 1863 at Cazenovia. Mustered in as Private, Co. M, February 23, 1864, to serve three years. Transferred to Co. I, March 29, 1864. Discharged at Portsmouth Grove, R.I. Also borne as Aldridge.

ALBRIDGE, EDWIN R.— Age 34 years. Enlisted January 4, 1864, at Syracuse, as Private, Co. K to serve three years. Rejected.

ALCOTT, GEORGE E., see Olcott, George E.

ALDEN, FRANK A.— Age 19 years, Enlisted, December 8, 1863, at Cazenovia. Mustered in as Private, Co. I, February 2, 1864, to serve three years. Transferred to Co. E. March 1864. Mustered out with company, as Sergeant, August 1, 1865, at Winchester, Virginia. Also borne as Alder.

ALDERMAN, F.— Age 18 years. Enlisted December 28, 1863, at Syracuse, as Private, Co. B, to serve three years. Rejected.

ALDRICH, GEORGE W., JR.— Age 18 years. Enlisted, January 8, 1864 at Plymouth. Mustered in as Private, Co. L. January 8, 1864, to serve three years. Name crossed with remark, "Did not accompany detachment."

ALDRICH, JAMES K.— Age 19 years. Enlisted, January 18, 1864, at Masonville. Mustered in as Private, Co. L, February 12, 1864, to serve three years. Mustered out with company August 1, 1865 at Winchester, Virginia.

ALDRICH, JOHN A.— Age 18 years. Enlisted January 5, 1864, at Plymouth. Mustered in as Private, Co. L, February 12, 1864, to serve three years. Mustered out with company August 1, 1865 at Winchester, Virginia.

ALDRICH, JOHN B.— Age 18 years. Enlisted January 18, 1864 at Masonville. Mustered in as Private, Co. L, February 12, 1864, to serve three years. Mustered out with company August 1, 1865 at Winchester, Virginia.

ALDRICH, EDWIN R. see Albridge, Edwin R.

ALEXANDER, GEORGE— Age 23 years. Enlisted November 19, 1863 at Rochester. Mustered in as Private, Co. F, January 10, 1864, to serve three years. Deserted, February 1864, from camp near Rochester.

ALGOE, LEWIS— Age 24 years. Enlisted December 14, 1863 at Rochester. Mustered in as Private Co. D, January 10, 1864 to serve three years. Discharged for disability as Saddler Sergeant, May 3, 1865.

ALLELY, HENRY— Age 18 years. Enlisted November 30, 1863 at Utica. Mustered in as a Private, Co. B, January 5, 1864, to serve three years. Mustered out with company August 1, 1865 at Winchester, Virginia.

ALLEN, ALONZO R.— Age 20 years. Enlisted February 1, 1864 at Rochester. Mustered in as First Lieutenant, Co. E, February 1, 1864 to serve three years. Discharged on July 27, 1864. Commissioned First Lieutenant on March 30, 1864, with rank from January 10, 1864.

ALLEN, CHARLES H.— Age 20 years. Enlisted January 4, 1864 at Avoca, as a Private, Co. G, to serve three years. Rejected.

ALLEN, DAVID W.— Age 27 years. Enlisted December 7, 1863 at Rochester, as a Private, Co. I, to serve three years. Rejected.

ALLEN, GEORGE C.— Age 31 years. Enlisted December 29, 1863 at Bath, as a Private Co. G, to serve three years. Rejected.

ALLEN, HENRY— Age 19 years. Enlisted April 12, 1865 at Albany. Mustered in as Private "unassigned," April 12, 1865, to serve for two years. Mustered out with detachment, May 6, 1865 at Hart's Island, New York Harbor.

ALLEN, IRA J.— Age 19 years. Enlisted December 11, 1863 at Ontario. Mustered in as Private, Co. H, February 2, 1864 to serve three years. Transferred with remark, "records of company lost."

ALLEN, JAMES— Age 20 years. Enlisted February 27, 1865 at New York. Mustered in as Private, Co. K, February 27, 1865 to serve three years. Absent at muster out of company.

ALLEN, LOUIS B.— Age 18 years. Enlisted December 10, 1863 at Ontario. Mustered in as Private, Co. H, February 2, 1864, to serve three years. Promoted to Corporal December 27, 1864. Mustered out with company, August 1, 1865 at Winchester, Virginia.

ALLEN, R. ALFRED— Age 30 years. Enlisted January 14, 1864 at New York. Mustered in as Private, Co. H, February 2, 1864 to serve three years. Appointed Hospital Steward, February 2, 1864. Mustered out August 1, 1865 at Winchester, Virginia. Commissioned Second Lieutenant, June 30, 1865 with rank from June 25, 1865.

ALLEN, TRUMAN H.— Age 32 years. Enrolled February 9, 1864 at Rochester. Mustered in as Captain, Co. K, January 9, 1864 to serve three years. Discharged July 27, 1864. Commissioned Captain March 30, 1864, with rank from January 29, 1864.

ALLEN, WILLIAM— Age 18 years. Enlisted December 30, 1863 at Cazenovia. Mustered in as Sergeant, Co. E, January 10, 1864 to serve three years. Died at Andersonville Georgia. No date given.

AMSDEN, CHARLES— Age 27 years. Enlisted December 19, 1863 at Syracuse. Mustered in as Private, Co. B, January 5, 1864 to serve three years. Mustered out with company on August 1, 1865 at Winchester, Virginia.

AMSDEN, LOUIS H.— Age 17 years. Enlisted December 16, 1863 at Rochester. Mustered in as Private, Co. F, January 10, 1864, to serve three years. Mustered out as a Bugler on June 28, 1865 at Winchester, Virginia.

ANDERSON, BENJAMIN— Age 18 years. Enlisted February 23, 1864 at Rochester. Mustered in as Private, Co. M, March 9, 1864, to serve three years. Appointed Corporal, April 10, 1865. Mustered out with company on August 1, 1865 at Winchester, Virginia.

ANDERSON, CHARLES— Age 22 years. Enlisted March 18, 1865 at Tarrytown. Mustered in as Private "unassigned," March 18, 1865 to serve three years. No further record.

ANDERSON, HENRY— Age 19 years. Enlisted April 3, 1865 at Jamaica. Mustered in as Private "unassigned," April 3, 1865 to serve three years. No further record.

ANDERSON, JAMES— Age 29 years. Enlisted February 18, 1864 at Rochester. Mustered in as Private, Co. M, February 23, 1864 to serve three years. No further record.

ANDERSON, LEWIS— Age 28 years. Enlisted March 24, 1865 at New York. Mustered in as Private, Co. L, March 24, 1865 to serve three years. Mustered out with company August 1, 1865 at Winchester, Virginia.

ANDREW, OLIVER C.— Age 17 years. Enlisted December 11, 1863 at Rochester. Mustered in as Private, Co. A, December 20, 1863 to serve three years. Discharged while paroled prisoner, June 27, 1865 at Winchester, Virginia.

ANDREW, WALTER— Age 20 years. Enlisted February 15, 1865 at New York. Mustered in as Private "unassigned," February 15, 1865 to serve three years. No further record.

ANDREWS, CHARLES— Age 22 years. Enlisted December 22, 1863 at Lyons. Mustered in as Private, Co. F, February 2, 1864 to serve three years. Transferred to Co. G, May 27, 1865. Deserted June 9, 1865.

ANDREWS, CHARLES— Age 38 years. Enlisted November 18, 1864 at New York. Mustered in as a Private, "unassigned," November 18, 1864 to serve three years. No further record.

ANGUISH, HENRY— Age 20 years. Enlisted February 25, 1864 at Manlius. Mustered in as Private, Co. E, March 8, 1864 to serve three years. Mustered out with company August 1, 1865 at Winchester, Virginia.

ANSELL, EDMUND— Age 18 years. Enlisted December 7, 1863 at Rochester. Mustered in as Private, Co. A, December 20, 1863 to serve three years. Mustered out with company, August 1, 1865 at Winchester, Virginia. Also borne as Anseun, Edward.

ANSELL, GEORGE— Age 30 years. Enlisted December 17, 1864 at Syracuse. Mustered in as Private, Co. A, December 17, 1864 to serve two years. Appointed Corporal, May 19, 1865. Mustered out with company August 1, 1865 at Winchester, Virginia.

ANSELL, HENRY— Age 21 years. Enlisted December 20, 1863 at Rochester. Mustered in as Private, Co. A, December 20, 1863 to serve three years. Appointed Sergeant, no date given. Quartermaster Sergeant, July 21, 1865. Mustered out with company August 1, 1865 at Winchester, Virginia.

ANTHONY, JOHN B.— Age 21 years. Enlisted December 20, 1863 at Avoca. Mustered in as Private, Co. G, February 2, 1864 to serve three years. Mustered out with company August 1, 1865 at Winchester, Virginia.

APPLEMAN, ADAM— Age 25 years. Enlisted December 29, 1863 at Lyons. Mustered in as Private, Co. H, February 2, 1864 to serve three years. Transferred to Co. F, no date given. Appointed Corporal, July 1, 1865. Mustered out with company August 1, 1865 at Winchester, Virginia.

APPLETON, A. J.— Age18 years. Enlisted January 5, 1864 at Rochester as a Private in Co. E, to serve three years. Rejected

ARMITAGE, JOSEPH C.— Age 22 years. Enlisted September 6, 1864 at Avon. Mustered in as Private, Co. G, September 6, 1864 to serve one year. Under sentence of G.M.C. at Fort Delaware, May 12, 1865. Discharged August 9, 1865 at Rochester New York.

ARMOLT, PETER— Age 32 years. Enlisted February 21, 1865 at New York. Mustered in as Private, Co. E, February 21, 1865 to serve three years. Absent at muster out of company. Also borne as Armoalt.

ARMSTRONG, ELIPHALET D.— Age 19 years. Enlisted December 30, 1863 at Avoca. Mustered in as Private, Co. G February 2, 1864 to serve three years. Mustered out with company August 1, 1865 at Winchester, Virginia.

ARMSTRONG, SELNER— Age 18 years. Enlisted November 6, 1863 at Rochester. Mustered in as Quartermaster Sergeant, Co. A December 20, 1863 to serve three years. Reduced, date not stated. appointed Sergeant, August 31, 1864, Regimental Quartermaster Sergeant, October23, 1864. Reduced and transferred to Co. A, December 29, 1864. Appointed First Sergeant July 21, 1865. Mustered out with company August 1, 1865 at Winchester,Va. Also borne as Samuel G. Armstrong prior service in Co. H Twenty Seventh New York Volunteers.

ARND, FREDERICK— Age 34 years. Enlisted January 4, 1864 at Bath. Mustered in as a First Sergeant in Co. G. February 2, 1864 to serve three years. Captured June 29,1864, paroled November 30, 1864. Mustered in as a Second Lieutenant to date July 12, 1864. Was reduced to Sergeant, December 1,1864. Reinstated First Sergeant April 24, 1864. Honorably discharged as Second Lieutenant to date June 28, 1865, at Winchester, Virginia. Prior service in Co. A, Twenty-Third New York Volunteers. Commissioned Second Lieutenant June 29, 1864 with rank from January 14, 1864.

ASHLEY, LUCAS W.— Age 20 years. Enlisted November 28, 1863 at Brockport. Mustered in as Sergeant, Co. C January 5, 1864 to serve three years. Reduced, date not stated. Mustered out May 18, 1865 at Baltimore, Maryland.

ASHTON, PETER— Age 20 years. Enlisted January 4,1864 at Syracuse. Mustered in as Private, Co. E January 10, 1864 to serve three years. Deserted January 13, 1864 at Rochester, NY.

ATTRIDGE, WILLIAM— Age 18 years. Enlisted December 7, 1863 at Rochester. Mustered in as Private, Co. A December 20, 1863 to serve three years. Died of disease April 28, 1865 in a Rebel prison.

AUSTIN, JAMES— Age 31 years. Enrolled April 23, 1865 at Winchester. Mustered in as First Lieutenant, Co. G to date April 23, 1865 to serve three years. Mustered out with company August 1, 1865 at Winchester, Virginia. Prior service in Battery E Fifth Artillery. Commissioned Second Lieutenant January 25, 1865 with rank from January 15, 1865. First Lieutenant February 18, 1865 with rank from February 1, 1865.

AYRES, SAMUEL— Age 29 years. Enlisted December 29, 1863 at Dunkirk as a Private in Co. K to serve three years. Rejected.

BABCOCK, IRA S.— Age 34 years. Enlisted January 5, 1864 at New Berlin. Mustered in as Private, Co. L, February 12, 1864 to serve three years. Appointed Commissary Sergeant, date not stated. Mustered out with company August 1, 1865 at Winchester, Virginia.

BABCOCK, JOHN R.— Age 24 years. Enlisted January 25, 1864 at Truxton. Mustered in as Private, Co. K February 6, 1864 to serve three years. Transferred to Co. E March 25, 1864. Mustered out June 22, 1865 at Washington, D.C. Prior service in Co. F, Twenty-Fourth New York Infantry Volunteers.

BABCOCK, LAWSON— Age 37 years. Enlisted January 22, 1864 at Syracuse. Mustered in as Private, Co. K February 6, 1864 to serve three years. Transferred to Co. E, March 25, 1864. Mustered out with company August 1, 1865 at Winchester, Virginia.

BABCOCK, WILLIAM— Age 25 years. Enlisted January 4, 1864 at Greene. Mustered in as Private, Co. L February 12, 1864 to serve three years. Mustered out with company August 1, 1865 at Winchester, Virginia.

BACHMAN, FREDERICK— Age 37 years. Enlisted December 1, 1863 at Rochester. Mustered in as Private, Co. F January 10, 1864 to serve three years. Mustered out August 22, 1865 at Elmira, New York.

BAER, ADOLPH— Age 20 years. Enlisted February 6, 1865, at New York. Mustered in as Private, "unassigned," February 6, 1865, to serve one year. No further record.

BAGEN, HUGH— Age 44 years. Enlisted November 10, 1863, at Brockport as Private, Co. C, to serve three years. Rejected.

BAINES, IRA— Age 18 years. Enlisted April 12, 1865, at Brooadalbin. Mustered in as Private, "unassigned," April 12, 1865, to serve one year; mustered out with detachment, May 6, 1865, at Hart's Island, New York Harbor.

BAKER, GEORGE T.— Age 21 years. Enlisted February 20, 1864, at Rochester. Mustered in as Private, Co. M, February 23, 1864, to serve three years. No further record.

BAKER, RICHARD— Age 22 years. Enlisted February 12, 1864, at Rochester. Mustered in as Corporal, Co. M, February 23, 1864, to serve three years. Transferred to Co. D, March 25, 1864. Mustered out with company, August 1, 1865, at Winchester Virginia.

BAKER, THOMAS— Age 23 years. Enlisted December 7, 1863, at Rochester. Mustered in as Corporal, Co. D, January 10, 1864, to serve three years. Appointed Sergeant, date not stated, discharged for disability, May 20, 1865, near Winchester, Virginia.

BAKER, WILLIAM— Age 24 years. Enlisted February 16, 1865 at New York. Mustered in as Private, Co. C, February 16, 1865, to serve three years. Deserted, June 7, 1865 near Winchester, Virginia.

BALDWIN, LYMAN M.— Age 20 years. Enlisted December 24, 1863, at Rochester. Mustered in as Corporal, Co. I, February 2, 1864, to serve three years. Appointed Quartermaster Sergeant, date not stated. Mustered out with company, August 1, 1865, at Winchester, Virginia. Also borne as Lyman W. Baldwin.

BALDWIN, PHILANDER R.— Age 20 years. Enlisted January 26, 1864, at Middlefield. Mustered in as Private, Co. L, February 12, 1864, to serve three years. Mustered out with company, August 1, 1865, at Winchester, Virginia.

BALK, ABRAHAM— Age 36 years. Drafted, date not stated. Mustered in at Lockport, as Private, "unassigned," February 27, 1865, to serve one year. Mustered out with detachment, May 9, 1865, at Elmira, NY.

BA[????] — Age 26 years. Enlisted December 21, 1863, at Brockport as Private, Co. C, to serve three years. Rejected.

BANNON, EDWARD— Age 19 years. Enlisted February 2, 1865, at New York. Mustered in as Private, Co. B, February 3, 1865, to serve three years. Mustered out with company, August 1, 1865, at Winchester, Virginia.

BANTEN, EDWARD— Age 21 years. Enlisted December 16, 1864 at New York. Mustered in as Private, "unassigned," December 16, 1864, to serve three years. No further record.

BARBEAU, MAURICE— Age 18 years. Enlisted, November 13, 1863, at Rochester. Mustered in as Corporal, Co. F, January 10, 1864, to serve three years. Deserted, February, 1865, from Parole Camp, Annapolis, Maryland.

BARBER, JOEL— Age 44 years. Enlisted December 15, 1863, at Hamilton, as Private, Co. E, to serve three years. Rejected.

BARBER, JOHN— Age 36 years. Enlisted December 30 at Smithfield. Mustered in as Private, Co. K, February 6, 1864, to serve three years. Transferred to Co. H, March 25, 1864. No further record.

BARBER, THOMAS N.— Age 21 years. Enlisted December 29, 1863 at Pomfret, as Private, Co. K, to serve three years. Rejected.

BARBER, WILLIAM S.— Age 20 years. Enlisted September 7, 1864, at Avon. Mustered in as Private, "unassigned," September 7, 1864, to serve one year. No further record.

BARDEEN, LEWIS— Age 16 years. Enlisted November 30, 1863 at Bath. Mustered in as Private, Co. G, February 2, 1864, to serve three years. Mustered out with company, August 1, 1865, at Winchester, Virginia.

BATES, JUSTUS— Age 36 years. Enlisted January 5, 1864 at Norwich. Mustered in as Private, Co. L, February 12, 1864 to serve three years. Mustered out July 19, 1865 at Washington, D.C.

BATHRICK, ROBERT— Age 21 years. Enlisted December 23, 1863 at Lee. Mustered in as Private, Co. C, January 5, 1864 to serve three years. Appointed Sergeant, January 1, 1865. Absent sick in hospital at date of muster out of company, August 1, 1865. No further record.

BAUM, JOHN— Age 18 years. Enlisted December 8, 1863 at Rochester. Mustered in as Private, Co. A, December 20, 1863 to serve three years. Captured, date not stated. Died of disease, April 28, 1865 in Rebel prison.

BAUPERLAND, FRANCIS— Age 40 years. Enlisted January 4, 1864 at Syracuse, as Private, Co. E, to serve three years. Rejected.

BAXTER, LLEWELLYN WEAVER— Age 17 years. Enlisted December 30, 1865 at Benton. Mustered in as Private, Co. C, January 5, 1864 to serve three years. Transferred to Co. A, March 22, 1864. Captured, date not stated. Died of disease, October 10, 1864 at Andersonville, Georgia.

BAYLIS, RICHARD B.— Age 25 years. Enlisted December 22, 1863 at Auburn as Private, Co. I, to serve three years. Rejected

BAYWATER, JOHN— Age 18 years. Enlisted December 14, 1863 at Rochester. Mustered in as Saddler, Co. F, January 10, 1864 to serve three years. Reduced, date not stated. Deserted, February 1865 from Parole Camp, Annapolis, Maryland.

BEACH, ANSEL— Age 28 years. Enlisted January 4, 1864 at Rochester. Mustered in as Corporal, Co. I, February 2, 1864 to serve three years. Mustered out with company, August 1, 1865 at Winchester, Virginia.

BEACH, VALENTINE— Age 15 years. Enlisted November 28, 1863 at Barre. Mustered in as Private, Co. K, February 6, 1864 to serve three years. Transferred to Co. F, March 25, 1864. Mustered out with company, August 1, 1865 at Winchester, Virginia.

BEADLE, JOHN G.— Age 24 years. Enlisted December 9, 1863 at Rochester. Mustered in as Private, Co. A, December 20, 1863 to serve three years. Deserted January 9, 1864 at Rochester, New York. Prior service in Co. I, Thirteenth New York Infantry Volunteers.

BEAMAN, SYLVANUS A.— Age 22 years. Enlisted January 2, 1864 at Avoca, as Private, Co. G to serve three years. Rejected.

BEAR, ADOLPH— Age 23 years. Enlisted February 6, 1865 at New York. Mustered in as Private, Co. B, February 6, 1865 to serve one year. Died June 16, 1865 in hospital at Winchester, Virginia.

BEARD, JAMES— Age 24 years. Enlisted December 9, 1863 at Rochester, as Private, Co. D, to serve three years. Rejected.

BECHOLD, ANTONI— Age 23 years. Enlisted March 14, 1865 at New York. Mustered in as Private, Co. K, March 14, 1865 to serve three years. Mustered out with company, August 1, 1865 at Winchester, Virginia.

BECKER, CHARLES— Age 22 years. Enlisted December 16, 1864 at New York. Mustered in as Private, "unassigned," December 16, 1864 to serve three years. No further record.

BECKWITH, LESTER— Age 25 years. Enlisted November 25, 1863 at Cuba. Mustered in as Private, Co. D, January 10, 1864 to serve three years. Transferred to Co. K, May 1, 1864. Appointed Corporal, June 1, 1865. Mustered out with company, August 1, 1865 at Winchester, Virginia.

BEEBY, HENRY E.— Age 24 years. Enlisted June 13, 1861, at Syracuse. Mustered in as Private, and appointed Sergeant, Co. B, Third Cavalry, July 30, 1861, to serve three years. Re-enlisted January 5, 1864. Mustered in as Second Lieutenant, Co. F, this regiment January 30, 1864. First Lieutenant, to date May 5, 1865. Mustered out with company, August 1, 1865 at Winchester, Virginia. Also borne as Henry W. Bee. Commissioned Second Lieutenant, March 30, 1864, with rank from January 19, 1864, original; First Lieutenant, April 22, 1865, with rank from April 14, 1865, vice Yates, killed.

BEEDLE, JAMES— Age 18 years. Enlisted November 26, 1863, at Brockport. Mustered in as Corporal, Co. C, January 5, 1864, to serve three years. Reduced March 1, 1865. Mustered out with company, August 1, 1865 at Winchester, Virginia.

BEERS, BENJAMIN F.— Age 44 years. Enlisted, December 30, 1863 at Jerusalem, as Private, Co. C, to serve three years. Rejected.

BEHUR, JOHN— Age 21 years. Enlisted March 28, 1865 at Rochester. Mustered in as Private, "unassigned," March 28, 1865, to serve two years. Mustered out with detachment, May 9, 1865, at Elmira New York.

BELDING, HENRY W.— Age 16 years. Enlisted December 2, 1863 at Lyons. Mustered in as Trumpeter, Co. H, February 2, 1864, to serve three years. Transferred to Co. B, Third Regiment V.R.C., date not recorded, from which discharged, August 20, 1865 at Augusta, Me.

BELITZ, CHARLES— Age 26 years. Enlisted March 7, 1865, at New York. Mustered in as Private, Co. K, March 7, 1865, to serve three years. Absent at Remount Camp at date of muster out of company. No discharge given, no further record.

BELL, FRANCIS G.— Age 18 years. Enlisted November 16, 1863 at Syracuse. Mustered in as Sergeant, Co. B, January 5, 1864, to serve three years. Reduced, date not stated. Mustered out with company, August 1, 1865, at Winchester, Virginia. Also borne as Frank G.

BELL, JOHN— Age 29 years. Enlisted December 7, 1863 at Rochester. Mustered in as Private, in Co. F, January 10, 1864, to serve three years. Deserted, February, 1864 from a camp near Rochester.

BELL, THOMAS— Age 25 years. Enlisted April 10,1864 at Albany. Mustered in as Private, "unassigned" April 10, 1864, to serve three years. Mustered out with detachment, May 6, 1865 at Hart's Island, New York Harbor.

BELLINGER, SAMUEL— Age 25 years. Enlisted December 19, 1863, at Lyons. Mustered in as Private, Co. H, February 2, 1864, to serve three years. Mustered out with company, August 1, 1865 at Winchester, Virginia.

BEMAN, ISAAC H.— Age 19 years. Enlisted January 2, 1864 at Avoca. Mustered in as Private, Co. G, February 2, 1864, to serve three years. Mustered out with company August 1, 1865 at Winchester, Virginia.

BEMIS, WASHINGTON— Age 37 years. Enlisted January 15, 1864 at Otswego. Mustered in as Private, Co. I, February 12, 1864 to serve three years. Mustered out with company, August 1, 1865 at Winchester, Virginia.

BEND, HENRY— Age 25 years. Enlisted December 9, 1863 at Riga. Mustered in as Private, Co. C, January 5, 1864 to serve three years. Died of disease on December 18, 1864 at Annapolis, Maryland.

BENHAM, FRANK H.— Age 18 years. Enlisted November 14, 1863 at Urbana. Mustered in as Private, Co. G, February 2, 1864 to serve three years. Captured and paroled, dates not stated. Discharged on June 14, 1865 at Elmira, New York.

BENNETT, ARTHUR— Age 20 years. Enlisted January 15, 1864 at Dunkirk. Mustered in as Private, Co. M, February 23, 1864, to serve three years. Transferred to Co. K, date not stated. Mustered out on June 28, 1865 at Winchester, Virginia.

BENNETT, THOMAS— Age 19 years. Enlisted January 9, 1864 at Otto. Mustered in as Private, Co. K, February 6. 1864, to serve three years. Deserted February 24,1864 at Rochester New York.

BENNETT, BENJAMIN— Age 36 years. Enrolled November 9,1863 at Bath. Mustered in as Captain, Co. G, to date January 29, 1864, to serve three years. Major to date April 14, 1865. Mustered out with regiment on August 1, 1865 at Winchester, Virginia. Commissioned Captain March 30,1864, with rank from January 29, 1864, original, Major, March 21, 1865 with rank from January 24, 1865.

BENTLEY, CALVIN— Age 19 years. Enlisted January 8,1864 at Plymouth. Mustered in as Private, Co. L, February 12, 1864, to serve three years. Captured, date not stated. Died August 16, 1864 at Andersonville, Georgia.

BENTON, JOHN— Age 20 years. Enlisted January 4, 1864 at Pomfret as Private in Co. K to serve three years. Rejected.

BERRY, JAMES F.— Age 20 years. Enlisted December 8, 1863 at Rochester. Mustered in as Sergeant, Co., I February 2, 1864 to serve three years. Appointed First Sergeant, date not stated. Mustered out with company August 1, 1865 at Winchester, Virginia.

BERRY, WILLIAM— Age 18 years. Enlisted April 12, 1864 at Giesboro Point D.C. Mustered in as Private, Co. K, April 12, 1864, to serve three years. No further record.

BEST, SAMUEL— Age 30 years. Enlisted April 10, 1865 at Kortright. Mustered in as a Private "unassigned," April 11, 1864 to serve three years. Mustered out with detachment, May 6, 1865 at Hart's Island, New York Harbor.

BETTS, THOMAS S.— Age 24 years. Enlisted December 21, 1863 at Lyons. Mustered in as Private, Co. H, February 2, 1864 to serve three years. Appointed Blacksmith, date not stated. Mustered out with company, August 1, 1865 at Winchester, Virginia.

BIDWELL, GEORGE W.— Age 29 years. Enlisted April 4, 1865 at Edinburgh. Mustered in as Private "unassigned," April 4, 1865 to serve three years. No further record.

BIER, PAUL— Age 28 years. Enlisted February 17, 1865 at New York. Mustered in as Private, Co. M, February 17, 1865 to serve three years. Deserted June 17, 1865 from camp near Winchester, Virginia.

BIGLOW, GEORGE— Age 18 years. Enlisted December 29, 1863 at Churchville. Mustered in as Private, Co. C, January 5, 1864, to serve three years. Died of disease February 24, 1864 at Rochester, New York.

BILBY, JOHN T.— Age 18 years. Enlisted April 3,1865 at Rochester. Mustered in as Private, Co. C, April 3, 1865 to serve three years. Absent sick in hospital at date of muster of company August 1, 1865. No further record. Also borne as John Bilbie.

BILLINGS, R. FLYNN— Age 18 years. Enlisted December 9, 1863 at Webster. Mustered in as Private, Co. H on February 2, 1864 to serve three years. Transferred to Co. F, date not stated. Mustered out with company August 1, 1865 at Winchester, Virginia. Also borne as Flynn R. and Floyd R. Billings.

BILLINGTON, EDWARD III— Enlisted November 23,1863at Brockport. Mustered in as Corporal, Co. C, January 5,1864 to serve three years. Reduced and captured, date not stated. Deserted while a prisoner of war and enlisted in the Rebel Army.

BIRDEE, JOHN— Age 22 years. Enlisted January 25, 1864 at Rochester as Private, Co. I to serve three years. Deserted January 29, 1864.

BIRDSALL, PERRY— Age 33 years. Enlisted February 14, 1865 at Binghamton. Mustered in as a Private, Co. H, February 14, 1865 to serve three years. Mustered out with company August 1, 1865 an Winchester, Virginia.

BISBEE, LEROY— Age 18 years. Enlisted December 22, 1863 at Lebanon. Mustered in as Private, Co. E, January 10, 1864 to serve three years. Discharged to date July 3, 1865. Also borne as Lerdy H. Bisby.

BISHOP, JOSEPH— Age 22 years. Enlisted February 25, 1864 at Rochester. Mustered in as Private, Co. M, March 8, 1864 to serve three years. Appointed Corporal, wounded, died in hospital, dates not stated.

BISHOP, THOMAS— Age 20 years. Enlisted December 25, 1863 at Rochester. Mustered in as Private, Co. F, January 10, 1864 to serve three years. Appointed Corporal, date not stated. Appointed Commissary Sergeant May 1, 1865. Mustered out with company August 1, 1865 at Winchester, Virginia.

BISSELL, FREDERICK H.— Age 20 years. Enlisted October 23, 1863 at Rochester. Mustered in as Private, Co. H, January 10, 1864 to serve three years. Deserted February 1864 from camp near Rochester New York. Prior service in Co. F, Thirty-Third New York Infantry Volunteers.

BLACK, THOMAS H.— Age 20 years. Enlisted January 28, 1864 at Brockport. Mustered in as Private, Co. K, February 6, 1864, to serve three years. Transferred to Co. A, March 25, 1864. No further Record.

BLAKELEY, ALEXANDER— Age 18 years. Enlisted December 18, 1863 at Rochester as Private, Co. I, to serve three years. Rejected.

BLAKESLEY, RILEY W.— Age 18 years. Enlisted December 24, 1863 at Rochester. Mustered in as Private, Co. I, February 2, 1864 to serve three years. Transferred to the First Battalion, V.R.C. August 1864.

BLEEKFIELD, RICHARD C.— Age 22 years. Enlisted March 24, 1865 at New York. Mustered in as Private, Co. L, March 24, 1865 to serve three years. Mustered out with company August 1, 1865 at Winchester, Virginia. Also borne as Blickfield.

BLELL, WILLIAM— Age 19 years. Enlisted March 22, 1865 at New York. Mustered in as Private, Co. K, March 22, 1865 to serve three years. Mustered out with company August 1, 1865 at Winchester, Virginia.

BLICKFELT, RICHARD C.— See Bleekfield, Richard C.

BLISS, JAMES H.— Age 26 years. Enlisted February 18, 1864 at Rochester. Mustered in as Private, Co. M, February 23, 1864 to serve three years. Transferred to Co. I, date not stated. Died August 6, 1864 at Andersonville, Ga.

BLIVEN, MILO— Age 19 years. Enlisted April 10, 1865 at New York. Mustered in as a Private "unassigned," April 10, 1865 to serve one year. No further record.

BLOOE, JOHN— Age 22 years. Enlisted February 13, 1864 at Sodus. Mustered in as Private, Co. M, February 14, 1864 to serve three years. No further record.

BOARDMAN, THERON— Age 18 years. Enlisted February 14, 1865 at Binghamton. Mustered in as Private, Co. H, February 14, 1865 to serve one year. Mustered out with company, August 1, 1865 at Winchester, Virginia.

BODEE, JOHN— Age 28 years. Enlisted February 27, 1865 at New York. Mustered in as Private, Co. H, February 27, 1865 to serve one year. Mustered out with company August 1, 1865 at Winchester, Virginia. Supposed to be identical with John Bodine of Co. D.

BODINE, JOHN— Age 29 years. Enlisted February 27, 1865 at New York. Mustered in as Private, Co. D, February 27, 1865 to serve three years. No further record. Supposed to be identical with John Bodee, Co. H.

BOGERT, ALBERT J.— Age 19 years. Enlisted March 7, 1865 at New York. Mustered in as Private, Co. K, March 7, 1865 to serve three years. Mustered out with company August 1, 1865 at Winchester, Virginia.

BOHLMAN, AUGUSTUS— Age 22 years. Enlisted January 4, 1864 at Rochester. Mustered in as Private, Co. F, January 10, 1864 to serve three years. Captured, date not stated. Died October __ 1864, at Florence, S.C.

BOLEAU, DANIEL B.— Age 24 years. Enlisted December 17, 1863 at Bath. Mustered in as Sergeant, Co. G, February 2, 1864 to serve three years. Captured June 29, 1864, paroled February 24, 1865. Discharged June 28, 1865 at Winchester, Virginia. Prior service in Co. A Twenty-Third New York Volunteers.

BOLLES, JASPER A.— Age 22 years. Enlisted February 25, 1864 at Rochester. Mustered in as Private, Co. I, March 8, 1864 to serve three years. Captured, date not stated. Died December 10, 1864 at Andersonville, Georgia.

BOND, JAMES— Age 25 years. Enlisted November 12, 1863 at Rochester. Mustered in as Private, Co. A, December 20, 1863 to serve three years. Mustered out with company August 1, 1865 at Winchester, Virginia.

BOOTH, MARTIN— Age 43 years. Enlisted December 20, 1863 at Moravia as Private in Co. I, to serve three years. Rejected.

BOPP, FREDERICK— Age 43 years. Enlisted December 28, 1863 at Rochester. Mustered in as Private, Co. K, February 6, 1864 to serve three years. Transferred to Co. F, date not stated. Died December 10, 1864 at Andersonville, Georgia.

BORDEN, WARUM— Age 21 years. Enlisted December 30, 1863 at Avon. Mustered in as Private, Co. G, February 2, 1863 to serve three years. In confinement at date of muster out of company, August 1, 1865 at Fort Delaware, by sentence of G.C.M.A.of S., May 12, 1865. Discharged with detachment, August 9, 1865 at Rochester, New York.

BOWDEN, ROBERT— Age 21 years. Enlisted April 10, 1965 at Lockport. Mustered in as Private, Co. F, April 10, 1865 to serve three years. Deserted June, 1865 from a camp near Winchester, Virginia.

BOWEN, E.J.— Age 28 years. Enlisted January 4, 1864 at Pomfret as a Private in Co. K to serve three years. Rejected.

BOWEN, LEROY— Age 19 years. Enlisted February 24, 1864 at Walton. Mustered in as Private, "unassigned," March 8, 1864 to serve three years. No further record.

BOWERS, THOMAS-Age 23 years. Enlisted February 17, 1865 at Stockton. Mustered in as Private, Co. H, February 17, 1865 to serve three years. Mustered out with company August 1, 1865 at Winchester, Virginia.

BOWERS, WILLIAM W.— Age 30 years. Enlisted February 1, 1864 at Middlefield. Mustered in as Corporal, Co. L, February 12, 1864 to serve three years. Deserted December 8, 1864 from hospital.

BOWLES, WILLIAM— Age 18 years. Enlisted December 14, 1863 at Rochester. Mustered in as Private, Co. C, January 5, 1864 to serve three years. Deserted February 6, 1864 at Rochester, New York.

BOWMAN, JACOB— Age 33 years. Enlisted December 7, 1863 at Lyons as a Private in Co. H to serve three years. Rejected.

BOYD, WILLIAM— Age 23 years. Enlisted December 6, 1863 at Utica. Mustered in as Private, Co. B, January 5, 1864 to serve three years. Deserted June 13, 1864 at Charles City Court House.

BOYD, WILLIAM R.— Age 25 years. Enlisted September 6, 1864 at Rochester. Mustered in as Private, Co. A, September 6, 1864 to serve one year. Captured November 12, 1864. Absent at date of muster out of company August 1, 1865. No discharge given. No further record.

BOYDEN, BRUCE O.— Age 18 years. Enlisted January 5, 1864, at Plymouth. Mustered in as Private, Co. I, February 12, 1864, to serve three years. Died of disease, March 4, 1864, at St. Mary's Hospital, Rochester, New York. Also borne as Bruce A. Boyden.

BOYER, JOSEPH H. W.— Age 19 years. Enlisted December 22, 1863 at Sodus. Mustered in as Private, Co. H, February 2, 1864, to serve three years. Mustered out with company, August 1, 1865, at Winchester, Virginia. Also borne as Joseph H. Boyer.

BOYLE, PETER— Age 20 years. Enlisted February 24, 1864, at Rochester. Mustered in as Private, Co. M, March 9, 1864, to serve three years. Mustered out with company, August 1, 1865, at Winchester, Virginia.

BOYLE, WILLIAM— Age 21 years. Enlisted February 13, 1865, at New York. Mustered in as Private, Co. H, February 13, 1865, to serve one year. Mustered out with company, August 1, 1865, at Winchester, Virginia.

BOYLIN, BERNARD— Age 33 years. Enlisted December 14, 1863 at Rochester. Mustered in as Private, Co. D, January 10, 1864, to serve three years. Captured June 27, 1864. Absent at date of muster out of company; no discharge given. No further record.

BRACKEN, JOHN— Age 18 years. Enlisted December 18, 1863 at Rochester. Mustered in as Private, Co. A, December 20, 1863, to serve three years. Discharged for disability, June 12, 1865, at Washington, D. C.

BRADIGAN, CHARLES— Age 20 years. Enlisted February 4, 1865 at Albany. Mustered in as Private, Co. C, February 13, 1865, to serve one year. Mustered out with company, August 1, 1865, at Winchester, Virginia.

BRADLEY, GEORGE— Age 26 years. Enlisted March 20, 1865 at Rochester. Mustered in as Private, "unassigned," March 20, 1865, to serve three years. No further record.

BRADLEY, ROBERT— Age 18 years. Enlisted January 7, 1864 at Rochester, as Private, Co. I, to serve three years. Rejected.

BRADY, ALEXANDER— Age 26 years. Enlisted November 22, 1863, at Rochester. Mustered in as Sergeant, Co. A, December 20, 1863, to serve three years. Reduced July 21, 1865. Mustered out with company, August 1, 1865, at Winchester, Virginia.

BRADY, THOMAS— Age 27 years. Enlisted December 3, 1863, at Syracuse. Mustered in as Private, Co. B, January 5, 1864, to serve three years. Transferred to Co. E, March 15, 1864. No further record.

BRAGG, LEWIS— Age 20 years. Enlisted December 18, 1863 at Rochester. Mustered in as Private, Co. A, December 20, 1863, to serve three years. Killed in action June 22, 1864, at Dinwiddie C.H., Virginia.

BRAMBLY, JOHN R.— Age 20 years. Enlisted December 2, 1863 at Rochester. Mustered in as Private. Co. A, December 20, 1863, to serve three years. Appointed Corporal, date not stated. Mustered out with company, August 1, 1865, at Winchester, Virginia.

BRANARD, MITCHELL— Age 25 years. Enlisted December 14, 1863 at Rochester. Mustered in as Corporal, Co. F, January 10, 1864, to serve three years. Deserted February 1864 from camp near Rochester, New York.

BRAND, GEORGE B.— Age 32 years. Enrolled September 28, 1863 at Rochester. Mustered in as First Lieutenant and Regimental Quartermaster, September 28, 1863, to serve three years. Resigned March 4, 1864. Commissioned First Lieutenant and Regimental Quartermaster, March 30, 1864, with rank from September 26, 1863, original.

BRANDEN, ALEXANDER— Age 25 years. Enlisted December 24, 1863, at Rochester. Mustered in as Private, Co. D, January 10, 1864, to serve three years. No further record.

BRANT, MASON— Age 19 years. Enlisted February 13, 1865 at New York. Mustered in as Private, Co. M, February 13, 1865, to serve one year. Mustered out with company, August 1, 1865, at Winchester, Virginia.

BRANT, MASON J.— Age 18 years. Enlisted February 24, 1865 at Auburn. Mustered in as Private, "unassigned," February 24, 1865, to serve three years. No further record.

BRATON, CHRISTOPHER— see Bruton, Christopher C.

BRAZER, CHARLES W.— Age 24 years. Enlisted November 18, 1863 at Rochester as Private, Co. I, to serve three years. Deserted December 1863 at Rochester, New York.

BRAZER, EDWARD S.— Age 21 years. Enlisted February 18, 1864 at Jerusalem. Mustered in as Private, "unassigned," February 19, 1864, to serve three years. No further record.

BRAZER, FREEMAN N.— Age 23 years. Enlisted November 18, 1863 at Rochester. Mustered in as Private, Co. I, February 2, 1864, to serve three years. Appointed Sergeant, date not stated. Deserted, July 1864 at Washington, D.C.

BRECK, SAMUEL A.— Age 18 years. Enlisted January 21, 1864 at Bath as Private, Co. G, to serve three years. Rejected.

BRECKLAY, AUSTIN— Age 29 years. Enlisted March 1, 1865 at New York. Mustered in as Private, Co. K, March 1, 1865, to serve one year. Mustered out with company, August 1, 1865, at Winchester, Virginia.

BREEN, JOHN— Age 25 years. Enlisted November 30, 1863 at Barre. Mustered in as Private, Co. F, January 10, 1864, to serve three years. Deserted, November 1864 from Remount Camp, Giesboro Point, D.C.

BRENN, JOHN— Age 25 years. Enlisted February 21, 1865 at New York. Mustered in as Private, Co. H, February 21, 1865, to serve one year. Mustered out with company, August 1, 1865, at Winchester, Virginia.

BRENNAN, ROBERT— Age 19 years. Enlisted February 13, 1865 at New York. Mustered in as Private, Co. M, February 13, 1865, to serve three years. Mustered out with company, August 1, 1865, at Winchester, Virginia.

BREWER, ROWLIN— Age 44 years. Enlisted January 4, 1864 at Rochester. Mustered in as Private, Co. D, January 10, 1864, to serve three years. Mustered out with company, August 1, 1865, at Winchester, Virginia.

BRIGGS, HALSEY— Age 30 years. Enlisted December 10, 1863 at Rochester. Mustered in as Wagoner, Co. D, January 10, 1864, to serve three years. Reduced, date not stated. Mustered out with company, August 1, 1865, at Winchester, Virginia.

BRIGMAN, CHARLES— Age 20 years. Enlisted February 12, 1864 at Rochester. Mustered in as Corporeal, Co. M, February 23, 1864, to serve three years. Reduced, date not stated. Discharged May 28, 1865.

BRINN, JACOB— see Brown, Jacob

BRINO, JOHN A.— Age 23 years. Enlisted January 30, 1864 at Bainbridge. Mustered in as Private, Co. L, January 30, 1864, to serve three years. No further record.

BRISTOL, JOSEPH— Age 22 years. Enlisted December 30, 1863 at OtisCo. Mustered in as Private, Co. E, January 10, 1864, to serve three years. Discharged for disability, June 12, 1865 at DeCamp General Hospital.

BRITON, JAMES— Age 18 years. Enlisted March 28, 1865 at Florida. Mustered in as Private, Co. M, March 28, 1865, to serve three years. Mustered out with company, August 1, 1865, at Winchester, Virginia.

BROCKWAY, HENRY— Age 18 years. Enlisted January 19, 1864 at Rochester as Private, Co. I, to serve three years. Rejected.

BRONSON, GILBERT— Age 18 years. Enlisted November 13, 1863 at Auburn. Mustered in as Private, Co. I, February 2, 1864, to serve three years. Deserted, May 18, 1865, at Winchester, Virginia.

BRONSON, JACOB— Age 41 years. Enlisted September 2, 1864, at Boonville. Mustered in as Private, "unassigned," September 2, 1864, to serve one year. Mustered out July 2, 1865, at Washington, D.C.

BROOKS, BENJAMIN— Age 20 years. Enlisted December 22, 1863, at Syracuse. Mustered in as Private, Co. B, January 5, 1864, to serve three years. Deserted, September 19, 1864, from artillery skirmish line, Winchester, Virginia.

BROWN, CHARLES— Age 21 years. Enlisted February 8, 1864, at Rochester. Mustered in as Private, Co. M, February 23, 1864; to serve three years. Transferred to Co. C, March 22, 1864. Appointed Bugler, date not stated. Mustered out with company, August 1, 1865 at Winchester, Virginia.

BROWN, CHARLES C.— Age 35 years. Enlisted December 31, 1863 at Rochester. Mustered in as Captain, Co. A, December 21, 1863 to serve three years. Mustered in as Major, February 23, 1864. Mustered out with company, August 1, 1865 at Winchester, Virginia. Not commissioned Captain; commissioned Major, March 30, 1864, with rank from January 29, 1864, original.

BROWN, CHARLES E.— Age 18 years. Enlisted November 16, 1863, at Auburn, as Private, Co. I, to serve three years. Rejected.

BROWN, DAVID— Age 27 years. Enlisted December 21, 1863, at Auburn, as Private Co. I, to serve three years. Rejected.

BROWN, GEORGE— Age 23 years. Enlisted December 14, 1863, at Syracuse. Mustered in as Private, Co. B, January 5, 1864, to serve three years. Reported transferred to Co. E, March 10, 1864. Found to have deserted, February 2, 1864, at Rochester, New York.

BROWN, GEORGE— Age 19 years. Enlisted April 10, 1865, at Albany. Mustered in as Private, "unassigned," April 10, 1865, to serve three years. Mustered out with detachment, May 6, 1865, at Hart's Island, New York Harbor.

BROWN, GEORGE S.— Age 21 years. Enlisted, April 10, 1865 at Rochester. Mustered in as Private, Co. C, April 10, 1865, to serve three years. Transferred to Co. D, June 9, 1865. Mustered out August 12, 1965, at Rochester, New York.

BROWN, HENRY E.— Age 30 years. Enlisted August 9, 1864, at Erwin. Mustered in as Private Co. G, August 15, 1865, to serve three years. Mustered out with company, August 1, 1865, at Winchester Virginia.

BROWN, JACOB— Age 30 years. Enlisted February 15, 1865, at New York. Mustered in as Private Co. H, February 15, 1865, to serve three years. No further record.

BROWN, JEROME W.— Age 27 years. Enlisted December 19, 1863 at Madison. Mustered in as Private, Co. E, January 10, 1864, to serve three years. Deserted January 13, 1864, at Rochester New York.

BROWN, JOHN— Age 25 years. Enlisted February 21, 1865, at New York. Mustered in as Private, "unassigned," February 21, 1865, to serve one year. No further record

BROWN, JOHN— Age 18 years. Enlisted December 16, 1863, at Lyons, as Private, Co. H, to serve three years. Rejected.

BROWN, JOHN E.— Age 18 years. Enlisted January 4, 1864, at Manlius. Mustered in as Private, Co. E, January 10, 1864, to serve three years. Died of disease, July 26, 1864, at McDougall General Hospital, New York Harbor.

BROWN, JOHNSON B.— Age 50 years. Enrolled February 17, 1864 at Rochester. Mustered in as Lieutenant Colonel, February 17, 1864, to serve three years. Discharged July 20, 1864. Commissioned Lieutenant Colonel, March 30, 1864, with rank from January 10, 1864, original.

BROWN, PATRICK— Age 21 years. Enlisted November 27, 1863 at Arcadia. Mustered in as Private, Co. H, February 2, 1864 to serve three years. Mustered out with company, August 1, 1865, at Winchester, Virginia. Prior service, in Co. H, Seventeenth New York Infantry Volunteers.

BROWN, ROBERT— Age 22 years. Enlisted March 11, 1865 at New York. Mustered in as Private, "unassigned," March 11, 1865, to serve three years. No further record.

BROWN, WILLIAM— Age 28 years. Enlisted March 12, 1864 at New York. Mustered in as Private, "unassigned," March 12, 1864, to serve three years. No further record.

BROWN, WILLIAM— Age 24 years. Enlisted December 19, 1863 at Syracuse, as Private, Co. B, to serve three years. Rejected.

BROWN, WILLIAM, P.— Age 26 years. Enlisted January 18, 1864, at Syracuse. Mustered in as First Sergeant, Co. H, February 2, 1864, to serve three years. Mustered in as Second Lieutenant, to date January to May, 1865, inclusive. Mustered out with company, August 1, 1865 at Winchester, Virginia.; prior service in Co. F Second United States Cavalry. Commissioned Second Lieutenant, December 19, 1864, with rank from November 23, 1864 vice Fox, promoted; First Lieutenant, January 20, 1865, with rank from December 21, 1864, vice Whitfield, discharged.

BROWN, WILLIAM, R.— Age 25 years. Enlisted, April 3, 1865 at Tarrytown. Mustered in as Private, Co. F, April 3, 1865, to serve one year. Appointed Quartermaster Sergeant, July1, 1865. Mustered out with company, August 1, 1865 at Winchester, Virginia.

BRUNDAGE, ADDISON— Age 20 years. Enlisted November 29, 1863 at Urbana. Mustered in a Private, Co. G, February 2, 1864, to serve three years. Mustered out with company August 1, 1865 at Winchester, Virginia.

BRUSH, JOSEPH— Age 18 years. Enlisted February 15, 1865 at New York. Mustered in a Private, "unassigned," February 15, 1865 to serve one year. Mustered out with detachment, May 6, 1865, at Hart's Island, New York Harbor.

BRUTON, CHRISTOPHER, C.— Age 22 years. Enlisted, January 6, 1864 at Rochester. Mustered in as First Lieutenant, Co. C, January 16, 1864, to serve three years. Captain, to date, November 4, 1864. Mustered out with company August 1, 1865 at Winchester, Virginia. Also borne as Braton. Commissioned First Lieutenant, March 30, 1864, with rank from January5, 1864, original. Captain, October 4, 1864, with rank from August 1, 1864. vice Allen, discharged.

BRYAN, JOHN— Age 22 years. Enlisted April 8, 1865 at New York. Mustered in as Private, Co. I, April 8, 1865, to serve one year. Mustered out with company August 1, 1865, at Winchester Virginia.

BRYAN, WILLIAM H.— Age 19 years, Enlisted February 21, 1865 at New York. Mustered in a Private, Co. H, February 21, 1865, to serve one year. Mustered out, July 28, 1865, at U.S. General Hospital, Cumberland, Maryland. Also borne as Bryam.

BRYANT, JAMES— Age 22 years. Enlisted January 28, 1864 at Walton. Mustered in as Private, "unassigned," February 29, 1864, to serve three years. No further record.

BRYANT, JOHN H.— Age 31 years. Enlisted, December 24, 1863, at Pomfret, as Private, Co. K, to serve three years. Rejected.

BRYANT, ROBERT— Age 18 years. Enlisted April 4, 1865 at Albany. Mustered in as Private, Co. F, April 4, 1865, to serve one year. Transferred to Co. G, May 27, 1865. Mustered out with company August 1, 1865 at Winchester, Virginia.

BUCKLA, ANSELM— Age 29 years. Enlisted March 1, 1865 at New York. Mustered in as Private, "unassigned," March 1, 1865 to serve three years. No further record.

BUCKLER, WILLIAM— Age 23 years. Enlisted April 15, 1864 at Greene. Mustered in as a Private in Co. M, April 15, 1864 to serve three years. Mustered out with company August 1, 1865 at Winchester, Virginia.

BUELL, CYRUS— Age 38 years. Enlisted December 3, 1863 at Albion. Mustered in as a Private in Co. K, February 6, 1864 to serve three years. Mustered out with company August 1, 1865 at Winchester, Virginia.

BULLER, HENRY— Age 21 years. Enlisted January 13, 1864 at Rochester. Mustered in as a Private in Co. I February 2, 1864 to serve three years. Transferred to Co. M, March __1864. Appointed Saddler date not stated. Transferred to Co. G Fourteenth Regiment Veteran Reserve Corps per order, January 28, 1865. Appointed Corporal July 1,1865. Mustered out August 12, 1865 at Washington, DC.

BUMP, CHARLES F.— Age 25 years. Enlisted December 28, 1863 at De Ruyter. Mustered in as a Private in Co. E, January 10, 1864 to serve three years. Mustered out May 11, 1865 at U.S.A. Hospital "Summit House" Philadelphia, Pa.

BUNDY, FRANK— Age 38 years. Enlisted March 11, 1865 at Tompkinsville. Mustered in as Private in Co. K, March 11, 1865 to serve three years. Mustered out July 29, 1865 at Elmira, New York.

BUNT, DAVID H.— Age 28 years. Enlisted January 23, 1864 at Fabius. Mustered in as a Private, Co. I, February 2, 1864 to serve three years. Transferred to Co. E, March__1864. Deserted, 1864 at Rochester, New York.

BURCH, WILLIAM— Age 34 years. Enlisted November 19, 1863 at Brockport, as Private, Co. C, to serve three years. Rejected.

BURCH, WILLIAM— Age 36 years. Enlisted March 30, 1864 at Sidney. Mustered in as Private "unassigned," March 30, 1864 to serve three years. No further record.

BURDICK, GEORGE W.— Age 18 years. Enlisted January 28, 1864 at Rochester. Mustered in as Corporal in Co. K, February 6, 1864 to serve three years. Reduced, date not stated. Mustered out with company August 1, 1865 at Winchester, Virginia.

BURDICK, JOSEPH— Age 26 years. Enlisted February 21, 1865 at Concord. Mustered in as Private in Co. H, February 21, 1865 to server, Virginia.

BURDICK, LAMONT— Age 18 years. Enlisted January 5, 1864 at Norwich. Mustered in as Private, Co. L, February 12, 1864 to serve three years. Captured, date not stated, died, date not stated, at Andersonville, Georgia.

BURDICK, WOLFORD W.— Age 24 years. Enlisted November 18, 1863 at Albion. Mustered in as Corporal, Co. F, January 10, 1864 to serve three years. Captured, date not stated. Died October__1864 at Florence, S.C. Prior service in Co. D, Fifth United States Artillery.

BURGESS, ANDREW— Age 27 years. Enlisted February 13, 1865 at New York. Mustered in as Private in Co. A, February 13, 1865 to serve three years. Deserted May 8, 1865 in the field, Virginia.

BURK, MARTIN— Age 22 years. April 3, 1865 at Schenectady. Mustered in as Private, Co. F, April 3, 1865 to serve three years. Appointed Corporal, June 1, 1865. Mustered out with company August 1, 1865 at Winchester, Virginia.

BURKE, THOMAS— Age 20 years. Enlisted April 12, 1865 at Brooklyn. Mustered in as Private, "unassigned," April 12, 1865, to serve three years. Mustered out with detachment, May 6, 1865, at Hart's Island, New York Harbor.

BURLEIGH, WILLIE J.— Age 18 years. Enlisted December 16, 1863 at Syracuse. Mustered in as Private, Co. B, January 5, 1864, to serve three years. Mustered out with company August 1, 1865 at Winchester, Virginia.

BURNE, JOHN— Age not stated. Enlisted March 15, 1865 at New York. Mustered in as Private, Co. I, March 15, 1865, to serve three years. Deserted, May 5, 1865 at Winchester, Virginia.

BURNS, JOHN— Age not stated. Enlisted April 5, 1865 at Williamsburgh. Mustered in as Private Co. C, April 1865, to serve three years. Mustered out with company August 1, 1865 at Winchester, Virginia.

BURNS, THOMAS— Age 21 years. Enlisted December 7, 1863 at Rome. Mustered in as Private Co. C, January 5, 1864, to serve three years. Deserted February 6, 1864 at Rochester, New York.

BURR, CHARLES— Age 22 years. Enlisted February 15, 1865 at New York. Mustered in as Private, Co. A, February 15, 1865, to serve one year. Transferred to Co. C, May 5, 1865, to Co. D, June 5, 1865. Mustered out with company August 1, 1865 at Winchester, Virginia.

BURR, NEVELL L.— Age 25 years. Enlisted December 21, 1863 at Portland. Mustered in as Sergeant, Co. K, February 6, 1864, to serve three years. Mustered out with company August 1, 1865 at Winchester, Virginia. Veteran volunteer.

BURROUGHS, AUGUTUS— Age 20 years. Enlisted February 23, 1864 at Sweden. Mustered in as Private Co. C, March 8, 1864, to serve three years. Discharged, July 20, 1865 at Harpers Ferry, Virginia.

BURTON, ED— Age 26 years. Enlisted January 24, 1864 at Syracuse. Mustered in as Private Co. E, February 2, 1864, to serve three years. Died of disease, October 1, 1864, at Judiciary Square Hospital, Washington, D.C.

BURTON, WILLIAM— Age 24 years. Enlisted December 21, 1863 at Rochester. Mustered in as Private, Co. I, February 2, 1864, to serve three years. Mustered out with company, August 1, 1865, at Winchester, Virginia. Prior service in Co. C, Third New York Artillery.

BUSH, CHARLES— Age 23 years. Enlisted January 2, 1864 at Waterloo, as Private Co. F, to serve three years. Rejected.

BUSH, PETER D.— Age 18 years. Enlisted February 16, 1864 at Rochester, as Private, Co. M, to serve three years. Rejected.

BUTLER, ALFRED— Age 20 years. Enlisted January 5, 1864 at Madison. Mustered in as Private, Co. E, January 10, 1864, to serve three years. Captured, date not stated. Died, date not stated, at Andersonville, Georgia.

BUTLER, DANIEL A.— Age 42 years. Enlisted December 5, 1863 at Brockport. Mustered in as Wagoner, Co. C, January 5, 1864, to serve three years. Reduced, date not stated. Mustered out with company, August 1, 1865, at Winchester, Virginia.

BUTLER, HENRY— Age 21 years. Enlisted February 18, 1864 at Rochester. Mustered in as Quartermaster Sergeant, Co. M, February 23, 1864, to serve three years. No further record.

BUTLER, NATHANIEL— Age 22 years. Enlisted January 30, 1864 at Cortlandville. Mustered in as Private, Co. M, February 23, 1864, to serve three years. No further record.

BUTLER, SIMEON— Age 33 years. Enlisted March 21, 1865 at Utica. Mustered in as Private, Co. G, March 24, 1865, to serve three years. Mustered out with company, August 1, 1865, at Winchester, Virginia.

BUTLER, THOMAS— Age 30 years. Enlisted February 3, 1864, at Rochester. Mustered in as Private, Co. K, February 6, 1864, to serve three years. Transferred to Co. M, March 25, 1864. Mustered out with company August 1, 1865, at Winchester, Virginia.

BUTLER, WILLIAM H.— Age 28 years. Enlisted July 26, 1864 at Albany. Mustered in as Private, Co. E, July 26, 1864, to serve one year. Deserted April 5, 1865, at Winchester Virginia.

BUTTON, ALBERT LEROY— Age 22 years. Enlisted January 21, 1864 at Lafayette. Mustered in as Private Co. H, February 2, 1984, to serve three years. Mustered out with company August 1, 1865 at Winchester, Virginia.

BUTTON, JOHN F.— Age 20 years. Enlisted January 4, 1864, at Plymouth. Mustered in as Corporal Co. L, February 12, 1864, to serve three years. Appointed Sergeant, June 1, 1865. Mustered out with company August 1, 1865 at Winchester, Virginia.

BUTTON, WILLIAM— Age 32 years. Enlisted January 16, 1864 at Lafayette. Mustered in as Private Co. H, February 2, 1864, to serve three years. Deserted, date not stated.

BYRAM, WILLIAM H.— see Bryam, William H.

CADWELL, CHARLES H.— Age 19 years. Enlisted January 13, 1864 at Pharsalia. Mustered in as Private Co. L, February 12, 1864, to serve three years. Mustered out July 5, 1865, at Baltimore, Maryland.

CADWELL, LUCIEN B.— Age 23 years. Enrolled January 15, 1864 at Rochester; mustered in as First Lieutenant Co. B, January 15, 1864, to serve three years; as Captain, to date September 27, 1864; mustered out with company August 1, 1865 at Winchester, Virginia. Commissioned First Lieutenant, March 30, 1864, with rank from January 5, 1864, original; Captain, September 16, 1864 with rank from July 27, 1864, vice Provost, discharged.

CAGER, JOHN— Age 23 years. Enlisted December 16, 1863 at Rochester. Mustered in as Private, Co. F, January 10, 1864, to serve three years. Deserted, February 1864, from camp near Rochester. Also borne as Coger and Cogen.

CAHILL, JOHN— Age 23 years. Enlisted March 31, 1865 at Auterlitz. Mustered in as Private, Co. F, April 1, 1865, to serve three years. Mustered out to date June 23, 1865 at Harpers Ferry, Virginia.

CAHILL, TIMOTHY— Age 18 years. Enlisted March 18, 1865 at New York. Mustered in as Private, Co. K, March 18, 1865, to serve one year. Absent at Remount Camp, on muster out of company, August 1, 1865 at Winchester, Virginia. No further record.

CAHOON, GEORGE— Age 25 years. Enlisted December 11, 1863 at Rochester. Mustered in as Private, Co. A, December 20, 1863, to serve three years. Mustered out with company August 1, 1865 at Winchester, Virginia. Prior to service, in Co. B, Thirty Fourth New York Infantry.

CALDWELL, CHARLES— Age 23 years. Enlisted April 8, 1865 at Syracuse. Mustered in as Private, Co. F, April 8, 1865, to serve three years. Mustered out with company August 1, 1865 at Winchester, Virginia.

CALDWELL, JAMES— Age 19 years. Enlisted November 20, 1863 at Brockport. Mustered in as Private, Co. C, January 5, 1864, to serve three years. Accidentally killed, February 17, 1864 at Rochester, New York.

CALDWELL, WILLIAM— Age 23 years. Enlisted December 26, 1863 at Brockport. Mustered in as Corporal, Co. C, January 5, 1864, to serve three years. Appointed Sergeant, date not stated. Captured, no date given. Mustered out with detachment, June 28, 1865, at Winchester, Virginia.

CALLAHAN, THOMAS— Age 21 years. Enlisted December 14, 1864 at New York. Mustered in as Private, Co. B, December 14, 1864, to serve three years. Appointed Corporal, March 1, 1865. Mustered out with company August 1, 1865 at Winchester, Virginia.

CALM, ARNOLD— Age 24 years. Enlisted March 25, 1865 at New York. Mustered in as Private, Co. K, March 25, 1865, to serve three years. Mustered out with company August 1, 1865 at Winchester, Virginia.

CAMERON, DANIEL— Age 21 years. Enlisted January 11, 1864 at Lenox. Mustered in as Wagoner, Co. K, February 6, 1864, to serve three years. Appointed Corporal, June 1, 1865. Mustered out with company August 1, 1865 at Winchester, Virginia.

CAMERON, MARTIN— Age 26 years. Enlisted as Private, Co. G, December 15, 1863, at Bath, to serve three years. Rejected.

CAMP, JOEL N.— Age 18 years. Enlisted December 11, 1863 at Syracuse. Mustered in as Private, Co. B, January 5, 1864 to serve three years. Appointed Corporal, March 1, 1865. Mustered out with company, August 1, 1865 at Winchester, Virginia.

CAMPBELL, CHESTER— Age 21 years. Enlisted January 5, 1865 at Oneida. Mustered in as Sergeant, Co. M, February 23, 1864 to serve three years. No further record.

CAMPBELL, CHESTER— Age 23 years. Enlisted March 25, 1864 at Oneida. Mustered in as Private, Co. M, March 25, 1864 to serve three years. Admitted to Lincoln General Hospital, December 2, 1864. Absent at date of muster out of company, August 1, 1865. No further record.

CAMPBELL, JAMES— Age 23 years. Enlisted March 25, 1865 at Rochester. Mustered in as Private, "unassigned," March 25, 1865 to serve three years. No further record.

CAMPBELL, ROBERT B.— Age 20 years. Enlisted January 1, 1864 at Bath. Mustered in as Private, Co. G, February 2, 1864, to serve three years. Appointed Corporal, February 1, 1865, reduced, May 12, 1865. In confinement at Fort Delaware under sentence of G.C.M.A. of S., May 30. 1865. Discharged, August 9. 1865 at Rochester, New York.

CAMPBELL, WILLIAM— Age 20 years. Enlisted January 13, 1864 at Rochester. Mustered in as Private, Co. I, February 2, 1864 to serve three years. Appointed Corporal, March—, 1864. Appointed Quartermaster Sergeant, date not stated. Appointed First Sergeant, July 1, 1865. Mustered out with company, August 1, 1865 at Winchester, Virginia.

CANAVAN, EDWARD— Age 22 years. Enlisted March 10, 1865 at Albany. Mustered in as Private, Co. I, March 10, 1865 to serve three years. Mustered out with company, August 1, 1865 at Winchester, Virginia.

CANAVAN, JAMES F.— Age 19 years. Enlisted April 5, 1865 at Albany. Mustered in as Private, "unassigned," April 10, 1865 to serve three years. Mustered out with detachment, May 6, 1865 at Hart's Island, New York Harbor.

CANTY, JAMES— Age 21 years. Enlisted December 16, 1863 at Rochester. Mustered in as Private, Co. F, January 10, 1864 to serve three years. Deserted, February, 1864 from camp near Rochester, New York.

CANTY, PATRICK— Age 35 years. Enlisted as Private, Co. F, January 4, 1864 at Waterloo, to serve three years. Rejected, February, 1864.

CANUTE, SAMUEL— Age 19 years. Enlisted January 8, 1864 at Hanover. Mustered in as Trumpeter, Co. K, February 6, 1864 to serve three years. Mustered out with company, August 1, 1865 at Winchester, Virginia.

CAPIN, KELLOG— Age 19 years. Enlisted as Private, Co. H, to serve three years, January 11, 1864 at Syracuse. Rejected.

CAREY, JOHN— Age 21 years. Enlisted March 11, 1865 at New York. Mustered in as Private, "unassigned," March 11, 1865 to serve one year. No further record.

CAREY, JOHN— Age 18 years. Enlisted February 25, 1865 at New York. Mustered in as Private, Co. K, February 25, 1865 to serve three years. Absent at date of muster out of company, August 1, 1865. No further record.

CAREY, MICHAEL— Age 31 years. Enlisted March 18, 1865 at New York. Mustered in as Private, Co. K, March 18, 1865 to serve one year. Absent at date of muster out of company, August 1, 1865. No further record.

CAREY, PHILLIP— Age 20 years. Enlisted March 14, 1865 at New York. Mustered in as Private, Co. K, March 14, 1865 to serve three years. Absent at Remount Camp, at date of muster out of company, August 1, 1865. No further record. Also borne as Cary.

CARLTON, GEORGE W.— Age 19 years. Enlisted December 8, 1863 at Riga. Mustered in as Private, Co. C, January 5, 1864, to serve three years. Appointed Corporal, March 1, 1865. Mustered out with company, August 1, 1865, at Winchester, Virginia. Prior service in Co. G, Thirteenth New York Infantry.

CARLTON, JAMES A.— Age 18 years. Enlisted December 8, 1863 at Riga. Mustered in as Private, Co. C, January 5, 1864, to serve three years. Mustered out with company, August 1, 1865, at Winchester, Virginia.

CARMICHAEL, GEORGE W.— Age 24 years. Enlisted December 11, 1863 at Rochester. Mustered in as Private Co. D, January 10, 1864, to serve three years. Mustered out with company, August 1, 1865, at Winchester, Virginia. Prior service in Co. E, Thirteenth New York Volunteers.

CARPENTER, ATWOOD— Age 19 years. Enlisted March 20, 1865 at Schenectady. Mustered in as Private, Co. I, March 20, 1865, to serve three years. Mustered out, August 9, 1865, at Rochester, New York.

CARPENTER, GEORGE W.— Age 32 years. Enlisted March 14, 1865 at New York. Mustered in as Private, Co. K, March 15, 1865, to serve three years. Appointed Sergeant, July 1, 1865. Mustered out with company, August 1, 1865, at Winchester, Virginia.

CARPENTER, JAMES— Age 18 years. Enlisted December 11, 1863 at Cazenovia. Mustered in as Private, Co. E, January 10, 1864, to serve three years. Died of disease, August 16, 1864, at Third Division General Hospital.

CARPENTER, JOHN— Age 33 years. Enlisted December 28, 1863 at Rome. Mustered in as Private, Co. C, January 5, 1864, to serve three years. Transferred to Co. D, June 9, 1865. Absent, prisoner of war, at date of muster out of company, August 1, 1865. No further record.

CARR, ALFRED— Age 38 years. Enlisted as Private, Co. G, to serve three years, January 14, 1864 at Urbana. Rejected, date not stated.

CARR, DAVID— Age 20 years. Enlisted December 26, 1863, at Syracuse. Mustered in as Private, Co. H, January 5, 1864, to serve three years. Missing in action, May 7, 1864, at Germana Ford. No further record.

CARR, HENRY— Age 18 years. Enlisted November 11, 1863, at Urbana. Mustered in as Private, Co. G, February 2, 1864, to serve three years. In confinement at Winchester, Virginia. at date of muster out of company. No further record.

CARR, JOHN— Age 41 years. Enlisted January 5, 1864 at Urbana. Mustered in as Farrier, Co. K, February 6, 1864, to serve three years. Transferred to Co. G, March 28, 1864. Captured, date not stated. Prisoner of war at Andersonville, from June 29, 1864 to April 28, 1865. Discharged June 12, 1865, at New York.

CARRAGIN, AVERY— Age 19 years. Enlisted November 14, 1863 at Urbana. Mustered in as Private, Co. G, February 2, 1864, to serve three years. Mustered out with company, August 1, 1865, at Winchester, Virginia.

CARROLL, JAMES A.— Age 24 years. Enlisted September 1, 1864 at Norwich. Mustered in as Private, Co. L, September 1, 1864, to serve one year. Died of disease, May 15, 1865, at Annapolis, Maryland., while a paroled prisoner. Also borne as James M.

CARROLL RICHARD— Age 27 years. Enlisted February 16, 1865 at New York. Mustered in as Private, Co. H, February 16, 1865, to serve three years. Mustered out with company, August 1, 1865, at Winchester, Virginia.

CARROLL, TIMOTHY— Age 18 years. Enlisted March 18, 1865 at New York. Mustered in as Private, Co. I, March 18, 1865, to serve one year. Mustered out with company, August 1, 1865, at Winchester, Virginia.

CARROLL, WILLIAM— Age 23 years. Enlisted January 2, 1864, at Johnston. Mustered in as Private, "unassigned," January 5, 1864, to serve three years. No further record.

CARRON, EDWARD— Age 18 years. Enlisted as Private, Co. D, to serve three years, December 15, 1863, at Rochester. Rejected.

CARTER,GEORGE— Age 21 years. Enlisted January 2, 1864 at Madison. Mustered in as Private Co. E, January 10, 1864, to serve three years. Died of disease, date not stated, at Rochester, New York.

CARTY, WILLIAM— Age 21 years. Enlisted December 12, 1864 at New York. Mustered in as Private, "unassigned," December 12, 1864, to serve three years. No further record.

CARVER, LEVI E.— Age 18 years. Enlisted December 8, 1863, at Rochester. Mustered in as Private, Co. D, January 10, 1864, to serve three years. Died of disease, February 29, 1864, at Cuba, New York. while on furlough.

CASE, GEORGE W.— Age 18 years. Enlisted December 22, 1863 at Syracuse. Mustered in as Private, Co. B, January 5, 1864 to serve three years. Mustered out with company, August 1, 1865, at Winchester, Virginia.

CASE, JOHN— Age 18 years. Enlisted February 19, 1864 at Rochester. Transferred in as Private, Co. M, February 23, 1864 to serve three years. No further record.

CASEY, ROBERT— Age 21 years. Enlisted April 12, 1865 at Kingston. Mustered in as Private, Co. C, April 12, 1865, to serve three years. Mustered out with detachment, May 6, 1865, at Hart's Island, New York Harbor.

CASSIDY, ANDREW— Age 18 years. Enlisted February 24, 1865 at New York. Mustered in as Private, Co. B, February 24, 1865, to serve three years. Deserted June 8, 1865, at Winchester, Virginia.

CASSIDY, WILLIAM— Age 32 years. Enlisted April 7, 1865 at Albany. Mustered in as Private, "unassigned," April 7,1865 to serve one year. Mustered out with detachment, May 6, 1865, at Hart's Island, New York Harbor. Also borne as Cassady.

CASSON, FRANK— Age 22 years. Enlisted December 8, 1863, at Rochester. Mustered in as Private, Co. F, January 10, 1864, to serve three years. Deserted, February 1864, from camp near Rochester, New York.

CASTON, JOHN— Age 26 years. Enlisted February 11, 1864 at Bath. Mustered in as Private, Co. M, February 23, 1864, to serve three years. Transferred to Co. G, March 24, 1864. Died, date not stated.

CASWELL, AUGUSTUS— Age 21 years. Enlisted December 4, 1863, at Cazenovia. Mustered in as Commissary Sergeant Co. E, January 10, 1864, to serve three years. Mustered out with company, August 1, 1865, at Winchester, Virginia.

CAVANAUGH, JOHN— Age 29 years. Enlisted December 7, 1863 at Rochester. Mustered in as Corporal, Co. D, January 10, 1864, to serve three years. Appointed Sergeant, no date given. Mustered out with company, August 1, 1865, at Winchester, Virginia.

CAWLEY, JOHN— Age 18 years. Enlisted January 14, 1864 at Rochester. Mustered in as Private, Co. K, February 6, 1864, to serve three years. Deserted, February 12, 1864 at Rochester.

CHAMBERLAIN, ISAAC— Age 18 years. Enlisted March 13, 1865 at Fishkill. Mustered in as Private, "unassigned," March 13, 1865, to serve three years. No further record.

CHAMBERLAIN, FRANK A.— Age 22 years. Enlisted December 8, 1863 at Rochester. Mustered in as Sergeant, Co. I, February 2, 1864, to serve three years. Appointed Quartermaster Sergeant, date not stated. Died of disease, July 25, 1864 at Mt. Pleasant Hospital, Washington, D.C.

CHAMBERLIN, J.E.— Age not stated. Enlisted March 12, 1865 at Fishkill. Mustered in as Private, Co. D, March 13, 1865, to serve three years. Mustered out June 2, 1865 at Washington, D.C.

CHAPHE, ELMORE— Age 18 years. Enlisted December 7, 1863 at Cazenovia. Mustered in as Wagoner in Co. E, January 10, 1864, to serve three years. Discharged for disability on May 12, 1864 at Washington, D.C.

CHAPIN, DAVID D.— Age 30 years. Enlisted as Private in Co. D, to serve three years, January 5, 1864 at Bath. Rejected.

CHAPMAN, ORRIN P.— Age 24 years. Enlisted February 8, 1864 at Rochester. Mustered in as Private, Co. M, February 23, 1864, to serve three years. Transferred to Co. C, March 22, 1864. Mustered out July 16, 1865 at Washington, D.C.

CHAPPEE, CHARLES— Age 18 years. Enlisted as Private, Co. H, to serve three years, January 27, 1864 at Syracuse. Deserted prior to muster of company.

CHAPPELL, EUGENE— Age 43 years. Enlisted at Rochester as Private, Co. F, October 12, 1863 to serve three years. Rejected.

CHAPPELL, SUMNER E.— Age 26 years. Enlisted December 4, 1863 at Rochester. Mustered in as Private, Co. F, January 10, 1864 to serve three years. Absent sick at date of muster out of company, August 1, 1865.

CHARLES, JOHN— Age 23 years. Enlisted December 17, 1863 at Rochester. Mustered in as Private, Co. A December 20, 1863 to serve three years. Mustered out with company, August 1, 1865, at Winchester, Virginia.

CHASE, GEORGE E.— Age 18 years. Enlisted as Private, Co. E, to serve three years, January 2, 1864 at Cazenovia. Rejected.

CHASE, JAMES— Age 19 years. Enlisted September 2, 1864 at Huron. Mustered in as Private, Co. H, September 3, 1864 to serve one year. Mustered out with company, June 6, 1865 at Winchester, Virginia.

CHESHIRE, JOHN F.— Age 23 years. Enlisted March 11, 1865 at New York. Mustered in as Private, Co. K, March 11, 1865, to serve three years. Absent at Remount Camp at date of muster out of company, August 1, 1865.

CHESTER, JERRY H.— Age 23 years. Enlisted as Private, Co. M, to serve three years, February 6, 1864 at Syracuse. Deserted, prior to muster in of company, February 23, 1864.

CHRISTENSON, JOHN— Age 22 years. Enlisted February 20, 1865 at New York. Mustered in as Private, "unassigned," February 20, 1865, to serve three years. No further record.

CHRISTMAN, HENRY R.— Age 18 years. Enlisted March 23, 1865 at New York. Mustered in as Private, "unassigned," March 25, 1865, to serve three years. Name crossed from roll without remark. No further record.

CHRISTMAN, WILLIAM— Age 23 years. Enlisted December 12, 1863 at Peterboro. Mustered in as Private, Co. H, February 2, 1864, to serve three years. Deserted, date not stated. Also borne as Chrisman, William.

CHRISTOPHER, JOHN— Age not stated. Enlisted as Private, Co. C, to serve three years, February 26, 1865, at New York. No record of muster in. Deserted, June 5, 1865 near Winchester, Virginia.

CHUBBUCK, JOHN— Age 44 years. Enlisted as Private Co. G, to serve three years, January 2, 1864 at Avoca. Rejected.

CHURCH, ALBERT L.— Age 18 years. Enlisted February 22, 1865 at New York. Mustered in as Private, Co. M, February 22, 1865, to serve three years. Mustered out with company, August 1, 1865, at Winchester, Virginia.

CHURCH, AMASA E.— Age 18 years. Enlisted November 17, 1863 at Urbana. Mustered in as Private, Co. G, February 2, 1864, to serve three years. Mustered out with company, August 1, 1865, at Winchester, Virginia.

CLARK, CHARLES D.— Age 28 years. Enrolled January 18, 1865 at Winchester, Virginia. Mustered in as first lieutenant and adjutant, January 18, 1865, to serve unexpired term; mustered out with regiment, August 1, 1865. Commissioned First Lieutenant and Adjutant, December 24, 1864, with rank from December 30, 1864, vice Suggett, dismissed.

CLARK, DELOS— Age 19 years. Enlisted December 16, 1863 at Cazenovia. Mustered in as Private, Co. H, January 10, 1864, to serve three years. Mustered out with company August 1, 1865 at Winchester Virginia.

CLARK, FRANK H.— Age 20 years. Enlisted December 14, 1863 at Rochester. Mustered in as Corporal, Co. A, December 20, 1863, to serve three years. Deserted February 28, 1864 from United States General Hospital, Washington, DC.

CLARK, GEORGE— Age 22 years. Enlisted December 7, 1863 at Rochester. Mustered in as Private Co. F, January 10, 1864, to serve three years. Deserted February-, 1864 from camp near Rochester, New York.

CLARK GEORGE D.— Age 23 years. Enlisted as Private Co. M, to serve three years, February 6, 1864 at Rochester. Deserted prior to muster in of company, February 23, 1864.

CLARK, GEORGE M.— Age 18 years. Enlisted January 12, 1864 at Rochester. Mustered in as Private, Co. G, February 2, 1864 to serve three years. Transferred to Co. D, March 6, 1864. No further record.

CLARK, HENRY— Age 32 years. Enlisted February 20, 1865 at New York. Mustered in as Private Co. H, February 20, 1865 to serve three years. Absent at date of muster out of company, August 1, 1865. No further record. Reported as transferred to Co. E, but no record found in that company.

CLARK, LEWIS— Age 38 years. Enlisted February 15, 1865 at Avon. Mustered in as Private, "unassigned", February 15, 1865 to serve one year. No record of muster out. Name erased from roll, without remark. No further record

CLARK, SAMUEL A.— Age 18 years. Enlisted February 26, 1864 at Walton. Mustered in as Private Co. L, February 26, 1865 to serve three years. Mustered out with company August 1, 1865 at Winchester Virginia.

CLARK, SEYMOUR— Age 26 years. Enlisted January 5, 1864 at Madison. Mustered in as Private Co. E, January 19, 1864 to serve three years. Mustered out with detachment, July 19, 1865 at Winchester Virginia., while parole prisoner.

CLAY, CHARLES, JR.— Age 18 years. Enlisted January 20, 1864 at Tully. Mustered in as Private Co. K, February 6, 1864 to serve three years. Transferred to Co. H, March 25, 1864. Died, date not stated.

CLICKNAR, THOMAS J.— Age 21 years. Enlisted January 20, 1864 at Bath. Mustered in as Farrier, Co. G, February 2, 1864 to serve three years. Died, date not stated.

CLIFFORD, CHARLES M.— Age 21 years. Enlisted March 2, 1865 at New York. Mustered in as Private Co. K, March 2, 1865 to serve three years. Absent at Remount Camp at date of muster out of company, August 1, 1865.

CLIFFORD LOUIS M.— Age 20 years. Enlisted November 10, 1863 at Albion. Mustered in as Corporal, Co. F, January 10, 1864, to serve three years. Mustered out with company August 1, 1865 at Winchester, Virginia. Prior service in Co. K, Twenty-Seventh, New York Volunteers.

CLUMP, THEODORE— see Klumpp, Theodore.

COATES, PHILANDER M.— Age 18 years. Enlisted November 25, 1863 at Urbana. Mustered in as Private Co. G, February 2, 1864, to serve three years. Deserted, August 16, 1864.

COCHERIN, JAMES— Age 20 years. Enlisted December 26, 1863 at Rochester. Mustered in as Private Co. D, January 10, 1864, to serve three years. Discharged for disability, May 20, 1865 at Winchester, Virginia. Also borne as Corcoran and Cocklin.

COCHRANE, JOHN— Age 20 years. Enlisted March 18, 1865 at New York. Mustered in as Private, Co. I, March 18, 1865, to serve one year. Mustered out with company, August 1, 1865, at Winchester, Virginia.

CORCORAN, JOHN— Age 29 years. Enlisted October 13, 1863 at Rochester. Mustered in as Sergeant, Co. A, December 20, 1863, to serve three years. Reduced in rank, July 21, 1865. Mustered out with company, August 1, 1865, at Winchester, Virginia.

COFFIN, REUBEN N.— Age 18 years. Enlisted March 26, 1865 at Syracuse. Mustered in as Private, Co. C, March 26, 1865, to serve three years. Mustered out with company, August 1, 1865, at Winchester, Virginia.

COGER, JOHN— see Cager, John

COHN, MAX— Age 23 years. Enlisted April 8, 1865 at Schenectady. Mustered in as Private, "unassigned," April 10, 1865, to serve three years. Mustered out with detachment, May 6, 1865 at Hart's Island, New York Harbor.

COLDGROVE, ALBERT— Age 18 years. Enlisted December 7, 1863 at Cazenovia. Mustered in as Private, Co. E, January 10, 1864, to serve three years. Appointed Corporal, date not stated. Mustered out with company, August 1, 1865, at Winchester, Virginia. Also borne as Colegrove.

COLE, URIAH R.— Age 19 years. Enlisted January 4, 1864 at Oxford. Mustered in as Sergeant, Co. L, February 12, 1864, to serve three years. Mustered out May 8, 1865 at Moore's U.S. General Hospital, Philadelphia, Pa. Prior service in Co. H, Twenty-Fourth, New York Infantry.

COLEGROVE, ALBERT— see Coldgrove, Albert

COLEMAN, JOSHUA L.— Age 22 years. Enlisted January 28, 1864 at Rochester. Mustered in as Private, Co. K, February 6, 1864, to serve three years. Mustered out June 15, 1865 at Harper's Ferry, Virginia. Prior service in Co. B, One Hundred Eighth New York Volunteers.

COLLIER, FREDERICK W.— Age 33 years. Enlisted December 31, 1865 at Avoca. Mustered in as Saddler, Co. G, February 2, 1864, to serve three years. Reduced, date not stated. Mustered out with company, August 1, 1865, at Winchester, Virginia.

COLLINS, JAMES— Age 22 years. Enlisted December 8, 1863 at Rochester. Mustered in as Private, Co. A, December 20, 1863, to serve three years. Deserted, December 18, 1863 at Rochester, New York.

COLLINS, PATRICK— Age 34 years. Enlisted December 23, 1863 at Livonia. Mustered in as Private, Co. D, January 10, 1864, to serve three years. Deserted, January 18, 1864.

COLLINS, WILLIAM— Age 26 years. Enlisted November 9, 1863 at Barre. Mustered in as Private, Co. F, January 10, 1864, to serve three years. Rejected.

COLLINS, WILLIAM— Age 21 years. Enlisted December 8, 1863 at Rochester. Mustered in as Private, Co. F, January 20, 1864, to serve three years. Deserted, February 1864, from camp near Rochester, New York.

COLLINS, WILLIAMS— Age 36 years. Enlisted December 15, 1863 at Rochester. Mustered in as Private, Co. D, January 10, 1864, to serve three years. Deserted, February 1, 1864.

COLLISTER, FRANK— Age 28 years. Enlisted November 23, 1863 at Riga; mustered in as First Sergeant, Co. C, January 5, 1864, to serve three years; mustered in as Second Lieutenant, February 24, 1864; discharged for disability September 8, 1864; disability removed and mustered in as First Lieutenant, Co. C, to date, January 12, 1865; transferred to Co. D, June 26, 1865; mustered out with company, August 1, 1865, at Winchester, Virginia. Also borne as Franklin A. Collister. Commissioned Second Lieutenant, March 30, 1864, with rank from January 1864, original. First Lieutenant, November 19, 1864, with rank from November 19, 1864, vice Bruton, promoted.

COLLISTER, JOHN— Age 21 years. Enlisted November 28, 1863 at Riga. Mustered in as Private, Co. C, January 5, 1864, to serve three years. Deserted, February 10, 1964 at Rochester, New York.

COLWELL, CHARLES— Age 23 years. Enlisted April 8, 1865 at Syracuse. Mustered in as Private, "unassigned," April 8, 1865 to serve three years. No further record.

COMBS, EDWARD F.— Age 17 years. Enlisted December 31, 1863 at Cazenovia. Mustered in as Trumpeter, Co. E, January 10, 1864 to serve three years. Mustered out with detachment, June 28, 1865 at Winchester, Virginia.

COMMISKY, DAVID— Age 23 years. Enlisted December 7, 1863 at Rochester. Mustered in as Corporal, Co. D, January 10, 1864 to serve three years. Appointed Commissary Sergeant, date not stated. Mustered out with company, August 1, 1865 at Winchester, Virginia.

COMSTOCK, ALBERT J.— Age 19 years. Enlisted January 18, 1864 at Rochester. Mustered in as Private, Co. H, February 2, 1864 to serve three years. Appointed Corporal, December 27, 1864. Mustered out with company, August 1, 1865 at Winchester, Virginia.

CONDON, ANDREW— Age 18 years. Enlisted February 18, 1865 at Canandaigua. Mustered in as Private, Co. B, February 18, 1865 to serve one year. Mustered out with company, August 1, 1865 at Winchester, Virginia.

CONDON, THOMAS— Age 28 years. Enlisted January 2, 1864 at Waterloo. Mustered in as Private, Co. F, January 10, 1864 to serve three years. Died of disease, July 18, 1864 at Andersonville, Georgia.

CONGERS, GEORGE W.— Age 19 years. Enlisted February 17, 1865 at New York. Mustered in as Private, Co. K, February 17, 1865 to serve one year. Absent at Remount Camp, at date of muster out of company, August 1, 1865.

CONINE, LORENZO D.— Age 19 years. Enlisted January 29, 1864 at Prattsburgh. Mustered in as Private, Co. G, February 2, 1864 to serve three years. Discharged with detachment, August 9, 1865 at Rochester.

CONLON, JOHN— Age 22 years. Enlisted December 11, 1863 at Rochester. Mustered in as Private, Co. D, January 10. 1864 to serve three years. Deserted, July 30, 1864.

CONNELL, EDWARD— Age 22 years. Enlisted February 9, 1865 at Albany. Mustered in as Private, Co. K, February 9, 1865 to serve three years. Mustered out with company, August 1, 1865 at Winchester, Virginia.

CONNELL, PATRICK— Age 21 years. Enlisted January 15, 1864 at Rochester. Mustered in as Private, Co. K, February 6, 1864 to serve three years. Deserted, February 15, 1864 at Rochester.

CONNELL, WILLIAM— Age 23 years. Enlisted February 9, 1865 at Albany. Mustered in as Private, Co. M, February 9, 1865 to serve three years. Transferred to Co. K, June 27, 1865. No further record.

CONNER, JOHN— Age 28 years. Enlisted March 29, 1865 at New York. Mustered in as Private, Co. I, March 29, 1865 to serve three years. Deserted, May 25, 1865 at Winchester, Virginia.

CONNER, MICHAEL— Age 22 years. Enlisted December 8, 1863 at Rochester. Mustered in as Private, Co. F, January 10, 1864 to serve three years. Deserted, February, 1864 from camp near Rochester. Also borne as Connors, John.

CONNERS, RICHARD— Age 23 years. Enlisted February 26, 1864 at Rochester. Mustered in as Private, Co. F, March 8, 1864 to serve three years. Deserted, June, 1865 from camp near Rochester, New York.

CONNERS, RICHARD— Age 21 years. Enlisted November 13, 1863 at Arcadia. Mustered in as Private, Co. H, February 2, 1864 to serve three years. Appointed Corporal, date not stated. Killed in action, September 19, 1864 at Winchester, Virginia. Prior service in Co. I, Seventeenth Regiment, New York Volunteers.

CONNORS, TIMOTHY— Age 23 years. Enlisted December 15, 1863 at Rochester. Mustered in as Trumpeter, Co. F, January 10, 1864, to serve three years. Deserted, February, 1864, from camp near Rochester, New York.

CONOVER, WILLIAM H.— Age 19 years. Enlisted January 4, 1864 at Norwich. Mustered in as private, Co. L, February 12, 1864, to serve three years; Second Lieutenant, February 12, 1864; First Lieutenant, Co. C, to date, May 5, 1865, mustered out with company, August 1, 1865, at Winchester, Virginia. Commissioned Second Lieutenant, March 30, 1864, with rank from January 29, 1864, original; First Lieutenant, April 23, 1865, with rank from April 14, 1865, vice Fox, discharge.

CONVERS, WILLIAM A.— Age 28 years. Enlisted January 12, 1864 at Rochester. Mustered in as Wagoner, Co. I, February 2, 1864, to serve three years. Mustered out, to date, June 6, 1865, from hospital at Frederick, Maryland.

CONWAY, JOHN— Age 22 years. Enlisted January 8, 1864 at New Albion. Mustered in as Private, Co. M, February 23, 1864, to serve three years. No further record.

COOK, DAVID A.— Age 25 years. Enlisted January 22, 1864 at Rochester. Mustered in as Private, Co. K, February 6, 1864, to serve three years. Transferred to Co. M, March 25, 1864. Mustered out with company, August 1, 1865, at Winchester, Virginia.

COOK, HARLO— Age 25 years. Enlisted October 29, 1863 at Clarkson. Mustered in as Private, Co. A, October 20, 1863, to serve three years. Deserted July 4, 1865 in the field, Virginia.

COOK, WILLIAM— Age 19 years. Enlisted September 5, 1864 at Rochester. Mustered in as Private, Co. H, September 5, 1864, to serve one year. Mustered out, June 6, 1865 at Winchester, Virginia. Also borne as Cook, William O.

COON, FRANCIS— Age 18 years. Enlisted April 12, 1865 at Rochester. Mustered in as Private, Co. D, April 12, 1865, to serve two years. Mustered out with company, August 1, 1865, at Winchester, Virginia.

COON, MILO— Age 33 years. Enlisted January 21, 1864 at Lenox. Mustered in as Sergeant, Co. M, February 23, 1864, to serve three years. No further record.

COONEY, MICHAEL— Commissioned First Lieutenant December 19, 1864, with rank from December 14, 1864, vice Fisher; promoted, not mustered.

COONEY, WILLIAM— Age 24 years. Enlisted February 16, 1865 at New York. Mustered in as Private, Co. M, February 16, 1865, to serve three years. Mustered out with company, August 1, 1865, at Winchester, Virginia.

COONS, SIMON— Age 23 years. Enlisted March 3, 1864 at Rochester. Mustered in as Private, Co. M, March 9, 1864, to serve three years. Mustered out, May 24, 1865 at Elmira, New York. Also borne as Kuntz, Simon.

COOPER, NICHOLAS— Age 37 years. Enlisted December 17, 1863 at Andes. Mustered in as Farrier, Co. L, February 12, 1864, to serve three years. Captured, date not stated. Died of disease December 13, 1864 at Andersonville Prison, Georgia.

COPELAND, GEORGE— Age 32 years. Enlisted February 18, 1865 at New York. Mustered in as Private, Co. C, February 18, 1865, to serve three years. Mustered out with company, August 1, 1865, at Winchester, Virginia.

CORBIN, JAMES— Age 22 years. Enlisted April 13, 1865 at New York. Mustered in as Private, "unassigned," April 13, 1865, to serve one year. Mustered out with detachment, May 6, 1865, at Hart's Island, New York Harbor.

CORCORAN, JAMES— see Cocherin, James

CORKERY, DANIEL— Age 22 years. Enlisted April 13, 1865 at New York. Mustered in as Private, "unassigned," April 13, 1865, to serve one year. Mustered out May 6, 1865 with detachment, at Hart's Island, New York Harbor.

CORKINS, GEORGE B.— Age 31 years. Enlisted November 18, 1863 at Syracuse. Mustered in as First Sergeant, Co. B, January 5, 1864 to serve three years. Mustered out with company August 1, 1865 at Winchester, Virginia. Prior service in Co. F Fifth Regiment, U.S. Cavalry. Commissioned Second Lieutenant December 19, 1864, with rank from December 1, 1864, vice Arnd, declined.

CORMANT, CARLOS B.— Age 20 years. Enlisted March 7, 1865 at New York. Mustered in as Private Co. K, March 7, 1865 to serve three years. Absent at Camp Remount at date of muster out of company. No further record.

CORNES, JAMES P.— Age 18 years. Enlisted January 22, 1864 at Brockport. Mustered in as Commissary Sergeant Co. K, February 6, 1864, to serve three years. Transferred to Co. C, March 25, 1864. Mustered in as Second Lieutenant Co. K, May 19, 1865. Mustered out with company August 1, 1865 at Winchester, Virginia. Commissioned Second Lieutenant, December 22, 1864, with rank from December 2, 1864, vice Dayton, not mustered. Commission revoked; Recommissioned February 25, 1865 with rank from February 1, 1865, vice Austin, promoted.

CORNISH, FRANK— Age 20 years. Enlisted December 23, 1863 at Western. Mustered in as Sergeant, Co. C, January 5, 1864 to serve three years. Died of disease December 2, 1864 at Annapolis, Maryland.

CORNWELL, JOHN— Age 40 years. Enlisted March 3, 1864 at Rochester. Mustered in as Private Co. M, March 9, 1864 to serve three years. Captured May 8, 1864. Mustered out, June 22, 1865 at U.S. General Hospital, York, Pa. Also borne as Cornwall.

CORRIGAN, THOMAS— Age 23 years. Enlisted February 3, 1864 at Rochester. Mustered in as Private, Co. K, February 6, 1864 to serve three years. Transferred to Co. M, March 25, 1864. Deserted, September 5, 1864 at Charleston, Virginia.

COUNTRYMAN, MARTIN V.— Age 27 years. Enlisted December 7, 1863 at Rochester. Mustered in as Private Co. I, February 2, 1864, to serve three years. Transferred to Two Hundred Thirty Ninth Co. , First Battalion V.R. C., date not stated. Retransferred to this company by order of Secretary of War. Mustered out with company August 1, 1865 at Winchester, Virginia.

COURTWRIGHT, JACOB H.— Age 18 years. Enlisted January 21, 1864 at Camillus. Mustered in as Private Co. I, February 2, 1864 to serve three years. Mustered out with company August 1, 1865 at Winchester, Virginia.

COVELL, JOHN D.— Age 18 years. Enlisted November 21, 1863 at Urbana. Mustered in as Corporal Co. G, February 2, 1864 to serve three years. Deserted July 27, 1864; also borne as Coville.

COVERT, ALONZO— Age 39 years. Enlisted January 1, 1864 at Greene. Mustered in as Private Co. L, February 12, 1864 to serve three years. Appointed Farrier, date not stated. Discharged for disability, December 31, 1864 at Philadelphia, Pa.

COYLE, EDWARD— Age 20 years. Enlisted February 25, 1865 at New York. Mustered in as Private Co. K, February 25, 1865 to serve three years. Absent at Remount Camp at date of muster out of company.

CRADOCK, MARTIN— Age 40 years. Enlisted November 25, 1863 at Rochester. Mustered in as Private Co. A, December 20, 1863 to serve three years. Mustered out with company August 1, 1865 at Winchester Virginia.

CRAFT, WILLIAM, JR.— Age 40 years. Enlisted February 25, 1965 at New York. Mustered in as Private Co. H, February 25, 1865 to serve three years. Mustered out June 23, 1865 at Harpers Ferry, Virginia. Also borne as Croft.

CRAIN, HENRY— Age 18 years. Enlisted January 18, 1864 at Masonville. Mustered in as Private Co. L, February 12, 1864 to serve three years. Discharged February 22, 1865 at McClellan General Hospital, Philadelphia, Pa.

CRAM, GEORGE CLARENCE—Officer Commissioned Colonel, August 13, 1864, with rank from August 13, 1864, vice Crooks, discharged; not mustered.

CRAM, JOHN F.— Age 26 years. Enlisted December 7, 1863 at Rochester. Mustered in as Sergeant Co. D, January 10, 1864 to serve three years. Mustered out June 28, 1865 at Winchester, Virginia.

CRANE, PETER— Age 18 years. Enlisted January 11, 1864 at Rochester. Mustered in as Private Co. G, February 2, 1864 to serve three years. Transferred to Co. D, March 6, 1864; captured June 13, 1864. Released April 28, 1864. Mustered out, June 29, 1865 at New York.

CRANSON, FREDERICK— Age 20 years. Enlisted December 30, 1863 at Cazenovia. Mustered in as Private Co. E, January 10, 1864 to serve three years. Mustered out May 14, 1865 at Baltimore, Maryland.

CRANSTON, JOSEPH S.— Age 22 years. Enlisted January 4, 1864 at Pomfret. Mustered in as Corporal Co. K, February 6, 1864 to serve three years. Deserted August 5, 1864 at Rochester, NY.

CRANTS, CORNELIUS— Age 20 years. Enlisted December 28, 1863 at Bath. Mustered in as Corporal Co. G, February 2, 1864 to serve three years. Appointed Sergeant, November 1, 1864, reduced April 23, 1865. Mustered out with company August 1, 1865 at Winchester, Virginia. Prior service in Co. G, Third New York Infantry Volunteers.

CRANTS, HENRY T.— Age 25 years. Enlisted December 19, 1863 at Bath. Mustered in as Quartermaster Sergeant Co. G, February 2, 1863 to serve three years. Died of disease, date not stated. Prior service in Co. A, Twenty Third New York Infantry Volunteers.

CRAUNCE, DELEVAN— Age 24 years. Enlisted September 1, 1864 at Norwich. Mustered in as Private, Co. F, September 3, 1864 to serve one year. Mustered out June 6, 1865 at Winchester, Virginia.

CRAY, WILLIAM HENRY— Age 20 years. Enlisted January 1, 1864 at Palmyra. Mustered in as Private Co. H, February 2, 1864 to serve three years. Appointed Corporal, date not stated. Mustered out with company August 1, 1865 at Winchester, Virginia.

CRAWFORD, EDWARD— Age 18 years. Enlisted November 2, 1863 at Penfield. Mustered in as Private Co. A, December 20, 1863 to serve three years. Died of disease, October 29, 1864 at Andersonville, Georgia.

CRAWLEY, WILLIAM— Age 21 years. Enlisted February 4, 1864 at Rochester. Mustered in as Private Co. K, February 6, 1864 to serve three years. Transferred to Co. M. No further record.

CRISTAL, JOHN— Age not stated. Enlisted September 3, 1864 at Rochester. Mustered in as Private Co. C, September 3, 1864 to serve three years. Mustered out with company August 1, 1865 at Winchester, Virginia.

CROFOOT, SAMUEL M.— Age 35 years. Enlisted December 10, 1863 at Syracuse. Mustered in as Sergeant Co. B, January 5, 1864 to serve three years. Mustered out with company August 1, 1865 at Winchester, Virginia. Prior service in Sixty First New York Volunteer Infantry.

CROFT, WILLIAM, JR.— see Craft, William, Jr.

CRONEN, JOHN— Age 18 years. Enlisted December 2, 1863 at Arcadia. Mustered in as Private Co. H, February 2, 1864 to serve three years. Mustered out with company August 1, 1865 at Winchester, Virginia.

CRONT, HENRY— Age 17 years. Enlisted April 12 1865 at Schenectady. Mustered in as private, "unassigned," April 12, 1865, to serve one year. Mustered out with detachment, May 6, 1865 at Harts Island, New York Harbor.

CROOKS, SAMUEL J.— Age not stated; enrolled March 4, 1863 at Rochester; mustered in as colonel, date not stated, to serve three years; discharged, to date March 21, 1865. Commissioned colonel May 4, 1865, with rank from January 29, 1864, original.

CROSBY, ALPHEUS H.— Age 38 years. Enlisted December 23, 1863 at Manchester. Mustered in as Private Co. H, February 2, 1864, to serve three years. Discharged, date not stated.

CROSSET, JEROME— Age 31 years. Enlisted January 24, 1864 at Manlius. Mustered in as Private Co. I, February 2, 1864, to serve three years. Transferred to Co. E. March, 1864. No further record.

CROTHER, GEORGE L.— Age 20 years. Enlisted December 26, 1863 at Sodus. Mustered in as Private Co. H. February 2, 1864, to serve three years. Mustered out, date not stated.

CROUSE CHARLES T.— Age 23 years. Enlisted February 29, 1864 at Lima. Mustered in as Private, Co. M, February 25, 1864, to serve three years. Discharged, date not stated, at Rochester New York. Also borne as Conice.

CROWE, JOHN— Age 28 years. Enlisted March 31, 1865 at New York. Mustered in as Private Co. F, March 31, 1865, to serve one year. Mustered out with company, August 1, 1865 at Winchester, Virginia.

CROWLEY, DANIEL— Age 34 years. Enlisted January 5, 1864 at Olean. Mustered in as Trumpeter, Co. K, February 6, 1864, to serve three years. Mustered out as Private, with detachment, May 19, 1865, at Satterlee General Hospital, Philadelphia, Pa.

CROWLEY, MICHAEL— Age 19 years. Enlisted December 4, 1863 at Rochester. Mustered in as Private, Co. A, December 20, 1863, to serve three years. Mustered out with company, August 1, 1865 at Winchester, Virginia.

CROYFORD, GEORGE— Age 21 years. Enlisted March 30, 1865 at New York. Mustered in as Private, Co. F, March 30, 1865, to serve three years. Mustered out with company, August 1, 1865 at Winchester, Virginia.

CRUMB, DE WITT— Age 18 years. Enlisted January 29, 1864 at Prattsburgh. Mustered in as Private, Co. G, February 2, 1864, to serve three years. Appointed Corporal, February 1, 1865. Mustered out with company, August 1, 1865 at Winchester, Virginia.

CUDDEBACK, ALBERT— Age 22 years. Enlisted December 16, 1863 at Rochester. Mustered in as Private, Co. I, February 2, 1864, to serve three years. Mustered out with company, August 1, 1865 at Winchester, Virginia.

CUDNEY, HARMAN— Age 18 years. Enlisted April 4, 1865 at Albany. Mustered in as Private, Co. F, April 4, 1865, to serve one year. Absent sick at muster out of company. No further record.

CULLEN, JAMES— Age 32 years. Enlisted March 18, 1865 at Brooklyn. Mustered in as Private, Co. K, March 18, 1865, to serve three years. Absent at Camp Remount at muster out of company, August 1, 1865. No further record.

CULLEN, JOHN C.— Age 20 years. Enlisted January 2, 1864 at New York. Mustered in as Private, "unassigned," January 2, 1864, to serve three years, no further record.

CUMMINGS, BIRDSALL— Age 18 years. Enlisted March 2, 1864 at Milford. Mustered in as Private, Co. L, February 12, 1864, to serve three years. Captured, date not stated, died of disease, date not stated, in Andersonville Prison, Georgia.

CURRY MICHAEL— Age 38 years. Enlisted as Private, Co. K, to serve three years, January 18, 1864 at Dunkirk. Rejected.

DAILEY, JAMES— Age 22 years. Enlisted March 25, 1865 at Rochester. Mustered in as Private, "unassigned," March 25, 1865 to serve three years. No further record.

DAILY, JOHN— Age 20 years. Enlisted February 2, 1864 at Rochester. Mustered in as Saddler, Co. K, February 6, 1864, to serve three years. Transferred to Co. M, March 25, 1864. Also borne as Dailey, no further record.

DAILY, RICHARD— Age 18 years. Enlisted December 22, 1863 at Verona. Mustered in as Private, Co. M, February 23, 1864, to serve three years. Mustered out with company, August 1, 1865 at Winchester, Virginia.

DAKINS, JONAH— Age 42 years. Enlisted September 14, 1864 at Albany. Mustered in as Private, "unassigned," September 21, 1864, to serve one year. No further record.

DAKINS, JONAH— Age 33 years. Enlisted January 2, 1864 at Waterloo. Mustered in as Private, Co. F, January 10, 1864, to serve three years, died February 5, 1865 at Salisbury, N.C.

DALTON, SAMUEL P.— Age 23 years. Enlisted December 8, 1863 at Buffalo. Mustered in as Corporal, Co. K, February 6, 1864, to serve three years. Died in prison at Florence, S.C., no date given.

DANIELS, CHARLES— Age 37 years. Enlisted January 4, 1864 at Preston. Mustered in as Private, Co. L, February 12, 1864, to serve three years. Discharged April 23, 1865 at McClellan Hospital, Philadelphia, Pa.

DANIELS, WILLIAM, H.— Age 23 years. Enlisted March 6, 1864 at Bath. Mustered in as Private, Co. G, April 6, 1864, to serve three years. Appointed Corporal, February 1, 1865, appointed Sergeant, July 1, 1865. Mustered out with company, August 1, 1865 at Winchester, Virginia.

DARBY, WILLIAM H.— Age 24 years. Enlisted February 28, 1865 at New York. Mustered in as Private, Co. D, February 28, 1865, to serve on year. Transferred to Co. M, date not stated. Mustered out with company, August 1, 1865 at Winchester, Virginia.

DAVID, ELIAS B.— Age 24 years. Enlisted December 23, 1863 at Syracuse. Mustered in as Private Co. B, January 5, 1864, to serve three years. Reported sick in hospital upon muster out of company, August 1, 1865, no further record.

DAVIDSON, DUNCAN— Age 35 year. Enlisted March 2, 1865 at Syracuse. Mustered in as Private, "unassigned," March 2, 1865, to serve three years. Mustered out with detachment May 9, 1865 at Elmira, New York.

DAVIDSON, JOHN— Officer Commissioned First Lieutenant May 20, 1865, with rank from April 15, 1865, vice Sperry; promoted; not mustered.

DAVIS, ALSON W.— Age 35 years. Enlisted December 30, 1865 at Avoca. Mustered in as Commissary Sergeant, Co. G, February 2, 1864, to serve three years. Died, date and place not stated. Also borne as Allison W.

DAVIS, GEORGE— Age 18 years. Enlisted December 24, 1863 at Utica. Mustered in as Private, Co. B, January 5, 1864, to serve three years. Died May 7, 1864 at Armory Square Hospital, Washington, D.C.

DAVIS, GEORGE— Age 25 years. Enlisted March 28, 1865 at New York. Mustered in as Private, Co. I, March 28, 1865, to serve three years. Transferred to Co. B, date not stated. Mustered out with company, August 1, 1865 at Winchester, Virginia.

DAVIS, HENRY— Age 21 years. Enlisted December 5, 1863 at Rochester. Mustered in as Private, Co. F, January 10, 1864, to serve three years. Deserted February, 1864 from camp near Rochester, New York.

DAVIS, JOHN— Age 19 years. Enlisted March 1, 1865 at Syracuse. Mustered in as Private, "unassigned," March 1, 1865, to serve three years, no further record.

DAVIS, JOHN— Age 21 years. Enlisted February 14, 1865 at New York. Mustered in as Private, Co. A, February 14, 1865, to serve three years. Transferred to Co. B, May 5, 1865. Mustered out with company, August 1, 1865 at Winchester, Virginia.

DAVIS, JOHN— Age 22 years. Enlisted February 24, 1864 at Rochester. Mustered in as Private, "unassigned," March 8, 1864, to serve three years. No further record.

DAVIS, LUCIAN— Age 18 years. Enlisted December 30, 1863 at Cazenovia. Borne as Private, Co. E, and rejected.

DAVIS, PATRICK— Age 20 years. Enlisted April 11, 1865 at New York. Mustered in as Private, "unassigned," April 11, 1865, to serve one year. Mustered out with detachment, May 6, 1865 at Hart's Island, New York Harbor.

DAVIS, THOMAS J.— Colored. Age 18 years. Enlisted January 14, 1864 at Rochester. Mustered in as Cook, Co. L, February 12, 1864, to serve three years. Deserted, December 8, 1864 at Camp Stoneman, D.C.

DAVIS, WILLIAM— Age 19 years. Enlisted February 28, 1865 at Plattsburgh. Mustered in as Private, Co. D, February 28, 1865, to serve one year. Mustered out August 21, 1865 at Elmira, New York.

DAVIS, WILLIAM H.— Age 23 years. Enlisted February 11, 1864 at Bath. Mustered in as Private, Co. M, February 23, 1864, to serve three years. Transferred to Co. G, March 24, 1864. Discharged for disability, June 22, 1865 at McClellan General Hospital, Philadelphia, Pa.

DAY, JULIUS S.— Age 21 years. Enlisted January 11, 1864 at Syracuse. Mustered in as Private, Co. H, to serve three years. Rejected.

DAY, MORGAN— Age 18 years. Enlisted December 30, 1863 as Private, Co. E, at Cazenovia, to serve three years. Discharged, January 8, 1864, underage.

DAYTON, EDWIN A.— Age 30 years. Enlisted December 21, 1863 at Brockport; mustered in as private, Co. C, January 5, 1864, to serve three years; appointed Sergeant Major, April 30, 1864; reduced, August 13, 1864; re-appointed February 1, 1865; mustered out with regiment, August 1, 1865 at Winchester, Virginia. Commissioned Second Lieutenant, August 13, 1864, with rank from July 24, 1864, vice Lamb. Discharged, not mustered, recommissioned July 15, 1865, with rank from June 25, 1865, vice Hazleton. Mustered out.

DEAL, WILLIAM— Age 22 years. Enlisted March 7, 1865 at New York. Mustered in as Private, Co. D, March 7, 1865, to serve three years. Mustered out with company, August 1, 1865 at Winchester, Virginia. Also borne as of Co. I.

DEAN, CHARLES G.— Age 17 years. Enlisted February 23, 1865 at Horseheads. Mustered in as Private, "unassigned," February 23, 1865, to serve one year. Mustered out with detachment, May 9, 1865 at Elmira, New York.

DE BOE, JOHN— Age 18 years. Enlisted February 3, 1864 at Rochester. Mustered in as Private, Co. K, February 6, 1864, to serve three years. Transferred to Co. H, March 25, 1864. No further record.

DE CLERCQ, WILLIAM E.— Age 17 years. Enlisted December 19, 1863 at Cazenovia. Mustered in as Private, Co. E, January 10, 1864, to serve three years. Died, date not known, at Andersonville, Georgia.

DEEGAN, WILLIAM— Age 44 years. Enlisted December 14, 1863 at Rochester, as Private, Co. D, to serve three years. Rejected.

DEERY, JAMES— Age 25 years. Enlisted March 2, 1865 at New York. Mustered in as Private, Co. D, March 2, 1865, to serve three years. Never joined company for duty.

DE GRAFF, JACOB— Age 38 years. Enlisted February 22, 1865 at Chemung. Mustered in as Private, Co. B, February 22, 1865, to serve one year. Mustered out with company August 1, 1865 at Winchester, Virginia.

DE GRAFF, WILLIAM— Age 18 years. Enlisted February 16, 1864 at Bath, as Private, Co. M, to serve three years. Rejected.

DEIOTIE, JAMES W.— See De Votie, James, W.

DE KAY, ALANSON— Age 24 years. Enlisted April 8, 1865 at Rochester. Mustered in as Private, Co. F, April 7, 1865 to serve one year. Mustered out with company August 1, 1865 at Winchester, Virginia.

DE LA KEVORDINA, NICHOLAS— Age 18 years. Enlisted February 22, 1865 at New York. Mustered in as Private, Co. H, February 22, 1865 to serve three years. Mustered out with company August 1, 1865 at Winchester, Virginia.

DELANEY, EDWARD— Age 28 years. Enlisted April 5, 1865 at New York. Mustered in as Private, Co. B, April 5, 1865 to serve three years. Died July 8, 1865 in hospital, at Winchester, Virginia.

DELANY, JOHN— Age 33 years. Enlisted March 15, 1865 at New York. Mustered in as Private, Co. D, March 15, 1865 to serve three years. Never joined company for duty.

DELEVAN, CHARLES H.— Age 21 years. Enlisted December 28, 1863 at Lyons. Mustered in as Private, Co. H, February 2, 1864 to serve three years. Mustered out with company August 1, 1865 at Winchester, Virginia. Prior service in Twenty Seventh New York Infantry.

DENNEY, JAMES, H.— Age 22 years. Enlisted January 12, 1864 at German. Mustered in as Private, Co. L, February 12, 1864 to serve three years. Appointed Corporal, June 1, 1865. Mustered out with company August 1, 1865 at Winchester, Virginia.

DENNING, JAMES— Age 23 years. Enlisted April 12, 1865 at Kingston. Mustered in as Private "unassigned," April 12, 1865 to serve three years. Mustered out with detachment, May 6, 1865 at Hart's Island, New York Harbor.

DENOIS, HENRY— Age 28 years. Enlisted March 2, 1865 at New York. Mustered in as Private, Co. C, March 2, 1865 to serve three years. Mustered out with company August 1, 1865 at Winchester, Virginia.

DEPEW, IRA— Age 21 years. Enlisted January 5, 1864 at Lyons. Mustered in as Private, Co. H, February 2, 1864 to serve three years. Mustered out with company August 1, 1865 at Winchester, Virginia.

DESBROW, THOMAS A.— Age 24 years. Enlisted December 21, 1863 at Utica. Mustered in as Private, Co. B, January 5, 1864 to serve three years. Discharged for disability, October 4, 1864 at New York.

DEUEL, ABRAM— Age 40 years. Enlisted December 24, 1863 at Rochester. Mustered in as Private, Co. I, February 2, 1864 to serve three years. In hospital at Philadelphia, Pa, on muster out of company, August 1, 1865. No further record.

DEVANE, HENRY— Age 29 years. Enlisted December 29, 1863 at Peterboro, as Private, Co. H, to serve three years. Rejected.

DEVINE, DANIEL— Age 20 years. Enlisted December 24, 1863 at Rochester. Mustered in as Private, Co. I, February 2, 1864 to serve three years. Captured, June 29, 1864. Mustered out July 18, 1865 at New York.

DEVLIN, JAMES— Age 21 years. Enlisted December 15, 1863 at Rochester. Mustered in as Private, Co. F, January 10, 1864 to serve three years. Deserted in November, 1864 from Remount Camp, Giesboro, D.C.

DEVOE, ISAAC— Age 23 years. Enlisted December 15, 1863 at Seneca Falls. Mustered in as Private, Co. I, February 2, 1864 to serve three years. Deserted in February, 1864 at Rochester.

DE VOTIE, JAMES W.— Age 18 years. Enlisted December 18, 1863 at Utica. Mustered in as Private, Co. B, January 5, 1864 to serve three years. Deserted August 24, 1864 from Chain Bridge, Virginia. Also borne as Deiotie.

DEWER, THOMAS— Age 21 years. Enlisted December 10, 1863 at Rochester. Mustered in as Sergeant, Co. F, January 10, 1864, to serve three years. Died, June 19, 1864 at Andersonville, Georgia.

DEXTER, JAMES R.— Age 28 years. Enlisted April 6, 1865 at Rochester. Mustered in as Private, Co. F, April 6, 1865, to serve three years. Transferred to Co. G, May 27, 1865. Mustered out with company August 1, 1865 at Winchester, Virginia.

DIBBLE, CHARLES H.— Age 18 years. Enlisted January 5, 1864 at Plymouth. Mustered in as Private, Co. L, February 12, 1864, to serve three years. Mustered out with company August 1, 1865 at Winchester, Virginia.

DICKINSON, DAVID H.— Age 23 years. Enlisted January 16, 1864 at Bath. Mustered in as Private, Co. G, February 2, 1864, to serve three years. Mustered out with detachment, August 9, 1865 at Rochester, NY. Prior service in Co. A, Twenty Third New York Infantry.

DIKEMAN, DAVID— Age 44 years. Enlisted December 4, 1863 at Rochester. Mustered in as Private, Co. F, January 10, 1864, to serve three years. Died, July 19, 1864 at Andersonville, Georgia.

DILDINE, ZACHARIAH— Age 25 years. Enlisted January 2, 1864 at Bath. Mustered in as Private, Co. G, February 2, 1864, to serve three years. Mustered out with company August 1, 1865 at Winchester, Virginia.

DILDIN, ZENAS W.— Age 31 years. Enlisted February 15, 1864 at Bath. Mustered in as Private, Co. M, February 23, 1864, to serve three years. Transferred to Co. G, March 24, 1864. Died, date and place not stated.

DILLINGHAM, RICHARD— Age 20 years. Enlisted December 5, 1863 at Rochester. Mustered in as Private, Co. H, December 5, 1863, to serve three years. Appointed Sergeant, date not stated. Mustered out with company August 1, 1865 at Winchester, Virginia. Also borne as Richard E.

DIME, FREDERICK— Age 23 years. Enlisted December 15, 1863 at Rochester. Mustered in as Private, Co. D, January 10, 1864, to serve three years. Mustered out with company August 1, 1865 at Winchester, Virginia.

DIMMOND, BENJAMIN, R.— Age 21 years. Enlisted March 31, 1865 at New York. mustered in as Private, Co. D, March 31, 1865, to serve three years. Discharged June 21, 1865.

DINGMAN, JAMES B.— Age 18 years. Enlisted November 2, 1863 at Rochester. Mustered in as Corporal, Co. A, December 20, 1863, to serve three years. Appointed Sergeant, date not stated. Mustered out with company August 1, 1865 at Winchester, Virginia.

DOAG, JAMES— Age 21 years. Enlisted January 7, 1864 at Rochester. Mustered in as Private, "unassigned," March 8, 1864, to serve three years. No further record.

DOBBIN, SAMUEL— Age 21 years. Enlisted January 1, 1864 at Riga. Mustered in as Private, Co. C, January 5, 1864, to serve three years. Appointed Sergeant, date not stated. Mustered out with company August 1, 1865 at Winchester, Virginia.

DOBBS, DEWITT CLINTON— Age 18 years. Enlisted December 7, 1863 at Lyons. Mustered in as Private, Co. H, February 2, 1864, to serve three years. Deserted, date not stated.

DODD, EDWARD, JR.— Age 19 years. Enlisted December 31, 1863 at Cortlandville. Mustered in as Private, Co. E, January 10, 1864, to serve three years. Transferred to Co. B, date not state. Mustered out June 15, 1865 at Jarvis General Hospital, Baltimore, Maryland. Also borne as Edmond.

DODD, JOHN J.— Age 23 years. Enlisted December 31, 1863 at Cortlandville. Mustered in as Private, Co. B, January 5, 1864, to serve three years. Appointed Corporal, March 1, 1865. Mustered out with company August 1, 1865 at Winchester, Virginia. Prior service in Co. H, Twenty Third Infantry.

DOHERTY, JOHN— Age 22 years. Enlisted March 11, 1865 at New York. Mustered in as Private, Co. D, March 11, 1865, to serve three years. Mustered out with company August 1, 1865 at Winchester, Virginia.

DOLAND, FRANK G.— Age 23 years. Enlisted November 23, 1863 at Barre. Mustered in as Corporal, Co. F, January 10, 1864, to serve three years. Reduced, date not stated. Appointed May 1, 1865. Sergeant, July 1, 1865. Mustered out with company August 1, 1865 at Winchester, Virginia.

DOLAND, JOHN— Age 18 years. Enlisted November 24, 1863 at Albion. Mustered in as Private, Co. F, January 10, 1864, to serve three years. Mustered out with company August 1, 1865 at Winchester, Virginia.

DOLPH, FRANCIS— Age 22 years. Enlisted December 7, 1863 at Brockport. Mustered in as Corporal, Co. C, January 5, 1864, to serve three years. Died of disease, April 30, 1864 at Lincoln Hospital, Washington, D.C. Prior service in Co. L, Seventeenth New York Volunteers.

DOLPH, JOHN W.— Age 16 years. Enlisted December 31, 1863 at Sweden. Mustered in as Private, Co. C, January 5, 1864, to serve three years. Mustered out with company August 1, 1865 at Winchester, Virginia.

DONAHUE, WILLIAM— Age 20 years. Enlisted April 13, 1865 at Kingston. Mustered in as Private, "unassigned," April 13, 1865, to serve three years. Mustered out with detachment, May 6, 1865, at Hart's Island, New York Harbor.

DONAHUGH, JOHN— Age 30 years. Enlisted January 15, 1864 at Rochester. Mustered in as Private, Co. K, February 6, 1864, to serve three years. Deserted, February 8, 1864.

DONALDSON, JOHN— Age 26 years. Enlisted December 25, 1863 at Fayetteville. Mustered in as Private, Co. E, to serve three years. Rejected.

DONALDSON, ROBERT H.— Age 24 years. Enlisted November 24, 1863 at Syracuse. Mustered in as Quartermaster Sergeant, Co. B, January 5, 1864, to serve three years. Mustered out with company August 1, 1865 at Winchester, Virginia.

DONK, CHARLES M.— Age 18 years. Enlisted March 31, 1865 at Schenectady. Mustered in as Private, "unassigned," March 31, 1865, to serve three years. Mustered out June 20, 1865 at U.S. General Hospital, Cumberland, Maryland.

DONNELLY, JAMES— Age 18 years. Enlisted April 14, 1865 at Kortright. Mustered in as Private, "unassigned," April 14, 1865, to serve three years. Mustered out with detachment, May 6, 1865 at Hart's Island, New York Harbor.

DONNELLY, JAMES— Age 20 years. Enlisted November 12, 1863 at Urbana. Mustered in as Corporal, Co. G, February 2, 1864, to serve three years. Appointed Sergeant, July 1, 1865. Mustered out with company August 1, 1865 at Winchester, Virginia. Prior service, Co. I, Thirty Fourth New York Volunteer Infantry.

DORA, ALFRED— see Dorn, Alfred

DORAS, CORNELIUS— Age 33 years. Enlisted March 15, 1865 at New York. Mustered in as Private, Co. D, March 15, 1865, to serve three years. Never joined company for duty. Also borne as Downs.

DORMER, JOHN— Age 23 years. Enlisted December 18, 1863 at Rochester. Mustered in as Private, Co. A, December 20, 1863, to serve three years. Appointed Corporal, February 29, 1864. Absent sick in hospital upon muster out of company, August 1, 1865.

DORN, ALFRED— Age 37 years. Enlisted March 8, 1865 at New York. Mustered in as Private, Co. G, March 8, 1865, to serve three years. Mustered out with company August 1, 1865 at Winchester, Virginia. Also borne as Dora and as of Co. D.

DOTY, ELISHA— Age 18 years. Enlisted December 22, 1863 at Syracuse. Mustered in as Private, Co. B, January 5, 1864, to serve three years. Mustered out with company August 1, 1865 at Winchester, Virginia. Also borne as Dotty.

DOUGLASS, GEORGE H.— Age 19 years. Enlisted April 7, 1865 at Syracuse. Mustered in as Private, Co. F, April 7, 1865, to serve three years. Absent sick in hospital upon muster out of company, August 1, 1865.

DOUGLASS, JOHN W.— Age 21 years. Enlisted February 15, 1865 at New York. Mustered in as Private, "unassigned," February 15, 1865, to serve three years. Deserted.

DOUGLASS, WALTER— Age 19 years. Enlisted April 8, 1865 at Albany. Mustered in as Private, "unassigned," April 10, 1865, to serve three years. Mustered out with detachment, May 6, 1865 at Hart's Island, New York Harbor.

DOWNEY, THOMAS E.— Age 19 years. Enlisted April 10, 1865 at Albany. Mustered in as Private, "unassigned," April 10, 1865, to serve one year. Mustered out with detachment, May 6, 1865 at Hart's Island, New York Harbor.

DOWNS, PETER J.— Age 22 years. Enlisted April 1, 1865 at Rochester. Mustered in as Private, Co. A, April 1, 1865, to serve one year. Mustered out with company August 1, 1865 at Winchester, Virginia.

DOYLE, EDWARD— Age 21 years. Enlisted April 11, 1865 at Kingston. Mustered in as Private, "unassigned," April 11, 1865, to serve three years. Mustered out with detachment, May 6, 1865 at Hart's Island, New York Harbor.

DOYLE, OWEN— Age 20 years. Enlisted December 17, 1863 at Rochester. Mustered in as Private, Co. A, December 20, 1863, to serve three years. Mustered out with company August 1, 1865 at Winchester, Virginia.

DRAKE, WALTER E.— Age 18 years. Enlisted January 5, 1864 at Plymouth. Mustered in as Private, Co. L, February 12, 1864, to serve three years. Reported deserted, December 8, 1864 from hospital. Also reported as died at Danville, Virginia.

DREW, WILLIAM H.— Age 24 years. Enlisted February 13, 1864 at Sodus. Mustered in as Private, Co. M, February 23, 1864, to serve three years. No further record.

DROST, ANDREW— Age 24 years. Enlisted March 2, 1865 at Rochester. Mustered in as Private, Co. A, March 2, 1865, to serve three years. Mustered out with company August 1, 1865 at Winchester, Virginia.

DROWN, HENRY C.— Age 20 years. Enlisted January 3, 1864 at Huron. Mustered in as Private, Co. H, February 2, 1864, to serve three years. Mustered out May 17, 1865 at USA General Hospital, York, Pa. Also borne as Droun.

DUCAN, ANTOINE— Age 35 years. Enlisted February 20, 1865 at New York. Mustered in as Private, Co. B, February 20, 1865, to serve three years. Mustered out with company August 1, 1865 at Winchester, Virginia. Also borne as Ducars.

DUCHRING, MAX— Age 25 years. Enlisted March 25, 1865 at New York. Mustered in as Private, Co. K, March 25, 1865, to serve three year. Mustered out with company August 1, 1865 at Winchester, Virginia. Also borne as During.

DUFFEY, LAWRENCE— Age 23 years. Enlisted December 15, 1863 at Rochester. Mustered in as Private, Co. A, December 20, 1863, to serve three years. Deserted, February 29, 1864 at Rochester.

DUMAS, EDWARD— Age 18 years. Enlisted February 26, 1865 at Harpersfield. Mustered in as Private, Co. D, February 26, 1865, to serve three years. Mustered out with company August 1, 1865 at Winchester, Virginia.

DUMAS, GEORGE— Age 29 years. Enlisted April 12, 1865 at Brooklyn. Mustered in as Private, "unassigned," April 12, 1865, to serve three years. Mustered out with detachment, May 6, 1865 at Hart's Island, New York Harbor.

DUMONT, MAXINE— Age 26 years. Enlisted December 1, 1863 at Rochester. Mustered in as Private, Co. F, January 10, 1864, to serve three years. Deserted, February 1864 from camp near Rochester.

DUNCAN, JOHN E.— Age 24 years. Enlisted December 4, 1863 at Arcadia. Mustered in as Corporal, Co. H, February 2, 1864, to serve three years. Discharged, date not stated.

DUNHAM, BENIJAH— Age 35 years. Enlisted December 15, 1863 at Rome. Mustered in as Private, Co. C, January 6, 1864, to serve three years. Absent sick upon muster out of company, August 1, 1865, no further record.

DUNN, EDWARD— Age 17 years. Enlisted November 6, 1863 at Rochester. Mustered in as Private, Co. A, December 20, 1863, to serve three years. Mustered out with company, August 1, 1865 at Winchester, Virginia.

DUNN, JOHN— Age 19 years. Enlisted April 11, 1865 at Kingston. Mustered in as Private, "unassigned," April 11, 1865, to serve three years. Mustered out with detachment, May 6, 1865 at Hart's Island, New York Harbor.

DUNNING, HERMAN R.— Age 27 years. Enrolled, date not stated, at Rochester; mustered in as 2nd Lieutenant, Co. H, February 2, 1864, to serve three years; discharged, August 9, 1864. Commissioned 2nd Lieutenant, March 30, 1864, with rank from January 19, 1864, original.

DUPER, PETER— Age 19 years. Enlisted March 20, 1865 at Malta. Mustered in as Private, Co. I, March 20, 1865, to serve one year. Mustered out with company, August 1, 1865, at Winchester, Virginia. Also borne as Dupee.

DU PLANTY, ALBERT— Age 22 years. Enlisted November 3, 1863 at Brockport. Mustered in as Sergeant, Co. C, November 5, 1863, to serve three years. Appointed Quartermaster Sergeant, date not stated. Mustered out with company, August 1, 1865, at Winchester, Virginia. Prior service in Co. D, Thirteenth New York Infantry. Also borne as DePluntz.

DURAN, HIRAM— Age 42 years. Enlisted December 12, 1863 at Brockport as Private, Co. C, to serve three years. Rejected.

DURING, MAX— See Duchring, Max.

DURKEE, SHUBUEL— Age 29 years. Enlisted November 30, 1863 at Lyons. Mustered in as Private, Co. H, February 2, 1864, to serve three years. Mustered out with company, August 1, 1865, at Winchester, Virginia. Prior service Co. I, Eighteenth New York Volunteers.

DURNING, OWEN— Age 26 years. Enlisted March 23, 1865 at New York. Mustered in as Private, Co. I, March 23, 1865, to serve three years. Mustered out with company, August 1, 1865, at Winchester, Virginia.

DURYEA, JAMES— Age 21 years. Enlisted February 23, 1865 at New York. Mustered in as Private, Co. C, February 23, 1865, to serve one year. Mustered out with company, August 1, 1865, at Winchester, Virginia.

DUVAL, ROBERT— Age 23 years. Enlisted December 19, 1863 at Rochester. Mustered in as Commissary Sergeant, Co. F, January 10, 1864, to serve three years. Deserted February, 1864 from camp near Rochester.

DWYER, JAMES— Age 32 years. Enlisted April 13, 1865 at New York. Mustered in as Private, "unassigned," April 13, 1865, to serve one years. Mustered out with detachment, May 6, 1865 at Hart's Island, New York Harbor.

DWYER, THOMAS— Age 19 years. Enlisted April 14, 1865, at Kingston. Mustered in as Private, Co. C, April 14, 1865, to serve three years. Mustered out with detachment, May 6, 1865, at Hart's Island, New York Harbor.

EARL, ROBERT— Age 24 years. Enlisted November 27, 1863 at Syracuse. Mustered in as Sergeant, Co. B, January 5, 1864, to serve three years. Mustered out with company, August 1, 1865, at Winchester, Virginia.

EASTMAN, NEIL, JR.— Age 27 years. Enlisted December 16, 1863 at Smithfield. Mustered in as Private, Co. E, January 10, 1864, to serve three years. Mustered out with company, August 1, 1865, at Winchester, Virginia.

EATER, ANTHONY— Age 40 years. Enlisted November 26, 1863 at Rochester as Private, Co. F, to serve three years. Rejected.

EATON, JOHN S.— Age 25 years. Enlisted April 13, 1865 at Albany. Mustered in as Private, "unassigned," April 13, 1865, to serve two years. Mustered out with detachment, May 6, 1865 at Hart's Island New York Harbor.

EAVES, FREDERICK— Age 18 years. Enlisted December 17, 1863 at Penn Yan. Mustered in as Private, Co. A, December 20, 1863, to serve three years. Killed in action, June 13, 1864 at White Oak Swamp, Virginia.

EBERLY, JOHN— Age 18 years. Enlisted January 1, 1864 at Rochester. Mustered in as Private, Co. D, January 10, 1864, to serve three years. No further record.

EBZ, CHARLES— Age 35 years. Enlisted February 3, 1864 at Cortlandville as Private. Co. K, to serve three years. Rejected.

EDGECOMB, ROBERT— Age 22 years. Enlisted January 10, 1864 at Rochester. Mustered in as Private, Co. I, February 2, 1864, to serve three years. Transferred to Co. E, March, 1864. Appointed Sergeant, no date stated. Mustered out with company, August 1, 1865, at Winchester, Virginia.

EDGERTON, HARRIS— Age 24 years. Enlisted November 16, 1863 at Urbana. Mustered in as Private, Co. G, February 2, 1864, to serve three years. Discharged for disability, June 8, 1865, at hospital, Baltimore, Maryland.

EDHA, JOHN— see Elide, John.

EDMOND, TRUMAN— see Edward, Truman.

EDMONSON, THOMAS— Age 44 years. Enlisted December 4, 1863 at Rochester. Mustered in as Private, Co. C, January 5, 1864, to serve three years. Deserted, February 4, 1864, at Rochester, New York. Also borne as Edmundson.

EDSON, HENRY— Age 18 years. Enlisted January 24, 1864 at Walton. Mustered in as Private, Co. L, February 12, 1864, to serve three years. Mustered out, August 17, 1865 at Elmira, New York.

EDWARDS, FRANKLIN— Age 25 years. Enrolled January 5, 1864 at Rochester. Mustered in as Captain, Co. C, January 5, 1864, to serve three years. Discharged for disability, March 29, 1865. Commissioned Captain, March 30, 1864, with rank from January 5, 1864, original.

EDWARDS, TRUMAN— Age 19 years. Enlisted February 14, 1865 at Albany. Mustered in as Private, Co. H, February 14, 1865, to serve one year. Died, June 16, 1865 at Winchester, Virginia.

EDWARDS, WILLIAM— Age 22 years. Enlisted January 27, 1864 at Middlefield. Mustered in as Sergeant, Co. L, February 12, 1864, to serve three years. Deserted, March 1, 1864 at Rochester, New York.

EHDE, JOHN— Age 27 years. Enlisted January 15, 1864 at Rochester. Mustered in as Private, Co. K, February 6, 1864, to serve three years. Transferred to Co. F, March 25, 1864. Mustered out with company, August 1, 1865, at Winchester, Virginia. Also borne as Edha.

EHINGER, CHARLES— Age 19 years. Enlisted February 25, 1865 at Tompkins. Mustered in as Private, Co. D, February 27, 1865, to serve three years. Mustered out with company, August 1, 1865, at Winchester, Virginia.

EHRENSBERGER, FREDERICK R.— Age 27 years. Enlisted March 18 1865 at New York. Mustered in as Private, Co. C, March 18, 1865, to serve three years. Mustered out with company, August 1, 1865, at Winchester, Virginia. Also borne as Errinberger.

EICHORN, HENRY H.— Age 19 years. Enlisted November 18, 1863 at Rochester. Mustered in as Sergeant, Co. D, January 10, 1864, to serve three years. Mustered out with company, August 1, 1865, at Winchester, Virginia. as First Sergeant.

EICKELBUERY, HENRY C.— Age 20 years. Enlisted December 12, 1863 at Lyons. Mustered in as Private, Co. H, February 2, 1864, to serve three years. Mustered out with company, August 1, 1865, at Winchester, Virginia., as Bugler. Also borne as Eickelburg.

ELDRIGE, MILO D.— Age 37 years. Enlisted January 4, 1864 at Green. Mustered in as Private, Co. L, February 12, 1864, to serve three years. Died, October 10, 1864 at Philadelphia, Pa. of wounds received in action.

ELIVEN, MILO— Age 19 years. Enlisted April 10, 1865 at New York City. Mustered in as Private, "unassigned," April 12, 1865, to serve one year. Mustered out with detachment, May 6, 1865 at Hart's Island, New York Harbor.

ELKINS, GEORGE— Age 27 years. Enlisted April 12, 1865 at Albany. Mustered in as Private, "unassigned," April 12, 1865, to serve one year. Mustered out with detachment, May 6, 1865 at Hart's Island, New York Harbor.

ELLERBECK, ROBERT E.— Age 28 years. Enrolled December 26, 1863 at Rochester. Mustered in as Captain, Co. M, February 23, 1864, to serve three years. Transferred to Co. K, April 9, 1865; discharged May 15, 1865. Commissioned Captain, March 30, 1864, with rank from January 29, 1864, original.

ELLIOTT, ROBERT— Age 25 years. Enlisted October 6, 1864 at Jamaica. Mustered in as Private, Co. M, October 6, 1864, to serve one year. Mustered out with company, August 1, 1865, at Winchester, Virginia. as Farrier.

ELLIS, ADDISON— Age 19 years. Enlisted January 20, 1864 at Pompey. Mustered in as Private, Co. H, February 2, 1864, to serve three years. Mustered out with company, August 1, 1865, at Winchester, Virginia.

ELLIS, DANIEL M.— Age 37 years. Enlisted January 5, 1864 at Bath. Mustered in as Private, Co. G, February 2, 1864, to serve three years. Died, date not stated.

ELLIS, JACOB E.— Age 20 years. Enlisted April 6, 1865 at Albany. Mustered in as Private, "unassigned," April 6, 1865, to serve one years. Mustered out with detachment, May 6, 1865 at Hart's Island, New York Harbor.

ELLIS, JAMES— Age 19 years. Enlisted November 30, 1863 at Utica. Mustered in as Private, Co. B, January 5, 1864, to serve three years. Discharged from Satterlee U.S. General Hospital, West Philadelphia, May 27, 1865.

ELLIS, JOHN L.— Age 33 years. Enlisted December 13, 1863 at Lyons as Private, Co. H, to serve three years. Rejected, February 2, 1864.

EMERSON, ANSEL— Age 35 years. Enlisted December 17, 1863 at Rochester. Mustered in as Corporal, Co. I, February 2, 1864, to serve three years. Deserted, May 17, 1865. Returned, no date. Tried by court-marshall, sentenced to be reduced two ranks. Dishonorably discharged and to be confined at Fort Delaware, Del. at hard labor for three years. No further record.

EMERSON, JOHN— Age 43 years. Enlisted December 26, 1863 at Rochester as Private, Co. I, to serve three years. Rejected.

EMERY, WILLIAM— Age 22 years. Enlisted January 16, 1864 at Lafayette, as Private, Co. H, to serve three years. Rejected, February 2, 1864.

EMMETT, ORAN— officer

ENGLES, WILLIAM— Age 22 years. Enlisted April 4, 1865 at New York. Mustered in as Private, Co. D, April 4, 1865 to serve one year. Mustered out with company August 1, 1865 at Winchester, Virginia.

ENGLISH, JOHN D.— Age 19 years. Enlisted April 14, 1865 at Kingston. Mustered in as Private, Co. C, April 14, 1865 to serve three years. Mustered out with detachment, May 6, 1865 at Hart's Island, New York Harbor.

ENNIST, GEORGE W.— Age 21 years. Enlisted January 21, 1864 at McDonough. Mustered in as Wagoner, Co. L, February 12, 1864 to serve three years. Mustered out with company August 1, 1865 at Winchester, Virginia.

ERRINBERGER, FREDERICK R.— See Ehrensberger, Frederick r.

ERWIN, DENNIS— See Irwin, Dennis.

ESTES, JOSEPH F.— Age 44 years. Enlisted December 21, 1863 at Rochester. Mustered in as Farrier, Co. I, February 2, 1864 to serve three years. Discharged for disability, May 12, 1865. Prior service in Co. K, Third New York Artillery.

EVANS, CLEM— (Colored) Age 35 years. Enlisted January 14, 1864 at Rochester. Mustered in as Cook, Co. H, February 2, 1864 to serve three years. Deserted, no date stated.

EVANS, KING D.— Age 25 years. Enlisted January 4, 1864 at Plymouth. Mustered in as First Sergeant, Co. L, February 12, 1864 to serve three years. Mustered out with company August 1, 1865 at Winchester, Virginia. Prior service in Co. D, Forty Fourth Infantry Volunteers.

EVANS, LUKE— Age 18 years. Enlisted January 19, 1864 at Prattsburgh. Mustered in as Private, Co. G, February 2, 1864 to serve three years. Captured, June 29, 1864, released, April 29, 1865. Discharged, July 1, 1865, at New York.

EVANS, RICHARD— Age 20 years. Enlisted January 22, 1864 at Rochester. Mustered in as Private, Co. G, February 2, 1864 to serve three years. Transferred to Co. D, March 6, 1864., Deserted, no date given. Also borne as Evens.

EVERETT, ISAAC D.— Age 18 years. Enlisted February 11, 1864 at Bath. Mustered in as Private, Co. M, February 23, 1864, to serve three years. Transferred to Co. G, March 24, 1864. Died, date not stated.

EVERSON, JOHN C.— Age 20 years. Enlisted January 25, 1864 at Syracuse. Mustered in as Private, Co. I, February 2, 1864 to serve three years. Transferred to Co. E, March, 1864. Appointed Quartermaster Sergeant, no date stated. Mustered out with company, August 1, 1865 at Winchester, Virginia.

FAHL, CHARLES— Age 21 years. Enlisted October 5, 1864 at Brooklyn. Mustered in as Private, "unassigned," October 5, 1864 to serve one year. No further record.

FAIRCHILD, HENRY N.— Age 18 years. Enlisted December 11, 1863 at Urbana. Mustered in as Private, Co. G, February 2, 1864 to serve three years. Captured, June 29, 1864. Paroled, December16, 1864. Discharged, June 28, 1865 at Winchester, Virginia.

FAIRCHILD, MARTIN— Age 26 years. Enlisted January 4, 1864 at Pomfret. Mustered in as Sergeant, Co. K, February 6, 1864, to serve three years. Died of disease, February 20, 1864 at hospital, Rochester, New York.

FALCONER, ALEXANDER— Age 17 years. Enlisted December 18, 1863 at Brockport. Mustered in as Private, Co. C, January 5, 1864, to serve three years. Mustered out with company, August 1, 1865 at Winchester, Virginia.

FANT, DAVID— Age 26 years. Enlisted December 22, 1863 at Utica. Mustered in as Private, Co. B, January 5, 1864, to serve three years. Transferred to Co. F, March 24, 1864. No further record.

FARLEY, TERRENCE— Age 21 years. Enlisted December 24, 1863 at Rochester. Mustered in as Private, Co. D, January 10, 1864, to serve three years. No further record.

FARLEY, WILLIAM— Age 22 years. Enlisted April 12, 1865 at Brooklyn. Mustered in as Private, "unassigned," April 12, 1865, to serve three years. Mustered out with detachment, May 6, 1865 at Hart's Island, New York Harbor.

FARRELL, JAMES— Age 18 year. Enlisted December 16, 1863 at Rochester. Mustered in as Private, Co. A, December 20, 1863, to serve three years. Died of disease, November 11, 1864, at Annapolis, Maryland.

FARRELL, JOHN— Age 44 years. Enlisted April 5, 1865 at New York. Mustered in as Private, Co. F, April 5, 1865, to serve one year. Mustered out with company, August 1, 1865 at Winchester, Virginia.

FARRELL, PATRICK— Age 29 years. Enlisted January 18, 1864 at Rochester. Mustered in as Private, Co. K, February 6, 1864, to serve three years. Transferred to Co. H, March 25, 1864. Mustered out with company, August 1, 1865 at Winchester, Virginia.

FARRELL, PATRICK— Age 20 years. Enlisted as Private, Co. I, January 25, 1864 at Rochester, to serve three years. Rejected.

FATTER, JOHN— Age 25 years. Enlisted April 8, 1865 at Rochester. Mustered in as Private, "unassigned," April 8, 1865, to serve three years. No further record.

FAUST, WILLIAM— Age 23 years. Enlisted January 16, 1864 at Albany. Mustered in as Private, "unassigned," January 21, 1864, to serve three years. No further record.

FAUTH, WILLIAM— Age 21 years. Enlisted November 27, 1863 at Lyons. Mustered in as Blacksmith, Co. D, January 10, 1864, to serve three years. Captured, May 6, 1864, released, date not stated. Mustered out September 4, 1865 at Rochester, New York. Prior service in Sixteenth Regiment, Michigan Volunteers.

FEATHERSON, THOMAS— Age 22 years. Enlisted April 3, 1865 at Tarrytown. Mustered in as Private, Co. F, April 3, 1865, to serve one year. Appointed Corporal, June 1, 1865; Sergeant, July 1, 1865. Mustered out with company, August 1, 1865 at Winchester, Virginia.

FEENANDER, MICHAEL— Age 18 years. Enlisted April 13, 1865 at Brooklyn. Mustered in as Private, "unassigned," April, 13, 1865, to serve one year. Mustered out with detachment, May 6, 1865, at Hart's Island, New York Harbor.

FEGER, FRANK J.— Age 21 years. Enlisted February 28, 1865 at New York. Mustered in as Private, Co. H, February 21, 1865, to serve three years. Mustered out with company, August 1, 1865 at Winchester, Virginia. Also borne as Feager.

FELLOWS, MILTON— Age 19 years. Enlisted November 18, 1863 at Albion. Mustered in as Private, Co. F, January 10, 1864, to serve three years. Mustered out May 13, 1865, at Baltimore, Maryland.

FENTON, FREDERICK— Age 18 years. Enlisted December 11, 1863 at Rochester. Mustered in as Bugler, Co. D, January 10, 1864, to serve three years. Mustered out with company, August 1, 1865 at Winchester, Virginia. Prior service, Co. F, Twenty Third Regiment, New York Infantry.

FERRIS, ISAAC— Age 42 years. Enlisted as private, Co. K, January 5, 1864 at Pomfret, to serve three years. Rejected.

FIELD, NELSON— Age 19 years. Enlisted January 6, 1864 at Verona. Mustered in as Sergeant, Co. M, February 23, 1864, to serve three years. Mustered out with company, August 1, 1865 at Winchester, Virginia.

FIELD, ROMANZO L.— Age 18 years. Enlisted August 29, 1864 at Verona. Mustered in as Private, Co. M, August 29, 1864, to serve one year. Mustered out June 6, 1865 at Winchester, Virginia.

FIESTER, JOHN— Age 42 years. Drafted at Lockport. Mustered in as Private, "unassigned," February 27, 1865, to serve three years. Mustered out with detachment, May 9, 1865 at Elmira, New York.

FINCH, DAVID S.— Age 32 year. Enlisted December 19, 1863 at Syracuse. Mustered in as Private, Co. B, January 5, 1864, to serve three years. Transferred to Co. F, March 24, 1864. No further record.

FINCH, HENRY— Age 18 years. Enlisted January 15, 1864 at German. Mustered in as Private, Co. L, February 12, 1864, to serve three years. Died, August 23, 1864 while a prisoner at Andersonville, Georgia.

FINCH, JAMES H.— Age 18 years. Enlisted February 15, 1864 at Bath. Mustered in as Private, Co. M, February 23, 1864, to serve three years. Transferred to Co. G, March 24, 1864. In confinement a Fort Delaware at time company was mustered out, August 1, 1865, by sentence of G.C.M.A.of S., May 12, 1865. Mustered out with detachment, August 9, 1865 at Rochester, New York.

FINCH, JONAS— Age 19 years. Enlisted January 11, 1864 at Unadilla. Mustered in as Private, Co. L, February 12, 1864, to serve three years. Died, September 14, 1864 while a prisoner at Andersonville, Georgia.

FINCH, SAMUEL— Age 18 year. Enlisted January 11, 1864 at Unadilla. Mustered in as Private, Co. L, February 12, 1864, to serve three years. Mustered out with detachment, June 28, 1865 at Winchester, Virginia.

FINCH, WILLIAM T.— Age 21 years. Enlisted September 1, 1864 at Sidney. Mustered in as Private, Co. L, September 19, 1864, to serve one year. Mustered out with detachment, June 6, 1865, at Winchester, Virginia.

FINGLETON, JAMES— Age 20 years. Enlisted January 5, 1864 at Lyons. Mustered in as Private, Co. D, January 10, 1864, to serve three years. Captured, May 6, 1864. No further record.

FINN, MICHAEL— Age 22 years. Enlisted April 12, 1865 at Kingston. Mustered in as Private, "unassigned," April 13, 1865, to serve three years. Mustered out with detachment, May 6, 1865 at Hart's Island, New York Harbor.

FINNEMORE, JOHN— Age 23 years. Enlisted March 15, 1865 at New York. Mustered in as Private, Co. D, March 15, 1865, to serve three years. Never joined for service; no further record. Also borne as Finimore.

FISHER, ADOLPHUS— Age 23 years. Enlisted April 8, 1865 at Rochester. Mustered in as Private, Co. F, April 8, 1865, to serve one year. Appointed Corporal, July 1, 1865. Mustered out with company, August 1, 1865 at Winchester, Virginia.

FISHER, JACOB— Age 25 years. Enrolled November 10, 1863 at Rochester; mustered in as First Lieutenant, Co. D, January 30, 1864, to serve three years; mustered in as Captain, Co. K, to date, November 29, 1864; transferred to Co. M, May 1865; re-transferred to Co. K, May 31, 1865; mustered out with company, August 1, 1865 at Winchester, Virginia. Commissioned First Lieutenant March 30, 1864, with rank from January 10, 1864, original; Captain, November 11, 1864, with rank from August 25, 1864, vice French, promoted.

FITZGERALD, CHARLES— Age 21 years. Enlisted December 15, 1863 at Rochester. Mustered in as Private, Co. F, January 10, 1864, to serve three years. Deserted, February 1864 from camp near Rochester, New York.

FITZGERALD, JOHN— Age 33 years. Enlisted December 23, 1863 at Rochester. Mustered in as Private, Co. F, January 10, 1864, to serve three years. Discharged for disability, May 15, 1865.

FITZGERALD, MICHAEL— Age 28 years. Enlisted October 24, 1863 at Rochester. Mustered in as Private, Co. A, December 20, 1863, to serve three years. Discharged, June 27, 1865 while a paroled prisoner at Winchester, Virginia.

FITZPATRICK, JOHN— Age 31 years. Enlisted December 10, 1863 at Rochester. Mustered in as Private, Co. F, January 10, 1864, to serve three years. Deserted in February 1864 from camp from Rochester, New York.

FITZSIMMONS, BARTHOLOMEW— Age 43 years. Enlisted October 27, 1863 at Rochester. Mustered in as Private, Co. A, December 20, 1863, to serve three years. Deserted February 27, 1864 at Rochester, New York.

FLANDERS, ORVILLE— Age 18 years. Enlisted December 7, 1863 at Albion. Mustered in as Private, Co. F, January 10, 1864, to serve three years. Died, November 9, 1864 at Florence, S.C.

FLEMING, JAMES— Age 19 years. Enlisted February 22, 1865 at New York. Mustered in as Private, Co. M February 22, 1865, to serve three years. Mustered out with company, August 1, 1865 at Winchester, Virginia. Also borne as Flemming.

FLEMMING, PETER— Age 30 years. Enlisted January 4, 1864 at Manlius. Mustered in as Private, Co. I, February 2, 1864, to serve three years. Transferred to Co. E, March 1864. Died, date not stated while prisoner at Andersonville, Georgia.

FLETCHER, DOUGLASS— Age 20 years. Enlisted November 26, 1863 at Syracuse. Mustered in as Corporal, Co. B, January 5, 1864, to serve three years. Deserted, August 13, 1864 from Chain Bridge, Virginia.

FLINN, THOMAS— Age 18 years. Enlisted November 28, 1863 at Syracuse. Mustered in as Private, Co. B, January 5, 1864, to serve three years. Mustered out with company, August 1, 1865 at Winchester, Virginia.

FLYNN, EDWARD— Age 18 years. Enlisted November 7, 1863 at Rochester. Mustered in as Private, Co. F, January 10, 1864, to serve three years. Died, October 1864 at Charleston, S.C.

FLYNN, WILLIAM— Age 20 years. Enlisted April 5, 1864 at Cape Vincent. Mustered in as Private, "unassigned April 6, 1864, to serve three years. No further record.

FLYNN, WILLIAM— Age 21 years. Enlisted March 14, 1865 at New York. Mustered in as Private, Co. D, March 14, 1865, to serve three years. Never joined for service. No further record.

FOLEY, PATRICK— Age 22 years. Enlisted April 3, 1865 at Kingston. Mustered in as Private, "unassigned," April 13, 1865, to serve three years. Mustered out with detachment, May 6, 1865 at Hart's Island, New York Harbor.

FOOSE, GEORGE C.— Age 18 years. Enlisted November 14, 1863 at Rochester. Mustered in as Private, Co. A, December 20, 1863, to serve three years. Discharged for disability, June 12, 1865 at Washington, D.C.

FOOTE, CHARLES R.— Age 21 years. Enlisted January 9, 1864 at Guilford. Mustered in as Corporal, Co. L, February 12, 1864, to serve three years. Died of disease, March 12, 1864 at St. Mary's Hospital, Rochester, New York.

FORBES, ISAIAH— Age 24 years. Enlisted December 23, 1863 at Fenner. Mustered in as Sergeant, Co. E, January 10, 1864, to serve three years. Reduced, date not stated. Mustered out with company, August 1, 1865 at Winchester, Virginia. Prior service in Co. H, 35th New York Infantry. Also borne as Isaac Forbes.

FORCE, JACOB A.— Age 32 years. Enlisted December 4, 1863 at Arcadia. Mustered in as Quartermaster Sergeant, Co. H, February 2, 1864, to serve three years. Discharged, date not known, records of company being lost.

FORD, ISAAC S.— Age 23 years. Enlisted December 14, 1863 at Madison. Mustered in as First Sergeant, Co. E, January 10, 1864, to serve three years. Reduced to Sergeant, May 14, 1865. Mustered out with detachment, June 28, 1865 at Winchester, Virginia. Prior service Co. I, Twenty Sixth New York Infantry.

FORSYTH, JOHN— Age 18 years. Enlisted April 8, 1865 at Albany. Mustered in as Private, "unassigned," April 8, 1865, to serve three years. Mustered out with detachment, May 6, 1865 at Hart's Island, New York Harbor.

FORWARD, JOHN— Age 23 years. Enlisted December 9, 1863 at Rochester. Mustered in as Private, Co. D, January 10, 1864, to serve three years. Deserted, date and place not stated.

FOSDICK, CHARLES H.— Age 17 years. Enlisted November 16, 1863 at Rochester. Mustered in as Private, Co. G, February 2, 1864, to serve three years. Transferred to Co. D, March 22, 1864. Dropped as a deserter, October 1, 1864. Also borne as Fostick.

FOSTER, ALBERT F.— Age 18 years. Enlisted November 30, 1863 at Rochester. Mustered in as Private, Co. I, February 2, 1864, to serve three years. Discharged May 28, 1865, Cleveland, Ohio.

FOSTER, FRANKLIN L.— Age 25 years. Enlisted March 15, 1865 at New York. Mustered in as Private, Co. D, March 15, 1865, to serve three years. Never joined for service. No further record.

FOWLER, ALDICE— Age 18 years. Enlisted January 5, 1864 at Sodus. Mustered in as Private, Co. H, February 2, 1864, to serve three years. Mustered out September 16, 1865 at Elmira, New York.

FOWLER, JOHN— Age 28 years. Enlisted March 25, 1865 at Auburn. Mustered in as Private, Co. F, March 25, 1865, to serve three years. Mustered out with company, August 1, 1865 at Winchester, Virginia.

FOX, NICHOLAS— Age 21 years. Enlisted April 5, 1865 at New York. Mustered in as Private, Co. F, April 5, 1865, to serve one year. Mustered out with company, August 1, 1865 at Winchester, Virginia.

FOX, REUBEN L.— Age 22 years. Enlisted, date not stated, at Rochester. Mustered in as Private, Co. B, January 5, 1864, to serve three years; mustered in as Second Lieutenant; January 15, 1864; First Lieutenant to date, January 7, 1865; discharged for disability, March 29, 1865. Commissioned Second Lieutenant, March 30, 1864, with rank from January 5, 1864, original. First Lieutenant, December 19, 1864, with rank from November 23, 1864, vice Neuman, promoted.

FRANCIS, CHARLES E.— Age 18 years. Enlisted as Private, Co. M, January 9, 1864 at Verona, to serve three years. Rejected.

FRANK, GILBERT L.— Age 19 years. Enlisted January 4, 1864 at Verona. Mustered in as First Sergeant, Co. M, February 23, 1864, to serve three years; mustered out with company, August 1, 1865 at Winchester, Virginia. as trumpeter.

FRANK, WILLIAM— Age 23 years. Enlisted April 8, 1865 at New York; mustered in as private, Co. A, April 8, 1865, to serve one year; mustered out with company, August 1, 1865 at Winchester, Virginia.

FRANKA, GEORGE— Age 35 years. Enlisted February 17, 1865 at New York; mustered in as private, Co. M, February 17, 1865, to serve three years. Mustered out with company, August 1, 1865 at Winchester, Virginia.

FRANKLIN, ALBERT— Age 19 years. Enlisted February 28, 1865 at New York. Mustered in as Private, Co. M, February 28, 1865, to serve three years. Mustered out with company, August 1, 1865 at Winchester, Virginia.

FRANKLIN, IRA O.— Age 32 years. Enlisted January 14, 1864 at Middlefield. Mustered in as Private, Co. L, February 12, 1864, to serve three years. Died, July 28, 1864, while a prisoner at Andersonville, Georgia.

FREEMAN, ALDERMAN— (Colored), age 19 years. Enlisted February 18, 1864 at Rochester. Mustered in as cook, Co. M, February 23, 1864, to serve three years. Transferred to Co. I, date not stated. Deserted as a private, May 31, 1865 at Winchester, Virginia.

FREEMAN, MILTON— Age 18 years. Enlisted December 18, 1863 at Westmorland. Mustered in as Private, Co. E, January 10, 1864, to serve three years. Killed in action, August 21, 1864, at Smithfield, Virginia.

FREER, JAMES A.— Age 18 years. Enlisted January 11, 1864 at Unadilla. Mustered in as Private, Co. L, February 12, 1864, to serve three years. Mustered out with company, August 1, 1865 at Winchester, Virginia.

FRENCH, GEORGE R.— Officer.

FRENCH, JAMES— Age 20 years. Enlisted January 4, 1864 at Urbana. Mustered in as Private, Co. G, February 2, 1864, to serve three years. Died, date and place not stated. Prior service in Co. B, Twenty Sixth New York Infantry.

FRIDLY, DAVID— Age 40 year. Enlisted as Private, Co. I, December 21, 1863 at Auburn, to serve three years. Rejected.

FRISCH, LAWRENCE— Age 44 years. Enlisted as Private, Co. D, January 8, 1864 at Rochester, to serve three years. Rejected.

FROST, AMASA— Age 21 years. Enlisted January 25, 1864 at Verona. Mustered in as Private, Co. M, February 23, 1864, to serve three years. Mustered out with company, August 1, 1865 at Winchester, Virginia.

FUFFON, ISIAH— Age 43 years. Enlisted January 18, 1864 at Syracuse. Mustered in as Private, Co. K, February 6, 1864, to serve three years. Transferred to Co. H, March 25, 1864. Mustered out June 19, 1865 at Buffalo, New York. Also borne as Triffon and Tuffon.

FULLER, HEBER— Age 24 years. Enlisted December 2, 1863 at Brockport. Mustered in as Commissary Sergeant, Co. C, January 5, 1864, to serve three years. Died of disease, December 12, 1864, at Baltimore, Maryland. Prior service in Thirteenth New York Infantry.

FULTER, JOHN— Age 25 years. Enlisted April 8, 1865 at Rochester. Mustered in as Private, "unassigned," April 8, 1865, to serve three years. No further record.

FURZES, WILLIAM— Age 22 years. Enlisted January 23, 1864 at Rochester. Mustered in as Farrier, Co. H, February 2, 1864, to serve three years. Deserted, date and place not known, records of company being lost.

GAHAN, PATRICK— Age 21 years. Enlisted December 15, 1863 at Syracuse. Mustered in as Private, Co. B, January 5, 1864, to serve three years. Transferred to Co. F, March 24, 1864. No further record.

GALARMAN, EDWARD— Age 28 years. Enlisted December 12, 1863 at Perrinton. Mustered in as Farrier, Co. A, December 20. 1863, to serve three years. Deserted, April 26, 1865 at United States General Hospital, Washington, D.C.

GALIVON, SAMUEL— (Colored), age 26, years. Enlisted January 30, 1864 at Rochester. Mustered in as Cook, Co. L, February 12, 1864, to serve three years. No further record.

GALLAGHER, FRANCIS— Age 18 years. Enlisted December 7, 1863 at Rochester. Mustered in as Private, Co. A, December 20, 1863 to serve three years. Mustered out with company, August 1, 1865 at Winchester, Virginia.

GALLAGHER, JEREMIAH— Age 19 years. Enlisted February 21, 1865 at New York City. Mustered in as Private, "unassigned," February 21, 1865, to serve one year. No further record.

GALLAGHER, JOHN— Age 23 years. Enlisted December 16, 1863 at Rochester. Mustered in as Private, Co. A, December 20, 1863, to serve three years. Deserted, December 20, 1864 at Snickersville, Virginia.

GALLIWA, SAMUEL— (Colored), age 26 years. Enlisted January 14, 1864 at Rochester. Mustered in as Under-Cook, Co. G, February 1864, to serve three years. Captured, June 29, 1864. Released, April 5, 1865; discharged June 28, 1865 at Winchester, Virginia. Also borne as Gallawa.

GAMS, JOHN— Age 23 years. Enlisted February 15, 1864 at Bath. Mustered in as Private, Co. M, February 23, 1864, to serve three years. Transferred to Co. G, March 24, 1864. In confinement at date of muster out of company at Fort Delaware, by sentence of G.C.M.A.of S., May 12, 1865. Discharged August 9, 1865 at Rochester.

GARBER, CHRISTIAN— Age 23 years. Enlisted February 20, 1865 at New York. Mustered in as Private, Co. M, February 20, 1865, to serve three years. On detached service at brigade hospital on muster out of company, August 1, 1865. No further record.

GARDNER, JOHN— Age 20 years. Enlisted April 11, 1865 at Rochester. Mustered in as Private, "unassigned," April 11, 1865, to serve three years. No further record.

GARDNER, JOSEPH— Age 26 years. Enlisted February 27, 1865 at New York. Mustered in as Private, Co. C, February 27, 1865, to serve three years. Deserted from United States Battery, June 12, 1865 while on detached service.

GARDINER, WILLIAM V.— Age 21 years. Enlisted December 19, 1863 at Utica. Mustered in as Private, Co. B, January 5, 1864, to serve three years. Confined in insane asylum at Washington, D.C. on muster out of company August 1, 1865. No further record.

GARRAD, JOSEPH— Age 44 years. Enlisted in Co. F, November 19, 1863 at Albion, to serve three years. Rejected.

GARRETTY, WILLIAM— Age 20 years. Enlisted February 20, 1865 at New York City. Mustered in as Private, Co. H, February 20, 1865, to serve three years. Mustered out with company, August 1, 1865 at Winchester, Virginia.

GARTSEE, HENRY— Age 29 years. Enlisted January 4, 1864 at Otsego. Mustered in as Commissary Sergeant, Co. L, February 12, 1864, to serve three years. Died, August 29, 1864 in confinement at Andersonville, Georgia., as a Private.

GASPER, PETER D.— Age 27 years. Enlisted as Private, Co. B, November 23, 1863, at Syracuse, to serve three years. Rejected.

GATES, ATLAS P.— Age 21 years. Enlisted December 24, 1863 at Syracuse. Mustered in as Private, Co. B, January 5, 1864, to serve three years. Mustered out with company, August 1, 1865 at Winchester, Virginia.

GATES, CHARLES— Age 35 years. Enlisted October 16, 1863 at Rochester. Mustered in as Private, Co. A, December 20, 1863, to serve three years. Deserted, January 7, 1864 at Rochester, New York.

GATES, HENRY P.— Age 23 years. Enlisted October 19, 1863 at Rochester. Mustered in as Private, Co. A, December 20, 1863 to serve three years. Mustered out with company, August 1, 1865 at Winchester, Virginia.

GATES, SQUIRE M.— See Yates, Squire M.

GAULT, FRANCIS N.— Age 18 years. Enlisted December 1, 1863 at Syracuse. Mustered in as Private, Co. B, January 5, 1864 to serve three years. Sick in hospital on muster out of company, August 1, 1865. No further record.

GAVITT, CHARLES E.— Age 18 years. Enlisted December 24, 1864 at Rochester. Mustered in as Private, Co. I, February 2, 1864 to serve three years. Died, July 17, 1864 at Poplar Lawn Hospital, Petersburg, Virginia.

GEORGE, HENRY S.— Age 33 years. Enlisted December 15, 1863 at Rochester. Mustered in as Private, Co. I, February 2, 1864 to serve three years. Deserted November 1864 at Alexandria, Virginia.

GERALD, JAMES M.— Age 19 years. Enlisted December 18, 1863 at Rochester. Mustered in as Private, Co. D, January 10, 1864 to serve three years. Deserted January 10, 1864. Also borne as Gerrold.

GERBER, CHRISTIAN— Age 23 years. Enlisted February 20, 1865 at New York City. Mustered in as Private, "unassigned," February 20, 1865 to serve three years. No further record.

GERE, BYRON M.— Age 21 years. Enlisted December 22, 1863 at Rochester. Mustered in as Corporal, Co. I, February 2, 1864 to serve three years. Appointed Sergeant, date not given. Mustered out with company, August 1, 1865 at Winchester, Virginia.

GETTY, JOSEPH— Age 18 years. Enlisted March 29, 1865 at Rochester. Mustered in as Private, Co. F, March 29, 1865 to serve three years. Transferred to Co. G, May 27, 1865. No further record.

GIBBS, MYRON H.— Age 26 years. Enlisted December 31, 1863 at Cazenovia. Mustered in as Private, Co. E, January 10, 1864 to serve three years. Died at Andersonville, Georgia., date not known.

GIBSON, HARVEY— Age 20 years. Enlisted, February 17, 1865 at New York. Mustered in as Private, Co. M, February 17, 1865 to serve three years. Sick in hospital on muster out of company, August 1, 1865. No further record.

GIDDING, ALBERT— Age 23 years. Enlisted as Private, "unassigned," December 23, 1865 at New York to serve three years. No further record.

GILBERT, CHARLES— Age 21 years. Enlisted December 21, 1863 at Syracuse. Mustered in as Private, Co. B, January 5, 1864 to serve three years. Captured on Wilson's raid, June 28, 1864. Died, September 20, 1864 in Andersonville, Georgia.

GILBERT, HENRY— Age 24 years. Enlisted March 22, 1865 at Rochester. Mustered in as private, Co F, March 22, 1865 to serve three years. Mustered out with company, August 1, 1865 at Winchester, Virginia.

GILBERT, NATHAN S.— Age 18 years. Enlisted January 18, 1864 at Milford. Mustered in as Private, Co. L, February 12, 1864 to serve three years. Appointed Corporal, July 1, 1865. Mustered out with company, August 1, 1865 at Winchester, Virginia.

GILLETT, JOHN N.— Age 21 years. Enlisted December 23, 1863 at Rochester. Mustered in as Private, Co. D, January 10, 1864 to serve three years. Mustered out July 18, 1865 at Washington, D.C.

GILLETT, NATHANIEL— Age 20 years. Enlisted December 16, 1863 at Brockport. Mustered in as Private, Co. C, January 5, 1864 to serve three years. Mustered out with company, August 1, 1865 at Winchester, Virginia. Also borne as Jillett, Nathaniel.

GILLING, JOHN— Age 34 years. Enlisted as Private, Co. M, January 7, 1864 at Rochester, to serve three years. Deserted prior to muster in of company, February 23, 1864.

GLAVEY, JAMES— Age 18 years. Enlisted January 4, 1864 at Rochester. Mustered in as Private, Co. D, January 10, 1864, to serve three years. Appointed Sergeant, date not stated. Mustered out with company, August 1, 1865 at Winchester, Virginia. Prior service in Co. G, Thirteenth Regiment, New York Volunteers.

GLEASON, EDWIN M.— Age 19 years. Enlisted January 5, 1864 at Oneida. Mustered in as Sergeant, Co. M, February 23, 1864, to serve three years. Reduced to ranks, date not stated. Mustered out with company, August 1, 1865 at Winchester, Virginia.

GLEASON, HARRISON— Age 19 years. Enlisted January 14, 1864 at Oneida. Mustered in as Sergeant, Co. M, February 23, 1864, to serve three years. Captured, June 25, 1864 and never heard from. No further record.

GLENNAN, PATRICK R.— Officer.

GOFF, WILIAM H.— Age 24 years. Enlisted December 7, 1863 at Urbana. Mustered in as Private, Co. G, February 2, 1864, to serve three years. Appointed Corporal, November 1, 1864. Appointed Sergeant, June 1, 1865. Mustered out with company, August 1, 1865 at Winchester, Virginia. Prior service in Co. I, Thirty Fourth New York Infantry.

GOIT, HENRY— Age 19 years. Enlisted as Private, Co. K, December 28, 1864 at Dunkirk, to serve three years. Rejected.

GOLDING, WILLIAM— Age 18 years. Enlisted March 13, 1865 at New York. Mustered in as Private, Co. K, March 13, 1865, to serve one year. Absent sick in hospital on muster out of company, August 1, 1865. No further record.

GOLLIGER, ANANIAS— Age 30 years. Enlisted, Private, Co. I, January 20, 1864 at Rochester, to serve three years. Rejected.

GOODE, THOMAS— Age 28 years. Enlisted as Private, Co. L, January 21, 1864 at McDonough, to serve three years. Deserted, February 9, 1864, prior to muster in of company.

GOODENOUGH, CALVIN— Age 19 years. Enlisted November 23, 1863 at Albion. Mustered in as Private, Co. F, January 10, 1864, to serve three years. Deserted, February 1864 from camp near Rochester. Prior service in Co. K, Twenty Fourth New York Infantry.

GOODRICH, HIRAM W.— Age 27 years. Enlisted December 10, 1863 at Syracuse. Mustered in as Corporal, Co. B, January 5, 1864, to serve three years. Died of wounds received in action, June 14, 1864, at Harrison's Landing, Virginia. Prior service in Co. I, Sixty First New York Volunteers.

GOODSELL, CHARLES H.— Age 24 years. Enlisted January 5, 1864 at Norwich. Mustered in as Sergeant, Co. L, February 12, 1864, to serve three years. Mustered out July 12, 1865 at Baltimore, Maryland.

GOODSELL, FRANKLIN J.— Age 21 years. Enlisted January 5, 1864 at Norwich. Mustered in as Private, Co. L, February 12, 1864, to serve three years. Died of disease, March 30, 1864 at Giesboro Point, D.C.

GOODWIN, CHARLES— Age 20 years. Enlisted December 4, 1863 at Penfield. Mustered in as Private, Co. A, December 20, 1863, to serve three years. Deserted, December 28, 1863 at Rochester, New York.

GOODWIN, PHILLIP— Age 27 years. Enlisted February 17, 1865 at New York City. Mustered in as Private, Co. H, February 17, 1865, to serve one year. Mustered out with company, August 1, 1865 at Winchester, Virginia.

GORDON, CHARLES— Age 23 years. Enlisted April 11, 1865 at Rochester. Mustered in as Private, Co. D, April 11, 1865, to serve three years. Mustered out with company, August 1, 1865 at Winchester, Virginia.

GORDON, CHARLES— Age 18 years. Enlisted as Private, Co. D, November 18, 1863 at Rochester, to serve three years. Rejected.

GORDON, JOHN— Age 21 years. Enlisted April 11, 1865 at Rochester. Mustered in as Private, Co. D, April 11, 1865, to serve three years. Mustered out with company, August 1, 1865 at Winchester, Virginia.

GORDON, RICHARD— Age 27 years. Enlisted March 2, 1864 at Rochester. Mustered in as Private, Co. F, March 8, 1864, to serve three years. Mustered out with company, August 1, 1865 at Winchester, Virginia. as Wagoner.

GORMAN, MARTIN— Age 19 years. Enlisted February 24, 1865 at New York City. Mustered in as Private, Co. H, February 24, 1865, to serve one year. Mustered out with company, August 1, 1865 at Winchester, Virginia.

GORZETTE, PETER— Age 21 years. Enlisted January 4, 1864 at Manlius. Mustered in as Farrier, Co. E, January 10, 1864, to serve three years. Deserted, January 13, 1864 at Rochester. Also borne as Goyt.

GOSNELL, JAMES— Age 21 years. Enlisted November 21, 1863 at Rochester. Mustered in as Private, Co. A, December 20, 1863, to serve three years. Appointed Corporal, June 30, 1864. Reduced, December 1, 1864. Mustered out with company, August 1, 1865 at Winchester, Virginia.

GOTT, ALEXANDER— Age 19 years. Enlisted January 18, 1864 at Rochester. Mustered in as Private, Co. K, February 6, 1864, to serve three years. Transferred to Co. F, March 25, 1864. Appointed Corporal, May 1, 1865. Appointed Sergeant, July 1, 1865. Mustered out with company, August 1, 1865 at Winchester, Virginia.

GOTT, DANIEL E.— Age 18 years. Enlisted February 16, 1864 at Yorkshire. Mustered in as Private, "unassigned," February 16, 1864, to serve three years. Rejected.

GOYT, PETER— See Gorzette, Peter

GRAHAN, CHARLES J.— Age 20 years. Enlisted Private, Co. M, February 22, 1864 at Rochester, to serve three years. Deserted prior to muster in of company, February 23, 1864.

GRAHAM, DAVID— Age 23 years. Enlisted January 22, 1864 at Lenox. Mustered in as Private, Co. M, January 22, 1864, to serve three years. No further record.

GRAHAM, JOHN— Age 22 years. Enlisted April 12, 1865 at Brooklyn. Mustered in as Private, "unassigned," April 12, 1865, to serve three years. Mustered out with detachment, May 6, 1865 at Hart's Island, New York Harbor.

GRAHAM, JOHN— Age 19 years. Enlisted February 14, 1865 at New York. Mustered in as Private, Co. C, February 14, 1865, to serve three years. Mustered out with company, August 1, 1865 at Winchester, Virginia.

GRAVEN GARRITT— Age 19 years. Enlisted December 14, 1863 at Rochester. Mustered in as Corporal, Co. A, December 20, 1863, to serve three years. Mustered out with company, August 1, 1865 at Winchester, Virginia.

GRAY, LEWIS— Age 23 years. Enlisted November 2, 1863 at Perrinton. Mustered in as Private, Co. A, December 20, 1863, to serve three years. Deserted, December 15, 1863 at Rochester.

GREEK, WILLIAM— Age 25 years. Enlisted December 24, 1863 at Bath. Mustered in as Corporal, Co. G, February 2, 1864, to serve three years. Died as Private, date not stated. Prior service in Co. A, Twenty Third New York Infantry.

GREEN, DANIEL— Age 36 years. Enlisted September 3, 1864 at Burlington. Mustered in as Private, Co. F, September 14, 1864, to serve one year. Mustered out June 5, 1865 at Winchester, Virginia.

GREEN, GEORGE M.— Age 18 years. Enlisted December 14, 1863 at Bath. Mustered in as Private, Co. G, February 2, 1864, to serve three years. Died, date not stated.

GREEN, GILBERT— Age 23 years. Enlisted November 16, 1863 at Urbana. Mustered in as Private, Co. G, February 2, 1864, to serve three years. Mustered out with company, August 1, 1865 at Winchester, Virginia.

GREEN, JOHN D.— Age 23 years. Enlisted February 13, 1864 at Bath. Mustered in as Private, Co. M, February 23, 1864, to serve three years. Transferred to Co. G, March 24, 1864. No further record.

GREEN SEELY D.— Age 25 years. Enlisted February 15, 1864 at Bath. Mustered in as Private, Co. M, February 23, 1864, to serve three years. Transferred to Co. G, March 24, 1864. In confinement on date of muster out of company at Fort Delaware, sentence G.C.M. Discharged August 9, 1865 at Rochester.

GREENFIELD, JOHN— Age 30 years. Enlisted January 11, 1864 at Smyrna. Mustered in as Private, Co. F, February 12, 1864, to serve three years. Mustered out with company, August 1, 1865 at Winchester, Virginia.

GREENWOOD, JOSHWAY— Age 21 years. Enlisted as Private, Co. H, December 20, 1863 at Peterboro, to serve three years. Deserted 1864, previous to muster in of company, February 2, 1864.

GREGORY, JOHN W.— Age 20 years. Enlisted January 11, 1864 at Colchester. Mustered in as Farrier, Co. L, February 12, 1864, to serve three years. Mustered out with company, August 1, 1865 at Winchester, Virginia.

GREY, JOHN— Age 21 years. Enlisted March 24, 1865 at Dunkirk. Mustered in as Private, Co. C, March 24, 1865, to serve three years. Mustered out with company, August 1, 1865 at Winchester, Virginia.

GRIDLEY, GEORGE E.— Age 19 years. Enlisted January 4, 1864 at Riga. Mustered in as Private, Co. C, January 5, 1864, to serve three years. Mustered out May 18, 1865 at Baltimore, Maryland. Also borne as George R.

GRIFFIN, MICHAEL— Age 23 years. Enlisted March 17, 1865 at Albany. Mustered in as Private, Co. I, March 17, 1865, to serve three years. Appointed Corporal, April 30. 1865. Mustered out with company, August 1, 1865 at Winchester, Virginia.

GRIFFITH, RICHARD— Age 22 years. Enlisted January 4, 1864 at OtisCo. Mustered in as Private, Co. E, January 10, 1864, to serve three years. Deserted, January 13, 1864 at Rochester.

GRIMM, GEORGE— Age 18 years. Enlisted March 2, 1865 at Rochester. Mustered in as Private, Co. A, March 2, 1865, to serve three years. Mustered out with company, August 1, 1865 at Winchester, Virginia.

GRISWOLD, JOHN E.— Age 24 years. Enlisted at Avoca, December 30, 1863, as Private, Co. G, to serve three years. Rejected.

GRISWOLD, SAMUEL Y.— Age 18 years. Enlisted February 11, 1864 at Bath. Mustered in as Private, Co. M, February 23, 1864, to serve three years. Transferred to Co. G, March 24, 1864. Died, date not stated.

GROVER, ABNER B.— Age 43 years. Enlisted as Private, Co. I, December 24, 1863 at Auburn, to serve three years. Rejected.

GUEST, JOSEPH— Age 49 years. Enlisted as Private, Co. H, December 28, 1863 at Lyons, to serve three years. Rejected.

GUILD, ELY T.— Age 42 years. Enlisted March 23, 1865 at Lockport. Mustered in as Private, Co. F, March 23, 1865 to serve one year. Transferred to Co. G, May 27, 1865. Mustered out with company, August 1, 1865 at Winchester, Virginia.

GULFAYLA, PATRICK— Age 37 years. Enlisted December 17, 1863 at Dunkirk, as Private, Co. K, to serve three years. Rejected.

GULICH, CHARLES— Age — years. Enlisted April 7, 1865 at New York City. Mustered in as Private, Co. I, April 7, 1865 to serve one year. Died June 16, 1865 at Harper's Ferry, Virginia.

GUNSULAS, MARTIN— Age 44 years. Enlisted November 20, 1863 at Syracuse. Mustered in as Blacksmith, Co. B, January 5, 1864 to serve three years. Mustered out with company, August 1, 1865 at Winchester, Virginia. Prior service in Co. H, One Hundred and Twenty Second New York Infantry.

GURNEE, SAMUEL— Age 22 years. Enlisted December 29, 1863 at Sodus. Mustered in as Private, Co. F, January 10, 1864 to serve three years. Discharged, June 8, 1865 at U.S. Hospital, at York, Pa. Also carried on Co. H rolls.

GUSTIN, FRANK— Age 18 years. Enlisted February 11, 1864 at Lebanon. Mustered in as Private, Co. M, February 23, 1864 to serve three years. Transferred at Co. E, March 25, 1864. Died at Andersonville, Georgia., date not stated.

GYURKONWITS, CARL VON— Age — years. Enlisted February 22, 1865 at New York. Mustered in as Private, Co. C, February 22, 1865 to serve one year. Mustered out with company, August 1, 1865 at Winchester, Virginia.

HACKER, JOHN— Age 18 years. Enlisted December 15, 1863 at Dunkirk. Mustered in as Private, Co. F, January 10, 1864 to serve three years. Transferred to Co. K, March, 1864. Mustered out with company, August 1, 1865 at Winchester, Virginia.

HADLEY, JOHN— Age 23 years. Enlisted April 8, 1865 at New York. Mustered in as Private, Co. C, April 8, 1865 to serve one year. Mustered out with company, August 1, 1865 at Winchester, Virginia.

HAGER, HENRY— See Hodges, Henry.

HALE, SIMEON— Age 38 years. Enlisted March 10, 1865 at Lockport. Mustered in as Private, "unassigned," March 10, 1865 to serve three years. Mustered out September 4, 1865 at Rochester, New York.

HALEY, DENNIS— Age 21 years. Enlisted April 14, 1865 at Kingston. Mustered in as Private, "unassigned," April 14, 1865 to serve three years. Mustered out May 6, 1865 at Hart's Island, New York Harbor.

HALL, HARVEY E.— Age 20 years. Enlisted August 31, 1864 at Verona. Mustered in as Private, Co. M, August 31, 1864 to serve one year. Mustered out June 6, 1865 at Winchester, Virginia.

HALL, ISAAC— Age 18 years. Enlisted December 23, 1863 at Syracuse, as Private, Co. B, to serve three years. Rejected.

HALL, SETH M.— Age 30 years. Enlisted September 16, 1864 at Avon. Mustered in as Private, Co. M, September 17, 1864 to serve one year. Died in prison, February 20, 1865 at Salisbury, N.C.

HALL, SIDNEY— Age 18 years. Enlisted January 18, 1864 at Rochester. Mustered in as Private, Co. I, February 2, 1864 to serve three years. Transferred to Co. M, March, 1864. Appointed Quartermaster Sergeant, July 1, 1865. Mustered out with company, August 1, 1865 at Winchester, Virginia.

HALLIDAY, MERVILLE W.— Age 18 years. Enlisted November 15, 1863 at Linden. Mustered in as Private, Co. D, January 10, 1864 to serve three years. Transferred to Co. K, May 1, 1864. Captured, November 7, 1864. Prisoner of war at time company was mustered out, August 1, 1865 at Winchester, Virginia.

HALLOCK, IRA J.— Age 18 years. Enlisted December 24, 1863 at Rochester. Mustered in as Private, Co. I, February 2, 1864 to serve three years. Mustered out June 10, 1865 at McClennan United States General Hospital, Philadelphia, Pa.

HALPIN, WILLIAM— Age 27 years. Enlisted February 18, 1864 at Rochester. Mustered in as Private, Co. M, February 23, 1864 to serve three years. No further record. Prior service in Co. A, Seventy Fifth Volunteers.

HAM, JOSEPH— Age 17 years. Enlisted December 14, 1863 at Benton. Mustered in as Private, Co. A, December 20, 1863 to serve three years. Deserted March 5, 1864 at Rochester

HAMILTON, BENJAMIN— Age 18 years. Enlisted December 21, 1863 at Pomfret, as Private, Co. K, to serve three years. Rejected.

HAMILTON, WILLIBY— Age 33 years. Enlisted January 4, 1864 at Pomfret, as Private, Co. K, to serve three years. Rejected.

HAMMOND, BERNARD D.— See Hanlon, Bernard D.

HAMMOND, HENRY C.— Age 21 years. Enlisted February 23, 1864 at Brockport. Mustered in as Private, Co. C, March 5, 1864 to serve three years. Appointed Sergeant, March 18, 1864, Quartermaster Sergeant, June 20, 1864, First Sergeant, June 16, 1865. Appointed Sergeant Major, date not stated. Captured, date or place not stated. Mustered out June 24, 1865 at Winchester, Virginia.

HANAVAN, JAMES— Age 22 years. Enlisted December 16, 1863 at Rochester. Mustered in as Private, Co. F, January 10, 1864 to serve three years. Deserted in February, 1864, from camp near Rochester.

HAND, GEORGE— Age 19 years. Enlisted March 14, 1865 at New York. Mustered in as Private, Co. K, March 14, 1865 to serve three years. Mustered out with company, August 1, 1865 at Winchester, Virginia.

HAND, THORNE— Age 36 years. Enlisted December 19, 1863 at Syracuse. Mustered in as Private, Co. B, January 5, 1864 to serve three years. Discharged May 24, 1865 at Whitehall United States Hospital, Philadelphia, Pa.

HANLON, BERNARD D.— Age 20 years. Enlisted April 10, 1865 at Albany. Mustered in as Private, "unassigned," April 10, 1865 to serve one year. Mustered out with detachment, May 6, 1865 at Hart's Island, New York Harbor. Also borne as Hammond.

HANNAH, CHARLES— Age 24 years. Enlisted December 10, 1863 at Rochester. Mustered in as Wagoner, Co. A, December 20, 1863 to serve three years. Mustered out with company, August 1, 1865 at Winchester, Virginia.

HANNON, DOMINICK— Age 39 years. Enlisted February 24, 1865 at New York City. Mustered in as Private, Co. B, February 24, 1865 to serve one year. Mustered out with company, August 1, 1865 at Winchester, Virginia.

HANYON, ADAM WAGE— Age 18 years. Enlisted December 24, 1863 at Rochester. Mustered in as Private, Co. I, February 2, 1864 to serve three years. Transferred to One Hundredth New York Volunteers, April 11, 1865.

HANYON, JOHN R.— Age 27 years. Enlisted December 7, 1863 at Rochester. Mustered in as Sergeant, Co. I, February 2, 1864 to serve three years. Discharged for disability, June 21, 1864.

HANYON, PETER, B.— Age 22 years. Enlisted December 7, 1863 at Rochester. Mustered in as Sergeant, Co. I, February 2, 1864 to serve three years. Mustered out with company, August 1, 1865 at Winchester, Virginia.

HARDEN, JAMES W.— Age 23 years. Enlisted January 4, 1864 at Smyrna. Mustered in as Private, Co. L, February 12, 1864 to serve three years. Mustered out June 6, 1865 at Frederick, Maryland.

HARE, JOHN Jr.— Age 20 years. Enlisted February 9, 1864 at Bath as Private, Co. M, to serve three years. Rejected.

HARFORD, GEORGE— Age 25 years. Enlisted February 20, 1865 at New York. Mustered in as Private, Co. M, February 20, 1865 to serve three years. Deserted, May 5, 1865.

HARMON, FRANCIS— Age 22 years. Enlisted December 26, 1863 at Syracuse. Mustered in as Private, Co. B, January 5, 1864 to serve three years. Appointed Corporal, March 1, 1865, reduced May 1, 1865. Mustered out with company, August 1, 1865 at Winchester, Virginia.

HARMON, WILLIAM H.— Age 31 years. Enlisted March 16, 1865 at New York. Mustered in as Private, Co. M, March 16, 1865 to serve three years. Transferred to Co. A, date not given. Reported as deserted, May 10, 1865 near Winchester, Virginia. No record of C.M. Appointed Corporal, July 1, 1865. Mustered out with company, August 1, 1865 at Winchester, Virginia.

HARRALL, HENRY H.— Age 27 years. Enlisted March 16, 1865 at New York. Mustered in as Private, "unassigned," March 16, 1865 to serve three years. No further record.

HARRINGTON, ALLEN R.— Age 27 years. Enlisted December 22, 1863 at Livonia. Mustered in a Private, Co. D, January 10, 1864 to serve three years. Mustered out with company, August 1, 1865 at Winchester, Virginia.

HARRINGTON, JAMES— Age 21 years. Enlisted April 13, 1865 at New York. Mustered in as Private, "unassigned," April 13, 1865 to serve one year. Mustered out with detachment, May 6, 1865 at Hart's Island, New York Harbor.

HARRINGTON, JAMES C.— Age 24 years. Enlisted November 12, 1863 at Urbana. Mustered in as Sergeant, Co. G, February 2, 1864 to serve three years. Mustered out as Commissary Sergeant, with company, August 1, 1865 at Winchester, Virginia. Prior service in Co. I, Thirty Fourth Infantry Volunteers.

HARRINGTON, RANSOM B.— Age 25 years. Enlisted November 27, 1863 at Rochester, as Private, Co. F, to serve three years. Rejected.

HARRINGTON, SILAS N.— Age 16 years. Enlisted December 21, 1863 at Rome. Mustered in as Private, Co. C, January 5, 1864 to serve three years. Mustered out with company, August 1, 1865 at Winchester, Virginia.

HARRIS, JOHN— (Colored) Age 25 years. Enlisted January 14, 1864 at Rochester. Mustered in as Cook, Co. H, February 2, 1864 to serve three years. Deserted, no date given.

HARRIS, JOHN H.— Age 20 years. Enlisted March 31, 1865 at New York City. Mustered in as Private, Co. H, March 31, 1865 to serve one year. Mustered out with company, August 1, 1865 at Winchester, Virginia.

HARRIS, THOMAS— Age 20 years. Enlisted April 12, 1865 at Kingston. Mustered in as Private, "unassigned," April 13, 1865 to serve three years. Mustered out with detachment, May 6, 1865 at Hart's Island, New York Harbor.

HARRISON, JOHN— Age 20 years. Enlisted February 18, 1865 at New York. Mustered in as Private, Co. E, February 18, 1865 to serve three years. Deserted June 1, 1865 at Winchester, Virginia.

HART, ALONZO— Age 20 years, Enlisted January 20, 1864 at Arcadia. Mustered in as Saddler, Co. H, February 2, 1864 to serve three years. Mustered out with company, August 1, 1865 at Winchester, Virginia.

HART, JOHN— Age 27 years. Enlisted April 10, 1865 at Albany. Mustered in as Private, "unassigned," April 10, 1865 to serve three years. Mustered out with detachment, may 6, 1865 at Hart's Island, New York Harbor.

HART, ROMAINE B.— Age 18 years. Enlisted December 9, 1863 at Webster. Mustered in as Sergeant, Co. H, February 2, 1864, to serve three years. Mustered out with company, August 1, 1865 at Winchester, Virginia.

HART, THEODORE— Age 23 years. Enlisted February 14, 1865 at New York. Mustered in as Private, Co. C, February 14, 1865 to serve three years. Mustered out with company, August 1, 1865 at Winchester, Virginia.

HARTMAN, ERNEST— Age 21 years. Enlisted February 28, 1865 at New York. Mustered in as Private, Co. M, February 28, 1865, to serve three years. Deserted, May 8, 1865, from Remount Camp, Maryland.

HARVEY, HARRY— Age 20 years. Enlisted December 24, 1863 at Rochester. Mustered in as Private, Co. C, January 5, 1864, to serve three years. Transferred to Co. A, March 22, 1864. Mustered out with company, August 1, 1865 at Winchester, Virginia.

HARVEY, WILIAM— Age 44 years. Enlisted January 19, 1864 at Syracuse, as Private, Co. H, to serve three years. Rejected.

HASKIN, JOHN G.— Age 33 years. Enlisted January 29, 1864 at Syracuse. Mustered in as Private, Co. K, February 6, 1864, to serve three years. Transferred to Co. B, March 25, 1864. Appointed Saddler, no date given. Discharged June 9, 1865 at Washington, D.C. Also borne as John J. Haskins.

HAUGHTON, WILLIAM R.— Age 26 years. Enlisted April 5, 1865 at New York. Mustered in as Private, "unassigned," April 5, 1865, to serve one year. Mustered out with detachment, May 6, 1865 at Hart's Island, New York Harbor. Also borne as Houghton.

HAVENS, ALONOZO— Age 23 years. Enlisted November 17, 1864 at Syracuse. Mustered in as Sergeant, Co. B, January 5, 1864, to serve three years. Deserted, May 25, 1864, from Point Royal, Pa.

HAVENS, GEORGE A.— Age 19 years. Enlisted February 15, 1864 at Bath. Mustered in as Private, Co. M, February 23, 1864, to serve three years. Transferred to Co. G, March 24, 1864. Died, date not stated.

HAWKINGS, FERDINAND— Age 20 years. Enlisted February 8, 1864 at Rochester. Mustered in as Private, Co. C, February 26, 1864, to serve three years. Died while a prisoner of war, place not stated.

HAWKINS, GEORGE F.— Age 19 years. Enlisted February 8, 1864 at Rochester. Mustered in as Private, Co. M, February 23, 1864, to serve three years. Transferred to Co. C, March 22, 1864. Captured, date not stated. Died while prisoner of war, date and place not stated. Also borne as Hawkins, Ferdinand.

HAWKS, JAMES M.— Age 29 years. Enlisted December 17, 1863 at Syracuse. Mustered in as Sergeant, Co. B, January 5, 1864, to serve three years. Mustered out with company, August 1, 1865 at Winchester, Virginia.

HAYDEN, ROBERT— Age 21 years. Enlisted April 7, 1865 at Albany. Mustered in as Private, "unassigned," April 7, 1865, to serve one year. Mustered out with detachment, May 6, 1865 at Hart's Island, New York Harbor.

HAYES, JOHN— Age 41 years. Enlisted November 6, 1863 at Rochester. Mustered in as Private, Co. A, December 20, 1863, to serve three years. Deserted December 23, 1863 at Rochester. Prior service in Co. I, One Hundred and Fifth New York Volunteers.

HAYES, PATRICK— Age 26 years. Enlisted January 26, 1864 at Lenox. Mustered in as Private, Co. M, February 23, 1864, to serve three years. Mustered out while paroled prisoner of was August 1, 1865 at Annapolis, Maryland.

HAYES, THOMAS— Age 22 years. Enlisted April 14, 1865 at Kingston. Mustered in as Private, "unassigned," April 14, 1865, to serve three years. Mustered out with detachment, May 6, 1865 at Hart's Island, New York Harbor.

HAYWARD, ALFRED— Age 24 years. Enlisted December 24, 1863 at Sodus. Mustered in as Private, Co. H, February 2, 1864, to serve three years. Appointed Corporal, date not stated. Mustered out with company, August 1, 1865 at Winchester, Virginia.

HAZLETON, DWIGHT W.— Officer

HEARLD, JAMES— Age 18 years. Enlisted February 23, 1864 at Livingston. Mustered in as Private, Co. M, February 23, 1864, to serve three years. Transferred to Co. D, March 25, 1864. Mustered out with detachment, June 28, 1865 at Winchester, Virginia. Also borne Hearal or Herald.

HEARTY, PETER— Age 19 years. Enlisted January 6, 1864 at Dunkirk. Mustered in as Private, Co. A, March 8, 1864, to serve three years. Mustered out with company, August 1, 1865 at Winchester, Virginia.

HECKER, WILLIAM F.— Age 20 years. Enlisted November 30, 1863 at Rochester. Mustered in as Quartermaster Sergeant, Co. F, January 10, 1864 to serve three years. Mustered out as Sergeant, June 28, 1865 at Winchester, Virginia. Prior service in Co. A, Thirty Third New York Volunteers.

HECOX, CHARLES B.— Age 20 years. Enlisted December 2, 1863 at Lyons. Mustered in as Private, Co. H, February 2, 1864, to serve three years. Mustered out with company, August 1, 1865 at Winchester, Virginia.

HECOX, FRANKLIN— Age 21 years. Enlisted December 19, 1863 at Lyons. Mustered in as Corporal, Co. D, January 10, 1864, to serve three years. Mustered out with detachment as Private, June 28, 1865 at Winchester, Virginia. Prior service in Co. D, Twenty Seventh Volunteers.

HEIMER, AUGUSTUS— Age 27 years. Enlisted January 4, 1864 at Andes. Mustered in as Private, Co. L, February 12, 1864, to serve three years. Discharged May 19, 1865 at hospital, Frederick, Maryland.

HEMINGWAY, JAMES— Age 20 years. Enlisted December 19, 1863 at Camillus. Mustered in as Private, Co. H, February 2, 1864, to serve three years. Mustered out with company, August 1, 1865 at Winchester, Virginia. Also borne as Hemanway and James M. Hemminway.

HEMMING, FREDERICK— Age 21 years. Enlisted December 30, 1863 at Rochester. Mustered in as Private, Co. C, January 5, 1864, to serve three years. Transferred to Co. A, March 22, 1864. Appointed Corporal, June 1, 1865. Mustered out with company, August 1, 1865 at Winchester, Virginia. Also borne as Henning.

HENNESSEY, MICHAEL— Age 34 years. Enlisted February 20, 1865 at New York. Mustered in as Private, Co. E, February 20, 1865, to serve three years. Absent at muster out of company, August 1, 1865. No further record.

HENNING, FREDERICK— see Hemming, Frederick.

HENNING, PETER— see Fleming, Peter.

HENRY, WILLIAM— see Williams, Henry.

HERMAN, HERMAN— Age 36 years. Enlisted January 15, 1864 at Rochester. Mustered in as Private, Co. I, February 2, 1864, to serve three years. Transferred to Co. M, in March 1864. Appointed Sergeant, date not stated. Reduced in ranks, April 25, 1865. Absent sick in hospital from May 1, 1864 at muster out of company, August 1, 1865. No further record.

HESS, FREDERICK— Age 33 years. Enlisted April 6, 1865 at New York. Mustered in as Private, Co. L, April 6, 1865 to serve one year. Mustered out with company, August 1, 1865 at Winchester, Virginia.

HEWLET, WILLIAM H.— see Hulet, William H.

HICKEY, WILLIAM— Age 41 years. Enlisted November 12, 1863 at Brockport, as Private, Co. C, to serve three years. Rejected.

HIKOCK, ASHUR D.— Age 38 years. Enlisted January 4, 1864 at Rochester, Co. D, to serve three years. Rejected

HICKS, ALFORD— Age 25 years. Enlisted December 24, 1863 at Syracuse. Mustered in as First Sergeant, Co. B, January 5, 1864 to serve three years. Mustered out with company, August 1, 1865 at Winchester, Virginia. Prior service in Co. E, Twenty Third New York Volunteers.

HIGGINS, JOHN— Age 21 years. Enlisted March 13, 1865 at New York. Mustered in as Private, Co. K, March 13, 1865 to serve three years. Mustered out with company, August 1, 1865 at Winchester, Virginia.

HIGHLAND, PATRICK— See Hilan, Patrick.

HILAN, PATRICK— Age 18 years. Enlisted December 30, 1863 at Van Buren. Mustered in as Private, Co. E, January 10, 1864 to serve three years. Transferred to Co. B, September 1, 1864. Appointed Corporal, date not given. Mustered out with company, August 1, 1865 at Winchester, Virginia. also borne as Highland.

HILLE, LOUIS— Age 37 years. Enlisted February 15, 1864 at Bath. Mustered in as Private, Co. M, February 23, 1864 to serve three years. Transferred to Co. G, March 24, 1864. Died, date not stated.

HINES, ADOLPHUS W.— Age 18 years. Enlisted March 22, 1865 at Andes. Mustered in as Private, Co. A, March 22, 1865 to serve three years. Mustered out with company, August 1, 1865 at Winchester, Virginia.

HINMAN, JAMES B.— Age 18 years. Enlisted January 4, 1864 at Plymouth. Mustered in as Trumpeter, Co. L, February 12, 1864 to serve three years. Captured November 12, 1864. Paroled at Salisbury, N.C., March 2, 1865. Mustered out as paroled prisoner, July 31, 1865 at Elmira, New York.

HINNING, WILLIAM H.— See Kenning, Wm. H.

HITCHCOCK, RICHARD— Age 26 years. Enlisted December 22, 1863 at Auburn. Mustered in as Private, Co. M, February 23, 1864 to serve three years. Transferred to Co. I, March 28, 1864. Appointed Corporal, date not stated. Mustered out with company, August 1, 1865 at Winchester, Virginia. Prior service in Co. A, Seventy Fifth New York Volunteers.

HITCHCOCK, SAMUEL B.— Age 41 years. Enlisted January 1, 1864 at Smithfield, as Private, Co. H, to serve three years. Rejected.

HITT, WILLIAM— Age 28 years. Enlisted January 4, 1864 at Colchester. Mustered in as Private, Co. L, February 12, 1864 to serve three years. Discharged, February 21, 1865.

HOAG, TRUE— Age 25 years. Enlisted January 5, 1864 at Lyons as Private, Co. H, to serve three years. Deserted previous to muster of company, February 2, 1864.

HOCKNILL, RICHARD R.— Age 41 years. Enlisted December 28, 1863 at Rochester. Mustered in as Private. Co. D, January 10, 1864 to serve three years. Mustered out with company, August 1, 1865 at Winchester, Virginia.

HODGE, JACOB— Age 23 years. Enlisted December 26, 1863 at Potter. Mustered in as Private, Co. C, January 5, 1864 to serve three years. Transferred to Co. A, March 22, 1864. Died, August 23, 1864 at Andersonville, Georgia., of wounds received in action.

HODGE, MILES B.— Enlisted December 15, 1863 at PennYan. Mustered in as Private, Co. A, December 20, 1863 to serve three years. Captured, November 12, 1864. No discharge furnished at muster out of company, August 1, 1865. No further record.

HODGES, HENRY— Age 20 years. Enlisted March 28, 1865 at New York. Mustered in as Private, Co. C, March 28, 1865 to serve three years. Transferred to Co. D, June 9, 1865. Absent without leave since June 1865. No discharge furnished at muster out of company, August 1, 1865. Also borne as Hager.

HOFFMAN, BRUNO— Age 25 years. Enlisted December 28, 1863 at New York, as Private "unassigned," to serve three years. No further record.

HOGHKERK, CHARLES H.— Age 18 years. Enlisted January 18, 1864 at Syracuse as Private, Co. H, to serve three years. Rejected.

HOLDEN, LEVI— Age 22 years. Enlisted December 8, 1863 at Rochester, as Private, Co. D, to serve three years. Rejected.

HOLLAND, THOMAS— Age 26 years. Enlisted February 27, 1865 at New York. Mustered in as Private, Co. C, February 27, 1865 to serve three years. Mustered out with company, August 1, 1865 at Winchester, Virginia.

HOLMES, ROBERT— Age 24 years. Enlisted January 6, 1864 at Rochester. Mustered in as Private, Co. F, January 10, 1864 to serve three years. Mustered out June 28, 1865 at Winchester, Virginia.

HOOBER, JOSEPH— Age 18 years. Enlisted March 13, 1865 at Rochester. Mustered in as Private, "unassigned," March 13, 1865 to serve three years. Mustered out June 21, 1865 at Elmira, New York.

HOOD, JAMES— Age 20 years. Enlisted January 14, 1864 at Rochester. Mustered in as Private, Co. G, February 2, 1864 to serve three years. Transferred to Co. D, March 6, 1864. Deserted, January 28, 1865.

HOOD, WILLIAM, H.— Age 23 years. Enlisted March 14, 1865 at New York. Mustered in as Private, "unassigned," March 14, 1865 to serve three years. No further record.

HOOSI, ALEXANDER— Age 19 years. Enlisted November 19, 1863 at Syracuse. Mustered in as Private, Co. B, January 5, 1864 to serve three years. Died, August 23, 1864 at Army Square Hospital, Washington, D.C.

HOPKINS, JOHN— Age 22 years. Enlisted October 5, 1864 at Jamaica. Mustered in as Private, Co. M, October 5, 1864 to serve one year. Mustered out with company, August 1, 1865 at Winchester, Virginia.

HOPKINS, WILLIAM A.— Age 27 years. Enlisted December 21, 1863 at Bath. Mustered in as Private, Co. G, February 2, 1864 to serve three years. Appointed Sergeant, June 28, 1865. Mustered out with company, August 1, 1865 at Winchester, Virginia. Prior service in Co. A, Twenty Third New York Volunteers.

HOPPER, JOHN— Age 21 years. Enlisted December 12, 1863 at Rochester. Mustered in as Sergeant, Co. F, January 19, 1864 to serve three years. Mustered out as Private, July 28, 1865 at Rochester, New York. Prior service in Co. I, Third Cavalry.

HOPPER, JOHN— Age 28 years. Enlisted January 25, 1864 at Rochester. Mustered in as Corporal, Co. K, February 6, 1864 to serve three years. Died in prison at Andersonville, Georgia., date not stated.

HOPPER, JOHN C.— Age 18 years. Enlisted March 14, 1865 at New York. Mustered in as Private, Co. K, March 14, 1865 to serve three years. Mustered out with company, August 1, 1865 at Winchester, Virginia.

HORTON, WILLIAM— Age 31 years. Enlisted April 10, 1865 at New York. Mustered in as Private, "unassigned," April 10, 1865 to serve one year. Mustered out with detachment, May 6, 1865 at Hart's Island, New York Harbor.

HORTON, WILLIAM W.— Age 25 years. Enlisted February 20, 1864 at Binghamton. Mustered in as Private, Co. I, February 20, 1864 to serve three years. Died, January 22, 1865 at Salisbury Prison, S.C.

HOSFORD, HIRAM— Age 27 years. Enlisted February 25, 1864 at bath. Mustered in as Private, Co. I, March 8, 1864 to serve three years. Mustered out with company, August 1, 1865 at Winchester, Virginia.

HOUGHSON, WILLIAM D.— See Hughson, William D.

HOUGHTON, WILLIAM R.— See Haughton, William, R.

HOUSER, GEORGE M.— Age 18 years. Enlisted December 16, 1863 at Syracuse. Mustered in as Private, Co. B, January 5, 1864 to serve three years. Mustered out with company, August 1, 1865 at Winchester, Virginia.

HOUSER, JAMES E.— Age 22 years. Enlisted December 21, 1863 at Syracuse. Mustered in as Private, Co. B, January 5, 1864 to serve three years. Mustered out with company, August 1, 1865 at Winchester, Virginia.

HOWARD, JAMES— Age 23 years. Enlisted April 5., 1865 at Albany. Mustered in as Private, Co. A, April 5, 1865 to serve three years. Deserted may 11, 1865 in the field, Virginia.

HOWARD, WILLIAM— Age 18 years. Enlisted April8, 1865 at Albany. Mustered in as Private, "unassigned," April 10, 1865 to serve three years. Mustered out with detachment, May 6, 1865 at Hart's Island, New York Harbor.

HOWE, ELMER— Age 22 years. Enlisted January 4, 1864 at Otsego. Mustered in as Private, Co. L, January 5, 1864 to serve three years. Deserted, December 8, 1864 from hospital.

HOWES, ZALMON— Age 21 years. Enlisted February 22,1865 at New York. Mustered in as Private, Co. C, February 22, 1865 to serve one year. Mustered out with company, August 1, 1865 at Winchester, Virginia.

HOYT, MYRON H.— Age 20 years. Enlisted December 2, 1863 at Rochester. Mustered in as Private, Co. A, December 20, 1863 to serve three years. Died of disease, July 30, 1864 at Andersonville, Georgia.

HOYT, SAMUEL— Age 26 years. Enlisted March 3, 1864 at Rochester. Mustered in as Private, Co. M, March 6, 1864 to serve three years. Died in prison, September 30, 1864 at Andersonville, Georgia.

HUBBARD, LUKE— Age 16 years. Enlisted November 25, 1863 at Syracuse, as Private, Co. B, to serve three years. Rejected.

HUBER, JOHN A.— Age 24 years. Enlisted February 15, 1864 at Bath. Mustered in as Private, Co. M, February 23, 1864 to serve three years. Transferred to Co. G, March 24, 1864. In confinement at Fort Delaware since May 12, 1865 by sentence of G.C.M.A. of S. Discharged August 9, 1865 at Rochester.

HUDGINS,DAVID L.— Age 18 years. Enlisted November 23, 1863 at Syracuse. Mustered in as Private, Co. B, January 5, 1864 to serve three years. Deserted February 28, 1864 from Rochester.

HUDGINS, WILLIAM J.— Age 19 years. Enlisted December 3, 1863 at Syracuse. Mustered in as Private, Co. B, January 5, 1864 to serve three years. Deserted March 22, 1864 from Giesboro Point, D.C.

HUDSON, THOMAS— Age 26 years. Enlisted December 16, 1863 at Rochester. Mustered in as Private, Co. F, January 10, 1864 to serve three years. Deserted in February 1864 from camp near Rochester.

HUDSON, WILLIAM— Age 30 years. Enlisted November 23, 1863 at Rochester. Mustered in as Private, Co. A, December 20, 1863 to serve three years. Discharged for disability, August 10, 1864 at Plymouth Grove, R.I.

HUES, ADELBERT— Age 18 years. Enlisted December 8, 1863 at Cazenovia. Mustered in as Private, Co. E, January 10, 1864 to serve three years. Died at Andersonville, Georgia.

HUFF, NELSON— Age 22 years. Enlisted December 31, 1863 at Lyons. Mustered in as Private, Co. F, February 2, 1864 to serve three years. Absent, sick at muster out of company August 1, 1865. No further record.

HUFF, NELSON H.— Age 31 years. Enlisted December 31, 1865 at Lyons. Mustered in as Private, Co. H, February 2, 1864 to serve three years. Mustered out May 31, 1865 at New York City.

HUGHES, EDWARD— Age 18 years. Enlisted December 11, 1863 at Utica, as Private, Co. B, to serve three years. Rejected.

HUGHS, MICHAEL— Age 44 years. Enlisted December 11, 1863 at Rochester, as Private, Co. D, to serve three years. Rejected.

HUGHSON, WILLIAM D.— Age 19 years. Enlisted January 13, 1864 at Preston. Mustered in as Corporal, Co. L, February 12, 1864 to serve three years. Reduced, date not stated. Died of disease, March 20, 1864 at St. Mary's Hospital, Rochester, New York. Also borne as Houghson.

HULBERT, FREDERICK— Age 18 years. Enlisted January 3, 1863 at Rome. Mustered in as Private, Co. C, January 5, 1963 to serve three years. Mustered out with company, August 1, 1865 at Winchester, Virginia.

HULBERT, JOHN W.— Age 18 years. Enlisted February 22, 1864 at Rochester. Mustered in as Farrier, Co. M, February 23, 1864 to serve three years. Died in prison, September 10, 1864 at Andersonville, Georgia.

HULET, WILLIAM H.— Age 29 years. Enlisted January 11, 1864 at Unadilla. Mustered in as Private, Co. L, February 12, 1864 to serve three years. Died, June 27, 1864 while a prisoner at Andersonville, Georgia. Also borne as Hewlet.

HULL, BIRNEY— Age 21 years. Enlisted December 21, 1863 at Portland. Mustered in as Sergeant, Co. K, February 6, 1864 to serve three years. Mustered out May 18, 1865 from United States Hospital, Summit House, Philadelphia, Pa.

HUMMEL, LEWIS— Age 27 years. Enlisted January 4, 1864 at Avoca. Mustered in as Private, Co. K, February 6, 1864 to serve three years. Transferred to Co. G, March 25, 1864. In confinement at Fort Delaware, by sentence of G.C.M. from May 12, 1865. Discharged August 9, 1865 at Rochester.

HUMPHREY, EDWIN— See Umphrey, Edwin.

HUNT, ALVIN G.— Age 18 years. Enlisted November 9, 1863 at Dunkirk. Mustered in as Corporal, Co. F, January 10, 1864 to serve three years. Appointed Sergeant, March 1, 1864. Mustered out June 28, 1865 at Winchester, Virginia. Prior service in Co. K, Twenty Seventh New York Volunteers

HUNTER, ROBERT— Age 18 years. Enlisted December 22, 1863 at Lyons. Mustered in as Private, Co. K, February 6, 1864 to serve three years. Transferred to Co. H, March 25, 1864. Mustered out with company, August 1, 1865 at Winchester, Virginia.

HUNTINGTON, CHARLES S.— Age 19 years. Enlisted August 5, 1864 at Rochester. Mustered in as Private, Co. G, August 5, 1864 to serve one year. In confinement at Fort Delaware by sentence of G.C.M., from May 12, 1865. Discharged, August 9, 1865 at Rochester.

HUNINGTON, FRANK F.— Age 18 years. Enlisted August 5, 1864 at Syracuse. Mustered in as Private, Co. G, August 5, 1864 to serve one year. Discharged, June 6, 1865 from U.S.A. General Hospital, Frederick, Maryland.

HUNTLY, ARCELUS E.— Age 36 years. Enlisted January 16, 1864 at Syracuse. Mustered in as Private, Co. H, February 2, 1864 to serve three years. Mustered out with company, August 1, 1865 at Winchester, Virginia.

HURD, JOHN— Age 28 years. Enlisted December 8, 1863 at Rochester, as Private, Co. D to serve three years. Rejected.

HURLBERT, FREDERICK— See Hulbert, Frederick.

HURLBUTT, WELLINGTON— Age 19 years. Enlisted December 4, 1863 at Rochester. Mustered in as Private, Co. A, December 20, 1863 to serve three years. Mustered out June 27, 1865 at Satterlee United States Hospital, Philadelphia, pa.

HUSON, GEORGE BOWKER— Age 21 years. Enlisted December 2, 1863 at Lyons. Mustered in as Private, Co. H, February 2, 1864 to serve three years. Transferred to Co. F, date not stated. Absent, sick at muster out of company, August 1, 1865. No further record.

HUSTON, JOHN S.— Age 18 years. Enlisted January 2, 1864 at Avoca. Mustered in as Private, Co. G, February 2, 1864 to serve three years. Appointed Corporal, April 1, 1865, reduced, May 12, 1865. Undergoing sentence on G.C.M. Discharged August 9, 1865 at Rochester.

HUTCHINSON, AMASA— Age 23 years. Enlisted April 12, 1865 at Rochester. Mustered in as Private, Co. F, April 12, 1865 to serve three years. Mustered out with company, August 1, 1865 at Winchester, Virginia.

HUTCHINSON, SANFORD— Age 39 years. Enlisted April 1, 1865 at Rochester. Mustered in as Private, Co. D, April 1, 1865 to serve three years. Mustered out with company, August 1, 1865 at Winchester, Virginia.

INGRAHAM, ALEXANDER— Age 23 years. Enlisted December 21, 1863 at Rochester. Mustered in as Private, Co. A, December 20, 1863 to serve three years. Discharged for disability, June 12, 1865 at Washington, D.C.

INGRAHAM, DUNHAM— Age 20 years. Enlisted March 28, 1864 at New Haven. Mustered in as Private, Co. A, March 28, 1864 to serve three years. Captured, November 12, 1864. Mustered out August 4, 1865 at New York.

INGRAHAM, ISAAC J.— Age 21 years. Enlisted August 8, 1864 at Delhi. Mustered in as Private, "unassigned' August 8, 1864 to serve one year. No further record.

IRISH, HENRY— Age 21 years. Enlisted January 6, 1864 at Rochester. Mustered in as Corporal, Co. F, January 10, 1864 to serve three years. Appointed Sergeant, March 1, 1864. Mustered out June 28, 1865 at Winchester, Virginia.

IRWIN, DENNIS— Colored. Age 28 years. Enlisted January 14, 1864 at Rochester. Mustered in as Cook, Co. K, February 5, 1864, to serve three years. Deserted, August 9, 1864, at Washington, D.C. Also borne as Erwin.

ISELIN, SOLOMAN— Age not stated. Enlisted April 6, 1865 at New York. Mustered in as Private, Co. C, April 6, 1865, to serve one year. Mustered out with company, August 1, 1865 at Winchester, Virginia.

JACKSON, CHARLES— Age 29 years. Enlisted February 17, 1865 at New York. Mustered in as Private, "unassigned," February 17, 1865, to serve three years. No further record.

JACKSON, CHARLES— Age 23 years. Enlisted February 22, 1865 at New York. Mustered in as Private, Co. C, February 22, 1865, to serve one year. Mustered out with company, August 1, 1865 at Winchester, Virginia.

JACKSON, DAVID F.— Age 26 years. Enlisted April 1, 1865 at New York. Mustered in as Private, Co. H, April 1, 1865, to serve one year. Mustered out with company, August 1, 1865 at Winchester, Virginia.

JACKSON, WILLIAM H.— Age 23 years. Enlisted December 3, 1863 at Dunkirk. Mustered in as Private, Co. F, January 10, 1864, to serve three years. Transferred to Co. K, March 1864. Appointed Commissary Sergeant, date not stated. Mustered out June 28, 1865 at Winchester, Virginia. Prior service in Co. H, Eighteenth New York Volunteers.

JACOBS, BENJAMIN— Age 23 years. Enlisted January 19, 1864 at Verona. Mustered in as Private, Co. M, February 23, 1864, to serve three years. Appointed Wagoner, date not stated. Discharged for disability, December 1, 1864 at Camp Russell, Virginia.

JACOBS, CLARK H.— Age 29 years. Enlisted November 27, 1863 at Cuba. Mustered in as Private, Co. D, January 10, 1864, to serve three years. Transferred to Co. K, May 1, 1864. Appointed Corporal, June 1, 1865. Mustered out June 28, 1865 at Winchester, Virginia.

JACOBUS, SAMUEL— Age 17 years. Enlisted as Private, Co. G, to serve three years, January 20, 1864 at Urbana. Rejected.

JAMES, WILLIAM F.— Age 28 years. Enlisted, March 28, 1865 at New York. Mustered in as Private, Co. I, March 28, 1865, to serve three years. Never joined for service. No discharge furnished at muster out of company, August 1, 1865. No further record.

JEAGER, URBAN— Age 25 years. Enlisted December 30, 1863 at Syracuse. Mustered in as Private, Co. B, January 5, 1864, to serve three years. Discharged for disability, May 30, 1865, at U.S. General Hospital, Cumberland, Maryland. Also borne as Reuben Yeager.

JANNER, CHARLES H.— Age 18 years. Enlisted November 28, 1863 at Brockport. Mustered in as Private, Co. C, January 5, 1864, to serve three years. Died of disease, April 1, 1865 at Kalarama Hospital, D.C.

JEROME, HELOM B.— Age 26 years. Enlisted January 25, 1864 at Syracuse. Mustered in as Private, Co. M, February 23, 1864, to serve three years. Transferred Co. B, March 25, 1864. Wounded, August 25, 1864. Mustered out with company, August 1, 1865 at Winchester, Virginia. Prior service in Co. D, Third New York Volunteers. Also borne as Henry Jerome.

JETTY, JOSEPH— Age 18 years. Enlisted March 29, 1865 at Rochester. Mustered in as Private, Co. F, March 29, 1865, to serve three years. Transferred to Co. G, May 28, 1865. Mustered out with company, August 1, 1865 at Winchester, Virginia.

JEWETT, JOSEPH— Age 24 years. Enlisted January 4, 1864 at Rochester. Mustered in as Private, Co. K, February 6, 1864, to serve three years. Deserted, February 14, 1864 at Rochester.

JILLETT, NATHANIEL— See Gillett, Nathaniel.

JOCHEMSEN, FRITZ— Age 21 years. Enlisted March 25, 1865 at New York. Mustered in as Private, "unassigned," March 25, 1865, to serve three years. No further record.

JOHNSON, DAVID A.— Age 21 years. Enlisted October 27, 1863 at Rochester. Mustered in as Private, Co. A, December 20, 1863, to serve three years. Died, September 4, 1864 of wounds received in action at Charleston, S.C.

JOHNSON, DENNIS— Age 20 years. Enlisted February 16, 1865 at New York. Mustered in as Private, Co. A, February 16, 1865, to serve three years. Deserted, July 24, 1865 from Remount Camp, Maryland.

JOHNSON, FREEMAN M.— Age 32 years. Enlisted October 19, 1863 at Rochester. Mustered in as Corporal, Co. A, December 20, 1863, to serve three years. Discharged for disability, May 19, 1865 at Philadelphia, Pa.

JOHNSON, GEORGE— Age 22 years. Enlisted December 27, 1864 at Tarrytown. Mustered in as Private, Co. H, December 27, 1864, to serve three years. Discharged, May 2, 1865.

JOHNSON, GILBERT— Age 31 years. Enlisted February 19, 1864 at Rochester. Mustered in as Commissary Sergeant, Co. M, February 23, 1864, to serve three years. No further record.

JOHNSON, JOHN— Age 25 years. Enlisted December 7, 1863 at Riga. Mustered in as Private, Co. C, January 5, 1864, to serve three years. Appointed Corporal, date not state. Died August 6, 1864 in Mount Pleasant Hospital.

JOHNSON, JOHN A.— Age 23 years. Enlisted December 14, 1863 at Buffalo. Mustered in as Private, Co. F, January 10, 1864, to serve three years. Deserted in February 1864 from camp near Rochester. Date of return not shown. Appears on rolls of Co. D as transferred to Co. K, May 1, 1864. No further record.

JOHNSON, MILTON C.— Age 29 years. Enlisted April 7, 1865 at Rochester. Mustered in as Private, Co. F, April 7, 1865, to serve three years. Transferred to Co. G, May 27, 1865. Mustered out with company, August 1, 1865 at Winchester, Virginia.

JOHNSON, ROBERT— Age 22 years. Enlisted November 26, 1863 at Syracuse. Mustered in as Corporal, Co. B, January 5, 1864, to serve three years. Appointed Sergeant, date not stated. Mustered out with company, August 1, 1865 at Winchester, Virginia.

JOHNSON, WILLIAM G.— Age 18 years. Enlisted November 27, 1863 at Riga. Mustered in as Private, Co. C, January 5, 1864, to serve three years. Appointed Corporal, March 1, 1865. Mustered out with company, August 1, 1865 at Winchester, Virginia.

JOHNSTON, ROBERT— Age 28 years. Enlisted January 11, 1864 at Otto. Mustered in as Private, Co. K, February 6, 1864, to serve three years. Deserted, February 23, 1864 at Rochester, NY.

JOICE, THOMAS— Age 18 years. Enlisted December 2, 1863 at Brockport. Mustered in as Private, Co. C, January 5, 1864, to serve three years. Captured, date not stated. Died, date unknown, in Andersonville Prison, Georgia.

JONES, ALONZO— Age 22 years. Enlisted January 29, 1864 at Prattsburgh. Mustered in as Private, Co. G, February 2, 1864, to serve three years. Died, date and place not stated.

JONES, DAVID— Age 20 years. Enlisted December 14, 1863 at Utica. Mustered in as Corporal, Co. B, January 5, 1864, to serve three years. Mustered out with company, August 1, 1865 at Winchester, Virginia.

JONES, DAVID— Age 37 years. Enlisted January 8, 1864 at Rochester. Mustered in as Private, Co. I, February 2, 1864, to serve three years. Deserted, February 1864 at Rochester, NY.

JONES, FRANK— Age 19 years. Enlisted March 2, 1865 at Tompkinsville. Mustered in as Private, "unassigned," March 2, 1865, to serve three years. No further record.

JONES, FRED— Age 18 years. Enlisted April 6, 1865 at New York. Mustered in as Private, Co. I, April 6, 1865, to serve one year. Mustered out with company, August 1, 1865 at Winchester, Virginia.

JONES, GEORGE F.— Age 18 years. Enlisted December 4, 1863 at Cazenovia. Mustered in as Private, Co. E, January 10, 1864, to serve three years. Wounded in action, June 12, 1864. Died of such wounds, July 20, 1864 at Cazenovia, New York.

JONES, GILBERT— Age 22 years. Enlisted December 11, 1863 at Rochester. Mustered in as Private, Co. A, December 20, 1863, to serve three years. Deserted, December 26, 1863 at Rochester, New York.

JONES, HENRY— (Colored). Age 25 years. Enlisted January 23, 1864 at Rochester. Mustered in as Under-Cook, Co. G, February 2, 1864, to serve three years. Deserted, October 21, 1864.

JONES, JAMES— Age 21 years. Enlisted February 14, 1865 at New York. Mustered in as Private, Co. C, February 14, 1865, to serve three years. Mustered out with company, August 1, 1865 at Winchester, Virginia.

JONES, JAMES— Age 18 years. Enlisted April 7, 1865 at New York. Mustered in as Private, Co. A, April 7, 1865, to serve one year. Deserted, May 21, 1865 in the field, Virginia.

JONES, JAMES B.— Age 44 years. Enlisted December 24, 1863 at Rochester. Mustered in as Farrier, Co. F, January 10, 1864, to serve three years. Captured, date not stated. Died, July 1864 at Andersonville, Georgia.

JONES, JAMES D.— Not commissioned surgeon. Missing since December 21, 1863.

JONES, JOHN— Age 19 years. Enlisted April 7, 1865 at New York. Mustered in as Private, Co. A, April 7, 1865, to serve one year. Deserted, May 12, 1865, in the field, Virginia.

JONES, WILLIAM— Age 20 years. Enlisted March 14, 1865 at New York. Mustered in as Private, Co. B, March 14, 1865, to serve three years. Mustered out with company, August 1, 1865 at Winchester, Virginia.

JORDAN, JOHN— Age 21 years. Enlisted December 2, 1863 at Bath. Mustered in as Private, Co. G, February 2, 1864, to serve three years. Mustered out with company, August 1, 1865 at Winchester, Virginia.

JUDD, HAMILTON— Age 43 years. Enlisted July 30, 1864 at Smyrna. Mustered in as Private, "unassigned," August 1, 1864, to serve three years. No further record.

JUSTICE, JOHN— Age 18 years. Enlisted December 12, 1863 at Rochester. Mustered in as Corporal, Co. A, December 20, 1863, to serve three years. Reduced, May 19, 1865. Mustered out with company, August 1, 1865 at Winchester, Virginia.

KAHLER, JACOB— Age 18 years. Enlisted March 7, 1865 at Rochester. Mustered in as Private, "unassigned," March 7, 1865, to serve three years. Mustered out with detachment, May 9, 1865 at Elmira, New York.

KANE, PETER— Age 29 years. Enlisted February 20, 1865 at New York City. Mustered in as Private, Co. H, February 20, 1865, to serve one year. Mustered out June 23, 1865 at Harper's Ferry, Virginia.

KARNEY, WILLIAM E.— Age 18 years. Enlisted March 23, 1865 at Rochester. Mustered in as Private, Co. F, March 23, 1865, to serve one year. Transferred to Co. G, May 27, 1865. Mustered out with company, August 1, 1865 at Winchester, Virginia. Also borne as Kearney and Kerney.

KAVANAGH, JOHN H.— see Cavanaugh, John H.

KEANE, WILLIAM— Age 19 years. Enlisted March 15, 1865 at New York. Mustered in as Private, Co. I, March 15, 1865, to serve one year. Mustered out with company, August 1, 1865 at Winchester, Virginia.

KEARNEY, WILLIAM E.— see Karney, W.E.

KEARNS, JOHN— Age 18 years. Enlisted April 10, 1865 at Albany. Mustered in as Private, "unassigned," April 10, 1865, to serve three years. Mustered out with detachment, May 6, 1865 at Hart's Island, New York Harbor.

KEETON, JOHN F.— Age 18 years. Enlisted at Rochester, date not stated. Mustered in as Private, "unassigned," March 1, 1865, to serve one year. Mustered out with detachment, May 9, 1865 at Elmira. Substitute: never joined regiment.

KELLER, JACOB— Age 40 years. Enlisted December 18, 1863 at Lyons. Mustered in as Private, Co. D, January 10, 1864, to serve three years. Absent sick at muster out of company, August 1, 1865. No further record.

KELLER, NICHOLAS— Age 21 years. Enlisted January 12, 1864 at Rochester. Mustered in as Private, Co. K, February 6, 1864 to serve three years. Deserted, February 26, 1864 at Rochester.

KELLERBOORE, CONRAD— Age 32 years. Enlisted December 3, 1863 at Lyons as Private, Co. H, to serve three years. Rejected.

KELLY, JAMES— Age 36 years. Enlisted March 3, 1865 at New York City. Mustered in as Private, "unassigned," March 3, 1865, to serve three years. Mustered out, June 13, 1865, from Harewood Hospital, Washington, D.C.

KELLEY, JOHN— Age 25 years. Enlisted April 12, 1865 at Kingston. Mustered in as Private, "unassigned", April 12, 1865, to serve three years. Mustered out with detachment, May 6, 1865 at Hart's Island, New York Harbor. Also borne as Kelly, John.

KELLY, JOHN— Age 23 years. Enlisted February 15, 1865 at New York City. Mustered in as Private, "unassigned," February 15, 1865, to serve three years. Deserted en route to regiment.

KELLY, JOHN— Age 19 years. Enlisted February 13, 1865 at New York City. Mustered in as Private, Co. H, February 13, 1865, to serve three years. Mustered out with company, August 1, 1865 at Winchester, Virginia.

KELLY, MICHAEL— Age 22 years. Enlisted February 13, 1865 at New York City. Mustered in as Private, Co. H, February 13, 1865, to serve three years. Mustered out with company, August 1, 1865 at Winchester, Virginia.

KELLY, THOMAS— Age 20 years. Enlisted April 14, 1865 at Kingston. Mustered in as Private, Co. C, April 14, 1865, to serve three years. No further record.

KELLY, THOMAS— Age 26 years. Enlisted February 2, 1865 at Albany. Mustered in as Private, "unassigned," February 2, 1865, to serve three years. Mustered out with detachment, May 6, 1865 at Hart's Island, New York Harbor.

KEMP, WALTER— Age 26 years. Enlisted November 12, 1863 at Rochester. Mustered in as Saddler, Co. A, December 20, 1863, to serve three years. Captured at Stony Creek, Virginia. June 29, 1864; confined at Andersonville, Georgia.; released at N. E. Bridge, N.C. March 1, 1865; mustered out with detachment, June 7, 1865 at Annapolis, Maryland. Prior service in Co. H, Twenty Seventh New York Volunteers.

KENNEDY, JOHN— Age 32 years. Enlisted April 13, 1865 at New York City. Mustered in as private, "unassigned," April 13, 1865 to serve one year. Mustered out with detachment, May 6, 1865, Hart's Island, New York Harbor.

KENNEDY, WILLIAM— Age 23 years. Enlisted February 13, 1865 at Buffalo. Mustered in as Private, Co. H, February 13, 1865, to serve three years. Mustered out with company, August 1, 1865 at Winchester, Virginia.

KENNING, WILLIAM H.— Age 32 years. Enlisted January 25, 1864 at Syracuse. Mustered in as Trumpeter, Co. M, February 23, 1864, to serve three years. Transferred to Co. E., March 25, 1864. Mustered out with company, August 1, 1865 at Winchester, Virginia. Also borne as Hinning, William.

KENNING, WILLIAM H.— Age 32 years. Enlisted December 30, 1865 at Cazenovia as Private, Co. E, to serve three years. Rejected.

KENT, GEORGE W.— Age 31 years. December 24, 1863 at Rochester. Mustered in as Corporal, Co. I, February 2, 1864, to serve three years. Mustered out, June 7, 1865 at Washington, D.C.

KENYON, ERWIN— Age 18 years. Enlisted December 30, 1863 at Cazenovia. Mustered in as Private, Co. E, January 10, 1864, to serve three years. Mustered out with company, August 1, 1865 at Winchester, Virginia.

KENYON, FRANCIS W.— Age 18 years. Enlisted January 16, 1864 at Fabius. Mustered in as Private, Co. K, February 6, 1864, to serve three years. Transferred to Co. E, March 25, 1865. Mustered out with company, August 1, 1865 at Winchester, Virginia.

KEYES, GEORGE— Age 19 years. Enlisted January 5, 1864 at Lyons. Mustered in as Private, Co. H, February 2, 1864 to serve three years. Mustered out with company, August 1, 1865 at Winchester, Virginia.

KEYES, JAMES— Age 19 years. Enlisted December 28, 1863 at Rochester. Mustered in as Private, Co. D, January 10, 1864 to serve three years. Captured, June 22, 1864. Stopped for arrest as a deserter, $30. No discharge given at muster out of company, August 1, 1865.

KIMBERLY, CURTIS— Age 19 years. Enlisted November 24, 1863 at Syracuse. Mustered in as Private, Co. B, January 5, 1864 to serve three years. Sick in Camp Parole, Annapolis, Maryland., at muster out of company, August 1, 1865. No further record.

KING, EZRA— Age 19 years. Enlisted December 8, 1863 at Brockport. Mustered in as Private, Co. C, January 5, 1864 to serve three years. Died of disease, October 9, 1864 at Philadelphia, Pa.

KING, NATHAN— Age 18 years. Enlisted March 16, 1865 at New York. Mustered in as Private, Co. K, March 16, 1865 to serve three years. Mustered out October 20, 1865 at Elmira.

KING, WILLIAM— Age 20 years. Enlisted March 16, 1865 at Brooklyn. Mustered in as Private, "unassigned," March 16, 1865 to serve three years. No further record.

KINGMAN, GEORGE— Age not given. Enlisted August 18, 1864 at Onondaga. Mustered in as Private, Co. C, August 18, 1864 to serve three years. Mustered out with company, August 1, 1865 at Winchester, Virginia.

KIPP, HENRY— Age 44 years. Enlisted November 21, 1863 at Syracuse, as Private, Co. B, to serve three years. Rejected.

KLINE, JOSEPH— Age 39 years. Enlisted December 24, 1863 at Rochester, as Private, Co. D, to serve three years. Rejected.

KLUMPP, THEODORE— Age 22 years. Enlisted December 2, 1863 at Lyons. Mustered in as Sergeant, Co. D, January 10, 1864 to serve three years. Captured, June 12, 1864 at White Oak Swamp, Virginia. Confined at Andersonville, Georgia. Released, March 1, 1865 at Wilmington, N.C. Mustered out June 27, 1865 at Annapolis, Maryland. Also bone as Plumb and as Clump. Prior service in Co. B, Twenty Seventh New York Volunteers.

KNAPP, JOHN— Age 40 years. Enlisted December 18, 1863 at Rochester, as Private, Co. I, to serve three years. Rejected.

KNIGHT, JOHN H.— Age 30 years. Enlisted February 12, 1864 at Rochester. Mustered in as Private, Co. M, February 23, 1864 to serve three years. Transferred to Co. K, no date given. Captured at Stony Creek, Virginia. Confined at Andersonville, Georgia. Released March 2, 1865. Mustered out June 17, 1865 as Saddler, at Annapolis, Maryland.

KNIGHT, WILLIAM— Age 24 years. Enlisted December 13, 1863 at Syracuse, as Private, Co. B, to serve three years. Rejected

KNOLLIER, THEODORE F.— Age 17 years. Enlisted December 17, 1863 at Cazenovia. Mustered in as Private, Co. E, January 10, 1864 to serve three years. No further record.

KOLEMAN, JOHN— Age 24 years. Enlisted April 11, 1865 at New York City. Mustered in as Private, "unassigned," April 11, 1865 to serve one year. Mustered out with detachment, May 6, 1865 at Hart's Island, New York Harbor.

KRUCHTEN, JOHN— Age 24 years. Enlisted February 15, 1864 at Bath. Mustered in as Private, Co. M, February 23, 1864 to serve three years. Transferred to Co. G, March 24, 1864. Discharged as paroled prisoner, June 9, 1865 at Elmira. Also borne as Krutzen. Prior service in Co. H, Twenty Seventh New York Volunteers.

KUNCE, SIMON— Age 22 years. Enlisted March 3, 1864 at Rochester. Mustered in as Private, "unassigned," March 8, 1864 to serve three years. No further record.

KUNTZ, SIMON— See Coons, Simon.

LABRASH, JAMES-Age 24 years. Enlisted February 15, 1864 at New York. Mustered in as Private, Co. M, February 23, 1864 to serve three years. No further record.

LACKEY, JAMES— Age 36 years. Enlisted February 22, 1865 at New York. Mustered in as Private, "unassigned," February 22, 1865 to serve three years. No further record.

LACY, JOHN— Age 25 years. Enlisted February 15, 1865 at New York City. Mustered in as Private, "unassigned," February 15, 1865 to serve three years. No further record.

LADD, ALANSON— Age 18 years. Enlisted November 23, 1863 at Rochester. Mustered in as Private, Co. F, January 10, 1864 to serve three years. Died September, 1864 at Andersonville, Georgia.

LADD, GEORGE— Age 35 years. Enlisted January 4, 1864 at Camillus. Mustered in as Private, Co. H, February 2, 1864 to serve three years. Mustered out with company, August 1, 1865 at Winchester, Virginia.

LAKE, HENRY— Age 28 years. Enlisted December 21, 1863 at Lyons. Mustered in as Private, Co. H, February 2, 1864 to serve three years. Mustered out July 8, 1865 at Washington, D.C. Also borne as Henry James Lake.

LAKE, JAMES S.— Age 20 years. Enlisted December 14, 1863 at Madison. Mustered in as Private, Co. E, January 10, 1864 to serve three years. Appointed Regimental Quartermaster Sergeant, January 10, 1864. Mustered out with regiment, August 1, 1865 at Winchester, Virginia. Commissioned First Lieutenant, and R.M.Q., July 31, 1865, with rank from May 15, 1865, vice Nellis, discharged, not mustered.

LAMB, WARREN W.— Age 23 years. Enlisted December 9, 1863 at Rochester. Mustered in as Private, "unassigned," December 12, 1863 to serve three years. Mustered in as Second Lieutenant, Co. I, February 12, 1864. Discharged for disability, September 8, 1864. Commissioned Second Lieutenant, March 30, 1864, with rank from January 29, 1864, original.

LAMBERT, HENRY— Age 35 years. Enlisted December 28, 1863 as Private, Co. D, at Rochester, to serve three years. Rejected.

LAMOTT, FRANCIS— Age 18 years. Enlisted as Private, Co. C, November 20, 1863 at Riga, to serve three years. Rejected.

LAMPHIER, CORNELIUS— Age 21 years. Enlisted December 26, 1863 at Elbridge. Mustered in as Private, Co. B, January 5, 1864 to serve three years. Transferred to Fourteenth Veteran Reserve Corps, date not stated, from which mustered out August 15, 1865 on surgeon's certificate of disability at U.S.A. General Hospital, Finley, Washington, D.C. Also borne as Lamper.

LANDON, ALBERT— Age 35 years. Enlisted as Private, Co. C, November 19, 1863 at Brockport, to serve three years. Rejected

LANE, HARRY O. B.— Age 19 years. Enlisted January 5, 1864 at New York. Mustered in as Private, "unassigned," January 5, 1864 to serve three years. No further record.

LANNING, BENJAMIN— Age 41 years. Enlisted as Private, Co. C, December 11, 1863 at Rome to serve three years. Rejected.

LANING, JOHN P.— Age 20 years. Enlisted December 8, 1863 at Rome. Mustered in as Private, Co. C, January 5, 1864 to serve three years. Deserted February 10, 1864 at Rochester.

LAPE, JOHN— Age 30 years. Enlisted November 27, 1863 at Arcadia. Mustered in as Wagoner, Co. H, February 2, 1864 to serve three years. Mustered out with company, August 1, 1865 at Winchester, Virginia. Prior service in Co. I, Seventeenth New York Volunteers.

LARCOM, WILLIAM R.— Age 18 years. Enlisted December 22, 1863 at Syracuse. Mustered in as Private, Co. B, January 5, 1864 to serve three years. Died of wounds, September 19, 1864, received at battle of Winchester. Also borne as Larkham.

LAREGAN, EDWARD— Age 22 years. Enlisted December 15, 1863 at Rochester. Mustered in as Private, Co. F, January 10, 1864 to serve three years. Deserted in February, 1864 near Rochester.

LARKIN, ANDREW J.— Age 18 years. Enlisted as Private, Co. H, January 24, 1864 at Syracuse, to serve three years. Rejected.

LARKIR, JAMES W.— Age 18 years. Enlisted December 17, 1863 at Rochester. Mustered in as Private, Co. C, January 5, 1864 to serve three years. Discharged, May 26, 1865 at Fredericksburg, Virginia.

LATHAM, CHARLES W.— Age 26 years. Enlisted February 24, 1864 at Pitcher. Mustered in as Private, Co. E, March 9, 1864 to serve three years. Mustered out with company, August 1, 1865 at Winchester, Virginia.

LAW, RUFUS H.— Age 24 years. Enlisted December 8, 1863 at Rochester. Mustered in as First Sergeant, Co. I, February 2, 1864 to serve three years. Transferred in July, 1864 to Second Battalion, Veteran Reserve Corps.

LAWLES, JAMES— Age 27 years. Enlisted January 27, 1864 at Rochester. Mustered in as Private, Co. I, February 2, 1864 to serve three years. Deserted in February, 1864 at Rochester, New York.

LAWLESS, SAMUEL A.— Age 27 years. Enlisted January 15, 1864 at Lyons. Mustered in as Private, Co. H, February 2, 1864 to serve three years. Deserted, (records of company lost)

LAWRENCE, DAVID— Age 24 years. Enlisted November 30, 1863 at Rochester. Mustered in as Corporal, Co. I, February 2, 1864 to serve three years. Mustered out May 19, 1865 while in Satterlee U.S. General Hospital, Philadelphia, Pa.

LAWSON, LEWIS— Age 25 years. Enlisted December 30, 1863 at Cazenovia, as Private, Co. E, to serve three years. Rejected.

LAYTON, DANIEL— Officer.

LEACH, JAMES P.— Age 21 years. Enlisted September 7, 1864 at Norwich. Mustered in as Private, Co. E, September 7, 1864 to serve one year. Mustered out June 6, 1865 at Winchester, Virginia.

LEAK, JAMES— Age 29 years. Enlisted December 9, 1863 at Riga. Mustered in as Private, Co. C, January 5, 1864 to serve three years. Appointed First Sergeant, date not stated. Mustered out with company, August 1, 1865 at Winchester, Virginia.

LEAKE, FREDERICK— Officer.

LEARD, GEORGE L.— Age 17 years. Enlisted January 14, 1864 at Rochester. Mustered in as Private, Co. I, February 2, 1864 to serve three years. Transferred to Co. M, March, 1864. Appointed Corporal, date not given. Deserted July 6, 1865 at Winchester, Virginia.

LEAVY, ALVAH H.— Age 20 years. Enlisted September 2, 1864 at Huron. Mustered in as Private, Co. H, September 3, 1864 to serve one year. Mustered out June 6, 1865 at Winchester, Virginia.

LEE, DWIGHT M.— Officer

LEE, JOHN F.— Age 17 years. Enlisted November 14, 1863 at Rochester. Mustered in as Private, Co. A, December 20, 1863 to serve three years. Deserted June 25, 1865 in the field, Virginia.

LEHNER, GEORGE— See Sehner, George,

LEIBENTHAL, HERMAN— Age 20 years. Enlisted April 7, 1865 at New York. Mustered in as Private, "unassigned," April 7, 1865 to serve one year. No further record.

LEONARD, ISAAC— Age 23 years. Enlisted January 29, 1864 at Rochester. Mustered in as Private, Co. I, February 2, 1864 to serve three years. Deserted in February, 1864 at Rochester, New York.

LEONARD, JOHN— Age 35 years. Enlisted April 6, 1865 at New York. Mustered in as Private, Co. C, April 6, 1865 to serve one year. Deserted, June 7, 1865 near Winchester, Virginia.

LEONARD, JOHN D.— Age 31 years. Enlisted December 12, 1863 at Rochester. Mustered in as Private, Co. D, January 10, 1864 to serve three years. Appointed Regimental Commissary Sergeant, date not stated. Reduced and transferred to Co. D, July 4, 1864. Mustered out August 9, 1865 at Rochester.

LEONARD, PETER— Age 36 years. Enlisted December 26, 1863 at Rochester. Mustered in as Private, Co. D, January 10, 1864 to serve three years. Deserted January 15, 1864

LEOSER, CHRISTOPHER— See Looser, Christopher.

LETTIS, JAMES— Age 32 years. Enlisted December 26, 1863 at Rochester. Mustered in as Private, Co. D, January 10, 1864 to serve three years. Discharged for disability, May 20, 1865 at Winchester, Virginia.

LEVINE, PAUL— Age 19 years. Enlisted August 9, 1864 at Annapolis, Ma. Mustered in as Private, Co. K, August 9, 1864 to serve three years. Deserted February 22, 1865 while on furlough at Potsdam, New York.

LEWIS, CHARLES H.— Age 19 years. Enlisted March 3, 1864 at Cherry Valley. Mustered in as Private, Co. E, March 9, 1864 to serve three years. Mustered out June 28, 1865 at Winchester, Virginia.

LEWIS, MILO— Age 38 years. Enlisted March 23, 1865 at New York. Mustered in as Private, Co. I, March 23, 1865 to serve three years. Mustered out July 21, 1865 at Harpers Ferry, Virginia. Also borne as Louis.

LEWRRY, ANTOINE— Age 29 years. Enlisted April 4, 1865 at Albany. Mustered in as Private, Co. L, April 4, 1865 to serve three years. Transferred to Co. G, June 2, 1865. Deserted, June 9, 1865. Also borne as Levory, Lenny, and Laury.

LIMBACHER, JOHN P.— Age 40 years. Enlisted April 7, 1865 at New York. Mustered in as Private, "unassigned," April 7, 1865 to serve one year. Mustered out July 14, 1865 from U.S. General Hospital, Cumberland, Maryland.

LINA, RALPH— Age 39 years. Enlisted February 21, 1865 at New York. Mustered in as Private, Co. H, February 21, 1865 to serve three years. Mustered out with company, August 1, 1865 at Winchester, Virginia.

LINDSEY, DARIUS— Age 21 years. Enlisted December 24, 1863 at Syracuse. Mustered in as Private, Co. B, January 5, 1864 to serve three years. Deserted, May 18, 1865 from Remount Camp, Maryland. Prior service in Co. H, Twenty Third New York Volunteers.

LINES, JOHN D.— Age 21 years. Enlisted as Private, Co. D, December 9, 1863 at Rochester, to serve three years. Rejected.

LIVINGSTON, FRANK— Age 29 years. Enlisted February 15, 1864 at Rochester. Mustered in as Private, Co. M, February 23, 1864 to serve three years. Transferred to Co. C, date not stated. Deserted, February 28, 1864 at Rochester.

LIVINGSTON, JOHN, F.— Age 24 years. Enlisted November 20, 1863 at Rochester. Mustered in ass Sergeant, Co. F, January 10, 1864 to serve three years. Deserted February, 1864 from camp near Rochester.

LLOYD, EDWIN R.— Age 26 years. Enlisted February 21, 1865 at New York. Mustered in as Private, Co. C, February 21, 1865 to serve three years. Mustered out July 21, 1865 at Harper's Ferry, Virginia.

LLOYD, HARLAN P.— Officer

LOCKWOOD, DANIEL— Age 26 years. Enlisted December 24, 1863 at Cuba. Mustered in as Private, Co. K, February 6, 1864 to serve three years. Mustered out June 8, 1865 from Jarvis General Hospital, Baltimore, Maryland.

LOCKWOOD, GEORGE W.— Age 19 years. Enlisted November 23, 1863 at Lyndon. Mustered in as Private, Co. D, January 10, 1864 to serve three years. Transferred to Co. K, May 4, 1864. Deserted June 12, 1865 while on detached service at Howitzer Battery K, First United States Artillery.

LOCKWOOD, LEBBENS D.— Age 18 years. Enlisted November 28, 1863 at Urbana. Mustered in as Bugler, Co. G, February 2, 1864 to serve three years. Died, date not stated.

LOCKWOOD, WILLIAM B.— Age 20 years. Enlisted April 4, 1865 at Albany. Mustered in as Private, "unassigned," April 4, 1865 to serve three years. Mustered out September 25, 1865 at Rochester.

LOFTUS, PATRICK-Age 31 years. Enlisted March 8, 1865 at New York. Mustered in as Private, "unassigned," March 8, 1865 to serve two years. No further record.-

LOHMAN, ALBERT— Age 19 years. Enlisted March 2, 1865 at New York. Mustered in as Private, Co. G, March 2, 1865 to serve three years. Mustered out with company, August 1, 1865 at Winchester, Virginia.

LOOMIS, EDWIN J.— Age 19 years. Enlisted January 4, 1864 at Norwich. Mustered in as Private, Co. L, February 12, 1864 to serve three years. Absent, sick in hospital on muster out of company, August 1, 1865. No discharge furnished. No further record.

LOOSER, CHRISTOPHER— Commissioned First Lieutenant, June 29, 1865 with rank from June 1, 1865, vice Peck, promoted; not mustered. Also borne as Leoser.

LORD, HERBERT— Age 20 years. Enlisted December 24, 1863 at Manlius. Mustered in as Sergeant, Co. E, January 10, 1864 to serve three years. Mustered in as Second Lieutenant, Co. H, to date March 24, 1865. Mustered out with company, August 1, 1865 at Winchester, Virginia. Prior service in First Wisconsin Cavalry. Commissioned Second Lieutenant, March 21, 1865 with rank from January 24, 1865.

LOSEY, JESSE B.— Officer

LOUCKS, MORRIS B.— Age 22 years. Enlisted December 30, 1863 at Avoca. Mustered in as Private, Co. G, February 2, 1864 to serve three years. Died, date not stated.

LOUIS, ARTHUR— Age 20 years. Enlisted as Private, Co. F, November 11, 1863 at Barre, to serve three years. Rejected.

LOW, CHARLES— Age 19 years. Enlisted December 4, 1863 at Utica. Mustered in as Private, Co. M, February 23, 1864 to serve three years. Transferred to Co. B, March 24, 1864. Mustered out with company, August 1, 1865 at Winchester, Virginia.

LOWE, JOHN— Age 40 years. Enlisted December 14, 1863 at Syracuse. Mustered in as Private, Co. B, January 5, 1864 to serve three years. Mustered out with company, August 1, 1865 at Winchester, Virginia.

LOWERY, GEORGE— Age 23 years. Enlisted January 15, 1864 at Rochester. Mustered in as Private, Co. K, February 6, 1864 to serve three years. Deserted, February 9, 1864 at Rochester, New York.

LOWRY, WILLIAM— Age 18 years. Enlisted December 29, 1863 at Smithfield. Mustered in as Private, Co. E, January 10, 1864 to serve three years. Mustered out June 28, 1865 at Winchester, Virginia. Also borne as Lerroy.

LOZEAR, ALFRED— Age 22 years. Enlisted January 27, 1864 at Middlefield. Mustered in as Corporal, Co. L, February 12, 1864 to serve three years. Deserted March 1, 1864 at Rochester, New York.

LUKE, HENRY— Age 22 years. Enlisted December 12, 1863 at Lyons. Mustered in as Private, Co. F, February 2, 1864 to serve three years. Mustered out July 13, 1865.

LUSK, LYCURGUS D.— Officer.

LUTZ, CHRISTIAN— Age 27 years. Enlisted April 6, 1865 at New York. Mustered in as Private, Co. L, April 6, 1865 to serve one year. Mustered out with company, August 1, 1865 at Winchester, Virginia.

LYNCH, LAWRENCE— Age 18 years. Enlisted April 4, 1865 at Albany. Mustered in as Private, Co. A, April 4, 1865 to serve three years. Mustered out with company, August 1, 1865 at Winchester, Virginia.

LYONS, THOMAS— Age 21 years. Enlisted April 11, 1865 at Syracuse. Mustered in as Private, Co. F, April 11, 1865 to serve three years. Mustered out with company, August 1, 1865 at Winchester, Virginia.

MACK, EDWARD— Age 18 years. Enlisted November 30, 1863 at Syracuse. Mustered in as Private, Co. B, January 5, 1864 to serve three years. Mustered out with company, August 1, 1865 at Winchester, Virginia.

MACK, JAMES— Age 23 years. Enlisted December 31, 1863 at Portland. Mustered in as Corporal, Co. K, February 6, 1864 to serve three years. Deserted June 14, 1865 at Bottom Bridge, Virginia.

MACK, JOHN— Age 39 years. Enlisted as Private, Co. H, January 18, 1864 at Syracuse, to serve three years. Rejected.

MACKEY, MARTIN— Age 20 years. Enlisted January 4, 1864 at Syracuse. Mustered in as Private, Co. E, January 10, 1864 to serve three years. Deserted January 13, 1864 at Rochester, New York. Also borne as McKay.

MAHONEY, MICHAEL— Age 31 years. Enlisted December 31, 1863 at Poolville. Mustered in as Private, Co. F, January 10, 1864 to serve three years. Mustered out with company, August 1, 1865 at Winchester, Virginia.

MAHONEY, MICHAEL— Age 40 years. Enlisted February 22, 1865 at New York. Mustered in as Private, Co. H, February 22, 1865 to serve three years. Mustered out with company, August 1, 1865 at Winchester, Virginia.

MAIN, NELSON C.— Age 19 years. Enlisted January 4, 1864 at Norwich. Mustered in as Saddler, Co. L, February 12, 1864 to serve three years. Died, date not known, while a prisoner at Andersonville, Georgia.

MAKER, HIRAM— Age 28 years. Enlisted as Private, Co. H, January 5, 1864 at Huron, to serve three years. Rejected.

MALEY, JAMES— Age 22 years. Enlisted January 4, 1864 at OtisCo. Mustered in as Sergeant, Co. E, January 10, 1864 to serve three years. Reduced, date not stated. Deserted, January 13, 1864 at Rochester, New York.

MALLORY, CHARLES— Age 21 years. Enlisted April 12, 1865 at Brooklyn. Mustered in as Private, "unassigned," April 12, 1865 to serve three years. Mustered out with detachment, May 6, 1865 at Hart's Island, New York Harbor.

MALOY, MICHAEL— Age 18 years. Enlisted December 14, 1863 at Syracuse. Mustered in as Private, Co. B, January 5, 1864 to serve three years. Mustered out with company, August 1, 1865 at Winchester, Virginia.

MANCHESTER, JOSEPH— Age 27 years. Enlisted November 27, 1863 at Arcadia. Mustered in as Corporal, Co. H, February 2, 1864 to serve three years. Reduced, date not stated. Mustered out with company, August 1, 1865 at Winchester, Virginia. Prior service in Co. I, Seventeenth New York Infantry.

MANCHESTER, MARTIN A.— Age 20 years. Enlisted December 24, 1863 at Madison. Mustered in as Private, Co. E, January 10, 1864 to serve three years. Mustered out with company, August 1, 1865 at Winchester, Virginia.

MANDEVILLE, LUCIUS N.— Age 19 years. Enlisted August 3, 1864 at Rochester. Mustered in as Private, Co. A, August 3, 1864 to serve one year. Mustered out June 6, 1865 at Winchester, Virginia.

MANDEVILLE, NEWTON J.— Age 21 years. Enlisted December 31, 1863 at Rochester. Mustered in as Private, Co. C, January 5, 1864 to serve three years. Transferred to Co. A, March 22, 1864, to Co. H, April 8, 1865. Appointed Sergeant, date not stated. Discharged, date not known, records of company lost.

MANSHARDT, MICHAEL— Age 20 years. Enlisted April 13, 1865 at New York. Mustered in as Private, "unassigned," April 13, 1865 to serve one year. Mustered out with detachment, May 6, 1865 at Hart's Island, New York Harbor.

MANZER, HERMAN— Age 23 years. Enlisted January 25, 1864 at Syracuse. Mustered in as Private, Co. I, February 2, 1864 to serve three years. Transferred to Co. E, in March, 1864. Appointed Sergeant, date not stated. Transferred to Veteran Reserve Corps, September 1, 1864. Also borne as Mencer

MARCH, GEORGE— See Murch, George.

MARCH, HAMILTON— Age 23 years. Enlisted December 30, 1863 at Avoca. Mustered in as Sergeant, Co. G, February 2, 1864 to serve three years. Appointed First Sergeant, June 28, 1865. Mustered out with company, August 1, 1865 at Winchester, Virginia.

MARCH, HAMILTON— Age 19 years. Enlisted January 4, 1864 at Norwich. Mustered in as Teamster, Co. L, February 12, 1864 to serve three years. Mustered out with company as Wagoner, August 1, 1865 at Winchester, Virginia.

MARSH, ISAAC B.— Age 20 years. Enlisted December 29, 1863 at Smyrna. Mustered in as Private, Co. E, January 10, 1864 to serve three years. Deserted February 22, 1864 at Rochester, New York.

MARSH, JEROME D.— Age 23 years. Enlisted December 23, 1863 at Smithfield. Mustered in as Private, Co. E, January 4, 1864 to serve three years. Died, date not stated, at Andersonville, Georgia.

MARSH, LEWIS— Age 38 years. Enlisted as Private, Co. F, December 10, 1863 at Rochester, to serve three years. Rejected.

MARTIN, ARTEMUS— Age 36 years. Enlisted as Private, Co. E, December 30, 1863 at Cazenovia, to serve three years. Rejected.

MARTIN, GEORGE— Age 21 years. Enlisted November 24, 1863 at Syracuse. Mustered in as Private, Co. B, January 5, 1864 to serve three years. Deserted October 25, 1864 from Remount Camp, Giesboro Point, Maryland. Prior service in Co. D, Twenty Sixth New York Infantry.

MARTIN, HIRAM— Age 33 years. Enlisted March 29, 1865 at Rochester. Mustered in as Private, "unassigned," March 29, 1865 to serve three years. No further record.

MARTIN, JOHN— Age 39 years. Drafted at Lockport. Mustered in as Private, "unassigned," February 27, 1865 to serve one year. Mustered out with detachment, May 9, 1865 at Elmira, New York.

MARTIN, KERON— Age 18 years. Enlisted January 6, 1864 at Avon. Mustered in as Private, Co. D, January 10, 1864 to serve three years. Captured, June 30, 1864. No further record.

MARTIN, WILLIAM— Age 19 years. Enlisted as Private, Co. D, November 26, 1863 at Rochester, to serve three years. Rejected.

MASON, JEAN BAPTIST— Age 28 years. Enlisted December 1, 1863 at Rochester. Mustered in as Private, Co. F, January 10, 1864 to serve three years. Deserted in February, 1864 from camp near Rochester, New York.

MASON, WILLIAM A.— Age 42 years. Enlisted as Private, Co. C, December 21, 1863 at Rome to serve three years. Rejected.

MATER, JACOB— Age 23 years. Enlisted March 4, 1865 at Westfield. Mustered in as Private, "unassigned," March 4, 1865 to serve one year. No further record.

MATHEWS, ANDREW— Age 24 years. Enlisted December 19, 1864 at New York. Mustered in as Private, Co. B, December 19, 1864 to serve three years. Mustered out with company, August 1, 1865 at Winchester, Virginia.

MATHEWS ANTHONY— Age 24 years. Enlisted December 12, 1864 at New York. Mustered in as Private, "unassigned," December 12, 1864 to serve three years. No further record.

MAXWELL, HENRY— Age 18 years. Enlisted as Private, Co. M, February 20, 1864 at Rochester, to serve three years. Rejected.

MAXWELL, JOHN G.— Age 44 years. Enlisted as Private, Co. E, December 3, 1863 at Rochester, to serve three years. Rejected.

MAXWELL, JOHN R.— Age 19 years. Enlisted February 28, 1865 at New York. Mustered in as Private, Co. B, February 28, 1865 to serve one year. Absent sick at time company was mustered out, August 1, 1865. No further record.

MAY, ROBERT— Age 19 years. Enlisted as Private, Co. C, December 1, 1863 at Brockport, to serve three years. Rejected.

MAYHEW, MARTIN— Age 19 years. Enlisted March 29, 1865 at New York. Mustered in as Private, "unassigned," March 29, 1865 to serve one year. No further record.

McARTHUR, HENRY— Age 19 years. Enlisted November 10, 1863 at Rochester. Mustered in as Commissary Sergeant, Co. A, December 20, 1863 to serve three years. Reduced, date not stated. Mustered out with company, August 1, 1865 at Winchester, Virginia.

McCABE, JOHN— Age 20 years. Enlisted October 3, 1864 at Jamaica. Mustered in as Private, Co. M, October 3, 1864 to serve one year. Captured, November 12, 1864. No further record.

McCABE, MICHAEL— Age 18 years. Enlisted January 28, 1864 at Walton. Mustered in as Private, "unassigned," February 29, 1864 to serve three years. No further record.

McCARRACK, JOHN— Age 42 years. Enlisted December 11, 1863 at Rome. Mustered in as Saddler, Co. C, January 5, 1864 to serve three years. Mustered out with company, August 1, 1865 at Winchester, Virginia.

McCARTHY, FLORENCE— Age 24 years. Enlisted December 9, 1863 at Rochester. Mustered in as Sergeant, Co. D, January 10, 1864 to serve three years. Appointed First Sergeant, date not stated. Killed in action, September 22, 1864 at Luray Valley, Virginia. Prior service in Co. K, Thirteenth New York Infantry.

McCARTHY, JOHN— Age 20 years. Enlisted January 28, 1864 at Rochester. Mustered in as Private, Co. K, February 6, 1864 to serve three years. Transferred to Co. M, March 25, 1864. No further record.

McCARTHY, PATRICK— Age 18 years. Enlisted January 14, 1864 at Rochester. Mustered in as Private, Co. K, February 6, 1864 to serve three years. Deserted February 16, 1864 at Rochester, New York.

McCASNELL, CHARLES— See McConnell, Charles.

McCAULEY, JAMES-Age 18 years. Enlisted April 12, 1865 at Schenectady. Mustered in as Private, "unassigned," April 12, 1865 to serve one year. Mustered out with detachment, May 6, 1865 at Hart's Island, New York Harbor.

McCAULEY, JOHN— Age 22 years. Enlisted December 15, 1863 at Rochester. Mustered in as Private, Co. F, January 10, 1864 to serve three years. Deserted in February, 1864 from camp near Rochester, New York.

McCAUSEY, JAMES— Age 18 years. Enlisted February 1, 1864 at Syracuse. Mustered in as Private, Co. K, February 6, 1864 to serve three years. Transferred to Co. B, March 25, 1864. Discharged to date May 29, 1865 at United States General Hospital, Cumberland, Maryland.

McCOY, DONALD— Age 29 years. Enlisted March 13, 1865 at New York. Mustered in as Private, "unassigned," March 13, 1865 to served one year. No further record.

McCAY, JOSEPH A.— See McKay, Joseph A.

McCAY, WILLIAM, E.— Age 27 years. Enlisted November 26, 1863 at Rochester. Mustered in as Private, Co. F, January 10, 1864 to serve three years. Deserted in February 1864 from camp near Rochester, New York.

McCHESSNEY, WM. W.— Age 19 years. Enlisted as Private, Co. M, February 16, 1864 at Bath to serve three years. Rejected.

McCOLLUM, FRANK— Age 18 years. Enlisted September 1, 1864 at Norwich. Mustered in as Private. Co. F, September 3, 1864 to serve one year. Mustered out June 6, 1865 at Winchester, Virginia.

McCONEY, PHILANDER— Age 28 years. Enlisted November 30, 1863 at Syracuse. Mustered as Trumpeter, Co. B, January 5, 1864 to serve three years. Discharged June 29, 1865 at United States General Hospital, York, Pa. Prior service in Co. H, One Hundred and Seventy Sixth New York Infantry.

McCONNELL, CHARLES— Age 21 years. Enlisted December 15, 1863 at Rochester. Mustered in as Private, Co. F, January 10, 1864 to serve three years. Deserted in February, 1864 from camp near Rochester, New York. Also borne as McCasnell.

McCORMICK, ALBERT— Age 20 years. Enlisted December 16, 1863 at Rochester. Mustered in as Private, Co. F, January 10, 1864 to serve three years. Deserted in February 1864 from camp near Rochester, New York.

McCORMICK, RICHARD— Age 19 years. Enlisted December 21, 1863 at Rochester. Mustered in as Private, Co. D, January 10, 1864 to serve three years. Mustered out with company, August 1, 1865 at Winchester, Virginia.

McCOY, JOHN— Age 23 years. Enlisted December 3, 1864 at New York. Mustered in as Private, Co. I, December 3, 1864 to serve three years. Mustered out July 11, 1865 at United States General Hospital, Cumberland, Maryland.

McCUEN, AMBROSE S.— Age 22 years. Enlisted December 23, 1864 at Palmyra. Mustered in as Corporal, Co. H, February 2, 1864 to serve three years. Appointed Sergeant, date not stated. Mustered out with company, August 1, 1865 at Winchester, Virginia. Prior service in Co. I, Seventeenth New York Infantry.

McCUEN, MILES— See McQueen, Miles.

McCULLOUGH, SAMUEL— Age 43 years. Enlisted March 2, 1865 at Tompkinsville. Mustered in as Private, "unassigned," March 2, 1865 to serve three years. No further record.

McDERMOTT, JAMES— Age 21 years. Enlisted December 17, 1863 at Rochester. Mustered in as Private, Co. A, December 20, 1863 to serve three years. Deserted December 20, 1864 in the field.

McDERMOTT, JOHN— Age 24 years. Enlisted March 28, 1865 at New York. Mustered in as Private, "unassigned," March 28, 1865 to serve three years. No further record.

McDERMOTT, PATRICK— Age 24 years. Enlisted March 13, 1865 at New York. Mustered in as Private, "unassigned," March 13, 1865 to serve three years. No further record.

McDERMOTT, THOMAS— Age 21 years. Enlisted December 15, 1863 at Rochester. Mustered in as Private, Co. F, January 10, 1864 to serve three years. Deserted in February, 1864 from camp near Rochester, New York.

McDONALD, JOHN— Age 43 years. Enlisted as Private, Co. F, December 14, 1863 at Rochester, to serve three years. Rejected.

McDONALD, KENNETH— Age 30 years. Enlisted November 27, 1863 at Rochester. Mustered in as Private, Co. A, December 20, 1863 to serve three years. Mustered out with company, August 1, 1865 at Winchester, Virginia.

McDONOUGH, JAMES— Age 29 years. Enlisted February 16, 1865 at New York. Mustered on as Private, Co. A, February 16, 1865 to serve one year. Deserted July 24, 1865 at Remount Camp, Virginia.

McGIBBON, ALEXANDER— Age 27 years. Enlisted as Private Co. F, December 1, 1863 at Rochester, to serve three years. Rejected.

McGINNIS, ROBERT— Age 22 years. Enlisted December 24, 1863 at Rochester. Mustered in as Private, Co. D, January 10, 1864 to serve three years. No further record.

McGOVERN, CHARLES— Age 18 years. Enlisted March 11, 1865 at Andes. Mustered in as Private, Co. K, March 11, 1865 to serve three years. Mustered out with company, August 1, 1865 at Winchester, Virginia.

McGOWAN, PATRICK— Age 20 years. Enlisted as Private, Co. K, January 15 1864 at Rochester, to serve three years. Rejected.

McGRATH, WILLIAM— Age 25 years. Enlisted March 28, 1865 at New York. Mustered in as Private, Co. I, March 28, 1865 to serve three years. Never joined the service, no discharge furnished.

McGRAW, DANIEL— Age 22 years. Enlisted December 22, 1863 at Auburn. Mustered in as Private, Co. M, February 23, 1864 to serve three years. Transferred to Co. I, March 28, 1864. Mustered out with company, August 1, 1865 at Winchester, Virginia.

McGRAW, JAMES— Age 20 years. Enlisted December 21, 1863 at Auburn. Mustered in as Private, Co. M, February 23, 1864 to serve three years. Transferred to Co. I, March 28, 1864. Appointed Commissary Sergeant, April 30, 1865.

Mustered out with company, August 1, 1865 at Winchester, Virginia. Prior service in Co. K, Thirty Third New York Infantry.

McGRAW, WM. H.— Age 18 years. Enlisted December 19, 1863 at DeRuyter. Mustered in as Private, Co. E, January 10, 1864 to serve three years. Mustered out with company, August 1, 1865 at Winchester, Virginia.

McGUIRE, GEORGE— Age 18 years. Enlisted as Private, Co. I, January 21, 1864 at Rochester to serve three years. Rejected.

McGUIRE, JAMES— Age 20 years. Enlisted February 17, 1865 at New York. Mustered in as Private, Co. M, February 17, 1865 to serve three years. Deserted June 23, 1865 from camp near Winchester, Virginia.

McGUIRE, JOHN— Age 22 years. Enlisted March 25, 1865 at Rochester. Mustered in as Private, "unassigned," March 25, 1865 to serve three years. No further record.

McGUIRE, PETER— Age 28 years. Enlisted February 17, 1865 at New York. Mustered in as Private, Co. I, February 17, 1865 to serve three years. Never joined the service, no discharge furnished.

McINTYRE, THOMAS— Age 23 years. Enlisted January 23, 1864 at Verona. Mustered in as Private, "unassigned," January 23, 1864 to serve three years. No further record.

McKAY, JOSEPH A.— Age 18 years. Enlisted December 1, 1863 at Rochester. Mustered in as Private, Co. D, January 10, 1864 to serve three years. Absent sick at time company was mustered out, August 1, 1865. No further record. Also borne as McCay.

McKAY, ROBERT JR.— Age 18 years. Enlisted October 3, 1864 at Jamaica. Mustered in as Private, Co. M, October 3, 1864 to serve one year. Mustered out with company, August 1, 1865 at Winchester, Virginia. Also borne as Robert McKee

McKEY, MARTIN— See Mackey, Martin.

McKINLEY, JOHN— Age 21 years. Enlisted November 24, 1863 at Syracuse. Mustered in as Private, Co. B, January 5, 1864 to serve three years. Appointed Corporal, date not stated. Discharged November 19, 1864 to accept promotion as Second Lieutenant, Twenty Eighth Regiment, United States Colored Infantry.

McKINNON, DONALD— Age 21 years. Enlisted April 6, 1865 at New York. Mustered in as Private, Co. E, April 6, 1865 to serve one year. Mustered out with company, August 1, 1865 at Winchester, Virginia.

McLARREN, ANDREW H.— Age 34 years. Enlisted March 17, 1864 at Victor. Mustered in as Private, "unassigned," March 17, 1864 to serve three years. No further record.

McLENNAN, ANDREW— Age 28 years. Enlisted March 17, 1864 at Rochester. Mustered in as Private, Co. M, March 9, 1864 to serve three years. Died September 1864 while a prisoner at Andersonville, Georgia.

McLENNAN, PETER— Officer.

McMANNIS, JOHN L.— Age 24 years. Enlisted December 22, 1863 at Rochester. Mustered in as Corporal, Co. D, January 10, 1864, to serve three years. Captured July 5, 1864 at Nottoway Bridge. Confined at Charleston, S.C. Released March 1, 1865 at N.E Bridge, N.C. Mustered out June 28, 1865 at Annapolis, Maryland.

McMULLEN, JAMES— Age 33 years. Enlisted March 2, 1864 at Lyme. Mustered in as Private, "unassigned," March 2, 1864 to serve three years. No further record.

McMULLEN, MICHAEL— Officer

McNANY, PATRICK— Age 23 years. Enlisted December 31, 1863 at Auburn. Mustered in as Private, Co. M, February 23, 1863 to serve three years. Transferred to Co. I, March 28, 1864. Mustered out June 13, 1865 at Washington, D.C. Also borne as McManey.

McNINCH, ROBERT P.— Age 21 years. Enlisted February 15, 1865 at Lima. Mustered in as Private, Co. C, February 15, 1865 to serve three years. Absent sick in hospital at time company was mustered out, August 1, 1865 at Winchester, Virginia. Also borne as McCuen.

McQUEEN, MILES— Age 18 years. Enlisted March 20, 1865 at Rochester. Mustered in as Private, Co. F, March 20, 1865 to serve three years. Transferred to Co. G, May 27, 1865. Mustered out with company, August 1, 1865 at Winchester, Virginia.

McSHANE, PATRICK— Officer

McSORLEY, CHARLES— Age 22 years. Enlisted November 26, 1864 at New York. Mustered in as Private, Co. M, November 26, 1864 to serve three years. Mustered out with company, August 1, 1865 at Winchester, Virginia.

MEAD, VOLNEY— Age 31 years. Enlisted November 30, 1863 at Rochester. Mustered in as Private, Co. I, February 2, 1864 to serve three years. In confinement for desertion at time company was mustered out August 1, 1865. No further record.

MECHAM, NELSON J.— Age 25 years. Enlisted December 11, 1863 at Utica. Mustered in as Farrier, Co. B, January 5, 1864 to serve three years. Mustered out with company, August 1, 1865 at Winchester, Virginia. Also borne as Meachem.

MELAY, OWEN— Age 24 years. Enlisted March 13, 1865 at New York. Mustered in as Private, "unassigned," March 13, 1865 to serve three years. No further record.

MEILIKE, CARL— Age 36 years. Enlisted December 8, 1863 at Rochester. Mustered in as Private, Co. B, January 5, 1864 to serve three years. Appointed Corporal, March 1, 1865. Mustered out with company, August 1, 1865 at Winchester, Virginia. Also borne as Charles Meilike and Charles W. Merlike.

MENCER, HERMAN— See Manzer, Herman.

MERCER, RICHARD— Age 20 years. Enlisted March 29, 1865 at Rochester. Mustered in as Private, "unassigned," March 29, 1865 to serve three years. No further record.

MERGAWICK, CYRACK— Age — years. Enlisted March 16, 1865 at New York. Mustered in as Private, Co. C, March 16, 1865 to serve one year. Absent sick in hospital at time company was mustered out, August 1, 1865. No further record.

MERLIKE, CHARLES W.— See Meilike, Carl.

MERNIN, PATRICK— Age 18 years. Enlisted April 4, 1865 at New York. Mustered in as Private, Co. F, April 4, 1865 to serve one year. Mustered out with company, August 1, 1865 at Winchester, Virginia.

MERRIAM, IRVING— Age 21 years. Enlisted January 5, 1864 at Plymouth. Mustered in as Private, Co. L, February 12, 1864 to serve three years. Appointed Corporal, date not stated. Died August 23, 1864 while a prisoner at Andersonville, Georgia.

MERRILL, EDMUND W.— Age 21 years. Enlisted December 30, 1863 at Huron. Mustered in as Sergeant, Co. H, February 2, 1864 to serve three years. Transferred to Co. F, date not known, reduced, date not stated. Transferred to First Company Second Battalion, Veteran Reserve Corps, by P.M.G., November 4, 1864 from which discharged as Sergeant, July 24, 1865 at Washington, D.C. Also borne as Merville, Edward.

MERRILL, SYLVESTER— Age 18 years. Enlisted as Private, Co. H, January 18, 1864 at Rochester, to serve three years. Deserted previous to muster in of company, February 2, 1864.

METCALF, BENJAMIN— Age 38 years. Enlisted December 31, 1863 at Smithfield. Mustered in as Private, Co. K, February 6, 1864 to serve three years. Transferred to Co. H, March 25, 1864. Mustered out with detachment, June 15, 1865 at Jarvis United States Army General Hospital, Baltimore, Maryland.

MEYER, MORRIS— Age 19 years. Enlisted April 12, 1865 at New York. Mustered in as Private, "unassigned," April 12, 1865 to serve one year. Mustered out with detachment, May 6, 1865 at Hart's Island, New York Harbor.

MEYERS, JOSEPH— Age 19 years. Enlisted December 15, 1863 at Rochester. Mustered in as Private, Co. D, January 10, 1864 to serve three years. Mustered out with company, August 1, 1865 at Winchester, Virginia.

MEYERS, PETER T.— Age 21 years. Enlisted April 8, 1865 at Rochester. Mustered in as Private, Co. F, April 8, 1865 to serve three years. Mustered out with company, August 1, 1865 at Winchester, Virginia. Also borne as Peter Meyers.

MILBORYNE, JOSEPH— Age 21 years. Enlisted January 27, 1864 at Syracuse. Mustered in as Private, Co. I, February 2, 1864 to serve three years. Transferred to Co. E. in March 1864. Appointed Corporal, date not stated. Mustered out with company, August 1, 1865 at Winchester, Virginia. Also borne as Mybbyre and Milbyere. Prior service in Co. D, Third New York Infantry.

MILES, THEODORE J.— Age 18 years. Enlisted December 28, 1863 at Fabius. Mustered in as Private, Co. B, January 5, 1864 to serve three years. Mustered out with company, August 1, 1865 at Winchester, Virginia.

MILLER, GEORGE— Age 26 years. Enlisted April 8, 1865 at Syracuse. Mustered in as Private, Co. F, April 8, 1865 to serve three years. Mustered out with company, August 1, 1865 at Winchester, Virginia.

MILLER, GOTTLIER— Age 33 years. Enlisted February 20, 1865 at New York. Mustered in as Private, Co. H, February 20, 1865 to serve three years. Mustered out with company, August 1, 1865 at Winchester, Virginia.

MILLER, HIRAM— Age 25 years. Enlisted as Private, Co. I, November 27, 1863 at Rochester, to serve three years. Rejected.

MILLER, JOHN H.— Age 18 years. Enlisted November 30, 1863 at Brockport. Mustered in as Private, Co. C, January 5, 1864 to serve three years. Mustered out with company, August 1, 1865 at Winchester, Virginia. Also borne as John Miller

MILLER, MOSES— Age 22 years. Enlisted February 28, 1865 at Plattsburg. Mustered in as Private, Co. K, February 28, 1865 to serve one year. Mustered out with company, August 1, 1865 at Winchester, Virginia.

MILLMAN, GARDINER— Age 38 years. Enlisted December 31, 1863 at Rochester. Mustered in as Private, Co. B, January 5, 1864 to serve three years. Captured June 28, 1864 on Wilson Raid. Died as Farrier, September 7, 1864 while a prisoner at Andersonville, Georgia.

MILLS, JOHN— Age 35 years. Enlisted December 13, 1864 at New York. Mustered in as Private, Co. B, December 13, 1864 to serve three years. Mustered out with company, August 1, 1865 at Winchester, Virginia.

MILLS, RICEWICK— Age 21 years. Enlisted January 21, 1864 at Cazenovia. Mustered in as Private, Co. L, February 12, 1864 to serve three years. Absent sick in hospital at time of muster out of company. August 1, 1865. No further record.

MINOCH, WILLIAM— Age 21 years. Enlisted as Private, Co. D, December 24, 1863 at Rochester, to serve three years. Rejected.

MINOT, BARTLETT— Age 18 years. Enlisted November 13, 1863 at Brockport. Mustered in as Trumpeter, Co. C, January 5, 1864 to serve three years. Mustered out with company, August 1, 1865 at Winchester, Virginia.

MIRCH, HIRAM— Age 20 years. Enlisted November 25, 1863 at Brockport. Mustered in as Private, Co. C, January 5, 1864 to serve three years. Deserted, August 25, 1864 at Camp Stoneman, D.C.

MITCHELL, THOMAS— Age 23 years. Enlisted December 11, 1863 at Wayne. Mustered in as Private, Co. G, February 2, 1864 to serve three years. Died, date and place not stated.

MITCHELL, WILLIAM— Age 18 years. Enlisted as Private, Co. M, January 5, 1864, at Dunkirk to serve three years. Rejected.

MITCHELL, WILLIAM— Age 18 years. Enlisted March 6, 1864 at Bath. Mustered in as Private, Co. K, March 6, 1864 to serve three years. Mustered out with company, August 1, 1865 at Winchester, Virginia.

MOAT, WILLIAM— Age 23 years. Enlisted March 2, 1865 at New York. Mustered in as Private, Co. K, March 2, 1865 to serve one year. Mustered out with company, August 1, 1865 at Winchester, Virginia.

MONAHAN, THOMAS— Age 20 years. Enlisted January 5, 1864 at Oneida. Mustered in as Corporal, Co. K, February 6, 1864 to serve three years. Reduced, date not stated. Deserted, November 12, 1864 while on furlough to Oneida, New York.

MONCKTON, WILLIAM A.— Age 19 years. Enlisted March 9, 1865 at New York. Mustered in as Private, Co. I, March 9, 1865 to serve two years. Mustered out with company, August 1, 1865 at Winchester, Virginia.

MONK, EDWARD— Age — years. Enlisted September 9, 1864 at Albany. Mustered in as Private, Co. I, September 9, 1864 to serve one year. Captured March 23, 1865 at Goldsboro, N.C. Released April 2, 1865 at Aikens Landing, Virginia. Mustered out June 26, 1865 at Annapolis, Maryland.

MONROE, ANDREW J.— Age 27 years. Enlisted December 14, 1863 at Bath. Mustered in as Private, Co. G, February 2, 1864 to serve three years. Died, date and place not stated.

MONROE, CORNELIUS— Age 26 years. Enlisted December 4, 1864 at Riga. Mustered in as Private, Co. C, January 5, 1864 to serve three years. Appointed Commissary Sergeant, date not stated. Mustered out with company, August 1, 1865 at Winchester, Virginia.

MONTGOMERY, FRANK— Age 22 years. Enlisted April 10, 1865 at Rochester. Mustered in as Private, "unassigned," April 10, 1865 to serve three years. Mustered out with detachment, May 9, 1865 at Elmira, New York.

MOOCHLER, JOHN— Age 24 years. Enlisted December 18, 1863 at Cazenovia. Mustered in as Corporal, Co. E, January 10, 1864 to serve three years. Died, date not stated, while a prisoner at Andersonville, Georgia. Also borne as Muchner. Prior service in Co. H, Thirty Fifth New York Infantry.

MOODY, JOHN P.— Age 25 years. Enlisted March 13, 1865 at Fishkill. Mustered in as Private, Co. I, March 13, 1865 to serve three years. Mustered out with company, August 1, 1865 at Winchester, Virginia.

MOON, JACOB— Age 24 years. Enlisted September 14, 1864 at Coventry. Mustered in as Private, "unassigned," September 15, 1864 to serve one year. No further record.

MOON, SETH— Age 35 years. Enlisted December 31, 1863 at Smithfield. Mustered in as Private, Co. H, February 2, 1864 to serve three years. Mustered out with company, August 1, 1865 at Winchester, Virginia.

MOORA, HENRY L.— Age 22 years. Enlisted January 4, 1864 at bath. Mustered in as Corporal, Co. G, February 2, 1864 to serve three years. Appointed Sergeant, April 25, 1865. Mustered out with company, August 1, 1865 at Winchester, Virginia. Prior service in Co. A, Twenty Third New York Infantry.

MOORE, ABNER— (Colored) Age 33 years. Enlisted January 14, 1864 at Rochester. Mustered in as Cook, Co. I, February 2, 1864 to serve three years. No further record.

MOORE, ABRAM— Age 17 years. Enlisted March 2, 1864 at Delhi. Mustered in as Private, Co. I, March 31, 1864 to serve three years. Mustered out with company, August 1, 1865 at Winchester, Virginia.

MOORE, ARA— Age 18 years. Enlisted December 19, 1863 at Cazenovia. Mustered in as Trumpeter, Co. E, January 10, 1864 to serve three years. Died, date not stated, while a prisoner at Andersonville, Georgia.

MOORE, BRADLEY N.— Age 20 years. Enlisted January 4, 1864 at Norwich. Mustered in as Private, Co. L, February 2, 1864 to serve three years. Died of sun stroke, June 27, 1864 near Stony Creek, Virginia.

MOORE, CLINTON— Age 18 years. Enlisted December 9, 1863 at Rochester. Mustered in as Private, Co. I, February 2, 1864 to serve three years. Appointed Corporal, April 30, 1865. Mustered out with company, August 1, 1865 at Winchester, Virginia.

MOORE, HENRY— Age 23 years. Enlisted December 1, 1863 at Rochester. Mustered in as Private, Co. A, December 20, 1863 to serve three years. Appointed Sergeant, July 1, 1865. Mustered out with company, August 1, 1865 at Winchester, Virginia.

MOORE, JASON— Age 18 years. Enlisted December 16, 1863 at Cazenovia. Mustered in as Private, Co. E, January 10, 1864 to serve three years. Died, date not stated, while a prisoner at Andersonville, Georgia.

MOORE, JOHN— Age 26 years. Enlisted January 4, 1864 at Rochester. Mustered in as Private, Co. D, January 10, 1864 to serve three years. Appointed Sergeant, date not stated. Mustered out with company, August 1, 1865 at Winchester, Virginia.

MOORE, LEWIS— Age 26 years. Enlisted November 10, 1863 at Rochester. Mustered in as Sergeant, Co. A, December 30, 1863 to serve three years. Mustered in as Second Lieutenant to date, April 23, 1865. Mustered out with company, August 1, 1865 at Winchester, Virginia. Commissioned Second Lieutenant, April 22, 1865, with rank from April 14, 1865, original, vice Conover, promoted. First Lieutenant, July 15, 1865, with rank from July 11, 1865, vice Smythe, discharged; not mustered

MOORE, OLIVER— Age 3 years. Enlisted January 15, 1864 at Rochester. Mustered in as Sergeant, Co. K, February 6, 1864 to serve three years. Mustered out as Corporal, June 21, 1865 at Annapolis, Maryland. Also borne as Oliver G. and O.O.G. Moore.

MOORE, THOMAS— Age 26 years. Enlisted April 11, 1865 at Brooklyn. Mustered in as Private, "unassigned," April 11, 1865 to serve three years. Mustered out with detachment, May 6, 1865 at Hart's Island, New York Harbor.

MOORES, HENRY— Age 18 years. Enlisted April 12, 1865 at Rochester. Mustered in as Private, Co. D, April 12, 1865 to serve three years. Mustered out with company, August 1, 1865 at Winchester, Virginia.

MOORES, JEREMIAH— Age 17 years. Enlisted as Private, Co. M, February 18, 1864 to serve three years. Rejected.

MORAN, EDWARD— Age 32 years. Enlisted January 4, 1864 at Syracuse. Mustered in as Private, Co. H, February 2, 1864 to serve three years. Mustered out with company, August 1, 1865 at Winchester, Virginia.

MORGAN, JAMES— Age 24 years. Enlisted December 8, 1863 at Rochester. Mustered in as Private, Co. F, January 10, 1864 to serve three years. Deserted in February 1864 from camp near Rochester, New York.

MORGAN, MICHAEL— Age 27 years. Enlisted April 12, 1865 at Brooklyn. Mustered in as Private, "unassigned," April 12, 1865 to serve three years. Mustered out with detachment, May 6, 1865 at Hart's Island, New York Harbor.

MORGENWECK, CYRIACK— Age 22 years. Enlisted March 16, 1865 at New York. Mustered in as Private, "unassigned," March 16, 1865 to serve three years. No further record.

MORHE, PHILLIP— Age 18 years. Enlisted February 25, 1865 at Tompkins. Mustered in as Private, "unassigned," February 27, 1865 to serve three years. No further record.

MORIAN, CHARLES A.— Age 20 years. Enlisted January 28, 1864 at Rochester. Mustered in as Private, Co. M, February 23, 1864 to serve three years. Transferred to Co. K, date not stated. Appointed Commissary Sergeant, date not stated. Mustered out, August 2, 1865 at Buffalo, New York. Veteran.

MORRISON, HENRY— Age 18 years. Enlisted October 24, 1863 at Rochester. Mustered in as Bugler, Co. A, December 20, 1863 to serve three years. Died of disease, March 30 1864 at Rochester, New York.

MORRISON, HIRAM— Age 19 years. Enlisted February 29, 1864 at Urbana. Mustered in as Private, Co. G, March 8, 1864 to serve three years. Mustered out with company, August 1, 1865 at Winchester, Virginia.

MORRISON, IRA S.— Age 19 years. Enlisted December 19, 1863 at Rochester. Mustered in as Private, Co. A, December 20, 1863 to serve three years. Died of disease, September 25, 1864 at Andersonville, Georgia.

MOORSE, FRANK— Age 33 years. Enlisted December 23, 1863 at Syracuse. Mustered in as Private, Co. B, January 5, 1864 to serve three years. Discharged for disability, June 3, 1865 at Washington, D.C.

MORSE, GARRETT C.— Age 18 years. Enlisted December 1, 1863 at Wheeler. Mustered in as Private, Co. G, February 2, 1864 to serve three years. Appointed Corporal June 1, 1865. Mustered out with company, August 1, 1865 at Winchester, Virginia.

MOSES, MARK E.— Age 24 years. Enlisted November 30, 1863 at Rochester. Mustered in as Sergeant, Co. F, January 10, 1864 to serve three years. Appointed First Sergeant, date not stated. Deserted in February 1865 from Camp Parole, Annapolis, Maryland. Prior service in Co. F, Twenty-Third New York Infantry.

MOSHER, AMOS— Age 33 years. Enlisted December 12, 1863 at Brockport. Mustered in as Private, Co. C, January 5, 1864 to serve three years. Discharged, June 6, 1865 at Washington, D.C. Also borne as Mosier.

MOUCK, MATTHEW— Age 20 years. Enlisted April 3, 1865 at New York. Mustered in as Private, Co. I, April 3, 1865 to serve three years. Mustered out with company, August 1, 1865 at Winchester, Virginia.

MOWERS, DAVID H.— Age 19 years. Enlisted January 4, 1864 at Sweden. Mustered in as Private, Co. I, January 5, 1864 to serve three years. Appointed Corporal, March 1, 1865. Appointed Sergeant, July 12, 1865. Mustered out with company, August 1, 1865 at Winchester, Virginia.

MOWERS, JEREMIAH— Age 17 years. Enlisted February 18, 1864 at Bath. Mustered in as Private, Co. , March 8, 1864 to serve three years. Confined at Fort Delaware, By sentence of G.C.M.A. of S., May 12, 1865. Discharged, August 9, 1865 at Rochester, New York.

MOWERS, JOHN— Age 18 years. Enlisted November 30, 1863 at Brockport. Mustered in as Private, Co. C, January 5, 1864 to serve three years. Mustered out with company, August 1, 1865 at Winchester, Virginia.

MOWRY, JOHN J.— Age 22 years. Enlisted March 15, 1865 at New York. Mustered in as Private, "unassigned," March 1, 1865 to serve three years. No further record.

MOXCEY, GEORGE W.— officer

MOYNE, JAMES— Age 21 years. Enlisted March 31, 1865 at New York. Mustered in as Private, "unassigned," March 31, 1865 to serve three years. No further record.

MUCHNER, JOHN— See Moochler, John.

MUDFORD, WILLIAM H.— Age 18 years. Enlisted January 11, 1864 at Unadilla. Mustered in as Private, Co. L, February 12, 1864 to serve three years. Mustered out June 6, 1865 at Satterlee U.S.A. General Hospital, West Philadelphia, Pa.

MULER, JACOB— Age 23 years. Enlisted March 4, 1865 at Westfield. Mustered in as Private, Co. L, March 4, 1865 to serve one year. Mustered out with company, August 1, 1865 at Winchester, Virginia.

MULLANEY, FRANCIS— Age 24 years. Enlisted March 22, 1865 at New York. Mustered in as Private, "unassigned," March 22, 1865 to serve two years. No further record.

MULLEN, JAMES— Age 21 years. Enlisted March 22, 1865 at Rochester. Mustered in as Private, "unassigned," March 22 1865 to serve three years. No further record.

MULLONEY, JOHN— Age 39 years. Enlisted December 19, 1863 at Rochester. Mustered in as Private, Co. A, December 20, 1863 to serve three years. Deserted, December 20, 1864 in the field, Virginia.

MULLOY, JOHN— Age 21 years. Enlisted February 23, 1864 at Rochester. Mustered in as Private, Co. M, February 23, 1864 to serve three years. No further record.

MUNSON, JOHN— Age 30 years. Enlisted January 4, 1864 at Smithfield. Mustered in as Private, Co. K, February 6, 1864 to serve three years. Transferred to Co. H, March 25, 1864. Mustered out with company, August 1, 1865 at Winchester, Virginia.

MURCH, GEORGE— Age 31 years. Enlisted December 30, 1863 at Cazenovia. Mustered in as Corporal, Co. E, January 10, 1864 to serve three years. Mustered out with company, August 1, 1865 at Winchester, Virginia. Also borne as March

MURPHY, CHARLES— Age 19 years. Enlisted December 21, 1863 at Fredonia. Mustered in as Private, Co. F, January 10, 1864 to serve three years. Deserted in February 1864 from camp near Rochester, New York.

MURPHY, JAMES— Age 24 years. Enlisted April 3, 1865 at Tarrytown. Mustered in as Private, Co. F, April 3, 1865 to serve one year. Appointed Corporal, July 1, 1865. Mustered out with company, August 1, 1865 at Winchester, Virginia.

MURPHY, JAMES— Age 19 years. Enlisted April 8, 1865 at New York. Mustered in as Private, "unassigned," April 8, 1865 to serve one year. No further record.

MURPHY, JOHN— Age 18 years. Enlisted April 8, 1865 at Albany. Mustered in as Private, "unassigned," April 8, 1865 to serve three years. Mustered out with detachment, May 6, 1865 at Hart's Island, New York Harbor.

MURPHY, MICHAEL— Age 18 years. Enlisted April 11, 1865 at Brooklyn. Mustered in as Private, "unassigned," April 11, 1865 to serve one year. Mustered out with detachment, May 6, 1865 at Hart's Island, New York Harbor.

MURPHY, SAMUEL— Age 28 years. Enlisted February 17, 1865 at New York. Mustered in as Private, Co. M, February 17, 1865 to serve three years. Mustered out with company, August 1, 1865 at Winchester, Virginia.

MURRAY, CHARLES E.— Age 18 years. Enlisted April 8, 1865 at New York. Mustered in as Private, Co. G, April 8, 1865 to serve three years. Mustered out with company, August 1, 1865 at Winchester, Virginia.

MURRAY, JOHN— Age 21 years. Enlisted December 9, 1863 at Rochester. Mustered in as Private, Co. I, February 2, 1864 to serve three years. Transferred to Co. G, in April 1864. Appointed Saddler, date not stated. Mustered out with company, August 1, 1865 at Winchester, Virginia.

MURRAY, JOHN— Age 24 years. Enlisted March 16, 1865 at Brooklyn. Mustered in as Private, "unassigned," March 16, 1865 to serve three years. No further record.

MURRAY, THOMAS— Age 23 years. Enlisted September 13, 1864 at Beekman. Mustered in as Private, "unassigned," September 13, 1864 to serve one year. No further record.

MYBBYRE, JOSEPH— See Millboryne, Joseph.

MYERS, LEWIS— Age 18 years. Enlisted as Private, Co. D, January 4, 1864 at Rochester, to serve three years. Rejected.

MYNER, CHARLES— Age 19 years. Enlisted as Private, Co. B, December 21, 1863 at Syracuse to serve three years. Rejected.

NARRY, JAMES— Age 20 years. Enlisted April 14, 1865 at New York. Mustered in as Private, "unassigned," April 14, 1865 to serve one year. Mustered out with detachment, May 6, 1865 at Hart's Island, New York Harbor.

NASH, PETER— Age 25 years. Enlisted January 24, 1864 at McDonough. Mustered in as Private, Co. L, January 22, 1864 to serve three years. Deserted, February 9, 1864.

NEEDHAM, HENRY — Age 21 years. Enlisted April 13, 1865 at Brooklyn. Mustered in as Private, "unassigned," April13, 1865 to serve one year. Mustered out with detachment, May 6, 1865 at Hart's Island, New York Harbor.

NEIL, HENRY— Age 29 years. Enlisted December 8, 1863 at Riga. Mustered in as Private, Co. C, January 5, 1864 to serve three years. Discharged, December 17, 1864.

NELLIS, CLARK S.— Age 22 years. Enlisted March 4, 1864 at Rochester. Mustered in as Private, Co. A, March 4, 1864 to serve three years. Appointed Commissary Sergeant, October 23, 1864. Mustered out with regiment, August 1, 1865 at Winchester, Virginia. Also borne as Nellis, Clark J. Commissioned Second Lieutenant, September 18, 1865 with rank from June 25, 1865, vice Allen, not mustered.

NELLIS, JAMES H.— Officer

NELLIS, JOHN L.— Age 18 years. Enlisted as Private, Co. G, January 29, 1864 at Prattsburgh to serve three years. Rejected.

NELMS, SAMUEL— Age 20 years. Enlisted March 25, 1865 at Westfield. Mustered in as Private, Co. F, March 25, 1865 to serve three years. Transferred to Co. G, May 27, 1865. Died, date not stated.

NELSON, CHARLES— Age 19 years. Enlisted November 5, 1863 at Brockport. Mustered in as Sergeant, Co. C, January 5, 1864 to serve three years. Reduced to ranks, date not stated. Mustered out with company, August 1, 1865 at Winchester, Virginia. Prior service in Co. D, Thirteenth New York Infantry.

NEWELL, ALEXANDER— Age 18 years. Enlisted December 16, 1863 at Utica. Mustered in as Private, Co. B, January 5, 1864 to serve three years. Mustered out with company, August 1, 1865 at Winchester, Virginia.

NEWELL, ANDREW C.— Age 25 years. Enlisted as Private, Co. K, January 29 1864 at Rochester, to serve three years. Rejected.

NEWELL, GEORGE E.— Age 18 years. Enlisted December 16, 1863 at Utica. Mustered in as Private, Co. B, January 5, 1864 to serve three years. Mustered out with company, August 1, 1865 at Winchester, Virginia.

NEWMAN, CHAPPELL B.— Age 34 years. Enlisted February 24, 1865 at New York. Mustered in as Private, Co. H, February 24, 1865 to serve three years. Mustered out with company, August 1, 1865 at Winchester, Virginia.

NEWMAN, EDWARD W.— Officer

NEWMAN, GEORGE W.— Officer

NEWMAN, WILLIAM— Age 28 years. Enlisted April 4, 1865 at Syracuse. Mustered in as Private Co. K, April 1, 1865 to serve three years. Mustered out with company, August 1, 1865 at Winchester, Virginia.

NICHELSON, EDWARD— Age 21 years. Enlisted December 23, 1863 at Syracuse. Mustered in as Private, Co. B, January 5, 1864 to serve three years. Mustered out with company, August 1, 1865 at Winchester, Virginia.

NICHOLS, GEORGE— Age 20 years. Enlisted February 8, 1864 at Plymouth. Mustered in as Private, "unassigned," February 8, 1864 to serve three years. No further record.

NICHOLS, GEORGE S.— Age 18 years. Enlisted January 14, 1864 at Unadilla. Mustered in as Private, Co. L, February 12, 1864 to serve three years. Mustered out with company, August 1, 1865 at Winchester, Virginia.

NICHOLS, WASHINGTON I.— Age 27 years. Enlisted April 10, 1865 at Lewiston. Mustered in as Private, Co. F, April 10, 1865 to serve three years. Discharged, June 7, 1865.

NICHOLSEN, GEORGE— Age 23 years. Enlisted February 17, 1865 at New York. Mustered in as Private "unassigned," February 17, 1865 to serve one year. No further record.

NISBET, ROBERT E.— Age 17 years. Enlisted November 10, 1863 at Rochester. Mustered in as Sergeant, Co. I, February 2, 1864, to serve three years. Mustered out with company, August 1, 1865 at Winchester, Virginia.

NIX, ANGEVINE— Age 20 years. Enlisted December 7, 1863 at Rochester. Mustered in as Private, Co. D, January 10, 1864, to serve three years. Died of disease, August 18, 1864, in hospital at David Island, New York.

NOBLE, HENRY C.— Age 25 years. Enlisted October 5, 1864 at Jamaica. Mustered in as Private, Co. M, October 5, 1864 to serve one year. Mustered out with company, August 1, 1865 at Winchester, Virginia.

NOBLE, JOHN F.— Age 20 years. Enlisted December 16, 1863 at Syracuse. Mustered in as Private, Co. B, January 5, 1864, to serve three years. Mustered out with company, August 1, 1865 at Winchester, Virginia.

NOLAN, JOSEPH— Age 25 years. Enlisted December 8, 1863 at Rochester. Mustered in as Private, Co. A, December 20, 1863, to serve three years. Mustered out with company, August 1, 1865 at Winchester, Virginia.

NOLAN, THOMAS F.— Age 17 years. Enlisted December 17, 1863 at Cazenovia. Mustered in as Private, Co. E, January 10, 1864, to serve three years. Died of disease, March 12, 1864 at Rochester, New York.

NOONAN, MICHAEL— Age 25 years. Enlisted as Private, Co. I, at Rochester, January 8, 1864, to serve three years. Rejected.

NORRIS, JOSEPH B.— Age 36 years. Enlisted January 13, 1864 at Rochester. Mustered in as Private, Co. K, February 6, 1864, to serve three years. Mustered out with company, August 1, 1865 at Winchester, Virginia.

NORTHRUP, PORTER, H.— Age 18 years. Enlisted January 15, 1864, at German. Mustered in as Private, Co. L, February 12, 1864, to serve three years. Captured, date not stated. Died of disease, no date, at Andersonville, Georgia.

NORTHRUP, SAMUEL— Age 19 years. Enlisted January 22, 1864 at Franklin. Mustered in as Private, Co. L, February 12, 1864 to serve three years. Mustered out with detachment, June 21, 1865 at Washington, D.C.

NORTON, JOHN— Age 21 years. Enlisted March 24, 1865 at New York. Mustered in as Private, "unassigned," March 24, 1865 to serve three years. No further record.

NYE, CHARLES F.— Age 18 years. Enlisted November 13, 1863 at Brockport. Mustered in as Private, Co. I, February 2, 1864 to serve three years. Died of Disease, August, 1864 at Poplar Ridge, New York.

OBERNAUER, VALENTINE— Age 39 years. Enlisted March 8, 1865 at New York City. Mustered in as Private, Co. I, March 8, 1865 to serve one year. Mustered out with company, August 1, 1865 at Winchester, Virginia.

OBERLY, ANTOINE— Age 35 years. Enlisted February 27, 1865 at New York City. Mustered in as Private, Co. B, February 27, 1865 to serve three years. Mustered out with company, August 1, 1865 at Winchester, Virginia. Also borne as Oberle, Antone S.

O'BRIEN, JAMES— Age 18 years. Enlisted February 24, 1864 at Rochester. Mustered in as Private, Co. M, March 9, 1864 to serve three years. Deserted June 1864 at White House Landing, Virginia.

O'BRIEN, JAMES B.— Age 24 years. Enlisted January 2, 1864 at Fredonia. Mustered in as Private, Co. K, February 6, 1864 to serve three years. Deserted February 20, 1864 at Rochester.

O'BRIEN, JOHN— Age 20 years. Enlisted March 17, 1865 at Lockport. Mustered in as Private, "unassigned," March 17, 1865, to serve three years. No further record.

O'BRIEN, JOHN— Age 23 years. Enlisted as Private, Co. L, January 30, 1864 at Bainbridge, to serve three years. Deserted February 9, 1864 prior to muster in of company, February 12, 1864.

O'BRIEN, MICHAEL— Age 44 years. Enlisted December 7, 1863 at Rochester. Mustered in as Commissary Sergeant, Co. D, January 10, 1864 to serve three years. Discharged for disability, October 13, 1864 from hospital, Philadelphia, Pa.

O'BRIEN, PATRICK— Age 23 years. Enlisted April 6, 1865 at Rochester. Mustered in As Private, "unassigned," April 6, 1865 to serve three years. Mustered out July 17, 1865 at Albany, in hospital. Never assigned to company.

O'BRIEN, TERRENCE— Age 44 years. Enlisted December 5, 1863 at Private, Co. D at Rochester, to serve three years. Rejected.

O'CONNOR, HUGH— Age 18 years. Enlisted March 8, 1865 at New York. Mustered in as Private, Co. K, March 8, 1865 to serve one year. Mustered out with company, August 1, 1865 at Winchester, Virginia.

ODLE, DEMETRIUS— Age 43 years. Enlisted December 22, 1863 at Manlius. Mustered in as Corporal, Co. E, January 10. 1964 to serve three years. Mustered out with company, August 1, 1865 at Winchester, Virginia.

ODELL, JOTHAN— Age 18 years. Enlisted December 17, 1863 at Nelson. Mustered in as Private, Co. E, January 10, 1864 to serve three years. Mustered out with company, August 1, 1865 at Winchester, Virginia.

OGDEN, FRANK— Age 19 years. Enlisted December 21, 1863 at Rochester. Mustered in as Private, Co. C, January 5, 1864 to serve three years. Mustered out with company, August 1, 1865 at Winchester, Virginia.

OLCOTT, GEORGE E.— Age 23 years. Enlisted April 13, 1865 at Orangeville. Mustered in as Private, Co. F, April 13, 1865 to serve one year. Transferred to Co. G, May 27, 1865. Died, date not stated. Also borne as Alcott.

OLMSTEAD, HENRY H.— Age 19 years. Enlisted December 23, 1863 at Milo. Mustered in as Private, Co. C, January 5, 1864 to serve three years. Transferred to Co. A, March 22, 1864. Died of disease, August 25, 1864 at Andersonville, Georgia.

OLTON, GEORGE C.— Age 18 years. Enlisted January 27, 1864 at Rochester. Mustered in as Private, Co. M, February 23, 1864 to serve three years. Prisoner of war since October 5, 1864. No discharge furnished at muster out of company, August 1, 1865. No further record.

O'MALLEY, JAMES— Age 23 years. Enlisted March 4, 1864 at Rochester. Mustered in as Private, Co. M, March 9, 1864 to serve three years. Appointed Corporal, January 20, 1865. Mustered out with company, August 1, 1865 at Winchester, Virginia.

O'NEAL, WILLIAM H.— Age 23 years. Enlisted March 18, 1865 at Tarrytown. Mustered in as Private, "unassigned," March 18, 1865 to serve three years. No further record.

O'NEIL, JAMES— Age 19 years. Enlisted January 18, 1864 at Arcadia. Mustered in as Private, Co. H, February 2, 1864 to serve three years. Deserted, date not stated, records lost.

O'NEIL, PATRICK— Age 23 years. Enlisted December30, 1863 at Madison. Mustered in as Farrier, Co. E, January 10, 1864 to serve three years. Died at Andersonville, Georgia., date not stated.

O'NEIL, RICHARD— Age 30 years. Enlisted April 13, 1865 at New York City. Mustered in as Private, "unassigned," April13, 1865 to serve one year. Mustered out with detachment, May 6, 1865 at Hart's Island, New York Harbor.

ORMOND, THOMAS— Age 18 years. Enlisted April 9, 1865 at New York. Mustered in as Private, Co. F, April 9, 1865 to serve three years. Mustered out with company, August 1, 1865 at Winchester, Virginia.

O'ROURKE, JOHN— Age 19 years. Enlisted February 4, 1864 at Georgetown. Mustered in as Private, Co. M, February 12, 1864 to serve three years. Transferred to Co. E, March 25, 1864. Mustered out with detachment June 28, 1865 at Winchester, Virginia.

ORR, JOHN— Age 40 years. Enlisted April 12, 1865 at Albany. Mustered in as Private, "unassigned," April 12, 1865 to serve three years. Mustered out May 6, 1865 at Hart's Island, New York Harbor.

OSBORN, ROBERT H.— Age 23 years. Enlisted December 29, 1863 at Lysander. Mustered in as Quartermaster Sergeant, Co. E, January 10, 1864 to serve three years. Died at Andersonville, Georgia., date not stated.

OSTRANGER, CLINTON N.— Age 20 years. Enlisted November 20, 1863 at Bath. Mustered in as Private, Co. G, February 2, 1864 to serve three years. Captured, June 29, 1864. Paroled, February 28, 1865. Discharged, June 28, 1865 at Winchester, Virginia. Prior service in Co. I, Thirty Fourth New York Volunteer Infantry.

OSTRANDER, EDWARD E.— Age 32 years. Enlisted January 7, 1864 at Bath Mustered in as Sergeant, Co .G, February 2, 1864 to serve e three years. Appointed First Sergeant, date not stated. Transferred to Co. M, April 24, 1865. Reduced to ranks, May 11, 1865. Mustered out with company, August 1, 1865 at Winchester, Virginia.

OTTO, HOWARD— Age 19 years. Enlisted November 29 1863 at Rochester. Mustered in as Private, Co. D, January 10, 1864 to serve three years. Transferred to Co. K, May 1, 1864. Mustered out with company, August 1, 1865 at Winchester, Virginia.

OVERHISER, JOSEPH S.— Age 32 years. Enlisted January 2, 1864 at Avoca. Mustered in as Private, Co. G, February 2, 1864 to serve three years. Discharged for disability, June 23, 1865 at Island Hospital, Harpers Ferry, Virginia.

PACKARD, HART— Age 18 years. Enlisted December 3, 1863 at Rochester. Mustered in as Bugler, Co. D, January 10,1864 to serve three years. Mustered out July 13, 1865 at Mower U.S.A. General Hospital, Philadelphia, Pa.

PALMER, GEORGE— Age 19 years. Enlisted March 25, 1865 at Hopewell. Mustered in as Private, Co. F, March 25, 1865 to serve three years. Appointed Corporal, July, 1, 1865. Mustered out with company, August 1, 1865 at Winchester, Virginia.

PALMETER, JASON L.— Age 19 years. Enlisted December 23, 1863 at Madison. Mustered in as Private, Co. E, January 4, 1864 to serve three years. Died of disease, December 3, 1864 at Naval School Hospital, Annapolis, Maryland.

PANGBURN, MYRON N.— Age 27 years. Enlisted March 12, 1864 at Sidney. Mustered in as Private, "unassigned," March 29, 1864 to serve three years. No further record.

PARDY, JAMES— Age 27 years. Enlisted January 5, 1864 at Lenox. Mustered in as Private, Co. M, February 23, 1864 to serve three years. Wounded September 1, 1864. Mustered out August 1, 1865 at Elmira, New York. Also borne as Pardie.

PARKER, JOHN— Age 24 years. Enlisted March 12, 1864 at New York. Mustered in as Private, "unassigned," March 12, 1864, to serve three years. No further record.

PARKER, THOMAS— Age 14 years. Enlisted March 14, 1865 at New York. Mustered in as Private, "unassigned," March 14, 1865 to serve three years. No further record.

PARKER, WILLIAM J.— Age 25 years. Enlisted December 18, 1863 at Brockport. Mustered in as Farrier, Co. C, January 5, 1864 to serve three years. Reduced, date not stated. Mustered out with company, August 1, 1865 at Winchester, Virginia.

PARKHURST, HENRY S.— Age 29 years. Enlisted February 24, 1864 at Lima. Mustered in as Private, Co. M, February 25, 1864 to serve three years. Appointed First Sergeant, date not stated. Reduced to Sergeant, June 30, 1865. Mustered out with company, August 1, 1865 at Winchester, Virginia.

PARMELEE, STEPHEN— Age 45 years. Enlisted January 9, 1864 at Verona, as Private, Co. M, to serve three years. Rejected. Also borne as Parmley.

PARROT, JAMES— Age 21 years. Enlisted February 22, 1865 at New York. Mustered in as Private, "unassigned," February 22, 1865 to serve three years. No further record.

PATRICK. C.W.— Age 20 years. Enrolled October 1, 1864 at Cedar Creek. Mustered in as First Lieutenant, Co. B, October 26, 1864 to serve three years. Discharged for disability, July 5, 1865. Prior service in Eighty First New York Volunteers. Commissioned First Lieutenant, August 15, 1864 with rank from August 15, 1864, vice Lloyd, promoted. Captain, May 31, 1865, with rank from May 15, 1865, vice Wisner, discharged, not mustered.

PATTEN, GEORGE W.— Age 18 years. Enlisted October 12, 1863 at Auburn. Mustered in as Private, Co. I, February 2, 1864 to serve three years. Mustered out with company, August 1, 1865 at Winchester, Virginia.

PATTERSON, WILLIAM— Age 23 years. Enlisted March 2, 1865 at New York. Mustered in as Private, Co. I, March 2, 1865 to serve one year. Mustered out with company, August 1, 1865 at Winchester, Virginia.

PAYNE, ARTHUR B.— Age 23 years. Enlisted January 5, 1864 at New Berlin. Mustered in as Corporal, Co. L, February 12, 1864 to serve three years. Reduced, date not stated. Mustered out with company, August 1, 1865 at Winchester, Virginia.

PAYTON, JAMES— Age 19 years. Enlisted February 27, 1864 at Rochester. Mustered in as Private, "unassigned," March 8, 1864 to serve three years. No further record.

PEACHY, CHARLES— Age 19 years. Enlisted November 14, 1863 at Rochester. Mustered in as Private, Co. C, January 5, 1864 to serve three years. Appointed Corporal, March 1, 1865. Mustered out with company, August 1, 1865 at Winchester, Virginia.

PEACHEY, NOAH— Age 18 years. Enlisted November 30, 1863 at Brockport. Mustered in as Private, Co. C, January 5, 1864 to serve three years. Died of disease, June 14, 1865 at hospital, Baltimore, Maryland.

PEACOCK, EDWIN— Age 26 years. Enlisted December 14, 1863 at Seneca Falls. Mustered in as Private, Co. I, February 2, 1864 to serve three years. Deserted, February 1864 at Rochester, New York.

PEASE, GEORGE R.— Age 18 years. Enlisted November 23, 1863 at Brockport. Mustered in as Private, Co. C, January 5, 1864 to serve three years. Appointed Corporal, March 1, 1865. Mustered out with company, August 1, 1865 at Winchester, Virginia.

PECK, HERBERT D.— Officer

PECK, JAMES G.— Age 38 years. Enlisted January 6, 1864 at Rochester. Mustered in as Wagoner, Co. F, January 10, 1864 to serve three years. Reduced, date not stated. Captured, date not stated. Died, June 9, 1864 at Andersonville, Georgia.

PECK, WILLIAM G-Age 22 years. Enlisted February 16, 1864 at Guilford. Mustered in as Private, Co. E, February 18, 1964. Appointed Corporal, March 9, 1864. Died of wounds, December 9, 1864 at Philadelphia, Pa.

PECKHAM, HENRY C.— Age 18 years. Enlisted February 9, 1864 at Madison. Mustered in as corporal, Co. M, February 23, 1864 to serve three years. Transferred to Co. E, March 25, 1864. Mustered out with company, August 1, 1865 at Winchester, Virginia.

PEER, STEPHEN— Age 23 years. Enlisted December 19, 1863 at Lyons. Mustered in as Private, Co. H, February 2, 1864 to serve three years. Deserted, date not stated.

PENDELTON, WILLIAM H.— Age 19 years. Enlisted February 28, 1865 at New York. Mustered in as Private, "unassigned," February 28, 1865 to serve three years. Mustered out with detachment, May 6, 1865 at Hart's Island, New York Harbor.

PENNEFETHER, RICHARD— Age 25 years. Enlisted October 5, 1864 at Tompkinsville. Mustered in as Private, Co. M, October 5, 1864 to serve one year. Appointed Saddler, January 10, 1865. Mustered out with company, August 1, 1865 at Winchester, Virginia.

PENNY, SANFORD A.— Age 18 years. Enlisted, October 31, 1863 at Rochester. Mustered in as Sergeant, Co. A, December 20, 1863, to serve three years. Mustered out with company, August 1, 1865, at Winchester, Virginia.

PERKINS, FRANKLIN R.— Age 22 years. Enrolled,

PERKINS, RICHARD— Age 27 years. Enlisted, December 3, 1864 at New York. Mustered in as Private, Co. I, December 3, 1864, to serve three years. Died, June 20, 1865 at Winchester, Virginia.

PERRY, FRANKLIN— Age 18 years. Enlisted December 18, 1863 at Utica. Mustered in as Private, Co. B, January 5, 1864, to serve three years. Mustered out with company, August 1, 1865, at Winchester, Virginia.

PERSONS, MATTHEW— Age 19 years. Enlisted November 19, 1863 at Brockport. Mustered in as Corporal, Co. C, January 5, 1864, to serve three years. Reduced, date not stated. Deserted, February 6, 1864 at Rochester, New York.

PEW, THOMAS S.— Age 41 years. Enlisted March 8, 1865 at Persia. Mustered in as Private, Co. I, March 8, 1865, to serve one year. Mustered out, August 9, 1865 at Rochester, New York.

PHELGA, HIRAM N.— Age 23 years. Enlisted August 25, 1864 at Smyrna. Mustered in as Private, "unassigned," August 25, 1864, to serve three years. No further record.

PHELTEPLACE, FRANCIS E.— Age 20 years. Enlisted January 29, 1864 at Milford. Mustered in as Private, Co. L, February 12, 1864, to serve three years. Captured and paroled, date not stated. Died, December 24, 1864, at Annapolis, Maryland.

PHILIPS, EDSON— Age 19 years. Enlisted December 19, 1863 at Palmyra. Mustered in as Private, Co. H, February 2, 1864, to serve three years. Mustered out with company, August 1, 1865, at Winchester, Virginia.

PHILIPS, ETHAN— Age 19 years. Enlisted January 18, 1864 at Palmyra. Mustered in as Private, Co. H, February 2, 1864, to serve three years. Died, date and place not stated.

PHILLIPS, ALBERT— Age 19 years. Enlisted January 4, 1864 at Constantia. Mustered in as Private, Co. B, January 5, 1864, to serve three years. Transferred to Co. E, March 25, 1864. Discharged for disability, February 12, 1865.

PHILLIPS, GEORGE— Age 22 years. Enlisted December 19, 1863 at Syracuse. Mustered in as Private, to serve three years; discharged for disability, September 20, 1864.

PHILLIPS, GEORGE D.— Age 17 years. Enlisted February 7, 1865 at Milford. Mustered in as Private, Co. C, February 11, 1865, to serve three years. Mustered out, July 21, 1865, at Harper's Ferry, Virginia. Also borne as George W. Phillips.

PHILLIPS, LEONARD D.— Age 18 years. Enlisted January 9, 1864 at Plymouth. Mustered in as Private, Co. L, February 12, 1864, to serve three years. Mustered out with company, August 1, 1865, at Winchester, Virginia.

PHILLIPS, MARTIN— Age 20 years. Enlisted November 23, 1863 at Syracuse. Mustered in as Private, Co. B, January 5, 1864, to serve three years. Mustered out with company, August 1, 1865, at Winchester, Virginia.

PHILLIPS, NORMAN— Age 27 years. Enlisted December 30, 1863 at Sweden, As Private, Co. C, to serve three years. Rejected.

PHILLIPS, WILLIAM H.— Age 18 years. Enlisted January 2, 1864 at Manlius. Mustered in as Private, Co. E, January 10, 1864, to serve three years. Mustered out with company, August 1, 1865, at Winchester, Virginia.

PHEIN, FREDERICK— Age 18 years. Enlisted January 4, 1864 at French Creek. Mustered in as Private, Co. K, February 6, 1864, to serve three years. No further record.

PIERCE, ACHIBALD— Age 28 years. Enlisted December 4, 1863 at Rochester. Mustered in as Private, Co. A. December 20, 1863, to serve three years. Mustered out with company, August 1, 1865 at Winchester, Virginia.

PIERCE, DANIEL— Age 20 years. Enlisted January 22, 1864 at German. Mustered in as Private, Co. L, February 12, 1864 to serve three years. Deserted from hospital December 8, 1864. Prior service in Co. B, One Hundred and Forty Fourth New York Infantry Volunteers.

PIERCE, FRANK— Age 24 years. Enlisted January 22, 1864 at McDonough. Mustered in as Private, Co. L, January 22, 1864 to serve three years. No further record.

PIERCE, JANS— Age 18 years. Enlisted January 5, 1864 at Sodus, as Private, Co. H, to serve three years. Rejected.

PIERCE, JOHN A.— Age 44 years. Enlisted December 18, 1863 at Sodus, as Private, Co. H, to serve three years. Rejected.

PILATY, JOSEPH C.— Age 32 years. Enlisted December 24, 1863 at Auburn. Mustered in as Private, Co. D, January 10, 1864 to serve three years. Transferred to Co. I, and appointed Sergeant, May1,1865. Discharged for disability, May 12, 1865. Prior service in Co. F, First Regiment, Lancers.

PITCHER, DAVID— Age 31 years. Enlisted December 14, 1863 at Brockport, as Private, Co. C, to serve three years. Rejected.

PLATT, HORATIO N.— Age 19 years. Enlisted January 15, 1864 at Milford. Mustered in as Private, Co. L, February 12, 1864 to serve three years. Appointed Corporal, March 25, 1865. Mustered out August 28, 1865 at Rochester, New York.

PLATT, JOHN— Age 22 years. Enlisted April 8, 1865 at New York. Mustered in as Private, Co. L, April 8, 1865 to serve one year. Mustered out with company, August 1, 1865 at Winchester, Virginia.

PLAYER, CHARLES— Age 18 years. Enlisted April 11, 1865 at Rochester. Mustered in as Private, Co. D, April 11, 1865 to serve one year. Mustered out with company, August 1, 1865 at Winchester, Virginia.

PLOSS, SAMUEL J.— Age 26 years. Enlisted December 2, 1863 at Arcadia. Mustered in as Sergeant, Co. H, February 2, 1864 to serve three years. Appointed First Sergeant, date not stated. Mustered out with company, August 1, 1865 at Winchester, Virginia. Also borne as Samuel S. Ploss. Prior service in Co. I, Seventeenth New York Infantry Volunteers.

PLOYER, HENRY— Age 19 years. Enlisted January 4, 1864 at New York. Mustered in as Private, "unassigned," January 4, 1864 to serve three years. No further record.

PLUMB, BEN M.— Age 20 years. Enlisted January 4, 1864 at Norwich. Mustered in as Quartermaster Sergeant, Co. L, February 12, 1864 to serve three years. Appointed Regimental Quartermaster Sergeant, date not stated. Reduced and transferred to Co. L, October 20, 1864. No further record.

PLUMB, THEODORE— See Klumpp, Theodore.

POMROY, A.C.— Age 31 years. Enlisted August 20, 1864 at Lagrange. Mustered in as Private, "unassigned," August 20, 1864 to serve one year. No further record.

PORTER, HENRY— Age 19 years. Enlisted April 13, 1865 at Rochester. Mustered in a Private, Co. F, April 13, 1865 to serve three years. Deserted June 9, 1865 from camp near Winchester, Virginia.

PORTER, WILLIAM— Age 18 years. Enlisted March 28, 1865 at Rochester. Mustered in as Private, Co. C, March 29, 1865 to serve three years. Transferred to Co. D, June 9, 1865. Mustered out with company, August 1, 1865 at Winchester, Virginia.

PORTSMOUTH, WILLIAM— Age 22 years. Enlisted December 9, 1863 at Rochester. Mustered in as Farrier, Co. A, December 20, 1863 to serve three years. Mustered out with company, August 1, 1865 at Winchester, Virginia. Prior service in Co. D, Twenty Second New York Infantry Volunteers.

POTTER, CHARLES— Age 24 years. Enlisted November 25, 1863 at Rochester. Mustered in as Private, Co. F, January 10, 1864 to serve three years. Deserted, February, 1864 from camp near Rochester, New York.

POTTER, JAMES R.— Age 18 years. Enlisted December 2, 1863 at Palmyra as Private, Co. H, to serve three years. deserted prior to muster in of company, February 2, 1864.

PRATT, CHARLES K.— Age 40 years. Enlisted January 29, 1864 at Prattsburgh, as Private, Co. G, to serve three years. Rejected.

PRATT, JOHN— Age 19 years. Enlisted March 24, 1864 at New York. Mustered in as Private, "unassigned," March 24, 1864 to serve three years. No further record.

PRATT, WILLIAM W.— Age 22 years. Enlisted December 17, 1863 at bath. Mustered in a Corporal, Co. G, February2, 1864 to serve three years. Captured June 29, 1864. Paroled, March 2, 1865. Appointed Sergeant, May 1, 1865. Discharged with detachment, June 28, 1865 at Winchester, Virginia. Prior service in Co. A, Twenty-Third New York Volunteers.

PRESTON, BYRON I.— Age 20 years. Enlisted December 12, 1863 at Rochester. Mustered in as Private, Co. D, January 10, 1864 to serve three years. Appointed Hospital Steward, date not stated. Mustered out with regiment, August 1, 1865 at Winchester, Virginia.

PRESTON, DAVID— Age 18 years. Enlisted January 27, 1864 at Syracuse. Mustered in as Private, Co. I, February 2, 1864 to serve three years. Transferred to Co. E, and deserted, March 1864 at Rochester, Virginia.

PRESTON, WALLACE M.— Age 21 years. Enlisted December 30, 1863 at Huron. Mustered in as Corporal, Co. H, February 2, 1864 to serve three years. Killed September 19, 1864 at Winchester, Virginia.

PRICE, DAVID W.— Age 19 years. Enlisted March 8, 1865 at New York. Mustered in as Private Co. K, March 8, 1865 to serve one year. Deserted June 7, 1865 near Winchester, Virginia.

PRICE, ROBERT— Age 21 years. Enlisted March 6, 1865 at Masonville. Mustered in as Private, "unassigned," March 6, 1865 to serve three years. No further record.

PRIMMER, GEORGE C.— Age 22 years. Enlisted December 14, 1863 at Madison. Mustered in as Corporal, Co. E, July 10, 1864 to serve three years. Appointed Sergeant, date not stated. Mustered out with company, August 1, 1865 at Winchester, Virginia. Prior service in Co. D, Twenty Sixth New York Infantry Volunteers.

PRINZ, EWALD— Age 26 years. Enlisted February 21, 1865 at New York. Mustered in as Private, "unassigned," February 21, 1865 to serve three years. No further record.

PROSSER, MATHEW— Age 24 years. Enlisted December 17, 1863 at Rochester. Mustered in as Farrier, Co. I, February 2, 1864 to serve three years. Appointed Corporal, August 31, 1864. Veterinary Surgeon, May 1, 1865. Mustered out with regiment, August 1, 1865 at Winchester, Virginia.

PROVOST, ISADORE E.— Officer

PUGH, THOMAS H.— Age 22 years. Enlisted December 16, 1863 at Utica. Mustered in as Private, Co. B, January 5, 1864 to serve three years. Mustered out with company, August 1, 1865 at Winchester, Virginia.

PUTNAM, EDWARD C.— Age 18 years. Enlisted January 11, 1864 at Rochester. Mustered in as Private, Co. M, February 23, 1864 to serve three years. Mustered out with company, August 1, 1865 at Winchester, Virginia.

PUTMAN, WILLIAM G.— Age 43 years. Enlisted November 24, 1863 at Barre, as Private, Co. F, to serve three years. Rejected.

QUACKENBUSH, MYRON E.— Age 18 years. Enlisted December 12, 1863 at Syracuse. Mustered in as Private, Co. B, January 5, 1864 to serve three years. Mustered out with company, August 1, 1865 at Winchester, Virginia.

QUINLAN, JOHN— Age 22 years. Enlisted February 5, 1864 at Rochester. Mustered in as Private, Co. K, February 6, 1864 to serve three years. Transferred to Co. M, March 25, 1864. No further record.

QUINLAN, MICHAEL— Age 19 years. Enlisted February 5, 1864 at Rochester. Mustered in as Private, Co. K, February 6, 1864 to serve three years. Transferred to Co. M, March 25, 1864. No further record.

QUINLIN, PATRICK— Age 24 years. Enlisted December 7, 1863 at Rochester. Mustered in as Private, Co. F, January 10, 1864 to serve three years. Deserted, February —, 1864 from camp near Rochester, New York.

RABON, AUGUSTUS— Age 20 years. Enlisted February 15, 1864 at Rochester. Mustered in as Private, Co. M, February 23, 1864 to serve three years. Transferred to Co. D, March 25, 1864. Mustered out with company, August 1, 1865 at Winchester, Virginia.

RADENBACK, JACOB— Age 41 years. Enlisted as Private, Co. H, to serve three years, January 8, 1864 at Lyons. Rejected.

RADNER, JACOB G.— Age 24 years. Enlisted December 12, 1863 at Albion. Mustered in as Private, Co. F, January 10, 1864 to serve three years. Deserted in February 1864 from camp near Rochester, New York. Also borne as Roaney, Jacob J.

RADWAY, BERT— Age 24 years. Enlisted December 10, 1863 at Syracuse. Mustered in as Private, Co. B, January 5, 1864 to serve three years. Mustered out with company, August 1, 1865 at Winchester, Virginia.

RALEG, JAMES— Age 15 years. Enlisted as Private, Co. H, December 7, 1863 at Arcadia, to serve three years. Rejected.

RANDALL, OLIVER— Age 15 years. Enlisted as Private, "unassigned," December 28, 1863 at Rochester, to serve three years. Mustered out March 16, 1864, being under age.

RANNEY, ROBERT R.— Age 18 years. Enlisted February 28, 1865 at Canandaigua. Mustered in as Private, "unassigned," February 28, 1865 to serve three years. No further record.

RAY, HORACE— Age 22 years. Enlisted December 26, 1863 at Syracuse. Mustered in as Private, Co. B, January 5, 1864 to serve three years. Mustered out with company, August 1, 1865 at Winchester, Virginia.

RAY, JAMES M.— Age 20 years. Enlisted November 19, 1863 at Syracuse. Mustered in as Commissary Sergeant, Co. B January 5, 1864 to serve three years. Reduced to ranks, date not stated. Appointed Corporal, March 1, 1865. Reduced may 1, 1865. Mustered out with company, August 1, 1865 at Winchester, Virginia.

RAY, LUKE— Age 18 years. Enlisted as Private, Co. M, January 5, 1864 at Dunkirk, to serve three years. Rejected.

RAYMOND, WILLIAM— Age 20 years. Enlisted December 14, 1863 at Bath. Mustered in as Private, Co. G, February 2, 1864 to serve three years. Died, date and place not stated.

REA, JOHN— Age 25 years. Enlisted February 23, 1865 at Brooklyn. Mustered in as Private, "unassigned." February 23, 1865 to serve three years. Substitute. No further record.

READ, JAY, F.— Age 18 years. Enlisted November 16, 1863 at Brockport. Mustered in as Trumpeter, Co. C, January 5, 1864 to serve three years. Mustered out with company, August 1, 1865 at Winchester, Virginia.

REAGAN, DAVID— Age 26 years. Enlisted January 4, 1864 at Camillus. Mustered in as Private, Co. M, February 23, 1864 to serve three years. Transferred to Co. H, date not stated. Mustered out with detachment, June 28, 1865 at Winchester, Virginia. Also borne as Reagan, Daniel.

REDING, GEORGE W.— Age 29 years. Enlisted January 5, 1864 at Middletown. Mustered in as Private, Co. M, February 23, 1864 to serve three years. Transferred to Co. L, March 24, 1864. Discharged June 12, 1865. Prior service in Co. G, Fifty-Sixth New York Infantry.

REDINGTON, CHARLES F.— Officer

REED, CELEY T.— Age 22 years. Enlisted November 10, 1863 at Rochester. Mustered in as Private, Co. I, February 2, 1864 to serve three years. Appointed Corporal, April 30, 1865. Mustered out with company, August 1, 1865 at Winchester, Virginia. Prior service in Co. I, Third Cavalry.

REED, HORATIO B.— Officer

REED, JOHN— Age 26 years. Enlisted April 13, 1865 at Kingston. Mustered in as Private, Co. M, April 13, 1865 to serve three years. Mustered out with detachment, May 6, 1865 at Hart's Island, New York Harbor.

REED, JOHN— Age 22 years. Enlisted April 3, 1865 at Syracuse. Mustered in as Private, "unassigned," April 3, 1865 to serve three years. Mustered out with detachment, May 9, 1865 at Elmira, New York.

REED, ROBERT— Age 40 years, Enlisted December 21, 1863 at Cazenovia. Mustered in as Private, Co. E, January 4, 1864 to serve three years. Died, date not stated at Andersonville, Georgia.

REEDING, JAMES— Age 44 years. Enlisted as Private, Co. I, December 21,1863 at Rochester, to serve three years. Rejected.

REILEY, THOMAS— Age — years. Enlisted April 6, 1865 at Williamsburgh. Mustered in as Private, Co. I, April 6, 1865 to serve three years. Deserted, May 25, 1865 at Winchester, Virginia.

REILEY, WILLIAM— Age 28 years. Date and place of enlistment or muster in as Private Co. A, not stated. Deserted, February 28, 1865 at Remount Camp, Maryland.

REILMYER, ADOLPH— Age 24 years. Enlisted April 3, 1865 at Albany. Mustered in as Private, Co. L, April 3, 1865 to serve three years. Deserted June 8, 1865 at Winchester, Virginia.

REINWALL, MICHAEL— Age 32 years. Enlisted as Private, Co. H, December 16, 1863 at Lyons, to serve three years. Rejected.

REMINGTON, DARIUS— Age 22 years. Enlisted December 10, 1863 at Syracuse. Mustered in as Corporal, Co. B, January 5, 1864 to serve three years. Appointed Sergeant, March 1, 1865. Appointed Commissary Sergeant, date not stated. Mustered out with company, August 1, 1865 at Winchester, Virginia.

REMINGTON, NAPOLEON B.— Age 20 years. Enlisted March 21, 1865 at New York. Mustered in as Private, Co. I, March 21, 1865 to serve one year. Mustered out with company, August 1, 1865 at Winchester, Virginia.

REYNOLDS, GEORGE W.— Age 44 years. Enlisted as Private, Co. E, January 2, 1864 at Eaton, to serve three years. Rejected.

REYNOLDS, OCHLAND F.— Age 21 years. Enlisted February 25, 1864 at Rochester. Mustered in as Private, Co. K, March 10, 1864 to serve three years. Died, December 18, 1864 at Annapolis, Maryland.

REYNOLDS, THOMAS— Age 18 years. Enlisted March 20, 1865 at Duanesbury. Mustered in as Private, Co. I, March 20, 1865 to serve three years. Mustered out with company, August 1, 1865 at Winchester, Virginia.

RHILES, GEORGE H.— Age 18 years. Enlisted as Private, Co. C, December 18, 1863 at Brockport to serve three years. Rejected.

RHODES, SAMUEL D.— Age 22 years. Enlisted April 29, 1863 at Giesboro Point. Mustered in as Bugler, Co. H, April 29, 1864 to serve three years. Mustered out with company, August 1, 1865 at Winchester, Virginia.

RHODES, EDWARD— Age 18 years. Enlisted April 4, 1865 at Albany. Mustered in as Private, Co. A, April 4, 1865 to serve three years. Mustered out with company, August 1, 1865 at Winchester, Virginia.

RHYON, JAMES— See Ryan, James.

RICE, THOMAS— Age 19 years. Enlisted April 8, 1865 at Red Hook. Mustered in as Private, "unassigned," April 8, 1865 to serve one year. Mustered out with detachment, may 6, 1865 at Hart's Island, New York Harbor.

RICE, WILLIAM A.— Age 37 years. Enlisted November 13, 1863 at Urbana. Mustered in as Private, Co. G, February 2, 1864 to serve three years. Mustered out with company, August 1, 1865 at Winchester, Virginia.

RICH, BENJAMIN— Age 31 years. Enlisted December 31, 1863 at Lyons. Mustered in as Private, Co. H, February 2, 1864 to serve three years. Discharged to date July 10, 1865.

RICH, WILLIAM— Age 44 years. Enlisted January 19, 1864 at Rochester. Mustered in as Private, Co. K, February 6, 1864 to serve three years. Mustered out June 20, 1865 at hospital in Philadelphia, Pa.

RICHARD, JOACHIM P.— Age 22 years. Enlisted as Private, Co. D, November 14, 1863 at Rochester to serve three years. Rejected.

RICHARDS, JAMES— Age 27 years. Enlisted January 4, 1864 at Lee. Mustered in as private, Co. C, January 5, 1864 to serve three years. Deserted February 17, 1864 at Rochester, New York.

RICHARDS, LUKE— Age 18 years. Enlisted December 7, 1863 at Rochester. Mustered in as Private, Co. A, December 20, 1863 to serve three years. Mustered out with company, August 1, 1865 at Winchester, Virginia.

RICHARDS, VICTOR C.— Age 23 years. Enlisted December 10, 1863 at Rochester. Mustered in as Private, Co. A, December 20, 1863 to serve three years. Died of disease, May 10, 1864 at Giesboro Point, D.C.

RICHARDSON, DAVID C.— Age 24 years. Enlisted as Private, Co. C, December 1, 1863 at Brockport to serve three years. Rejected.

RICHARDSON, EGBERT— Age 18 years. Enlisted January 5, 1864 at Norwich. Mustered in as Private, Co. L, February 12, 1864 to serve three years. Mustered out with company, August 1, 1865 at Winchester, Virginia.

RICHMOND, WILLIAM— Age 25 years. Enlisted February 22, 1865 at New York. Mustered in as Private, Co. C, February 22, 1865 to serve one year. Mustered out with company, August 1, 1865 at Winchester, Virginia.

RICHMAIER, ADOLPH— Age 24 years. Enlisted April 3, 1865 at Albany. Mustered in as private, "unassigned," April 3, 1865 to serve three years. No further record.

RIDDLE, GEORGE B.— Age 28 years. Enlisted January 15, 1864 at Rochester. Mustered in as Private, Co. I. February 2, 1864 to serve three years. Transferred to Co. M, in March 1864. Absent sick at Rochester at time company was mustered out., August 1, 1865 at Winchester, Virginia.

RIDDLE, THOMAS— Age 18 years. Enlisted February 3, 1864 at Rochester. Mustered in as Private, Co. K, February 6, 1864 to serve three years. Transferred to Co. M, March 25, 1864. Appointed Corporal, April 10, 1865. Mustered out with company, August 1, 1865 at Winchester, Virginia.

RIDGWAY, JOHN— Age 33 years. Enlisted December 26, 1863 at Ontario. Mustered in as Private, Co. H, February 2, 1864 to serve three years. Died, date not known, records of company being lost.

RIGHT, JOHN W.— Age 20 years. Enlisted February 10, 1864 at Rochester. Mustered in as Trumpeter, Co. M, February 23, 1864 to serve three years. No further record.

RIGNOR, WILLIAM H.— Age 16 years. Enlisted January 30, 1864 at Rochester. Mustered in as Private, Co. I, February 2, 1864 to serve three years. Transferred to Co. M, March 1864. Died October 20, 1864 in prison at Charleston, S.C.

RILEY, JOHN— Age 25 years. Enlisted April 13, 1865 at New York. Mustered in as Private, "unassigned," April 13, 1865 to serve one year. Mustered out with detachment, May 6, 1865 at Hart's Island, New York Harbor.

RILEY, PATRICK— Age 19 years. Enlisted February 24, 1865 at New York. Mustered in as Private, Co. H, February 24, 1865 to serve one year. Mustered out with company, August 1, 1865 at Winchester, Virginia. Also borne as Rieley.

RITTER, MYRON— Age 18 years. Enlisted December 18, 1863 at Syracuse. Mustered in as Private, Co. B, January 5, 1864 to serve three years. Discharged June 14, 1865 at Annapolis, Maryland.

RITTER, WILLIAM A.— Age 18 years. Enlisted December 26, 1863 at Syracuse. Mustered in as Private, Co. B, January 5, 1864 to serve three years. Mustered out with company, August 1, 1865 at Winchester, Virginia.

RIVEST, JOSEPH E.— Age 28 years. Enlisted January 11, 1864 at Rochester. Mustered in as Private, Co. I, February 2, 1864 to serve three years. Transferred to Co. M, in March 1864. Appointed First Sergeant, January 11, 1864. Captured June 13, 1864 at White Oak Swamp, Virginia. Released February 24, 1865 at Wilmington, N.C. Reduced and appointed Sergeant, May 1, 1865. Mustered out July 26, 1865 at Rochester, New York.

ROACH EDWARD— Age 25 years. Enlisted January 15, 1864 at Rochester. Mustered in as Private, Co. K, February 6, 1864 to serve three years. Appointed Corporal, date not stated. Transferred to V.C.R., March 20, 1865.

ROACH, MARTIN— Age 19 years. Enlisted January 8, 1864 at Rochester. Mustered in as Private, Co. D, January 10, 1864 to serve three years. Captured June 30, 1864. No further record.

ROACH, MICHAEL— Age 29 years. Enlisted February 13, 1865 at New York. Mustered in as private, Co. H, February 13, 1865 to serve one year. Mustered out with company, August 1, 1864 at Winchester, Virginia.

ROBERTS, HIRAM— Age 27 years. Enlisted January 4, 1864 at Cohocton. Mustered in as Private, Co. G, February 2, 1864 to serve three years. Died, date and place not stated.

ROBERTS, THEODORE M.— Age 20 years. Enlisted January 4, 1864 at Norwich. Mustered in as Sergeant, Co. I, to serve three years. Appointed Quartermaster Sergeant, June 1, 1865. Mustered out with company, August 1, 1864 at Winchester, Virginia.

ROBERTS, THOMAS— Age 30 years. Enlisted January 4, 1864 at Avon. Mustered in as Private, Co. D, January 10, 1864 to serve three years. Captured June 22, 1864. No further record.

ROBERTS, TIMOTHY H.— Age 18 years. Enlisted November 27, 1863 at Rochester. Mustered in as Corporal, Co. I, February 2, 1864 to serve three years. Transferred to Co. A, Twenty-Fourth V.R.C. in July 1864, from which discharged, August 12, 1865 at Washington, D.C.

ROBERTSON, JAMES— Age 21 years. Enlisted February 28, 1864 at Rochester. Mustered in as Private, Co. M, March 8, 1864 to serve three years. Deserted in August, 1864 from hospital in Philadelphia, Pa.

ROBERTSON, JACKSON— Age 26 years. Enlisted January 15, 1864 at Rochester. Mustered in as Private, Co. K, February 6, 1864 to serve three years. Deserted, February 6, 1864 at Rochester, New York.

ROBBINS, LYMAN S.— Age 18 years. Enlisted December 7, 1863 at Sheridan. Mustered in as Private, Co. K, February 6, 1864 to serve three years. Mustered out with company, August 1, 1864 at Winchester, Virginia.

ROBINS, ELISHA A.— Age 44 years. Enlisted January 21, 1864 at Rochester. Mustered in as Private, Co. I, February 2, 1864 to serve three years. Discharged for disability, May 29, 1865.

ROBINSON, CHARLES— Age 19 years. Enlisted March 13, 1865 at Goshen. Mustered in as Private, "unassigned," March 13, 1865 to serve one year. No further record.

ROBINSON, DELOS L.— Age 23 years. Enlisted January 2, 1864 at Bath. Mustered in as Private, Co. K, February 6, 1864 to serve three years. Transferred to Co. G, March 25, 1864. Mustered out with company, August 1, 1864 at Winchester, Virginia.

ROBINSON, WILLIAM— Age 21 years. Enlisted February 23, 1864 at Rochester. Mustered in as Corporal, Co. M, February 23, 1864 to serve three years. Died September 15, 1864 in prison at Andersonville, Georgia.

RODGERS, JAMES— Age 20 years. Enlisted December 21, 1863 at Fredonia. Mustered in as Private, Co. F, January 10, 1864 to serve three years. Deserted, in February 1864 from camp near Rochester, New York. Also borne as Rogers.

ROGERS, OWEN— Age 19 years. Enlisted March 25, 1865 at Red Hook. Mustered in as Private, Co. I, March 25, 1865 to serve three years. Never joined for service. No discharge given at time company was mustered out August 1, 1865. No further record.

RODNER, JACOB J.— See Radner, Jacob G,

ROLSTON, ROBERT S.— Age 23 years. Enlisted November 24, 1863 at Syracuse. Mustered in as Corporal, Co. B, January 5, 1864, to serve three years. Reduced, date not stated. Deserted, August 3, 1864 at Chain Bridge, Virginia.

RONAN, JAMES— Age 24 years. Enlisted February 3, 1864 at Rochester. Mustered in as Private, Co. K, February 6, 1864 to serve three years. Transferred to Co. M, March 25, 1864. Mustered out June 28, 1865 at Winchester, Virginia.

ROONEY, WILLIAM— Age 23 years. Enlisted January 4, 1864 at Rochester. Mustered in as Private, Co. D, January 10, 1864 to serve three years. Mustered out with company, August 1, 1865 at Winchester, Virginia.

ROOT, LAWRENCE— Age 45 years. Enlisted October 5, 1864 at New York. Mustered in as Private, Co. A, October, 5, 1864 to serve one year. Mustered out to date July 27, 1865 at U.S. General Hospital, Cumberland, Maryland.

ROOT, RUBIN— Age 26 years. Enlisted December 21, 1863 at Brockport. Mustered in as Farrier, Co. C, January 5, 1864 to serve three years. Died of disease, as Private, April 9, 1864 at Giesboro, D.C. Prior service in Co. E, First New York Infantry.

RORKE, JOHN— Age 33 years. Enlisted March 15, 1865 at New York. Mustered in as Private, Co. G, March 15, 1865 to serve three years. Appointed Corporal, July 1, 1865. Mustered out with company, August 1, 1865 at Winchester, Virginia.

ROSE, HENRY H.— Age 17 years. Enlisted January 19, 1864 at Onondaga. Mustered in as Private, Co. H, February 2, 1864 to serve three years. Transferred to Co. E, date not stated. Died, date not stated at Andersonville, Georgia.

ROSE, MILLARD— Age !9 years. Enlisted September 14, 1864 at Norwich. Mustered in as Private, Co. F, September 15, 1864 to serve one year. Mustered out June 6, 1865 at Winchester, Virginia.

ROSE, NOAH C.— Age 13 years. Enlisted as Private, Co. I, January 14, 1864 at Rochester to serve three years. Rejected.

ROSE, WILLIAM— Age 22 years. Date and place of enlistment or muster in as Private, Co. A, not stated. Deserted, December 20, 1864 in the field.

ROSEGRANT HIRAM— Age 19 years. Enlisted January 19, 1864 at Rochester. Mustered in as Private, Co. I, February 2, 1864 to serve three years. Deserted May 31, 1865 at Winchester, Virginia.

ROURKE, MICHAEL— Age 18 years. Enlisted December 20, 1863 at Livonia. Mustered in as Private, Co. D, January 10. 1864 to serve three years. Mustered out with company, August 1, 1865 at Winchester, Virginia.

ROUSSEAU, JOHN— Age 22 years. Enlisted December 12, 1863 at Irondequoit. Mustered in as Private, Co. A, December 20, 1863 to serve three years. Appointed Corporal, May 19, 1865. Discharged June 28, 1865 while paroled prisoner at Winchester, Virginia.

ROUSSOU, FRANK— Age 29 years. Enlisted February 23, 1865 at new York. Mustered in as Private, Co. B, February 23, 1865 to serve three years. Mustered out with company, August 1, 1865 at Winchester, Virginia.

ROWE, WILLIAM H.B.— Age 19 years. Enlisted December 3, 1863 at Dunkirk. Mustered in as First Sergeant, Co. K, February 6, 1864 to serve three years. Mustered out June 28, 1865 at Winchester, Virginia.

ROWLEY, ANDREW H.— Age 20 years. Enlisted March 30, 1865 at Rochester. Mustered in as Private, Co. F, March 30, 1865 to serve three years. No further record.

ROYK, WARREN A.— Age 18 years. Enlisted November 23, 1863 at Urbana. Mustered in as Bugler, Co. G, February 2, 1864 to serve three years. Mustered out with company, August 1, 1865 at Winchester, Virginia.

RUNDELL, GEORGE— Age 24 years. Enlisted December 14, 1863 at Madison. Mustered in as Private, Co. E, January 10, 1864 to serve three years. Mustered out with company, August 1, 1865 at Winchester, Virginia.

RUNKIN, PETER— Age 22 years. Enlisted April 11, 1865 at Syracuse. Mustered in as Private, Co. F, April 11, 1865 to serve three years. Mustered out with company, August 1, 1865 at Winchester, Virginia.

RUSS, GEORGE L.— Age 18 years. Enlisted December 15, 1863 at Hamilton. Mustered in as Private, Co. E, January 10, 1864 to serve three years. Transferred to Co. A, Twentieth V.R.C. from which discharged, August 14, 1865 at Philadelphia, Pa.

RUSS, JOHN W.— Age 21 years. Enlisted December 15, 1863 at Hamilton. Mustered in as Private, Co. E, January 10, 1864 to serve three years. Died, date not stated, at Andersonville, Georgia.

RUSSELL, WILLIAM— Age 19 years. Enlisted December 14, 1864 at New York. Mustered in as Private, Co. B, December 14, 1864 to serve three years. Mustered out with company, August 1, 1865 at Winchester, Virginia.

RYAN, ANDREW J.— Age 21 years. Enlisted March 30, 1865 at Brooklyn. Mustered in as Private, Co. K, March 30, 1865 to serve three years. Mustered out June 15, 1865 at Harpers Ferry, Virginia.

RYAN, FRANCIS— Age 19 years. Enlisted February 21, 1865 at New York. Mustered in as Private, "unassigned," February 24, 1865 to serve three years. Admitted to McDougall General Hospital, New York, June 29, 1865. Mustered out July 26, 1865.

RYAN, FRANK— Age 19 years. Enlisted January 5, 1864 at Rochester. Mustered in as Farrier, Co. F, January 10, 1864 to serve three years. Deserted in February 1864 from camp near Rochester, New York.

RYAN, GEORGE N.— Age 21 years. Enlisted January 4, 1864 at Pomfret. Mustered in as Private, Co. L, February 12, 1864 to serve three years. Transferred to Co. K, March 15, 1864. Captured, June 30, 1864. Released, date not stated. Appointed Sergeant, date not stated. Mustered out July 12, 1865 at new York. Also borne as George A.

RYAN, JAMES— Age 24 years. Enlisted April 14, 1865 at Kingston. Mustered in as Private, Co. C, April 14, 1865 to serve three years. Mustered out with detachment, May 6, 1865 at Hart's Island, New York Harbor.

RYAN, JAMES— Age 18 years. Enlisted December 16, 1863 at Cazenovia. Mustered in as Private, Co. E, January 10, 1864 to serve three years. Died, date not stated, at Andersonville, Georgia. Also borne as Ryaur and Rhyon.

RYAN, JEREMIAH— Age 24 years. Enlisted March 25, 1865 at Auburn. Mustered in as Private, "unassigned," March 25, 1865 to serve one year. No further record.

RYAN, JOHN— Age 19 years. Enlisted February 2, 1864 at Rochester. Mustered in as Private, Co. K, February 6, 1864 to serve three years. Transferred to Co. M, March 25, 1864. No further record.

RYAN,MARTIN— Age 33 years. Enlisted December 29, 1863 at Rochester. Mustered in as Private, Co. C, January 5, 1864 to serve three years. Transferred to Co. A, March 22, 1864. Died of disease, September 10, 1864 at Sandy Hook, Maryland.

RYAN, MICHAEL— Age 21 years. Enlisted February 22, 1864 at Rochester. Mustered in as Farrier, Co. M, February 23, 1864 to serve three years. Mustered out with company, August 1, 1865 at Winchester, Virginia.

RYAN, PETER— Age 28 years. Enlisted February 22, 1864 at New York. Mustered in as Private, Co. E, February 22, 1864 to serve three years. Mustered out with company, August 1, 1865 at Winchester, Virginia.

RYAN, THOMAS— Age 38 years. Enlisted as Private, Co. E, December 14, 1863 at Syracuse, to serve three years. Rejected.

RYAN, THOMAS— Age 21 years. Enlisted October 27, 1863 at Rochester. Mustered in as Private, Co. A, December 20, 1863 to serve three years. Mustered out with company, August 1, 1865 at Winchester, Virginia. Prior service in Co. H, Twenty Seventh New York Infantry.

RYAN, WILLIAM— Age 21 years. Enlisted February 22, 1864 at Rochester. Mustered in as Corporal, Co. M, February 23, 1864 to serve three years. Reduced, date not stated. Mustered out with company, August 1, 1865 at Winchester, Virginia.

SAFFORD, MANLEY A.— Age 20 years. Enlisted November 11, 1863 at Barre. Mustered in as Private, Co. F, January 10, 1864, to serve three years. Appointed Sergeant, March 1, 1864. Mustered out June 28, 1865 at Winchester, Virginia. Veteran.

SAFFORD, WILLIAM— Age 18 years. Enlisted November 16, 1863 at Albion. Mustered in as Corporal, Co. F, January 10, 1864 to serve three years. Mustered out with company, August 1, 1865 at Winchester, Virginia.

SAGER, WILLIAM— Age 21 years. Enlisted December 14, 1863 at Rochester. Mustered in as Private, Co. C, January 5, 1864 to serve three years. Died in captivity at Florence, S.C., date not known.

SAIERS, ROBERT— See Swires, Robert.

SALISBURY, CHARLES F.— Age 16 years. Enlisted December 14, 1863 at Cazenovia. Mustered in as Private, Co. E, January 10, 1864 to serve three years. Mustered out with company, August 1, 1865 at Winchester, Virginia.

SAMPSON, SIMEON— Age 18 years. Enlisted March 1, 1865 at Syracuse. Mustered in as Private, Co. B, March 1, 1865 to serve three years. Mustered out with company, August 1, 1865 at Winchester, Virginia.

SANDERSON, WILLIAM— Age 18 years. Enlisted January 4, 1864 at Manlius. Mustered in as Private, Co. E, January 10, 1864 to serve three years. Discharged for disability, November 12, 1864 at Washington, D.C.

SANFORD, WILLARD— Age 22 years. Enlisted November 6, 1863 at Brockport. Mustered in as Sergeant, Co. C, January 5, 1864 to serve three years. Died in hospital at Baltimore, Maryland. Prior service in Co. D, Thirteenth New York Infantry.

SARTCHFIELD, JAMES— Age 18 years. Enlisted December 10, 1863 at Rochester. Mustered in as Private, Co. A, December 20, 1863 to serve three years. Captured at Stony Creek, Virginia., June 29, 1864. Confined at Andersonville, Georgia. Released at N.E.Bridge, N.C., March 1, 1865. Mustered out June 7, 1865 at Annapolis, Maryland.

SARTWELL, JOHN E.— Age 19, years. Enlisted as Private, Co. K, January 31, 1864 at Rochester, to serve three years. Rejected.

SAUR, HENRY— Age 28 years. Enlisted March 7, 1865 at New York. Mustered in as Private, "unassigned," March 7, 1865 to serve three years. Mustered out September 20, 1865 at Elmira, New York.

SAWDEY, JAMES K.— Age 18 years. Enlisted December 18, 1863 at Hamilton. Mustered in as Private, Co. E, January 10, 1864 to serve three years. Appointed Corporal, date not stated. Mustered out with company, August 1, 1865 at Winchester, Virginia.

SAWYER, ELMER— Age 18 years. Enlisted February 22, 1864 at Rochester. Mustered in as Private, Co. M, February 23, 1864 to serve three years. Died in prison, November 25, 1864 at Florence, S.C.

SAWYER, HENRY— Age 22 years. Enlisted as Private, Co. D, December 25, 1863 at Rochester, to serve three years. Rejected.

SAXTON, RANSOM— Age 19 years. Enlisted December 22, 1863 at Rome. Mustered in as Private, Co. C, January 5, 1864 to serve three years. No further record.

SAYLES, ALBERT G.— Age 19 years. Enlisted February 25, 1864 at Manlius. Mustered in as Private, Co. F, March 9, 1864 to serve three years. Died at Andersonvile, Georgia., date not stated.

SAYLES, AMOS G.— Age 44 years. Enlisted as Private, Co. K, December 20, 1863 at Smithfield, to serve three years. Rejected.

SAYRUSCH, JAMES W.— Age 33 years. Enlisted February 21, 1865 at new York. Mustered in as Private, "unassigned," February 21, 1865 to serve three years. No further record.

SCANTLIN, JOHN— Age 19 years. Enlisted February 21, 1865 at Canandaigua. Mustered in as Private, Co. H, February 21, 1865 to serve one year. Mustered out with company, August 1, 1865 at Winchester, Virginia. Also borne as Scantyn.

SCHARET, WILLIAM— See Schurer, William.

SCHEIB, WILLIAM H.— Age 17 years. Enlisted January 25, 1864 at Rochester. Mustered in as Private, Co. K, February 6, 1864 to serve three years. Transferred to Co. M, March 25, 1864, to Fifty-fifth Company, Veteran Reserve Corps, January 7, 1865, from which discharged, September 15, 1865 at Chester, Pa.

SCHERMERHORN, DAVID F.— Age 19 years. Enlisted April 10, 1865 at Albany. Mustered in as Private, "unassigned," April 10, 1865 to serve one year. Mustered out May 6, 1865 at Hart's Island, New York Harbor.

SCHENCK, VALENTINE— Age 41 years. Enlisted April 6, 1865 at Brooklyn. Mustered in as Bugler, April 6, 1865 to serve one year. Mustered out with company, August 1, 1865 at Winchester, Virginia.

SCHENISH, JAMES— Enlisted as Private, Co. C, to serve three years, February 21, 1865 at New York. No record of muster in. Mustered out with company, August 1, 1865 at Winchester, Virginia.

SCHEPMUS, NELSON— Age 19 years. Enlisted April 12, 1865 at New York. Mustered in as Private, "unassigned," April 12, 1865 to serve one year. Mustered out, May 6, 1865 at Hart's Island, New York Harbor.

SCHLICK, THEODORE— Officer

SCHLOUT, GEORGE I.— Age 34 years. Enlisted March 4, 1865 at Ellicottsville. Mustered in as Private, Co. L, March 4, 1865 to serve three years. Mustered out with company, August 1, 1865 at Winchester, Virginia.

SCHMITH, JACOB— Age 26 years. Enlisted December 2, 1863 at Rochester. Mustered in as Private, Co. A, December 20, 1863 to serve three years. Deserted, December 20, 1863 at Rochester, New York.

SCHOLL, FREDERICK— Age 22 years. Enlisted March 7, 1864 at Rochester. Mustered in as Private, Co. M, March 9, 1864 to serve three years. Sent to Brigade Hospital, June 1, 1865. Absent on muster out of company, August 1, 1865. No further record.

SCHOLL, WILLIAM— Age 18 years, Enlisted January 27, 1864 at Rochester. Mustered in as Private, Co. M, February 23, 1864 to serve three years. Died in prison, October 20, 1864 at Charleston, S.C.

SCHORN, JACOB— Age 18 years. Enlisted as Private, Co. L, April 3, 1865 at Norwich. No record of muster in. Mustered out with company, August 1, 1865 at Winchester, Virginia.

SCHRADER, HENRY— Age 27 years. Enlisted March 3, 1864 at New York. Mustered in as Private, "unassigned," March 3, 1865 to serve three years. No further record.

SCHUH, JOHN— Age 25 years. Enlisted April 4, 1865 at Albany. Mustered in as Private, Co. L, April 4, 1864, to serve three years. Mustered out with company, August 1, 1865 at Winchester, Virginia.

SCHUPPERT, CHARLES— Age 22 years. Enlisted March 15, 1865 at New York. Mustered in as Private, "unassigned," March 15, 1865 to serve one year. No further record.

SCHURER, WILLIAM— Age 18 years. Enlisted April 10, 1865 at Albany. Mustered in as Private, "unassigned," April 10, 1865 to serve one year. Mustered out May 6, 1865 at Hart's Island, New York Harbor. Also borne as Scharet.

SCHUYLER, CHARLES M.— Age 15 years. Enlisted January 22, 1864 at Rochester. Mustered in as Private, Co. K, February 6, 1864 to serve three years. Transferred to Co. M, March 25, 1864. Mustered out with company, August 1, 1865 at Winchester, Virginia.

SCHWARTZ, CARL— Age 21 years. Enlisted February 20, 1865 at New York. Mustered in as Private, "unassigned," February 20, 1865 to serve three years. No further record.

SCHWENBERGER, LEONHARD— Age 20 years. Enlisted March 3, 1865 at New York. Mustered in as Private, Co. I, March 3, 1865 to serve three years. Mustered out with company, August 1, 1865 at Winchester, Virginia. Also borne as Shonberger.

SCOTT, CHARLES N.— Age 18 years. Enlisted January 4, 1864 at Rochester. Mustered in as Private, Co. D, January 10, 1864 to serve three years. Mustered out with company, August 1, 1865 at Winchester, Virginia.

SCOTT, HARRY E.— Age 18 years. Enlisted April12, 1865 at Canandaigua. Mustered in as Private, Co. F, April 12, 1865 to serve three years. Mustered out with company, August 1, 1865 at Winchester, Virginia.

SCOTT, HENRY C.— Age 18 years. Enlisted January 5, 1864 at Plymouth. Mustered in as Private, Co. L, February 12, 1864 to serve three years. Mustered out with company, August 1, 1865 at Winchester, Virginia.

SCOTT, JAY M JR.— Age 18 years. Enlisted January 14, 1864 at Preston. Mustered in as Private, Co. L, February 12, 1864 to serve three years. Discharged, December 9, 1864.

SCOTT, THOMAS— Age 29 years. Enlisted March 24, 1865 at New York. Mustered in as Private, "unassigned," March 24, 1865 to serve three years. No further record.

SCOTT, WILLIAM H.— Age 18 years. Enlisted December 10, 1863 at Rochester. Mustered in as Private, Co. I, February 2, 1864 to serve three years. Deserted March 22, 1864 at Rochester, New York.

SCOVILLE, FRANK— Age 44 years. Enlisted February 13, 1864 at Verona. Mustered in as Private, Co. M, February 13, 1864 to serve three years. Discharged at Washington, D.C., date not stated.

SCRIBNER, J.D.P.— Age 38 years. Enlisted December 4, 1863 at Arcadia. Mustered in as Private, Co. H, February 2, 1864 to serve three years. Mustered out with company, August 1, 1865 at Winchester, Virginia.

SCULLIN, PAUL— Age 22 years. Enlisted January 2, 1864 at Andes. Mustered in as Private, Co. L, February 12, 1864 to serve three years. Mustered out with detachment, June 28, 1865 at Winchester, Virginia.

SEARY, ALVAH H.— See Leary, Alvah H.

SEEDORE, WILLIAM F.— Age 35 years. Enlisted January 29, 1864 at Prattsburgh. Mustered in as Private, Co. G, February 2, 1864 to serve three years. Captured June 29, 1864. Discharged May 30, 1865 at United States General Hospital, Cumberland, Maryland.

SEELEN, FREDERICK— Age 35 years. Enlisted March 31, 1865 at New York. Mustered in as Private, "unassigned," March 31, 1865 to serve three years. Mustered out June 22, 1865 at United States General Hospital, Cumberland, Maryland.

SEELY, LUCEAN B.— Age 18 years. Enlisted December 15, 1865 at Fredonia. Mustered in as Private, Co. F, January 10, 1864 to serve three years. Transferred to Co. K, March, 1864 as Bugler. Deserted, June 24, 1865 near Winchester, Virginia.

SEGER, ADAM— Age 37 years. Enlisted December 28, 1863 at Palmyra. Mustered in as Corporal, Co. H, February 2, 1864 to serve three years. Reduced to ranks, date not stated. Mustered out with company, August 1, 1865 at Winchester, Virginia. Also borne as Seager.

SEHNER, GEORGE— Age 21 years. Enlisted November 27, 1863 at Lyons. Mustered in as Blacksmith, Co. D, January 10, 1864 to serve three years. Mustered out with company, August 1, 1865 at Winchester, Virginia. Prior service in Co. B, Twenty Seventh New York Volunteers.

SEIVER, LORENZO— Age 20 years. Enlisted as Private, Co. C, at Rome, November 30, 1863 to serve three years. Rejected for rupture.

SEIZE, GEORGE— Age 22 years. Enlisted February 14, 1865 at New York. Mustered in as Private, Co. M, February 17, 1865 for serve three years. Mustered out to date July 21, 1865 at Harpers Ferry, Virginia.

SEMS, JOHN— Age 18 years. Enlisted December 17, 1863 at Rochester. Mustered in as Private, Co. D, January 10, 1864 to serve three years. Prisoner of war on muster out of company, August 1, 1865. No further record.

SERENSON, WILLIAM M.— Age 27 years. Enlisted February 28, 1865 at New York. Mustered in as Private, Co. M, February 28, 1865 to serve three years. Deserted, June 17, 1865 near Winchester, Virginia.

SERGEANT, IRA S.— Age 28 years. Enlisted January 23, 1864 at New Lisbon. Mustered in as Private, Co. I, February 12, 1864 to serve three years. Mustered out June 23, 1865 at Harper's Ferry, Virginia. Also borne as Sargeant.

SERGEANT, JAMES H.— Age 24 years. Enlisted December 21, 1863 at Sodus. Mustered in as Commissary Sergeant, Co. H, February 2, 1864 to serve three years. Mustered out with company, August 1, 1865 at Winchester, Virginia.

SERGEANT, WILLIAM H.— Age 20 years. Enlisted December 21, 1863 at Sodus. Mustered in as Corporal, Co. H, February 2, 1864 to serve three years. Mustered out with company, August 1, 1865 at Winchester, Virginia.

SHADDERS, HENRY C.— Age 37 years. Enlisted December 12, 1863 at Rochester. Mustered in as Trumpeter, Co. I, February 2, 1864 to serve three years. Appointed Sergeant, to date March 1, 1865. Mustered out with company, August 1, 1865 at Winchester, Virginia.

SHAEFER, CHARLES— Age 20 years. Enlisted March 14, 1865 at New York. Mustered in as Private, Co. I, March 14, 1865 to serve one year. Died June, 1865 at Winchester, Virginia. Also borne as Shaffer, Carl.

SHAFFER, PETER -Age 35 years. Enlisted December 31, 1863 at Nelson. Mustered in as Corporal, Co. E, January 10, 1864 to serve three years. Captured and paroled, no dates stated. Mustered out July 18, 1865 at Elmira, New York.

SHALOWS, JOSEPH -Age 17 years. Enlisted December 14, 1863 at Rochester. Mustered in as Private, Co. K, February 6, 1864 to serve three years. Name transferred to Co. C, March 25, 1864. Found to have deserted February 28, 1864 at Rochester, New York.

SHANNON, EDWARD -Age 18 years. Enlisted April 5, 1865 at Albany. Mustered in as Private "unassigned" April 10, 1865 to serve three years. Mustered out with detachment May 6, 1865 at Harts Island, New York Harbor.

SHANNON, JOHN -Age 18 years. Enlisted April 14, 1865 at Kortright. Mustered in as Private, "unassigned" April 14, 1865 to serve three years. Mustered out with detachment, May 6, 1865 at Harts Island, New York Harbor.

SHAREFF, FRANK A -See Sherff, Frank A.

SHATTUCK, HARRISON A -Age 18 years. Enlisted January 29, 1864 at Plattsburgh. Mustered in as a Private, Co. G, February 2, 1864 to serve three years. Discharged for disability, December 24, 1864 at Philadelphia, Pa.

SHAVER, ELIAS -Age 18 years. Enlisted January 2, 1864 at Avoca. Mustered in as Private, Co. G, February 2, 1864 to serve three years. Died, date not stated.

SHAVER, BENJAMIN N-Age 18 years. Enlisted December 18, 1863 at Cazenovia. Mustered in as a Private, Co. E, January 4, 1864 to serve three years. Died at Andersonville, Georgia.

SHAW, BERNARD -Age 32 years. Enlisted March 14, 1865 at New York. Mustered in as a Private, "unassigned" to serve one year, March 14, 1865. No further record.

SHAW, LEWIS -Age 17 years. Enlisted December 28, 1863 at Bath. Mustered in as Private, Co. G, February 2, 1864 to serve three years. In confinement at Fort Delaware, May 12, 1865 under sentence of court-martial. Discharged August 9, 1865 at Rochester, New York.

SHAW, WILLIAM -Age 25 years. Enlisted January 15, 1864 at Rochester. Mustered in as Private, "unassigned" January 16, 1864 to serve three years. No further record.

SHEAR, JOHN -Age 30 years. Enlisted as Private, Co. B, December 19, 1863 at Syracuse to serve three years. Rejected.

SHIELS, EDMOND -Age 23 years. Enlisted January 15, 1864 at Rochester. Mustered in as Corporal Co. K, February 6, 1864 to serve three years. Appointed Sergeant, date not given. First Sergeant, July 1, 1865. Mustered out with company, August 1, 1865 at Winchester, Virginia.

SHELDON, CHARLES N -Age 44 years. Enlisted as Private in Co. I, December 26, 1863 at Rochester, to serve three years. Rejected.

SHELDON, FRANK -Age 18 years. Enlisted January 4, 1864 at OtisCo. Mustered in as Private, Co. E, January 10, 1864 to serve three years. Mustered out with detachment, June 28, 1865 at Winchester, Virginia.

SHEPARD, MILLER -Age 18 years. Enlisted April 11, 1865 at Rochester. Mustered in as Private, Co. F, April 11, 1865 to serve two years. Mustered out with company, August 1, 1865 at Winchester, Virginia.

SHEPARDSON, LORENZO -Age 23 years. Enlisted December 17, 1863 at Hamilton. Mustered in as Private, Co. E, January 10, 1864 to serve three years. Appointed Corporal, no date given. Died, date not stated at Andersonville, Georgia.

SHEPHARD, CHARLES -Age 22 years. Enlisted March 15, 1865 at New York. Mustered in as Private, Co. A, March 15, 1865 to serve one year. Deserted July 24, 1865 at Remount Camp, Maryland.

SHEPHERD, WILLIAM H -Age 17 years. Enlisted December 9, 1863 at Cazenovia. Mustered in as Private, Co. E, January 10, 1864 to serve three years. Mustered out with detachment, June 28, 1865 at Winchester, Virginia.

SHERFF, FRANK A — Age 18years. Enlisted December 28 at Syracuse. Mustered in as Private, Co. B, January 5, 1864 to serve three years. Mustered out with company, August 1, 1865 at Winchester, Virginia.

SHERIDAN, EDWARD — Age 28 years. Enlisted March 17, 1865 at Lockport. Mustered in as Private, Co. C, March 17, 1865 to serve three years. Mustered out with company, August 1, 1865 at Winchester, Virginia.

SHERWOOD, GEORGE H — Age 18 years. Enlisted November 3, 1863 at Auburn. Mustered in as Private, Co. I, February 2, 1864, to serve three years. Deserted, August, 1864 at Harpers Ferry, Virginia.

SHERWOOD, MARVIN R -Officer

SHIPP, HENRY -Age 17 years. Enlisted at Barre, as Private, Co. F, December 7, 1863 to serve three years. Rejected.

SHIPP, HENRY — Age 16 years. Enlisted December 1, 1863 at Brockport as Private, Co. C, to serve three years. Rejected, under age.

SHOALS, WILLIAM — Age 43 years. Enlisted as Private, Co. I, to serve three years. December 21, 1863 at Rochester. Rejected, disease.

SHOAT, CHARLES S.— Age 22 years. Enlisted December 25, 1863 at Rochester. Mustered in as Private, Co. D, January 10, 1864 to serve three years. Mustered out with company, August 1, 1865 at Winchester, Virginia.

SHONBERGER, LEONHARD — See Schwenberger, Leonhard.

SHULTS, ELIAS — Age 22 years. Enlisted January 7, 1864 at Bath. Mustered in as Farrier, Co. G, February 2, 1864 to serve three years. Captured June 29, 1864, paroled March 1, 1865. Discharged, June 28, 1865 at Winchester, Virginia.

SHWEIKERT, CHARLES— Age 26 years. Enlisted March 7, 1865 at New York. Mustered in as Private, Co. I, March 7, 1865 to serve one year. Mustered out with company, August 1, 1865 at Winchester, Virginia.

SILVERNAH, DAVID — Age 18 years. Enlisted December 13, 1863 at Syracuse. Mustered in as Private, Co. B, January 5, 1864 to serve three years. Mustered out with company, August 1, 1865 at Winchester, Virginia.

SIMMONS, AARON — Age 29 years. Enlisted October 21, 1863 at Rochester. Mustered in as Private, Co. A, December 20, 1863 to serve three years. Deserted, February 6, 1864 at Rochester.

SIMMONS, MYRON — Age 18 years. Enlisted December 8, 1863 at Brockport. Mustered in as Private, Co. C, January 5, 1864 to serve three years. Mustered out with company, August 1, 1865 at Winchester, Virginia.

SIMPSON, ZACHARIAH T — Age 21 years. Enlisted February 23, 1864 at Rochester. Mustered in as Private, Co. M, February 23, 1864 to serve three years. No further record.

SIMS, LEWIS — Age 36 years. Enlisted February 13, 1865 at Buffalo. Mustered in as Private, Co. H, February 13, 1865, to serve three years. Mustered out with company, August 1, 1865 at Winchester, Virginia.

SINCLAIR, CHARLES — Age 26 years. Enlisted February 23, 1865 at new York. Mustered in as Private "unassigned" February 23, 1865 to serve three years. No further record.

SINGLE, JOSEPH — Age 41 years. Enlisted March 7, 1865 at New York. Mustered in as Private, Co. I, March 7, 1865, to serve three years. Mustered out with company, August 1, 1865 at Winchester, Virginia.

SINZER, JAMES — Age 26 years. Private, Co. A, date and place of enlistment not shown. Deserted February 28, 1865 at Remount Camp, Virginia.

SISSON, PERRY V.— Age 26 years. Enlisted January 7, 1864 at Rochester. Mustered in as Private, Co. I, February 2, 1864 to serve three years. Transferred to Co. M, March 1864. Appointed Sergeant, date not stated. Died in prison, July 1864 at Andersonville, Georgia. Also borne as Sissen, Terry V. Prior service in Co. C, Sixth Indiana Volunteers.

SKEEL, ALBERT — Age 33 years. Enlisted December 14, 1863 at Syracuse. Mustered in as Private, Co. B, January 5, 1864 to serve three years. Appointed Corporal, date not stated. Mustered out with company, August 1, 1865 at Winchester, Virginia.

SKELLION, CHARLES — Age 18 years. Enlisted December 8, 1863 at Brockport. Mustered in as Private, Co. C, January 5, 1864, to serve three years. Mustered out with company, August 1, 1865 at Winchester, Virginia.

SKINNER, JAMES G — Age 24 years. Enlisted January 11, 1864 at North Norwich. Mustered in as Private, Co. L, January 11, 1864 to serve three years. Died in hospital at City Point, Virginia. of wounds received in action, June 20, 1864.

SLATER, TRUMAN — Age 19 years. Enlisted December 10, 1863 at Jerusalem. Mustered in as Private, Co. A, December 20, 1863 to serve three years. Mustered out with company, August 1, 1865 at Winchester, Virginia.

SLAVIN, FRANCIS — Age 33 years. Enlisted December 14, 1863 at Rochester. Mustered in as Private, Co. D, January 10, 1864 to serve three years. Prisoner of war since June 30, 1864. No further record.

SLEEPER, CHARLES C — Age 23 years. Enlisted March 1, 1865 at Schenectady. Mustered in as Private, Co. E, March 1, 1865 to serve three years. Mustered out with company, August 1, 1865 at Winchester, Virginia.

SLOAN, GEORGE W — Age 18 years. Enlisted January 20, 1864 at Pompey. Mustered in as Private, Co. B, February 2, 1864 to serve three years. Mustered out with detachment, June 28, 1865 at Winchester, Virginia.

SLOCUM, ELISHA— Age 36 years. Enlisted as Private, Co. E, December 29, 1863 at Cazenovia, to serve three years. Rejected, to feeble.

SLOUT, GEORGE, J — Age 34 years. Enlisted March 4, 1865 at Elliotville. Mustered in as Private "unassigned" March 4,1865 to serve three years. No further record.

SLOVER, HENRY — Age 20 years. Enlisted January 18, 1864. Mustered in as Private, Co. G, February 2, 1864, to serve three years. Transferred to Co. E, March 22, 1864. Mustered out with detachment, June 28, 1865 at Winchester, Virginia.

SMALTZ, CARL — Age — years. Enlisted February 24, 1865 at New York. Mustered in as Private, Co. C, February 24, 1865, to serve three years. Mustered out with company, August 1, 1865 at Winchester, Virginia.

SMITH, ADELBERT L — Age 18 years. Enlisted January 5, 1864 at Norwich. Mustered in as Private, Co. L, February 12, 1864 to serve three years. Mustered out with company, August 1, 1865 at Winchester, Virginia.

SMITH, ALEXANDER M — Age 28 years. Enlisted November 18, 1863 at Bath. Mustered in as Corporal, Co. G, February 2, 1864 to serve three years. Reduced, date not stated. Died about July 24, 1865. Prior service in Eighty-Fourth Pennsylvania Infantry.

SMITH, BENJAMIN F — Age 18 years. Enlisted December 15, 1863, at Albion, as Private, Co. F, to serve three years. Rejected.

SMITH, CHARLES — Age 18 years. Enlisted November 29, 1863 at Rochester. Mustered in as Private, Co. I, February 2, 1864 to serve three years. Mustered out as Bugler, June 3, 1865 at Washington, D.C.

SMITH, CHARLES V — Age 27 years. Enlisted January 5, 1864 at Smithfield. Mustered in as Private, Co. L, February 12, 1864 to serve three years. Appointed Corporal, no date given. Deserted, December 8, 1864 from hospital.

SMITH, EMERSON — Age 18 year. Enlisted January 21, 1864 at Lafayette. Mustered in as Private, Co. H, February 2, 1864 to serve three years. Mustered out with company, August 1, 1864 at Winchester, Virginia.

SMITH, FRANCIS M — Age 21 years. Enlisted January 1, 1864 at Syracuse. Mustered in as Private, Co. B, January 5, 1864 to serve three years. Transferred to Co. I, March 29, 1864. Appointed Corporal, date not stated. Mustered out with company, August 1, 1864 at Winchester, Virginia.

SMITH, FREDERICK — Age 21 years. Enlisted December 21, 1863 at Riga. Mustered in as Corporal, Co. C, January 5, 1864 to serve three years. Died of disease, as Private, October 18, 1864 at Annapolis, Maryland.

SMITH, GEORGE — Age 42 years. Enlisted as Private Co. K, December 21, 1863 at Dunkirk, to serve three years. Rejected.

SMITH, GEORGE — Age 27 years. Enlisted February 18, 1864 at Rochester. Mustered in as Private, Co. M, February 23, 1864 to serve three years. No further record.

SMITH, GEORGE — Age 21 years. Enlisted March 14, 1865 at New York. Mustered in as Private, "unassigned" March 14, 1865 to serve three years. No further record.

SMITH, GEORGE N — Age 22 years. Enlisted December 14, 1863 at Lyons. Mustered in as Private, Co. H, February 2, 1864 to serve three years. Deserted, records lost.

SMITH, JAMES — Age 19 years. Enlisted December 15, 1863 at Syracuse. Mustered in as Private, Co. B, January 5, 1864 to serve three years. Deserted January 6, 1864 at Rochester, New York.

SMITH, JAMES — Age 22 years. Enlisted January 4, 1864 at OtisCo. Mustered in as Private, Co. E, January 10, 1864 to serve three years. Deserted, January 13, 1864 at Rochester, New York.

SMITH, JAMES — Age 22 years. Enlisted April 8, 1865 at Brooklyn. Mustered in as Private, Co. I, April 8, 1865 to serve three years. Mustered out May 6, 1865 at Hart's Island, New York Harbor.

SMITH, JAMES — Age 23 years. Enlisted April 12, 1865 at Brooklyn. Mustered in as Private, "unassigned", April12, 1865 to serve three years. Mustered out May 6, 1865 at Hart's Island, New York Harbor.

SMITH, JAMES A — Age 19 years. Enlisted December 14, 1863 at Lyons. Mustered in as Trumpeter, Co. H, February 2, 1864 to serve three years. Died, records lost.

SMITH, J. MONTRYSON — officer

SMITH, JOHN — Age 20 years. Enlisted December 8, 1863 at Rochester. Mustered in as Private, Co. F, January 10, 1864 to serve three years

SMITH, JOHN — Age 29 years. Enlisted January 2, 1864 at Pomfret. Mustered in as Corporal, Co. K, February 6, 1864 to serve three years. Deserted, September 18, 1864 at Washington, D.C.

SMITH, JOHN — Age 20 years. Enlisted February 17, 1865 at New York. Mustered in as Private, Co. M, February 17, 1865 to serve three years. Deserted, June 26, 1865 near Winchester, Virginia.

SMITH, JUDSON — Age 18 years. Enlisted December 14, 1863 at Elmira. Mustered in as Private, Co. M, December 18, 1863 to serve three years. Mustered out with company, August 1, 1865 at Winchester, Virginia.

SMITH, NATHANIEL — Age 44 years. Enlisted as Private, Co. H, at Syracuse, January 6, 1864 to serve three years. Rejected, February 2, 1864.

SMITH, RICHARD — Age 20 years. Enlisted January 15, 1864 at Rochester as Private Co. K, to serve three years. Rejected.

SMITH, SAMUEL — Age 18 years. Enlisted March 27, 1865 at Syracuse. Mustered in as Private, "unassigned", March 27, 1865 to serve three years. Mustered out August 4, 1865 at Elmira, New York.

SMITH, THEODORE — Age 22 years. Enlisted March 18, 1864 at Giesboro Point, D.C. Mustered in as Private, Co. F, March 18, 1865 to serve three years. Died October, 1864 at Florence, S.C.

SMITH, THOMAS — Age 23years. Enlisted February 28, 1865 at New York. Mustered in as Private, Co. I, February 28, 1865 to serve three years. Deserted, May 25, 1865 at Winchester, Virginia.

SMITH, THOMAS C — Age 16 years. Enlisted January 21 1864 at Rochester. Mustered in as Private, Co. I, February 2, 1864 to serve three years. Transferred to Co. M, March 1864. Transferred to Co. C, Third Company Provisional Cavalry, Veteran Reserve Corps, date not stated. Retransferred to Co. M, Twenty Second New York Cavalry, April 22, 1865. Mustered out with company, August 1, 1865 at Winchester, Virginia.

SMITH, VAN DE MARK — Age 21 years. Enlisted November 14, 1863 at Rochester. Mustered in as Quartermaster Sergeant, Co. D, January 10, 1864 to serve three years. Discharged for disability, May 20, 1865 at hospital in Philadelphia, Pa.

SMITH, WALLACE W — Age 25 years. Enlisted September 16, 1864 at Albany. Mustered in as Private, "unassigned", September 20, 1864 to serve one year. No further record.

SMYTH, MONTRESSON -See Smith, J. Montryson— See Smith, J.Montryson.

SNOW, THOMAS J — Age 40 years. Enlisted December 23, 1863 at Riga. Mustered in as Private, Co. C, January 5, 1864 to serve three years. Mustered out with company, August 1, 1865 at Winchester, Virginia.

SNYDER, ASA R.— Age 21 years. Enlisted February 19, 1864 at Rochester. Mustered in as Private, Co. M, February 23, 1864 to serve three years. Appointed Corporal, date not stated. Transferred to Co. F, January 8, 1865. Appointed First Sergeant, date not stated. Mustered out with company, August 1, 1865 at Winchester, Virginia. Veteran.

SNYDER, JOHN — Age 28 years. Enlisted April7, 1865 at Lapeer. Mustered in as Private, Co. E, April 7, 1865 to serve three years. Mustered out with company, August 1, 1865 at Winchester, Virginia.

SNYDER, MILES W — Age 18 years. Enlisted January 13, 1864 at Rochester. Mustered in as Private, Co. I, February 2, 1864 to serve three years. Transferred to Co. M, March, 1864. Absent, sick in hospital since June 1, 1865 and upon muster out of company August 1, 1865. No further record.

SOGGS, EDWARD — Age 18 years Enlisted March 20, 1865 at Duanesburg. Mustered in as Private, Co. K, March 20, 1865, to serve three years. Mustered out with company, August 1, 1865 at Winchester, Virginia.

SOGGS, WILLIAM — Age 18 years. Enlisted December 31, 1863 at Lyons. Mustered in as Private, Co. H, February 2, 1864 to serve three years. Mustered out with company, August 1, 1865 at Winchester, Virginia.

SOMERS, JAMES — Age 18 years. Enlisted March 14, 1865 at Alabama, New York. Mustered in as Private, Co. I, March 14, 1865 to serve three years. Mustered out with company, August 1, 1865 at Winchester, Virginia.

SOUTHWORTH, ROBERT — Age 21 years. Enlisted December 11, 1863 at Cazenovia. Mustered in as Sergeant, Co. E, January 10, 1864 to serve three years. Died, date not stated at Andersonville, Georgia. Prior service in Co. A, Sixth New York Infantry.

SPAFFORD, HENRY C — Age 20 years. Enlisted February 14, 1865 at Binghamton. Mustered in as Private, Co. H, February 14, 1865 to serve one year. Mustered out with company, August 1, 1865 at Winchester, Virginia.

SPAULDING, JAMES A — Age 27 years. Enlisted December 17, 1863 at Rochester. Mustered in as Private, Co. A, December 20, 1863 to serve three years. Appointed Corporal, December 20, 1863. Appointed Sergeant, May 1, 1865.

Captured and paroled, dates not stated. Discharged, June 28, 1865 at Winchester, Virginia.

SPENCER, GEORGE O -Age 18 years. Enlisted March 14, 1865 at New York. Mustered in as Private, Co. I, March 14, 1865 to serve three years. Mustered out with company, August 1, 1865 at Winchester, Virginia.

SPERRY, GEORGE- Age 38 years. Enrolled July 4, 1864 at Light House Point, Virginia. Mustered in as First Lieutenant, Co. I, to date June 25, 1864, to serve three years. Transferred January 4, 1865 to Co. C, to Co. A, date not stated. Mustered in as Captain, Co. F, to date April 29, 1865. Mustered out with company August 1, 1865 at Winchester, Virginia. Commissioned First Lieutenant March 20, 1864 with rank from January 10, 1864, original. Captain, April 22, 1865, with rank from March 29, 1865, vice Edwards, discharged.

SPERRY, JAMES S- Age 19 years. Enlisted February 28, 1865 at Concord. Mustered in as Private, Co. M, February 28, 1865 to serve three years. Deserted May 20, 1865 near Winchester, Virginia.

SPINDLER, JACOB- Age 42 years. Enlisted February 24, 1865 at New York City. Mustered in as Private, Co. A, February 24, 1865 to serve three years. Mustered out with company, August 1, 1865 at Winchester, Virginia.

SPOONER, JOHN P- Age 23 years. Enlisted April 10, 1865 at Albany. Mustered in as Private, "unassigned", April 10, 1865 to serve three years. Mustered out with detachment, May 6, 1865 at Hart's Island, New York Harbor.

SPOORE, ADDISON- Age 25 years. Enlisted January 25, 1864 at New Lisbon. Mustered in as Private, Co. L, February 12, 1864 to serve three years. Mustered out with detachment, June 27, 1865 at Satterlee United States General Hospital, Philadelphia, Pa. Also borne as Spoon.

SPREADBURY, JOHN Officer

SPRING, CHARLES E- Age 18 years. Enlisted January 22, 1864 at Sweden. Mustered in as Sergeant, Co. K, February 6, 1864 to serve three years. Reduced in ranks, November 19, 1864. Transferred to Co. C, November 20, 1864. Mustered out with company, August 1, 1865 at Winchester, Virginia.

SQUAIN, ELEXANDER- Age 22 years. Enlisted January 8, 1864 at Rochester. Mustered in as Private, Co. D, January 10, 1864 to serve three years. No further record.

STALLMAN, FREDERICK P- Age 22 years. Enlisted December 8, 1863 at Rochester. Mustered in as Corporal, Co. D, January 10, 1864 to serve three years. Mustered out with company, August 1, 1865 at Winchester, Virginia.

STANSEL, JOHN- Age 44 years. Enlisted December 31, 1863 at Avoca as Private, Co. G to serve three years. Rejected.

STANTON, HIRAM M - Age 22 years. Enlisted January 22, 1864 at Syracuse. Mustered in as Private, Co. K, February 6, 1864 to serve three years. Transferred to Co. E, March 25, 1864. Died of disease, July 12, 1864 at Richmond, Virginia.

STANTON, RUBEN- Age 19 years. Enlisted January 4, 1864 at Constantia. Mustered in as Corporal, Co. E, January 10, 1864, to serve three years. Died of disease, date not stated at United States General Hospital, Annapolis, Maryland. Also borne as Stanton, Rubert.

STANTON, SYLVESTER - Age 44 years. Enlisted as Private, Co. H, to serve three years January 4, 1864 at Solon. Rejected.

STAPLETON, JOHN F -Age 19 years. Enlisted April 5, 1865 at Albany. Mustered in as Private "unassigned" April 10, 1864 to serve three years. Mustered out with detachment May 6, 1865 at Harts's Island, New York Harbor.

STARKS, WILLIAM -Age 38 years. Enlisted December 22, 1863 at Rochester. Mustered in as Corporal Co. I, February 2, 1864 to serve three years. Discharged to date September 15, 1864.

STARR, HENRY -Age 22 years. Enlisted March 15, 1865 at New York. Mustered in as Private, "unassigned" March 15, 1865 to serve three years. No further record.

STARR, HENRY P -Age 21 years. Enlisted August 12, 1862 at Rochester. Mustered in as Private, Co. M, Third Cavalry, September 10, 1862 to serve three years. Muster in as Second Lieutenant, Co. A, this regiment, to date April 16, 1864. Transferred to Co. K, November 2, 1864. Mustered out with company, August 1, 1865 at Winchester, Virginia.

Commissioned Second Lieutenant March 30, 1864, with rank from January 5, 1864, original.

STEELE, FRANK -Age 24 years. Enlisted October 26, 1863 at Rochester. Mustered in as First Sergeant, Co. F, January 10, 1864 to serve three years. Discharged April 20, 1864 at Giesboro Point, D.C.

STEELE, JAMES H -Age 42 years. Enlisted January 5, 1864 at Plymouth. Mustered in as Private, Co. L, February 12, 1864 to serve three years. Died of disease, May 27, 1864 at Washington, D.C.

STEENBURGH, HIRAM -Age18 years. Enlisted December 24, 1863 at Madison. Mustered in as Private, Co. E, January 10, 1864 to serve three years. Mustered out with company, August 1, 1865 at Winchester, Virginia. Also borne as Steenburgh and Steamburg.

STEEMBURGH, WILLIAM -Age 26 years. Enlisted December 30, 1863 at Manlius. Mustered in s Private, Co. E, January 10, 1864 to serve three years. Mustered out with company, August 1, 1865 at Winchester, Virginia. Also borne as Steenburgh and Steamburg.

STEIN, FREDERICK -Age 35 years. Enlisted March 30, 1865 at Albany. Mustered in as Private, "unassigned", March 30, 1865 to serve three years. No further record.

STELLRECHT, DAVID -Age 18 years. Enlisted January 27, 1864 at Morris. Mustered in as Private, Co. L, February 12, 1864 to serve three years. Captured, date not stated. Died of disease, August 16, 1864 at Andersonville, Georgia.

STEPHENS, JOHN -Age 23 years. Enlisted April 12, 1865 at Albany, Mustered in as Private, "unassigned" April 12, 1865 to serve two years. Mustered out with detachment, May 6, 1865 at Harts Island, New York Harbor.

STERLING, ADAM H -Age 18 years. Enlisted December 24, 1863 at Rome. Mustered in as Private, Co. C, January 5, 1864 to serve three years. Captured, date not stated. mustered out with detachment, June 28, 1865 at Winchester, Virginia.

STETSON, RICHARD -Age 20 years. Enlisted December 7, 1863 at Rome. Mustered in as Corporal, Co. C, January 5, 1864 to serve three years. Mustered out with company, August 1, 1865 at Winchester, Virginia.

STEVENS, CHARLES -Age 19 years. Enlisted December 29, 1863 at Rochester. Mustered in as Private, Co. F, January 10, 1864 to serve three years. Died of disease, November 5, 1864 at Florence, S.C.

STEVENS, E.B. -Age 21 years. Enlisted November 30, 1863 at Syracuse. Mustered in as Private, Co. B, January 5, 1864 to serve three years. Died of disease, November 28, 1864 in Cavalry Corps Hospital, Winchester, Virginia.

STEVENS, JOHN -Age 21 years. Enlisted November 24, 1863 at Rochester. Mustered in as Private, Co. C, January 5, 1864 to serve three years. Deserted January 7, 1864 at Rochester, New York.

STEVENS, WARREN -Age 18 years. Enlisted December 31, 1863 at Nelson. Mustered in as Saddler, Co. E, January 10, 1864 to serve three years. Reduced, date not stated. Mustered out with company, August 1, 1865 at Winchester, Virginia.

STEVENS, WILLIAM H -Age 18 years. Enlisted February 24, 1865 at Harpersfield. Mustered in as Private, Co. I, February 24, 1865 to serve three years. Mustered out with company, August 1, 1865 at Winchester, Virginia.

STEWART, ALEXANDER -Age 33 years. Enlisted January 4, 1864 at Bath. Mustered in as Wagoner, Co. G, February 2, 1864 to serve three years. Mustered out with company, August 1, 1865 at Winchester, Virginia. Prior service in Co. G, Twenty Third New York Infantry.

STEWART, IVORY M -Age 18 years. Enlisted January 5, 1864 at Peterboro. Mustered in as Private, Co. K, February 6, 1864 to serve three years. Died of disease February 15, 1864 at Rochester, New York.

STEWART, THOMAS -Age 32 years. Enlisted January 16, 1864 at Bath. Mustered in as Private, Co. G, February 2, 1864 to serve three years. Died, date not stated. Prior service in Co. I, Thirty Fourth New York Infantry.

STIEFVATER, NICHOLAS -Age 18 years. Enlisted as Private, Co. B to serve three years, December 17, 1863 at Utica. Rejected.

STODDARD, JOHN -Age 16 years, Enlisted February 22, 1865 at Harpersfield. Mustered in as Private, Co. K, February 22, 1865 to serve three years. Mustered out with company, August 1, 1865 at Winchester, Virginia.

STODDER, HENRY -Age 27 years. Enlisted March 3, 1865 at New York. Mustered in as Private, Co. I, March 3, 1865 to serve three years. Mustered out with company, August 1, 1865 at Winchester, Virginia.

STOKES, JONATHAN A -Age 37 years. Enlisted December 9, 1863 at Ontario. Mustered in as Sergeant, Co. H, February 2, 1864 to serve three years. Discharged, date not stated.

STONE, HEDDING A -Age 20 years. Enlisted February 24, 1864 at Lima. Mustered in as Private, Co. M, February 25, 1864 to serve three years. Mustered out with company, August 1, 1865 at Winchester, Virginia.

STONE, JOHN -Age 34 years. Enlisted February 2, 1865 at Masonville. Mustered in as Private, Co. D, February 2, 1865 to serve three years. Died of disease in hospital at Winchester, Virginia.

STONE, LAWRENCE -Age 18 years. Enlisted February 20,1865 at New York. Mustered in as Private, Co. E, February 20, 1865 to serve three years. Absent upon muster out of company August 1, 1865. No discharge furnished. No further record.

STONE, OMER O -Age 18 years. Enlisted January 2, 1864 at Madison. Mustered in as Private Co. E, January 10, 1864 to serve three years. Mustered out June 27, 1865 at Satterlee United Stated Army General Hospital, West Philadelphia, Pa.

STONE, THOMAS J -Age 20 years. Enlisted April 11, 1865 at New York. Mustered in as Private, "unassigned", April1, 1865 to serve one year. Mustered out May 6, 1865 at Harts Island, New York Harbor.

STONE, WILLIAM HENRY -Age 33 years. Enlisted January 5, 1864 at Lyons. Mustered in as Private, Co. H, February 2, 1864 to serve three years. Discharged, records lost.

STONE WILLIAM H -Age 20 years. Enlisted December 9, 1863 at Rochester. Mustered in as Corporal, Co. D, January 10,1864 to serve three years. Appointed Bugler, date not stated. Mustered out with company, August 1, 1865 at Winchester, Virginia.

STORMONT, William -Age 27 years. Enlisted January 21, 1864 at Rochester. Mustered in as Private, Co. I, February 2, 1864 to serve three years. Transferred to Co. M, March 1864. Appointed Sergeant, date not stated. Died of wounds, date not stated.

STRATTON, ISAAC -Age 17 years. Enlisted December 21, 1863 at Urbana. Mustered in as Private, Co. G, February 2, 1864 to serve three years. Died, date not stated.

STRONG, MONSON -Age 23 years. Enlisted as Private, Co. M, February 12, 1864 at Bath to serve three years. Rejected for disability.

STUDER, FREDERICK -Age 18 years. Enlisted December 22, 1883 at Lyons. Mustered in as Private, Co. H, February 2, 1864 to serve three years. Deserted, records lost.

STUFFER, CHRISTOPHER -Age 43 years. Enlisted as Private, Co. F, October 30,1863 at Rochester to serve three years. Rejected for disability.

SUGGETT, JOSEPH H -Age 21 years. Enrolled September 26, 1863 at Rochester. Mustered in as First Lieutenant and Adjutant, September 26, 1863 to serve three years. Dismissed July 25, 1864 for incompetency. Commissioned First Lieutenant and Adjutant March 30, 1864 with rank from September 26, 1863, original.

SUITS, JOHN H -Age 27 years. Enlisted March 7, 1864 at Rochester. Mustered in as Private, Co. B, March 8, 1864 to serve three years. Absent at Camp Parole, Annapolis, Maryland. on muster out of regiment, August 1, 1865. No further record.

SULLIVAN, FRANKLIN -Age 18 years. Enlisted March 17, 1864 at Lockport. Mustered in as Private, "unassigned" March 17, 1864 to serve three years. No further record.

SULLIVAN, JAMES -Age 19 years. Enlisted January 26, 1864 at Rochester. Mustered in as Private, Co. D, February 2, 1864 to serve three years. Deserted, March 5, 1864

SULLIVAN, MICHAEL -Age 19 years. Enlisted January 27, 1864 at Rochester. Mustered in as Private, Co. G, February 2, 1864 to serve three years. Transferred to Co. D, March 22, 1864. No further Record.

SULLIVAN, WILLIAM -Age 22 years. Enlisted February 22, 1865 at New York. Mustered in as Private, "unassigned" February 22, 1865 to serve three years. No further record.

SUMNER, JEREMIAH A (Colored) -Age 24 years. Enlisted January 14, 1864 at York. Mustered in as Cook Co. K, February 6, 1864 to serve three years. Deserted February 18, 1864 at Rochester.

SUMMERS, JAMES -Age 38 years. Enlisted March 10, 1865 at Lockport. Mustered in as Private, "unassigned" March 10,1865, to serve three years. No further record.

SUTPHIN, BENJAMIN -Age 24 years. Enlisted January 25, 1864 at Lyons. Mustered in as Farrier, Co. H, February 2, 1864 to serve three years. Mustered out with company, August 1, 1865 at Winchester, Virginia.

SWAN, HENRY -Age 21 years. Enlisted March 20, 1865 at New York. Mustered in as Private, "unassigned" March 20, 1865 to serve three years. No further record

SWAN, HENRY -Age 30 years. Enlisted January 11, 1864 at Edmeston. Mustered in as Sergeant, Co. L, February 12, 1864 to serve three years. Mustered out June 28,1865 at Winchester,Va. Prior service in Co. G, 6th New York Infantry.

SWAN, THOMAS -Age 18 years. Enlisted April 8, 1865 at Rochester. Mustered in as Private, Co. D, April 8, 1865 to serve three years. Mustered out July 21, 1865 at Harpers Ferry, Virginia.

SWARTZ. JOHN -Age 25 years. Enlisted February 29, 864 at Bath. Mustered in as Private, Co. G, March 8, 1864 to serve three years. Died, date not stated.

SWEENEY, MICHAEL -Age 27 years. Enlisted December 28, 1863 at Rochester. Mustered in as Private, Co. C, January 5, 1864 to serve three years. Transferred to Co. D, June 9, 1865. Captured June 28, 1864 at Reams Station, Virginia. Released May 5, 1865 at Raleigh, N.C. Mustered out July 10, 1865 at Rochester.

SWEET, CROSBY -Age 19 years. Enlisted as Private, Co. K at Pomfret, to serve three years. Rejected for disability.

SWEEZY GEORGE W -Age 22 years. Enlisted January 5, 1864 at Bath. Mustered in as Private, Co. G, February 2, 1864, to serve three years. Captured, June 29, 1864. Confined at Andersonville, paroled February 27, 1865. Discharged, August 4, 1865 at Elmira, New York.

SWEEZY, NATHAN -Age 18 years. Enlisted March 7, 1865 at New York. Mustered in as Private, Co. K, March 7, 1865 to serve three years. Mustered out with company, August 1, 1865 at Winchester, Virginia.

SWIFT, EBER J -Age 18 years. Enlisted September 30, 1863 at Cuba. Mustered in as Private, Co. D, January 10, 1864 to serve three years. Transferred to Co. K, May 1, 1864. Died of Disease, August 10, 1864 at Giesboro Point, D.C.

SWIFT, THOMAS -Age 44 years. Enlisted as Private Co. I, November 17, 1863 at Auburn to serve three years. Rejected.

SWIRES, ROBERT -Age 27 years. Enlisted November 27, 1863 at Rochester. Mustered in as Private, Co. F, January 10, 1864 to serve three years. Deserted, February 1864 from camp near Rochester. New York.

SYLVANUS, JOHN -Age 32 years. Enlisted March 3, 1865 at Tompkinsville. Mustered in as Private "unassigned" March 3, 1865 to serve three years. No further record.

SYLVESTER, ALBERT -Age 19 years. Enlisted August 24, 1864 at Truxton. Mustered in as Private, "unassigned" August 24, 1864 to serve three years. No further record.

SYLVESTER, CHARLES -Age 20 years. Enlisted as Private Co. E, December 8, 1863 at Cazenovia, to serve three years. Rejected for disability.

SYPHERS, GILBERT -Age 19 years. Enlisted February 20, 1865 at Goshen. Mustered in as Private, Co. H, February 20, 1865 to serve one year. Mustered out with company, August 1, 1865 at Winchester, Virginia.

TACK, JACOB -Age 18 years. Enlisted August 18, 1863 at Troy. Mustered in as Private Co. C, August 28, 1863 to serve three years. Mustered out June 6, 1865 at Satterlee U.S.A. General Hospital, West Philadelphia, Pa.

TALBOT, JOSEPH -Age 17 years. Enlisted January 9, 1864 at Smyrna. Mustered in as Private, Co. L, February 12, 1864 to serve three years. Died of disease, April 12, 1864 at Giesboro Point, D.C.

TALLMAN, BYRON -Age 25 years. Enlisted October 12, 1863 at Perrington. Mustered in as First Sergeant, Co. A, December 20, 1863 to serve three years. Mustered in as Second Lieutenant, Co. H, to date August 10, 1864. Mustered out with company, August 1, 1865 at Winchester, Virginia. Commissioned Second Lieutenant August 18, 1864 with rank from August 9, 1864, vice Dunning, discharged

TALLMAN, GEORGE WAGE -Age 18 years. Enlisted February 12, 1864 at Rochester. Mustered in as Wagoner, Co. M, February 23, 1864 to serve three years. Transferred to Co. H, no date given. Mustered out with company, August 1, 1865 at Winchester, Virginia.

TALLMAN, HENRY M -Age 25 years. Enlisted March 29, 1865 at Canandaigua. Mustered in as Private, Co. M. March 29, 1865 to serve one year. Mustered out with company, August 1, 1865 at Winchester, Virginia.

TALLMAN, WILLIAM -Age, date and place of enlistment and muster in as Private in Co. M not stated. Transferred to Co. H, March 22, 1864. No further record.

TAPPAN, FRANK -Age 18 years. Enlisted November 27, 1863 at Syracuse. Mustered in as Private, Co. B, January 5, 1864 to serve three years. Mustered out with company, August 1, 1865 at Winchester, Virginia. Also borne as Tappen.

TARBEL, SAMUEL SAGE -Age 44 years. Enlisted December 19, 1863 at Syracuse. Mustered in as Trumpeter, Co. B, January 5, 1864 to serve three years. Transferred as Private to Veteran Reserve Corps, June 26, 1864.

TARBOX, ROBERT -Age 18 years. Enlisted January 21, 1864 at Rochester. Mustered in as Private Co. I, February 2, 1864 to serve three years. Transferred April 11, 1865 to One Hundred New York Volunteers.

TAYLOR, ADELBERT, Age 19 years. Enlisted December 19, 1863 at Syracuse. Mustered in as Private, Co. B, January 5, 1864 to serve three years. Discharged May 19, 1865 at Rulison General Hospital, Annapolis Junction, Maryland.

TAYLOR, ALBERT P -Age 18 years. Enlisted April 4, 1865 at Albany. Mustered in as Private Co. C, April 4, 1865 to serve three years. Mustered out with company, August 1, 1865 at Winchester, Virginia.

TAYLOR, CALVIN -Age 21 years. Enlisted January 5, 1864 to Lyons. Mustered in as Private, Co. H, February 2, 1864 to serve three years. Mustered out with company, August 1, 1865 at Winchester, Virginia.

TAYLOR, FAYETTE -Age 17 years. Enlisted December 11, 1863 at Utica. Mustered in as Private, Co. B, January 5, 1864 to serve three years. Mustered out September 19, 1865 at Elmira, New York.

TAYLOR, GAYNE H -Age 18 years, Enlisted February 19, 1864 at Rochester. Mustered in as Private, Co. M, February 23, 1864 to serve three years. Absent in hospital on muster out of company, August 1, 1865. No further record.

TAYLOR, HENRY -Age 26 years. Enlisted February 20, 1865 at New York. Mustered in as Private Co. C, February 20, 1865 to serve one year. Discharged July 18, 1865 at U.S.A. General Hospital, Frederick, Maryland.

TAYLOR, ISRAEL B -Age 40 years. Enlisted December 8, 1863 at Rochester. Mustered in as Commissary Sergeant, Co. I, February 2, 1864 to serve three years.

Promoted Second Lieutenant, Co. F, May 16, 1865. Resigned May 24, 1865. Commissioned Second Lieutenant December 7, 1864 with rank from September 26, 1864, vice Redington dismissed.

TAYLOR, JOHN -Age 18 years. Enlisted March 31, 1865 at Rochester. Mustered in as Private, Co. A, March 31, 1865 to serve three years. Mustered out with company, August 1, 1865 at Winchester, Virginia.

TAYLOR, JOHN -Age 19 years. Enlisted January 5, 1864 at Lyons. Mustered in as Private Co. H, February 2, 1864 to serve three years. Mustered out with company, August 1, 1865 at Winchester, Virginia.

TAYLOR, JOHN LAMSON -Age 19 years. Enlisted April 11, 1865 at Albany. Mustered in as Private, "unassigned" April 11, 1865 to serve two years. Mustered out with detachment, May 6, 1865 at Harts Island, New York Harbor.

TAYLOR, ORVILLE -Age 21 years. Enlisted January 11, 1864 at Unadilla. Mustered in as Private, Co. L, February 12, 1864 to serve three years. Captured, June 23, 1864. Released August 22,1864. Mustered out with company, August 1, 1865 at Winchester, Virginia.

TAYLOR, ROBERT B -Age 18 years. Enlisted February 16, 1864 at Bath. Mustered in as Private, Co. M, February 23, 1864 to serve three years. Transferred to Co. G, March 24, 1864. Mustered out with company, August 1, 1865 at Winchester, Virginia.

TERRIL, WILLIAM M -Age 25 years. Enlisted November 24, 1863 at bath. Mustered in as Private, Co. G, February 2, 1864 to serve three years. Captured, June 29, 1864. Released August 22, 1864. Mustered out with company, August 1, 1865 at Winchester, Virginia.

TERRILL, MILES T -Age 20 years. Enlisted December 18, 1863 at Jerusalem. Mustered in as Private, Co. A, December 20, 1863 to serve three years. Died of disease, October 8, 1864 at Florence S.C. Prior service in Co. A, 23rd New York Infantry.

TERWILLIGER, IRA -Age 38 years. Enlisted December 31, 1863 at Auburn, as Private, Co. I, to serve three years. Rejected.

THANVETTE, DAVID -See Thonvett, David.

THAYER, RICHARD J -Age 19 years. Enlisted January 11, 1864 at Unadilla. Mustered in as Private Co. M, January 12, 1864 to serve three years. Line drawn through name with remark, "did not accompany detachment."

THETGA, HIRAM N -Age 23 years. Enlisted August 25, 1864 at Norwich. Mustered in as Private, Co. M, September 2, 1864 to serve three years. Mustered out with company, August 1, 1865 at Winchester, Virginia.

THOMAS, HUGH -Age 25 years. Enlisted December 12, 1863 at Rochester. Mustered in as Private, Co. C, January 5, 1864 to serve three years. Deserted, February 3, 1864 at Rochester.

THOMPSON, ANDREW -Age not given. Enlisted March 28, 1865 at Albany. Mustered in as Private, Co. C, March 28, 1865 to serve three years. Mustered out with company, August 1, 1865 at Winchester, Virginia.

THOMPSON, BYRON -Age 18 years. Enlisted January 18, 1864 at Rochester as Private, Co. H to serve three years. Rejected.

THOMPSON, JAMES -Age 23 years. Enlisted February 22, 1865 at New York City. Mustered in as Private, "unassigned" February 22, 1865 to serve three years. No further record.

THOMPSON, JOHN -Age 23 years. Enlisted November 27, 1863 at Rochester. Mustered in as Private, Co. D, January 10, 1864 to serve three years. Captured June 30, 1864, paroled January 25, 1865. Mustered out July 11, 1865 at United States General Hospital, York, Pa.

THOMPSON, MILTON -Age 18 years. Enlisted March 3, 1864 at Rochester. Mustered in as Corporal, Co. E, March 8, 1864 to serve three years. Mustered out with company, August 1, 1865 at Winchester, Virginia.

THOMPSON, SAMUEL W -Age 20 years. Enlisted December 5, 1863 at Walworth. Mustered in as Corporal Co. H, February 2, 1864 to serve three years. Mustered out with company, August 1, 1865 at Winchester, Virginia. Also borne as Thompson, Wellington.

THOMPSON, ANDREW -Age 18 years. Enlisted March 23, 1865 at Auburn. Mustered in as Private, "unassigned" March 23, 1865 to serve three years. No further record.

THONVETT, DAVID -Age 44 years. Enlisted January 1, 1864 at Dunkirk as Private, Co. H, to serve three years. Rejected. Also borne as Thanvette and as Thorvitt.

THORNS, WILLIAM -Age 27 years. Enlisted November 27, 1863 at Lyons. Mustered in as Saddler, Co. D, January 10, 1864 to serve tree years. Appointed Saddler Sergeant, June 1, 1865. Mustered out with company, August 1, 1865 at Winchester, Virginia.

Prior service in Co. B, Twenty Seventh New York Volunteers.

THORVITT, DAVID, See Thonvet, David.

THURNSTON, THEODORE W -Age 33 years. Enlisted December 31, 1863 at Manlius. Mustered in as Private Co. E, January 10, 1864 to serve three years. Appointed Corporal no date stated. Mustered out with company, August 1, 1865 at Winchester, Virginia.

Prior service in Co. I, Sixty First New York Volunteers.

TIFFT, GEORGE C -Age 18 years. Enlisted January 18, 1864 at Masonville. Mustered in as Private, Co. L, February 12, 1864 to serve three years. Appointed Corporal, no date given. Died of disease, May 19, 1864 at Portsmouth Grove, R.I. Also borne as George L. Tift.

TILESTON, ARTHUR T -Age 21 years. Enrolled September 29, 1864 at Middleton. Mustered in as First Lieutenant, Co. L, to date September 29, 1864 to serve three years. Transferred to Co. K, May 10, 1865. Mustered out with company, August 1, 1865 at Winchester, Virginia. Commissioned First Lieutenant September 17, 1864, vice Allen, discharged.

TINDALL, EDWARD -Age 28 years. Enlisted March 28, 1865 at New York. Mustered in as Private Co. C, March 28, 1865 to serve one year. Transferred to Co. D, June 9, 1865. Mustered out with company, August 1, 1865 at Winchester, Virginia. Also borne as Yendal.

TOBIN, JOHN -Age 25 years. Enlisted December 23, 1863 at Rochester. Mustered in as Private, Co. F, January 10, 1864 to serve three years. Appointed Corporal, May 1, 1865. Mustered out June 28, 1865 at Winchester, Virginia.

TOBIN, THOMAS -Age 18 years. Enlisted April 1, 1865 at Albany. Mustered in as Private, Co. C, April 1, 1865, to serve three years. Mustered out with company, August 1, 1865 at Winchester, Virginia.

TODD, ROBERT -Age 14 years. Enlisted January 23, 1864 at Newark as Private, Co. H to serve three years. Rejected.

TODD, ROBERT, R -Age 23 years. Enlisted December 9, 1863 at Arcadia. Mustered in as Private, Co. H, February 2, 1864 to serve three years. Discharged to date October 5, 1864.

TOMBRIDGE, JOHN S -Age 19 years. Enlisted March 11, 1865 at New York. Mustered in as Private Co. I, March 11, 1865 to serve three years. Never joined for service. No discharge furnished. No further record.

TOMLINSON, WILBUR F- Age 32 years. Enlisted February 9, 1864 at Urbana. Mustered in as a Private, Co. M, February 23, 1864 to serve three years. Transferred to Co. G, March 24, 1864. Died, date and place not stated. Prior service in Co. I, Thirty Fourth New York Infantry.

TOPHAM, THOMAS -Age 29 years. Enlisted December 15, 1863 at Rochester. Mustered in as Corporal, Co. D, January 10, 1864 to serve three years. Mustered out with company, August 1, 1865 at Winchester, Virginia.

TOPPING, MARTIN M- Age 22 years. Enlisted January 25, 1864 at Cortlandville. Mustered in as Private, Co. K, February 6, 1864 to serve three years. Transferred to Co. B, March 22, 1864. Mustered out with detachment, May 19, 1865 at Saterlee U.S.A. General Hospital, Philadelphia, Pa. as of Co. K.

TOWER, ANSON -Age 22 years. Enrolled March 4, 1864 at Rochester. Mustered in as First Lieutenant and Regimental Commissary to date January 29, 1864 to serve three years. Mustered out with regiment, August 1, 1865 at Winchester, Virginia. Commissioned First Lieutenant and Regimental Commissary. March 29, 1864, with rank from January 29, 1864, original.

TOWNSEND, JAMES H -Age 17 years. Enlisted January 21, 1864 at McDonough. Mustered in as Private, Co. L, February 12, 1864 to serve three years. Captured, May 10, 1864 at Wilderness, Virginia. Released September 12, 1864 at Aikens

Landing, Virginia. but did not rejoin regiment. Discharged, August 12, 1865 at Rochester, Virginia.

TOWNSEND, LUTHER -Age 27 years. Enlisted January 29, 1864 at Plattsburgh. Mustered in as Private, Co. G, February 2, 1864 to serve three years. Died date and place not stated.

TRACY, DANIEL -Age 18 years. Enlisted 18 years, Enlisted February 16, 1865 at Tompkins. Mustered in as Private "unassigned" February 16, 1865 to serve three years. No further record.

TRACY, GEORGE -Age 23 years. Enlisted February 27, 1864 at Vernon. Mustered in as Private Co. B, February 27, 1864 to serve three years. Deserted September 3, 1864 at Boonsboro, Maryland. Prior service in Co. G, Fourteenth New York Infantry.

TRACY, HENRY -Age 18 years, Enlisted February 27, 1864 at Vernon. Mustered in as Private, Co. B, February 27, 1864 to serve three years. Absent sick in hospital at time company was mustered out, August 1, 1865. No further record. Also borne as Henry C.

TRASK, DEXTER -Age 23 years. Enlisted as Private, Co. H, December 29, 1863 at Lyons to serve three years. Absent at time company was mustered in February 2, 1864. Borne with remark, "taken for deserter."

TRASS, HARVEY -Age 18 years. Enlisted January 5, 1864 at Plymouth. Mustered in as Private, Co. L, February 12, 1864 to serve three years. Mustered out with company, August 1, 1865 at Winchester, Virginia.

TRIBLE, FREDERICK, -Age 22 years. Enlisted March 15, 1865 at New York. Mustered in as Private, Co. A, March 15, 1865 to serve three years. Deserted July 21, 1865 at Remount Camp, Virginia.

TRIFFORD, ISIAH, See Fufford, Isiah.

TRIMBLE, JOHN -Age 25 years. Enlisted December 29, 1863 at Rochester. Mustered in as Private, Co. C, January 5, 1864 to serve three years. Transferred to Co. A, March 22, 1864. Appointed Commissary Sergeant, Date not stated. Mustered out with company, August 1, 1865 at Winchester, Virginia. Also borne as Trumble.

TRIPP, ROBERT H -Age 33 years. Enlisted as Private Co. F, January 2, 1864 at Waterloo to serve three years. Rejected.

TROST, ANDREW -Age 24 years. Enlisted March 3, 1865 at Rochester. Mustered in as Private, "unassigned" March 3, 1865, to serve three years. No further record.

TRUMAN, CHARLES -Age 35 years. Enlisted February 22, 1865 at New York. Mustered in as Private, "unassigned" February 22, 1865 to serve three years. No further record.

TRUMAN, EDWARDS, see Edwards, Truman.

TRUMBLE, DANIEL -Age 20 years. Enlisted January 4, 1864 at Murray. Mustered in as Private, Co. C, January 5, 1864 to serve three years. Mustered out with company, August 1, 1865 at Winchester, Virginia.

TRUMBLE, FREDERICK -Age -years. Enlisted September 30, 1864 at Rochester. Mustered in as Private Co. C, October 31, 1864 to serve one year. Mustered out with company, August 1, 1865 at Winchester, Virginia.

TRUMBLE, JOHN, See Trimble, John.

TRUMBLE, RUEBEN -Age 20 years. Enlisted December 29, 1863 at Westmoreland. Mustered in as Private Co. E, January 10, 1864 to serve three years. Mustered out with company, August 1, 1865 at Winchester, Virginia.

TRUMPP, ERNEST, -Age 19 years. Enlisted December 29, 1863 at Rochester. Mustered in as Private, Co. F, January 10, 1864 to serve three years. Died, August 30, 1864 at Andersonville, Georgia.

TUBBS, JAMES H -Age 23 years. Enlisted as Private, Co. H, December 21, 1863 at Newark, to serve three years. Rejected.

TUCKER, ALMOND A -Age 31 years. Enlisted as Private Co. E, December 30, 1863 at Cazenovia, to serve three years. Rejected.

TUCKER, JOHN -Age 26 years. Enlisted March 15, 1865 at New York. Mustered in as Private, "unassigned" March 15, 1865 to serve one year. No further record.

TUCKER, LEROY -Age 21 years. Enlisted February 28, 1865 at Rochester. Mustered in as Private, "unassigned" February 28, 1865 to serve one year. No further record.

TUFFORD, ISIAH -See Fufford, Isiah.

TURNBELL, JOSEPH B. -Age 18 years. Enlisted December 13, 1863 at Arcadia. Mustered in as Private, Co. H, February 2, 1864 to serve three years. Mustered out with company, August 1, 1865 at Winchester, Virginia. Also borne as Turnbull

TURNBRIDGE, JOHN S -Age 19 years. Enlisted March 11, 1865 at New York. Mustered in as Private, "unassigned" March 11, 1865 to serve three years. No further record.

TURNER, HENRY -Age 28 years. Enlisted February 16, 1865 at New York. Mustered in as Private, Co. A, February 16, 1865 to serve three years. Deserted, July 24, 1864 at Remount Camp, Maryland.

TURNER, JAMES -Age 20 years. Enlisted January 22, 1864 at Rochester. Mustered in as Private, Co. G, February 2, 1864 to serve three years. Transferred to Co. D, March 22, 1864. Deserted March 28, 1864, place not stated.

TURNER, JOHN -Age 21 years. Enlisted February 24, 1865 at New York. Mustered in as Private, "unassigned" February 24, 1865 to serve three years. No further record.

TURNER, JOHN J -Age 41 years. Enlisted January 28, 1864 at Verona. Mustered in as Private, Co. M, February 2, 1864 to serve three years. Died September, 1864 at Andersonville, Georgia. Also borne at John Turner.

TURNER, LEVI -Age 40 years. Enlisted as Private, Co. C, December 21, 1863 at Rome, to serve three years. Rejected.

TURNEY, ADDISON -Age 28 years. Enlisted January 13, 1864 at Rochester. Mustered in as Private, Co. K, February 6, 1864 to serve three years. Transferred to Co. C, March 25, 1864. Deserted March 28, 1864 at Rochester, New York.

TUTHILL, CHARLES -Age 33 years. Enlisted January 29, 1864 at Prattsburg. Mustered in as Private, Co. K, February 6, 1864 to serve three years. Transferred to Co. G, March 25, 1864. Died, date and place not stated.

TUTT, WILLIAM H -Age 30 years. Enlisted March 17, 1865 at Lockport. Mustered in as Private, Co. K, March 17, 1865 to serve three years. Mustered out June 28, 1865 at United States General Hospital Cumberland, Maryland.

TWEED, SAMUEL -Age 23, years. Enlisted March 24, 1865 at Brooklyn. Mustered in as Private, "unassigned" March 24, 1865 to serve three years. No further record.

TYNDALL, EDWARD -Age 26 years. Enlisted March 18, 1865 at New York. Mustered in as Private "unassigned" March 18, 1865 to serve three years. No further record

UMPHREY, EDWIN -Age 20 years. Enlisted March 25, 1865 at Kortright. Mustered in as Private Co. K, March 25, 1865 to serve three years. Mustered out with company, August 1, 1865 at Winchester, Virginia. Also borne as Edwin Humphreys

VALLANCE, JAMES -Age 40 years. Enlisted as Private Co. K, January 8, 1864 at Rochester, to serve three years. Rejected.

VALKER, JOHN -Age 26 years. Enlisted April 8, 1865 at Riga. Mustered in as Private, Co. D, April 8, 1865 to serve three years. Mustered out with company, August 1, 1865 at Winchester, Virginia.

VAN ALSTYNE, FRANK -Age 18 years. Enlisted January 29, 1864 at Rochester. Mustered in as Private, Co. M, February 23, 1864 to serve three years. Mustered out with company, August 1, 1865 at Winchester, Virginia.

VAN AUKER, JOHN -Age 22 years. Enlisted November 16, 1863 at Rochester. Mustered in as Private, Co. D, January 10, 1864, to serve three years. Mustered out with detachment, June 28, 1865 at Winchester, Virginia.

VAN CORTLAND, JAMES S -Age 21 years. Enrolled January 1, 1865 at Winchester, Virginia. Mustered in as First Lieutenant Co. E, to date January 1, 1865 to serve three years. Mustered out with company, August 1, 1865 at Winchester, Virginia. Prior service in Co. G 155th new York Infantry. Commissioned First Lieutenant, August 25, 1864 with rank from August 23, 1864, vice Lusk, promoted. Captain, September 18, 1865, with rank from August 31, 1865, vice Vaughn, discharged, not mustered.

VANDENBERG, JANS -Age 43 years. Enlisted January 23, 1864 at Syracuse as Private in Co. H, to serve three years. Rejected.

VANDERMARK, SMITH -Age 21 years. Enlisted November 14, 1863 at Rochester. Mustered in as Sergeant, Co. D, January 10, 1864 to serve three years. Mustered out May 29, 1865 at Satterlee U.S.A. General Hospital, West Philadelphia, Pa.

VAN GELDER, JOHN J -Age 22 years. Enlisted February 3, 1864 at Dunkirk as Private Co. M, to serve three years. Rejected.

VAN GELDER, JOHN S -Age 18 years. Enlisted February 15, 1864 at Bath. Mustered in as Private, Co. G, March 8, 1864 to serve three years. Died, date and place not stated.

VAN GELDER, TOBIAS T Age 16 years. Enlisted January 18, 1864 at bath. Mustered in as Private Co. G, February 2, 1864 to serve three years. Absent in confinement at date of muster out of company August 1, 1865 at Fort Delaware by sentence of G.C.M.A.of S. May 12, 1865. Discharged August 9, 1865 at Rochester, New York.

VAN MARTER, JAMES G -Age 28 years. Enrolled at Rochester. Mustered in as Captain, Co. H, February 2, 1864 to serve three years. Dismissed July 26, 1864. Commissioned Captain, March 30, 1864, with rank from January 29, 1864, original.

VAN RENSAELER, FRANK -(Colored)-Age not stated. Enlisted February 23, 1864 at Rochester. Mustered in as Cook, Co. M, February 23, 1864 to serve three years. No further record.

VAN SLYCK, DAVID B -Age 34 years. Enrolled November 7, 1863 at Rochester. Mustered in as Surgeon, November 7, 1863 to serve three years. Mustered out with regiment, August 1, 1865 at Winchester, Virginia. Commissioned Surgeon, March 30, 1864 with rank from October 24, 1863, original.

VAN STEENBURGH, WILLIAM H -Age 18 years. Enlisted January 5, 1864 at Middletown. Mustered in as Private, Co. L, February 12, 1864 to serve three years. Mustered out with detachment, June 28, 1865 at Winchester, Virginia.

VAN VRANKEN, GEORGE R -Age 21 years. Enlisted November 26, 1863 at Syracuse as Private Co. B, to serve three years. Rejected.

VARNER, ROBERT -Age 38 years. Enlisted March 10, 1865 at New York. Mustered in as Private, Co. I, March 10, 1865 to serve three years. Absent at date of muster out of company August 1, 1865. No further record.

VASSER, MATHEW -Age 21 years. Enlisted February 21, 1865 at Brooklyn. Mustered in as Private, Co. K, February 21, 1865 to serve one year. Appointed Corporal, June 1, 1865. Mustered out with company, August 1, 1865 at Winchester, Virginia.

VAUGHAN, HENRY S -Age 26 years. Enrolled December 30, 1863 at Norwich. Mustered in as Captain, Co. L, February 15, 1864 to serve three years. Discharged, August 31, 1865. Commissioned Captain, March 30, 1864, with rank from January 29, 1864, original.

VIBBORI, GEORGE -Age 21 years. Enlisted January 1, 1864 at Fenner. Mustered in as a Private, Co. E, January 10, 1864, to serve three years. Captured, date not stated. Died date not stated at Andersonville, Georgia.

VICE, GEORGE -Age 18 years. Enlisted December 8, 1863 at Cazenovia. Mustered in as a Private, Co. E, January 10, 1864 to serve three years. Died of wounds, February 20, 1864 at Jarvis Hospital, Baltimore, Maryland.

VIDWELL, GEORGE W -Age 39 years. Enlisted April 4, 1865 at Edenburg. Mustered in as Private "unassigned" April 4, 1865, to serve three years. Mustered out with detachment, May 6, 1865 at Harts Island, New York Harbor

VOGT, JOHN H -Age 17 years. Enlisted April 5, 1865 at Rotterdam. Mustered in as Private, "unassigned" April 5, 1865 to serve three years. Mustered out with detachment May 6, 1865 at Harts Island New York Harbor.

VON GYURKOWITZ, CARLOS -Age 20 years. Enlisted February 22, 1865 at New York. Mustered in as Private "unassigned" February 22, 1865, to serve one year. No further record.

WADDLE, FRANK J -Age 19 years. Enlisted January 18, 1864 at Rochester. Mustered in as a Private, Co. K, February 6, 1864 to serve three years. Transferred to Co. A, March 25, 1864. Captured and paroled, dates not stated. Discharged June 27, 1865 at Winchester, Virginia.

WADE, FREDERICK -Age 21 years. Enlisted January 20, 1864 at Bath as Private Co. G to serve three years. Rejected.

WADE, ISAAC C -Age 18 years. Enlisted February 23, 1864 at Rochester. Mustered in as Corporal, Co. M, February 23, 1864 to serve three years. Mustered out with company, August 1, 1865 at Winchester, Virginia.

WADE, WILLIAM D -Age 10 years. Enlisted December 29, 1863 at Pomfret, as Private, Co. K, to serve three years. Rejected.

WAFFLES, GEORGE A -Age 18 years. Enlisted December 5, 1863 at Riga, as Private Co. C, to serve three years. Rejected.

WAGNER, RANT -Age 26 years. Enlisted December 26, 1863 at Syracuse. Mustered in as Private, Co. B, January 5, 1864 to serve three years. Transferred to Co. F, March 24, 1864. No further record.

WAHL, FRANZ -Age 18 years. Enlisted February 25, 1865 at Tompkins. Mustered in as Private, "unassigned" February 27, 1865 to serve three years. No further record.

WAILMAN, THOMAS -Age 18 years. Enlisted January 19, 1864 at Lenox as Private "unassigned" to serve three years. Rejected.

WALKER, CHARLES F -Age 18 years. Enlisted December 11, 1863 at Syracuse. mustered in as a Private Co. B, January 5, 1864 to serve three years. Mustered out with company, August 1, 1865 at Winchester, Virginia.

WALKER, EBENEZER -Age 21 years. Enlisted December 7, 1863 at Rochester. Mustered in as Saddler, Co. I, February 2, 1864, to serve three years. Mustered out June 27, 1865 at Satterlee U.S. General Hospital, Philadelphia., Pa.

WALKER, GEORGE -Age 33 years. Enlisted December 15, 1863 at Syracuse. Mustered in as Private, Co. B, January 5, 1864 to serve three years. Transferred to Co. F, March 24, 1864. No further record.

WALKER, GEORGE W -Age 34 years. Enlisted December 25, 1863 at Dunkirk. Mustered in as a Private, Co. F, January 10, 1864 to serve three years. Deserted, February, 1864 from camp near Rochester, New York. Prior service in Co. G, Sixty Sixth New York Infantry.

WALKER, GEORGE W -Age 30 years. Enlisted December 25, 1863 at Dunkirk. Mustered in as Private, Co. I, February 2, 1864 to serve three years. Deserted June 24, 1865 near Winchester, Virginia.

WALKER, TIMOTHY D -Age 24 years. Enlisted December 7, 1863 at Rochester. Mustered in as Sergeant, Co. I, February 2, 1864 to serve three years. Mustered out with company, August 1, 1865 at Winchester, Virginia. Prior service in Co. A, Third New York Artillery.

WALKER, WILLIAM - (Colored)-Age 25 years. Enlisted January 20, 1864 at Rochester. Mustered in as Cook, Co. I, February 2, 1864 to serve three years. No further record.

WALKER, WILLIAM -Age 19 years. Enlisted January 4, 1864 at OtisCo. Mustered in as a Private Co. E, January 10, 1864 to serve three years. Deserted, January 13, 1864 at Rochester, New York.

WALKER, WILLIAM V -Age 27 years. Enlisted December 11, 1863 at Cazenovia. Mustered in as a Corporal, Co. E, January 10, 1864 to serve three years. Captured, date not stated. Died, date not stated at Andersonville, Georgia.

WALLACE, CALEB M -Age 27 years. Enlisted December 22, 1863 at Urbana. Mustered in as a Private, Co. G, February 2, 1864 to serve three years. Died, date and place not stated.

WALLACE, HENRY -Age 26 years. Enlisted March 6, 1865 at Masonville. Mustered in as Private, "unassigned" March 6, 1865 to serve three years. No further record.

WALSH, LUKE -Age 20 years Enlisted March 22 1865 at New York. Mustered in as Private, Co. I, March 22, 1865 to serve three years. Mustered out with company, August 1, 1864 at Winchester, Virginia.

WALSH, MICHAEL -Age 27 years. Enlisted April 1, 1865 at New York. Mustered in as a Private, "unassigned", April 1, 1865 to serve one year. No further record.

WALTER, AUDREY -Age not stated. Enlisted February 15, 1865 at New York. Mustered in as Private, Co. C, February 15, 1865 to serve three years. Mustered out with company, August 1, 1865 at Winchester, Virginia.

WALTERS, GEORGE J -Age 18years. Enlisted January 5, 1863 at Rochester. Mustered in as Private, Co. D, January 10, 1864 to serve three years. Captured, November 12, 1864 at Winchester, Virginia. Released March 1, 1865. Mustered out with company, August 1, 1865 at Winchester, Virginia.

WALWORTH, WALTER C -Age 18 years. Enlisted January 5, 1864 at Plymouth. Mustered in as Private, Co. L, February 12, 1864 to serve three years. Appointed Corporal, date not stated, Sergeant, June 1, 1865. Mustered out with company, August 1, 1865 at Winchester, Virginia.

WARD, HENRY -Age 21 years. Enlisted December 11, 1863 as Syracuse, as Private, Co. B, to serve three years. Rejected.

WARD, ISRAEL -Age 19 years. Enlisted December 24, 1863 at Cazenovia. Mustered in as a Private, Co. E, January 10, 1864 to serve three years. Died of wounds, May 7, 1864 at Fredericksburg, Virginia.

WARDEN, WILLIAM R -Age 19 years. Enlisted April 5, 1865 at New York. Mustered in as a Private "unassigned" April 5, 1865 to serve one year. No further record.

WARDWELL, MYRON F -Age 32 years. Enlisted September 3, 1864 at Pittsfield. Mustered in as a Private, Co. L, September 15, 1864 to serve one year. Mustered out with detachment, June 6, 1865 at Winchester, Virginia.

WARNER, JOSHUA -Age 38 years. Enlisted January 23, 1864 at Syracuse. Mustered in as a Private, Co. E, February 6, 1864 to serve three years. Transferred to 243rd Company First Battalion, Veteran Reserve Corps, September 1, 1864, from which discharged, August 19, 1865 at Washington, D.C. Supposed to be identical with Joshua Warner, Co. I.

WARNER, JOSHUA -Age 44 years. Enlisted January 27, 1864 at Onondaga. Mustered in as a Private Co. I, February 2, 1864 to serve three years. deserted, March, 1864 at Rochester, New York.

WARNER, STEWART -Age 19 years. Enlisted December 23, 1863 at Auburn. Mustered in as a Saddler, Co. M, February 23, 1864 to serve three years. Reduced, date not stated. Transferred to Co. I, March 22, 1864. Mustered out with company, August 1, 1865 at Winchester, Virginia.

WARNER, WILLIAMS -See Warren, William.

WARNER, WILLIAM -Age 22 years. Enlisted December 19, 1863 at Lyons. Mustered in as Private, Co. D, January 10, 1864 to serve three years. Mustered out with company, August 1, 1865 at Winchester, Virginia.

WARREN, ALFRED -Age 18 years. Enlisted November 3, 1863 at Brockport. Mustered in as a Corporal, Co. C, January 5, 1864 to serve three years. Reduced, date not stated. Mustered out with company, August 1, 1865 at Winchester, Virginia.

WARREN, GEORGE -Age 18 years. Enlisted April 5, 1865 at Albany. Mustered in as Private, Co. D, April 5, 1865 to serve three years. Absent, sick at hospital at date of muster out of company, August 1, 1865. No further record.

WARREN, WILLIAM -Age 23 years. Enlisted December 8, 1863 at Rochester. Mustered in as a Private, Co. F, January 10, 1864 to serve three years. Deserted, February, 1864 from camp near Rochester. Also borne as Warner.

WASHBURN, GEORGE W -Age 22 years. Enlisted December 21, 1863 at Sodus. Mustered in as a Private, Co. K, February 6, 1864 to serve three years. Transferred to Co. H, March 25, 1864. Transferred to One Hundred Ninety Second New York Volunteers, April, 1865. Also borne as George H. Washburn.

WASTENS, ENDRERAS -Age 12. Enlisted December 15, 1863 at Buffalo, as Private, Co. K, to serve three years. Rejected.

WATERMAN, JOHN S -Age 32 years. Enlisted February 23, 1865 at New York. Mustered in as a Private, "unassigned", February 23, 1865 to serve one year. No further record.

WATERS, EDWIN -Age 21 years. Enlisted March 6, 1865 at Albany. Mustered in as a Private "unassigned " March 6, 1865 to serve one year. No further record.

WATTERS, CHARLES B -Age 25 years. Enlisted December 17, 1863 at Rochester as Private, Co. I to serve three years. Rejected.

WATTERS, WILLIAM -Age 26 years. Enlisted December 10, 1863 at Rochester as Private, Co. K, to serve three years. Rejected.

WATSON, FREDERICK -Age 21 years. Enlisted March 14, 1865 at New York. Mustered in as a Private, Co. K, March 14, 1865 to serve three years. Mustered out with company, August 1, 1865 at Winchester, Virginia.

WATSON, JOHN -Age 21 years. Enlisted December 8, 1863 at Rochester, as Private Co. F, to serve three years. Rejected.

WATSON, THOMAS -Age 18 years. Enlisted March 4, 1864 at Rochester. Mustered in as a Private, Co. M, March 9, 1864 to serve three years. Mustered out June 28, 1865 at Winchester, Virginia.

WEAVER, CALEB -Age 34 years. Enlisted February 12, 1864 at Cohocton. Mustered in as a Private, Co. M, February 23, 1864 to serve three years. Transferred to Co. G, March 24, 1864. In confinement at date of muster out of company at Fort Delaware by sentence of G.C.M.A. of S., May 30, 1865. Discharged August 9, 1865 at Rochester, New York. Also borne as Caleb M. Weaver.

WEAVER, CHARLES -Age 18 years. Enlisted January 14, 1864 at Otsego. Mustered in as a Private, Co. L, February 12, 1864 to serve three years. Transferred to Two Hundred Forty Third Company, First Battalion Veteran Reserve Corps, December 3, 1864, from which discharged August 8, 1865 at Washington, D.C.

WEAVER, MARTIN -Age 30 years. Enlisted April 8, 1865 at New York. Mustered in as a Private, Co. L, April 8, 1865 to serve one year. Mustered out with company, August 1, 1865 at Winchester, Virginia.

WEBB, CHARLES M -Age18 years. Enlisted December 21, 1863 at Brockport. Mustered in as a Private, Co. C, January 5, 1864 to serve three years. Appointed Corporal, February 29, 1864. Reduced, January 3, 1865. Mustered out with company, August 1, 1865 at Winchester, Virginia. Also borne as Charles W. and William Webb.

WEBB, HENRY -Age 18 years. Enlisted March 22, 1865 at Franklin. Mustered in as a Private, Co. A, March 23, 1865, to serve three years. Absent, sick in hospital at Winchester, Virginia., at date of muster out of company, August 1, 1865. No further record.

WEBB, ORSON -Age 19 years. Enlisted January 13, 1864 at Rochester, as Private, Co. K, to serve three years. Rejected.

WEBB, SAMUEL Jr. -Age 23 years. Enlisted December 31, 1863 at Smithfield. Mustered in as a Private, Co. E, January 10, 1864 to serve three years. Deserted, January 13, 1864 at Rochester, New York.

WEBER, HENRY -Age 39 years. Enlisted January 4, 1864 at New York. Mustered in as a Private "unassigned" January 4, 1864 to serve three years. No further record.

WEBER, MARTIN -Age 30 years. Enlisted April 8, 1865 at New York. Mustered in as a Private "unassigned", April 8, 1865 to serve one year. No further record.

WEBSTER, HENRY -Age 18 years. Enlisted February 23, 1864 at Rochester. Mustered in as Corporal, Co. M, February 23, 1864 to serve three years. Reduced, date not stated. Captured, date not stated. Died, August 15, 1864 at Andersonville, Georgia.

WEBSTER, JEROME -Age 18 years. Enlisted December 14, 1863 at Sweden. Mustered in as a Private, Co. C, January 5, 1864 to serve three years. Mustered out with company, August 1, 1865 at Winchester, Virginia.

WEEDEN, JAMES M -Age 19 years. Enlisted January 4, 1864 at Norwich. Mustered in as Corporal, Co. L, February 12, 1864 to serve three years. Appointed Sergeant, date not stated. Mustered out June 7, 1965 at Annapolis, Maryland.

WEEKES, FRANK -Age 20 years. Enlisted December 26, 1863 at Syracuse. Mustered in as a Private, Co. B, January 5, 1864 to serve three years. Mustered out with company, August 1, 1865 at Winchester, Virginia. Also borne as Frank Wicks

WEEKS, JAMES E -Age 26 years. Enrolled January 29, 1864 at Rochester. Mustered in as First Lieutenant, Co. M, March 4, 1864 to serve three years. Discharged October 31, 1864 at Washington, D.C. Commissioned First Lieutenant March 30, 1864, with rank from January 29, 1864, original.

WELCH, JOHN -Age 28 years. Enlisted April 7, 1865 at New York. Mustered in as a Private "unassigned" April 7, 1865, to serve one year. No further record.

WELCH, JOHN E -Age 18 years, Enlisted April 12, 1865 at Wilton. Mustered in as Private "unassigned" April 12, 1865 to serve one year. Mustered out with detachment, May 6, 1865 at Harts Island, New York Harbor.

WELCH, WILLIAM -Age 12 years. Enlisted December 12, 1863 at Brockport as Private in Co. C to serve three years. Rejected.

WELCHIM, ADAM F -Age 22 years. Enlisted February 15, 1865 at New York. Mustered in as Private, Co. A, February 15, 1865 to serve three years. Deserted July 24, 1865 at Remount Camp, Maryland.

WELL, HENRY -Age 33 years. Enlisted March 8, 8165 at New York. Mustered in as Private, Co. I, March 8, 1865 to serve three years. Mustered out with company August 1, 1865 at Winchester, Virginia.

WELLMAN, EDWARD -Age 19 years. Enlisted January 14, 1864 at Lenox. Mustered in as a Private, Co. K, February 6, 1864 to serve three years. Wounded, June 13, 1864. Died from wounds, June 20, 1864 at Hampton, Virginia.

WELLMAN, FRANK -Age 23 years. Enlisted March 7, 1865 at New York. Mustered in as Private, Co. I, March 7, 1865 to serve three years. No further record.

WELLMAN, THOMAS -Age 18 years. Enlisted January 19, 1864 at Lenox. Mustered in as Private "unassigned" February 22, 1864 to serve three years. No further record.

WELLS, CHARLES -Age 27 years. Enlisted December 4, 1863 at Rochester. Mustered in as Private Co. A, December 20, 1863 to serve three years. Deserted, December, 1863 at Rochester, New York.

WELLS, LYMAN -Age 18 years. Enlisted December 21, 1863 at Madison. Mustered in as Private, Co. E, January 10, 1864 to serve three years. Mustered out with company August 1, 1865 at Winchester, Virginia.

WELLS, WILLIAM -Age 29 years. Enlisted December 21, 1863 at Syracuse. Mustered in as Private, Co. B, January 5, 1864 to serve three years. Deserted, March 22, 1864 at Giesboro Point, D.C.

WENDENBERGER, FRANK -Age 20 years. Enlisted April 10, 1865 at Albany. Mustered in as Private "unassigned" April 10, 1865 to serve one year. Mustered out with detachment, May 6, 1865 at Hart's Island, New York Harbor.

WENKILMANN, HENRY -Age 28 years. Enlisted March 8, 1865 at New York. Mustered in as Private "unassigned", March 8, 1865 to serve three years. Mustered out with detachment, May 6, 1865 at Hart's Island, New York Harbor.

WESCOTT, DECALYUS -Age 18 years. Enlisted September 6, 1864 at Otsego. Mustered in as Private, Co. F, September 6, 1864 to serve one year. Died February 2, 1865 at Salisbury, N.C.

WESTON, GEORGE M -Age 21 years. Enlisted March 10, 1865 at New York. Mustered in as Private in Co. I, March 10, 1865 to serve three years. Mustered out with company, August 1, 1865 at Winchester, Virginia.

WEVER, SPENCER C -Age 23 years. Enlisted November 30, 1863 at Syracuse. Mustered in as Private, Co. B, January 5, 1864 to serve three years. Appointed Sergeant, date not stated. Mustered out with company, August 1, 1865 at Winchester, Virginia. Also borne as Weaver. Prior service in Co. B 27th New York Volunteers.

WEYMAN, FREDERICK -Age 18 years. Enlisted November 25, 1863 at Rochester. Mustered in as Private, Co. D, January 10, 1864 to serve three year. Mustered out with company, August 1, 1865 at Winchester, Virginia. Prior service in 22nd New York Volunteer Infantry.

WHALAN, JOHN -Age 23 years. Enlisted January 12, 1864 at Rochester. Mustered in as Private, Co. G, February 2, 1864 to serve three years. Transferred to Co. D, March 22, 1864. Mustered out with company, August 1, 1865 at Winchester, Virginia.

WHALEN, LARRY -Age 21 years. Enlisted January 2, 1864 at Rochester. Mustered in as Private, Co. D, January 10, 1864 to serve three years. Absent without leave at date of muster out of company, August 1, 1865. No Further record.

WHALEN, PETER -Age 19 years. Enlisted April 5, 1865 at Hudson. Mustered in as Private Co. F, April 5, 1865 to serve one year. Mustered out with company August 1, 1865 at Winchester, Virginia. Also borne as Whelan.

WHEATON, WELLINGTON -Age 21 years. Enlisted December 5, 1863 at Bath. Mustered in as Corporal, Co. G, February 2, 1864 to serve three years. Appointed Quartermaster Sergeant, July 1, 1864. Mustered out with company August 1, 1865 at Winchester, Virginia. Prior service in Co. I, Thirty Fourth New York Infantry.

WHEDON, CHARLES E -Age 18 years. Enlisted December 29, 1863 at Syracuse. Mustered in as Farrier, Co. B, January 5, 1864 to serve three years. Appointed Bugler, date not stated. Mustered out with company August 1, 1865 at Winchester, Virginia. Also borne as Wheedon.

WHEDON, HENRY E -Age 23 years. Enlisted December 14, 1863 at Syracuse. Mustered in as Corporal, Co. B, January 5, 1864 to serve three years. Appointed Sergeant, date not stated. Mustered out with company August 1, 1865 at Winchester, Virginia. Also borne as Wheedon.

WHEELER, AMOS E -Age 24, years. Enlisted December 9, 1863 at Penn Yan. Mustered in as Corporal, Co. A, December 20, 1863 to serve three years. Appointed Sergeant, March 15, 1865. Captured and paroled dates not stated. Discharged, June 27, 1865

WHEELER, CHARLES -Age 24 years. Enlisted April 10, 1865 at Rochester. Mustered in as Private in Co. F, April 10, 1865 to serve three years. Mustered out with company August 1, 1865 at Winchester, Virginia.

WHEELER, CHARLES M -Age 26 years. Enlisted January 22, 1864 at Rochester. Mustered in as Private, Co. K. February 6, 1865, to serve three years. Transferred to Co. M, March 25, 1864. Absent in hospital at Washington, D.C. at date of muster out of company, August 1, 1865. No further record.

WHEELER, GEORGE R -Age 28 years. Enlisted August 31, 1864 at Unadilla. Mustered in as Private, Co. F, September, 3, 1864 to serve one year. Appointed Corporal, date not stated. Mustered out with detachment, June 6, 1865, at Winchester, Virginia.

WHEELER, HENRY -Age 21 years. Enlisted October 4, 1864 at Jamaica. Mustered in as a Private, Co. M, October 4, 1864 to serve one year. Mustered out with company August 1, 1865 at Winchester, Virginia.

WHEELER, HUBERT -Age 19 years. Enlisted December 4, 1863 at Syracuse. Mustered in as Private, Co. B, January 5, 1864 to serve three years. Appointed Corporal, date not stated. Mustered out with company August 1, 1865 at Winchester, Virginia.

WHEELER, RUDEN E -Age 19 years. Enlisted January 1, 1864 at Rochester. Mustered in as Private, Co. I, February 2, 1864 to serve three years. Transferred to Co. M, March, 1864. Appointed Sergeant, June 1, 1865. Mustered out with company August 1, 1865 at Winchester, Virginia.

WHEELOCK, NOEL B -Age 19 years. Enlisted February 23, 1864 at Pitcher. Mustered in as Private, Co. E, February 24, 1864 to serve three years. Died of disease, April 20, 1865 at St. Elizabeth.

WHELAN, PETER -See Whalen, Peter.

WHIPPLE, EMMETT -Age 18 years. Enlisted April 12, 1865 at New York. Mustered in as Private "unassigned" April 12, 1865, to serve one year. Mustered out with detachment, may 6, 1865 at Hart's Island, New York Harbor.

WHIPPLE, MARVIN D -Age 21 years. Enlisted January 2, 1864 at Rochester. Mustered in as Private, Co. D, January 10, 1864 to serve three years. Captured June 22, 1865, place not stated. No further record.

WHITE, ALONZO -Age 31 years. Enlisted August 31, 1864 at Pharsalia. Mustered in as a Private, Co. I, September 16, 1864 to serve one year. Appointed Farrier, date not stated. Mustered out with detachment, June 6, 1865 at Winchester, Virginia.

WHITE, CORNELIUS - Age 18 years. Enlisted January 5, 1864 at Rochester. Mustered in as a Private, Co. I, February 2, 1864 to serve three years. Mustered out May 29, 1865 at Jarvis U.S.A. General Hospital, Baltimore, Maryland. Also bone as C.J. White.

WHITE, DAVID C -Age 18 years. Enlisted January 13, 1864 at German. Mustered in as a Private, Co. L, February 12, 1864 to serve three years. Captured and paroled, date not stated. Died December 31, 1864 at Annapolis, Maryland.

WHITE, DAVID R- Age 28 years. Enlisted February 28, 1865 at New York. Mustered in as a Private, "unassigned," February 28, 1865 to serve three years. No further record.

WHITE, GEORGE -Age 20 years. Enlisted September 7, 1864 at New Lisbon. Mustered in as Private, Co. E, September 20, 1864 to serve three years. Died, date not stated at Salisbury, N.C.

WHITE, NAPOLEON B -Age 19 years. Enlisted January 4, 1864 at Norwich. Mustered in as a Private, Co. L, February 12, 1864 to serve three years. Appointed Corporal, June 1, 1865. Mustered out with detachment, June 28, 1865 at Winchester, Va.

WHITE, OSSIAN CHARLES -Age 16 years. Enlisted December 30, 1863 at Cazenovia. Mustered in as a Private, Co. E. January 10, 1864 to serve three years. Mustered out with company August 1, 1865 at Winchester, Virginia.

WHITE, PETER -Age 30 years. Enlisted April 12, 1865 at Kingston. Mustered in as a Private, Co. C, April 13, 1865 to serve three years. Mustered out with detachment, May 6, 1865 at Harts Island, New York Harbor.

WHITE, WILLIAM R-Age 21 years. Enlisted December 21, 1863 at Hamilton. Mustered in as a Private, Co. E, January 10, 1864 to serve three years. Died of disease, date not stated at Hamilton, New York.

WHITFIELD, EBEN -Age 28 years. Age 28 years. Enrolled April 16, 1864 at Camp Stoneman, D.C. Mustered in as First Lieutenant Co. I, April 16, 1864 to serve three years. Discharged for disability, December 19, 1864. Commissioned First Lieutenant March 30, 1864, with rank from January 29, 1864, original.

WHITING, WILLIAM -Age 18 years. Enlisted December 30, 1863 as Private, Co. B to serve three years, at Syracuse. Rejected.

WHITING, WILLIAM S -Age 18 years. Enlisted as Private Co. E, December 30, 1863, at Fayetteville, to serve three years. Rejected.

WHITMAN, WILLIAM S -Age 18 years. Enlisted October 3, 1864 at Jamaica. Mustered in as Private, Co. M, October 3, 1864 to serve one year. Mustered out with company August 1, 1865 at Winchester, Virginia.

WHITMORE, ALONZO -Age 20 years. Enlisted January 5, 1864 at Lenox. Mustered in as Private, Co. K, February 6, 1864 to serve three years. Died of disease, August 20, 1865 at Portsmouth Grove, R.I.

WHITMORE, ANSEL -Age 18 years. Enlisted December 4, 1863 at Rochester. Mustered in as Private, Co. A, December 20, 1863 to serve three years. Mustered out with company August 1, 1865 at Winchester, Virginia.

WHITNEY, GEORGE -Age 19 years. Enlisted November 16, 1863 at Albion. Mustered in as Trumpeter, Co. F, January 10, 1864 to serve three years. Mustered out June 22, 1865 at McClennan U.S.A. Hospital, Philadelphia. Pa.

WHITNEY, JOHN J -Age 31 years. Enlisted April 1, 1865 at Rochester. Mustered in as Private, Co. F, April 1, 1865 to serve three years. Appointed Sergeant June 1, 1865. Mustered out with company August 1, 1865 at Winchester, Virginia.

WICKS, FRANK, See Weekes, Frank.

WIGHTMAN, CHARLES H -Age 17 years. Enlisted as Private, Co. K to serve three years, December 28, 1863 at Pomfret. Rejected.

WILBER, HORACE V -Age 26 years. Enlisted December 19, 1863 at Syracuse. Mustered in as Private, Co. B, January 5, 1864 to serve three years. Mustered out with company August 1, 1865 at Winchester, Virginia.

WILBUR, GEORGE- Age 30 years. Dates of enlistment and muster in not stated. Appears as Private, Co. A. Captured, November 12, 1864. Absent at date of muster out of company August 1, 1865. No further record.

WILCOX, ELIAS -Age 24 years. Enlisted January 21, 1864 at Rochester. Mustered in as Private, Co. I, February 2, 1864 to serve three years. Deserted, March 1864 at Rochester, New York.

WILCOX, HENRY M -Age 18 years. Enlisted August 1, 1864 at Norwich. Mustered in as Private, Co. L, August 18, 1864 to serve one year. No further record.

WILCOX, SILOAM E -Age 23 years. Enlisted January 4, 1863 at Rochester. Mustered in as Private, Co. I, February 2, 1864 to serve three years. Transferred to Co. M, March 1864. Appointed Quartermaster Sergeant, date not stated. Mustered out with company, August 1, 1865 at Winchester, Virginia. Prior service in Co. K, Third New York Cavalry Volunteers.

WILBERT, WILLIAM -Age 16 years. Enlisted as Private, Co. I, November 24, 1863 at Auburn to serve three years. Rejected

WILHELM, ADAM JOSEPH -Age 22 years. Enlisted February 15, 1865 at New York. Mustered in as Private "unassigned," February 15, 1865 to serve three years. No further record.

WILKINS, TERRENCE D -Age 19 years. Enlisted November 11, 1863 at Rochester. Mustered in as Private, Co. A, December 20, 1863 to serve three years. Captured June 23, 1864. Released December 8, 1864 at Florence, S.C. Mustered out July 15, 1865 at Buffalo, New York.

WILL, PAUL - Age 18 years. Enlisted December 18, 1863 at Cazenovia. Mustered in as Private, Co. E, January 10, 1864 to serve three years. Deserted, January 13, 1864 at Rochester, New York.

WILL, REINHOLD - Age 27 years. Enlisted April 11, 1865 at Rochester. Mustered in as Private, Co. K, April 11, 1865 to serve three years. Mustered out with company August 1, 1865 at Winchester, Virginia.

WILLARD, GEORGE- Age 32 years. Enlisted February 23, 1864 at Rochester. Mustered in as Corporal, Co. M, February 23, 1864 to serve three years. Absent, sick at date of muster out of company August 1, 1865.

WILLETT, JOHN- Age 28 years. Enlisted December 22, 1863 at Rochester. Mustered in as Private, Co. D, January 10, 1864 to serve three years. No further record.

WILLIAMS, A.J.- Age 29 years. Enlisted February 23, 1865 at New York. Mustered in as Private, Co. H, February 23, 1865 to serve three years. Mustered out with company August 1, 1865 at Winchester, Virginia.

WILLIAMS, CHARLES- Age 30 years. Enlisted April 5, 1865 at New York. Mustered in as Private "unassigned" April 5, 1865, to serve one year. Mustered out with detachment, May 6, 1865 at Harts Island, New York Harbor. Also borne as Williams, Charles U.

WILLIAMS, GEORGE W- Age 24 years. Enlisted November 30, 1863 at Rochester. Mustered in as Sergeant, Co. H, February 2, 1864 to serve three years. Transferred to Co. F, date not stated. Mustered out as Private, April 21, 1866 at Albany New York. Prior service in Co. B, Twenty Seventh New York State Volunteers.

WILLIAMS, HANSON- Age 24 years. Enlisted December 14, 1863 at Peterboro. Mustered in as Private, Co. H, February 2, 1864 to serve three years. Appointed Corporal, December 27, 1864. Mustered out with company August 1, 1865 at Winchester, Virginia.

WILLIAMS, HENRY -Age 23 years. Enlisted December 19, 1863 at Rochester. Mustered in as Sergeant, Co. F, January 10, 1864 to serve three years. Appointed Commissary Sergeant, date not stated. Deserted February 1864, from camp near Rochester, New York. Also borne as Henry William.

WILLIAMS, JOHN- Age 28 years. Enlisted October 17, 1863 at Rochester. Mustered in as Corporal, Co. A, December 20, 1863 to serve three years. Mustered out as Private with company, August 1, 1865 at Winchester, Virginia.

WILLIAMS, JOHN A- Age 29 years. Enlisted February 23, 1865 at new York. Mustered in as Private, "unassigned," February 23, 1865 to serve three years. No further record.

WILLIAMS, LORENZO D- (Colored)- Age 29 years. Enlisted January 4, 1864 at Rochester. Mustered in as Cook, Co. D, January 10, 1864 to serve three years. Deserted. August 10, 1864

WILLIAMS, WILLIAM- Age 43 years. Enlisted January 4, 1864 at Florida. Mustered in as Private "unassigned" January 5, 1864, to serve three years. No further record.

WILLIAMSON, ALANSON J- Age 23 years. Enlisted April 3, 1865 at Hudson. Mustered in as Private, Co. K, April 3, 1865, to serve one year. Appointed Corporal, June 1, 1865, Sergeant, July 1, 1865. Mustered out with company August 1, 1865 at Winchester, Virginia.

WILLIAMSON, WILLIAM H- Age 38 years. Enlisted as Private, Co. D, January 1, 1864 at Rochester to serve three years. Rejected.

WILLOUGHBY, THOMAS- Age 23 years. Enlisted December 9, 1863 at Rochester. Mustered in as Sergeant, Co. D January 10, 1864 to serve three years. Mustered out June 13, 1865 at Annapolis, Maryland. Prior service in Co. G, Twenty Seventh Regiment New York Volunteers.

WILLIS, GEORGE- Age 25 years. Enlisted January 2, 1864 at Rochester. Mustered in as Private, Co. F, January 10, 1864 to serve three years. Deserted February, 1864 from camp near Rochester.

WILLITTS, INGRAHAM, -Age 19 years. Enlisted March 2, 1865 at Auburn. Mustered in as Private, Co. B, March 2, 1865 to serve one year. Mustered out with company August 1, 1865 at Winchester, Virginia.

WILLITTS, LOTTS-Age 18 years. Enlisted February 24, 1865 at Auburn. Mustered in as Private, Co. B, February 24, 1865 to serve one year. Mustered out with company August 1, 1865 at Winchester, Virginia.

WILLMOT, HENRY-Age 20 years. Enlisted March 24, 1865 at Brooklyn. Mustered in as Private, Co. K, March 24, 1865 to serve three years. Mustered out with company August 1, 1865 at Winchester, Virginia.

WILSON, CONRAD-Age 18 years. Enlisted January 15, 1864 at Rochester. Mustered in as Private, Co. I, February 2, 1864 to serve three years. Transferred to Co. M, March 1864. Appointed Corporal, date not stated. Mustered out June 28, 1865 at Winchester, Virginia.

WILSON, HENRY-Age 21 years. Enlisted January 15, 1864 at Rochester. Mustered in as Farrier, Co. K, February 6, 1864 to serve three years. Deserted, February 10, 1864 at Rochester, New York.

WILSON, JOHN- Age 20 years. Enlisted April 1, 1865 at Kingston. Mustered in as Private, Co. A, April 1, 1865 to serve three years. Mustered out with detachment, May 6, 1865 at Hart's Island, New York Harbor.

WINKLEMAN, H.— See Wenkilmann, Henry

WINN, JAMES-Age 21 years. Enlisted March 13, 1865 at Manlius. Mustered in as Private,"unassigned," March 13, 1865 to serve three years. Mustered out with detachment, May 9, 1865 at Elmira, New York. Never joined regiment.

WINTERS, URNEST -Age 19 years. Enlisted December 15, 1863 as Private, Co. H at Lyons. Rejected.

WISE, SIDNEY V- Age 21 years. Enlisted January 4, 1864 at Lenox. Mustered in as Quartermaster Sergeant, Co. K, February 6, 1864 to serve three years. Mustered out with company August 1, 1865 at Winchester, Virginia.

WISNER, OSCAR F-Age 38 years. Enrolled February 10, 1864 at Rochester. Mustered in as Captain, Co. I, February 10, 1864 to serve three years. Discharged to date May 15, 1865. Commissioned Captain, March 30, 1864 with rank from January 29, 1864 original.

WOLFF, JOHN- Age 19 years. Enlisted January 4, 1864 at New York. Mustered in as Private, "unassigned," January 4, 1864, to serve three years. No further record.

WOOD, EDGAR A -Age 18 years. Enlisted as Private, Co. K, December 24, 1863 at Pomfret to serve three years. Rejected.

WOOD, GEORGE- Age 30 years. Enlisted January 9, 1864 at Verona. Mustered in as Private, Co. M, January 9, 1864 to serve three years. Mustered out June 3, 1865 from United States general Hospital, Cumberland, Maryland.

WOOD, HENRY- Age 29 years. Enlisted February 13, 1864 at Sodus. Mustered in as Private, Co. M, February 23, 1864 to serve three years. No further record.

WOOD, JOHN S- Age 19 years. Enlisted November 11, 1863 at Auburn. Mustered in as Bugler, Co. I February 2, 1864 to serve three years. Transferred March 29, 1865 to 192nd New York Volunteers.

WOODARD, GEORGE- Age 30 years. Enlisted March 23, 1864 at Giesboro Point, D.C.

Mustered in as Private, Co. F, March 23, 1864 to serve three years. Appointed Sergeant, date not stated. Mustered in as Second Lieutenant, July 30, 1865. Mustered out with company, August 1, 1865 at Winchester, Virginia. Also borne as George F. Woodward. Commissioned Second Lieutenant, November 10, 1864 with rank from September 10, 1864, vice Collister, discharged. Commission revoked; Recommissioned, May 31, 1865, with rank from May 22, 1865, vice Taylor, missing.

WOODEN, WILLIAM-Age 38 years. Enlisted as Private, Co. E, January 2, 1864 at Madison. Rejected.

WOODERSON, CHARLES G-Age 18 years. Enlisted December 5, 1863 at Rochester. Mustered in as Private, Co. A December 20, 1863, to serve three years. Mustered out with company August 1, 1865 at Winchester, Virginia.

WOODRUFF, SAMUEL-Age 30 years. Enlisted November 30, 1863 at Urbana. Mustered in as Private, Co. G, February 2, 1864 to serve three years. Died, date and place not stated.

WOOLFER, WILLIAM-Age 30 years. Enlisted as Private, Co. M, January 30, 1864 at Dunkirk, to serve three years. Rejected.

WORDEN, VERNON- Age 18 years. Enlisted January 11, 1864 at Smyrna. Mustered in as Private, Co. L February 12, 1864 to serve three years. Died of disease at St. Mary's Hospital, March 2, 1864 at Rochester.

WORDEN, WILLIAM R-Age 19 years. Enlisted April 5, 1865 at New York City. Mustered in as Private, Co. B April 5, 1865 to serve one year. Deserted June 6, 1865 at Winchester, Virginia.

WRENN, JOHN- Age 23 years. Enrolled October 9, 1863 at Rochester. Mustered in as First Lieutenant, Co. A, December 31, 1863 to serve three years. Mustered in as Captain, February 23, 1864. Resigned, July 13, 1864 at City Point, Virginia.

Commissioned First Lieutenant, with rank from December 21, 1863 original; Captain, March 30, 1864 with rank from January 5, 1864, original.

WRIGHT, ADELBERT- Age 18 years. Enlisted January 4, 1864 at Manlius. Mustered in as Private, Co. E, January 10, 1864 to serve three years. Appointed Bugler, date not stated. Mustered out with company, August 1, 1865 at Winchester, Virginia.

WRIGHT, GEORGE- Age 28 years. Enlisted March 10, 1865 at New York. Mustered in as Private "unassigned," March 10, 1865 to serve three years. No further record.

WRIGHT, HENRY- Age 25 years. Enlisted as Private, Co. C December 19, 1863 at Rochester to serve three years. Rejected.

WRIGHT, JOHN-Age 20 years. Enlisted February 10, 1864 at Hamlin. Mustered in as Private, Co. M, February 23, 1864 to serve three years. Transferred to Co. C, March 22, 1864. Mustered out with company, August 1, 1865 at Winchester, Virginia.

WRIGHT, JOHN- Age not stated. Enlisted February 8, 1864 at Rochester. Mustered in as Private, Co. C, February 23, 1864 to serve three years. Mustered out with company, August 1, 1865 at Winchester, Virginia.

WRIGHT, JOHN N.- Age 33 years. Enlisted January 22, 1864 at Van Buren. Mustered in as Corporal, Co. H February 2, 1864 to serve three years. Transferred as Sergeant to Co. E date not stated. Appointed First Sergeant, date not stated. Mustered out with company August 1, 1865 at Winchester, Virginia. Commissioned Second Lieutenant, July 31, 1865 with rank from July 11, 1865, vice Moore, promoted, not mustered.

WRIGHT, SILAS- Age 18 years. Enlisted January 14, 1864 at bath. Mustered in as Private, Co. K, February 6, 1864 to serve three years. Transferred to Twenty Second Company second Battalion Veteran reserve corps, March 25, 1864 from which discharged, November 21, 1865 at Washington, D.C.

WRIGHT, WALTER- Age 16 years. Enlisted as Private in Co. K, December 17, 1863 at Sheridan to serve three years. Rejected.

WURTH, JOHN- Age 25 years. Enlisted December 21, 1863 at Syracuse. Mustered in as Private, Co. B, January 5, 1864 to serve three years. Discharged at New York City, date not stated. Also borne as Worth.

WYGANT, WILLIAM- Age 19 years. Enlisted March 25, 1862 at New York. Mustered in as Private, Co. K, March 28, 1865 to serve three years. Mustered out with company August 1, 1865 at Winchester, Virginia.

YAGER, EUGENE- Age 18 years. Enlisted February 22, 1864 at Rochester as Private, Co. M to serve three years. Rejected, under age.

YATES, SQUIRE M.- Age 21 years. Enlisted November 15, 1861 at Smyrna. Mustered in as Private, Co. I, Eighth New York Cavalry, November 28, 1861 to serve three years. Appointed Regimental Quartermaster Sergeant April 14, 1862.

Re-enlisted December 1, 1863, transferred to and mustered in as First Lieutenant in Co. K this regiment February 17, 1864. Killed April 7, 1865. Commissioned First Lieutenant March 30, 1864 with rank from January 29, 1864, original.

YAW, ELIJAH F.-Age 23 years. Enlisted December 28, 1863 at Palmyra. Mustered in as Private, Co. H, February 2, 1864 to serve three years. Mustered out June 27, 1865 from Satterlee United States General Hospital, at West Philadelphia, Pa.

YEAGER, RUEBEN- see Jeager, Urban

YENDALL. EDWARD- see Tindall, Edward.

YACHUNSON, FLITZ- Age 21 years. Enlisted March 25, 1865 at New York. Mustered in as Private, Co. L March 25, 1865 to serve three years. Deserted June 25, 1865 at Winchester, Virginia.

YORK, FAYETTE G.-Age 18 years. Enlisted January 4, 1864 at Norwich. Mustered in as Corporal, Co. I, February 12, 1864 to serve three years. Appointed Sergeant, no date given. Died while prisoner of war at Andersonville, Georgia. Also borne as Fayette C.

YOUNG, BENJAMIN L.— Age 24 years. Enlisted January 4, 1864 at Syracuse, as Private, Co. E, to serve three years. Rejected.

YOUNG, CHRISTOPHER— Age 27 years. Enlisted December 1, 1863 at Urbana. Mustered in as Private, Co. G, February 2, 1864, to serve three years. Mustered out with company, August 1, 1865 at Winchester, Virginia.

YOUNG, ROBERT— Age 19 years. Enlisted December 16, 1863 at Rome, as Private, Co. C, to serve three years; rejected for disability.

YOUNG, WILLIAM— Age 18 years. Enlisted November 10, 1863 at Rochester. Mustered in as Private, Co. A, December 20, 1863 to serve three years. Appointed Corporal, no date given. Appointed Sergeant, July 1, 1865. Mustered out with company, August 1, 1865 at Winchester, Virginia.

YOUNGS, GEORGE C.— Age 26 years. Enlisted January 4, 1864 at Elbridge. Mustered in as Private, Co. H, February 2, 1864 to serve three years. Died, no date given.

YOUNGS, JOSEPH N.— Age 19 years. Enlisted December 16, 1863 at Rome. Mustered in as Private, Co. C, January 5, 1864 to serve three years. Mustered out with company, August 1, 1865 at Winchester, Virginia.

ZACHER, VICTOR— Age 27 years. Enlisted January 19, 1864 at Rochester. Mustered in as Private, Co. K, February 6, 1864 to serve three years. Transferred to Co. M, March 25, 1864. Mustered out with company, August 1, 1865 at Winchester, Virginia. Also borne as Zacker.

ZEPFEL, ROBERT— see Ziffle, Robert.

ZIFFLE, ROBERT— Age 26 years. Enlisted December 19, 1863 at Lyons. Mustered in as Private, Co. D, January 10, 1864 to serve three years. Mustered out, August 28, 1865 at Rochester, New York. Also borne as Zepfel.

Appendix E

My Civil War Ancestor

In 1863, James Herald lived in Riga, New York. He worked as a farm hand and attended school during the winter. He enlisted in Company M, 22nd New York Cavalry Regiment in Company M, on February 23, 1864 to serve for three years. On March 25, 1864 he was transferred to Company D. His first taste of the real war came during the battle of the Wilderness, where the regiment was briefly engaged with the Rebels. His most extreme experience came during the raid on the railroads south of Petersburg, Va. James was assigned, along with First Lieutenant Patrick Glennan, as a messenger carrying dispatches from General James Harrison Wilson to General Grant's headquarters. They were apart from the regiment for about eight to ten days during that campaign, but rejoined their company in time for Lieutenant Glennan to be killed at Dinwiddie Court House, and for James to be captured at Stony Creek, Va., near the Sappony Baptist Church on June 29, 1864.

Now a prisoner of war, James was sent, along with numerous other soldiers of the regiment, to Andersonville Prison. He would endure many hardships during his confinement there, and on the date of his parole, in March of 1865 he weighed only 98 pounds. James was sent to Camp Parole, at Annapolis, Md., and spent the next eight weeks recovering.

He received a 4 week furlough, which he spent at his home in Riga, then rejoined the regiment at Winchester, Va. He was discharged from the army on June 28, 1865 at Winchester.

James returned to Riga, and remained there until the following spring, when He and his brother and his brother's family moved to Hubbardston, Michigan. He worked as a farm hand again, and saved his money with the hope of purchasing his own land. He was married in April of 1873, and bought a farm the following year. By 1882, his wife, Elizabeth, had given birth to six children.

In 1884, lightning struck their farmhouse burning it to the ground. Everyone escaped the flames safely. However, Elizabeth, who fled the house into the snow in bare feet and nightclothes took ill soon after and died of pneumonia in December 1884. James was now a 39 year old widower with 6 children to raise alone. James soon married again, and with his second wife Mary had 10 more children.

James was plagued with health problems for most of his life. He died on September 10, 1910 at the age of 65. His legacy however lives on in Michigan, where many of his descendants still reside.

I was told a story that James' cavalry uniform and a company flag was passed on to one of his sons. These cherished possessions were unfortunately the innocent victim, when after a family dispute, his wife set fire to the whole lot, and burned them to a crisp.

James Herald did not end up as a great war hero. He was a simple man who came to the aid of his country in it's hour of need, and I am deeply proud to be one of his descendants, and equally proud to be able to tell his story.[1]

Endnotes

Chapter 1

[1] Frederick Phisterer, *New York in the War of the Rebellion 1861-1865*, 5 Volumes and Index, (Albany, 1912), p. 1065.

Chapter 2

[1] Rochester (NY) Union&Advertiser, 26 Sept 1864. U&A, 30 Sept 1864. Hereafter cited U&A.
[2] U&A, 08 Oct 1864
[3] U&A, 19 Nov 1864, U&A 4 Dec 1864, U&A 8 Feb 1864, U&A 24 Feb 1864, U&A 26 Feb 1864
[4] U&A, 01 Mar 1864
[5] U&A, 04 Mar 1864
[6] U&A, 07 Mar 1864
[7] Dewitt Crumb, MD., *Historical Addresses, Reminiscences, and Roster of survivors of the 22nd New York Volunteer Cavalry, 2d Brig. 3d Div. Cavalry Corps.* (New York 1894), p. 3. Hereafter to be cited as Crumb, *Reminiscences*.
[8] U&A, 23 April 1864
[9] *War of the Rebellion: A Compilation of the Official Records of the Union and Confederate Armies*, 129 vols. (Washington, D.C., 1880-1901) pt.1, vol. XXXIII, pp. 966-967, 994. Hereafter cited as *OR*., U&A 2 May 1864.

Chapter 3

[1] Crumb, *Reminiscences*, p. 4.
[2] *OR*, XXXVI, pt. 2, p. 329.
[3] *OR*, XXXVI, pt.2, p. 326.
[4] Crumb, *Reminiscences*, p. 6-8.
[5] *OR*, XXXVI, pt.2, pp. 508-509.
[6] *OR*, XXXVI, pt.1, pp. 995-996, Steven Starr, *The Union Cavalry in the Civil War*, Vol.II (New York,1994) p.8. Hereafter cited as Steven Starr, *Union Cavalry*, *OR*, XXXVI, pt.1, pp. 995-996.
[7] Crumb, *Reminiscences*, p. 8. *OR*, XXXVI, pt.3, p. 883.
[8] Crumb, *Reminiscences*, p. 8, U&A, 27 June 1864, *OR*, XXXVI, pt.3, p. 884.
[9] Frederick Dyer, *A Compendium of the War of the Rebellion*, (Des Moine,Iowa) 1908, pp. 1381-1382. Crumb, *Reminiscences*, p. 8.

Chapter 4

[1] Edward G. Longacre, *Wilson-Kautz Raid*, Civil War Times Illustrated, May,1970, p. 32. Hereafter cited as Longacre, Wilson-Kautz Raid.
[2] *OR, XXXX*, pt.1, p. 644.
[3] Crumb, *Reminiscences*, p. 9. Longacre, *Wilson-Kautz Raid*, p. 35. A.A. Humphreys, *The Virginia Campaign of '64 and '65*, (New York 1883), p. 237. *OR,XXXX*, pt.1, pp. 20-622.
[4] William C. Davis, *Death in the Trenches, Grant at Petersburg*, Time Life Books (Alexandria Va. 1986), p.55.
[5] A.A. Humphreys, *The Virginia Campaign of '64 and '65*, (New York 1883), pp. 238-239. - Crumb, *Reminiscences*, pp. 9-12. Longacre, *Wilson-Kautz Raid*, pp. 38-40. *OR, XXXX*, pt 1. pp. 646-647.
[6] A.B. Cummins, *The Wilson-Kautz Raid, More commonly referred to as the Battle of the Grove*. (Blackstone, Va.), 1961, pp. 28-30, Noah Andre Trudeau, *The Last Citadel*, (Boston), pp. 9-10.Crumb, *Reminiscences*, pp. 13-15. Longacre, *Wilson-Kautz Raid*, pp. 39-42, Steven Starr, *Union Cavalry*, pp. 197-199.

Chapter 5

[1] *OR, XXXX*, pt.1, pp. 624,625.
[2] Crumb, *Reminiscences*, p. 15. *U&A*, 8 July 1864, *U&A*, 9 July 1864. *U&A*, 1 Aug 1864. *U&A*, 8 Aug 1864. *OR*, XXXIII, pt.1, p. 104.
[3] *OR*, XLIII, pt.1, p. 516.

Chapter 6

[1] Crumb, *Reminiscences*, pp. 13-18.
[2] Jeffery Wert, *From Winchester to Cedar Creek, The Shenandoah Campaign of 1864*, (Mechanicsburg, Pa.) 1987. pp. 32,33.
[3] Crumb, *Reminiscences*, pp. 18,19, *OR*, XLIII, pt1, pp. 911-912.
[4] Crumb, *Reminiscences*, pp. 18,19, *OR*, XXXXIII pt.1, pp. 104-105.
[5] Crumb, *Reminiscences*, pp. 20, 21.
[6] Thomas A. Lewis, *The Shenandoah in Flames, The Valley Campaign of 1864*. Time Life Books, (Alexandria Va.), 1987, p.139. Hereafter cited as Lewis, *Shenandoah in Flames*, Crumb, *Reminiscences*, pp. 21-23.
[7] Crumb, Reminiscences, pp. 23-24, Lewis, *Shenandoah in Flames*, p. 145.
[8] Joseph P. Cullen, *Battle Chronicles of the Civil War 1864, Cedar Creek*, (New York, 1989), pp. 118-119. Lewis, *Shenandoah in Flames*, p. 145. Crumb, *Reminiscences*, p. 24. *OR*, XLIII pt.1, pp. 433-435.

⁹ Crumb, *Reminiscences*, pp. 24-25.
¹⁰ Crumb, *Reminiscences*, pp. 24-25.
¹¹ Crumb, *Reminiscences*, pp. 25-25. *OR*, XLIII, pt.1, pp. 674-677.
¹² Harlan Page Lloyd, *The Battle of Waynesboro*, p. 194 hereafter cited as Lloyd, *The Battle of Waynesboro*, Crumb, *Reminiscences*, pp. 25-26.
¹³ Lloyd, *The Battle of Waynesboro*, p. 194.

Chapter 7

¹ Lloyd, *The Battle of Waynesboro*, pp. 199,200.
² Lloyd, *The Battle of Waynesboro*, pp. 201-203, Crumb, *Reminiscences*, p. 26, *OR*, XLIII pt.1, pp. 543,544.
³ Crumb, *Reminiscences*, p. 27. Lloyd, *The Battle of Waynesboro*, pp. 204-206.
⁴ Lloyd, *The Battle of Waynesboro*, p. 206, Crumb, *Reminiscences*, pp. 26-27.
⁵ Crumb, *Reminiscences*, pp. 27-28, Lloyd, *The Battle of Waynesboro*, p. 207, *OR*, XLVI, pt.1, pp. 528-529.
⁶ *OR*, XLVI, pt.1, pp. 454-455.
⁷ *OR*, XLVI, pt.1, pp. 1322-1323.

Chapter 8

¹ OR, XLVI, pt.1, p. 1285.
² U&A, 4 August 1865, U&A, 5 August, 1865.
³ Crumb, *Reminiscences*, p. 57.
⁴U&A, 9 August 1865.
⁵Crumb, *Reminiscences*, pp. 55,56.

Chapter 9

¹OR, Series II, Vol. VII, pp. 593,669-670, Military Service Record of Colonel Samuel Crooks, National Archives, Washington, D.C.
²Military Service Record of Colonel Samuel Crooks, National Archives, Washington, D.C.

Appendix A

¹Annual Report of the Adjutant General of the State of New York for the Year1894. Vol. 5. Registers of the 20th, 21st, 22d, 23d, 24th, 25th and 26th Regiments of Cavalry, Volunteers in War of the Rebellion. (Albany, 1895), pp. 470-720.

Appendix B

[1] Seth M. Hall, *Diary of Seth Hall, 22nd New York Cavalry*, In Fifth Annual Report of the New York Bureau of Military Statistics. 1868. Pp. 613-617.

Appendix C

[1] Frederick Phisterer, *New York in the War of the Rebellion 1861-1865*, 5 Volumes and Index, (Albany, 1912), pp. 1065-1078.

Appendix D

[1] Frederick Phisterer, *New York in the War of the Rebellion 1861-1865*, 5 Volumes and Index, (Albany,1912), pp. 1065-1078. Annual Report of the Adjutant General of the State of New York for the Year1894. Vol. 5. Registers of the 20th, 21st, 22d, 23d, 24th, 25th and 26th Regiments of Cavalry, Volunteers in War of the Rebellion. (Albany, 1895), pp. 470-720.

Appendix E

[1] Kathryn Gayeanne Stillwell, *The Heralds,* (1978), pp. 8-11. Military Record and Pension File of James Herald, National Archives, Washington, D.C.

Unidentified, 22nd N.Y. Cavalry
[Div. Military-Naval Affairs, N.Y. State Adjt. Gen. Office, Albany, N.Y.]

Index

100th New York
Volunteers, 125,
199
105th New York
Volunteers, 127
108th New York
Volunteers, 90
122nd New York
Infantry, 123
13th New York
Infantry, 68, 84,
85, 106, 116,
119, 150, 162,
182
144th New York
Infantry
Volunteers, 170
14th New York
Infantry, 203
14th Regiment
Veteran Reserve
Corps, 79, 142
155th New York
Infantry, 205
16th Michigan
Volunteers, 111
176th New York
Infantry, 151
17th New York
Infantry, 78, 92,
103, 143, 148,
151, 171
18th New York
Volunteers, 106,
135
192nd New York
Volunteers, 219
192th New York
Volunteers, 210

1st Battalion
Veteran Reserve
Corps, 209, 211
1st New York
Infantry, 96, 179
1st United States
Artillery, 145
1st Wisconsin
Cavalry, 146
20th Veteran
Reserve Corps,
180
22nd New York
Cavalry, 191
22nd New York
Infantry
Volunteers, 171
22nd New York
Volunteer
Infantry, 213
23rd New York
Infantry, 65, 95,
101, 102, 111,
121, 129, 131,
145, 157, 160,
171, 195, 200
23rd New York
Volunteers, 73
24th New York
Infantry, 66, 90,
120
24th Veteran
Reserve Corps,
178
26th New York
Infantry, 114,
116, 149, 172
27th New York
Infantry, 65, 89,
100, 128, 133,
140, 141, 201,
217, 218

27th New York
Volunteers, 213
2nd Battalion
Veteran Reserve
Corps, 220
2nd United States
Cavalry, 78
33rd New York
Infantry, 72, 128,
153
34th New York
Infantry, 82, 103,
119, 126, 166,
195, 202, 213
35th New York
Infantry, 114,
157
3rd Cavalry, 69,
131, 174, 194
3rd New York
Artillery, 81,
109, 208
3rd New York
Cavalry, 216
3rd New York
Infantry, 95, 136,
155
3rd Veteran
Reserve Corps,
69
56th New York
Infantry, 174
5th U. S. Artillery,
66, 80
5th U. S. Cavalry,
94
61st New York
Volunteers, 120,
201
66th New York
Infantry, 208
6th Indiana
Volunteers, 189

Index

6th New York
Infantry, 192, 197
75th New York
Volunteers, 124, 129
81st New York
Volunteers, 167
84th Pennsylvania
Infantry, 190
8th New York
Cavalry, 220

A

Abbott
  Charles, 61
Abell
  Frederick, 61
Aber
  George, 61
Able
  Christopher, 61
  Frederick, 61
Ackerman
  Fred, 61
  Frederick, 61
Ackley
  John, 61
Active
  James, 61
Adams
  Edwin, 61
  Frederick, 61
  John, 61
Adison
  John, 61
Albridge
  Edwin, 62
Alcott
  George, 62
Alden
  Frank, 62

Alderman
  F., 62
Aldrich
  Edwin, 62
  George, 62
  James, 62
  John, 62
Alexander
  George, 62
Algoe
  Lewis, 62
Allely
  Henry, 62
Allen
  Alonzo, 51, 62
  Charles, 63
  David, 63
  George, 63
  Henry, 63
  Ira, 63
  James, 63
  Louis, 63
  R. Alfred, 63
  Truman, 56, 60, 63
  William, 32, 63
Amsden
  Charles, 63
  Louis, 63
Anderson
  Benjamin, 63
  Charles, 64
  Henry, 64
  James, 64
  Lewis, 64
  Andrew
  Oliver, 64
  Walter, 64
Andrews
  Charles, 64
Anguish
  Henry, 64

Ansell
  Edmond, 64
  George, 64
  Henry, 64
Anseun
  Edward, 64
Anthony
  John, 65
Appleman
  Adam, 65
Appleton
  A. J., 65
Armitage
  Joseph, 65
Armolt
  Peter, 65
Armstrong
  Eliphalet, 65
  Samuel, 65
  Selner, 65
Arnd
  Frederick, 54, 65
Ashley
  Lucas, 65
Ashton
  Peter, 65
Attridge
  William, 32, 66
Augusta
  Me., 69
Austin
  James, 54, 66
Ayres
  Samuel, 66

B

Babcock
  Ira, 66
  John, 66
  Jon, 60
  Lawson, 66
  William, 66

Index

Bachman
  Frederick, 66
Baer
  Adolph, 66
Bagen
  Hugh, 66
Baines
  Ira, 66
Baker
  George, 66
  Richard, 67
  Thomas, 67
  William, 67
Baldwin, 37
  Lyman, 67
  Philander, 67
Balk
  Abraham, 67
Bannon
  Edward, 67
Banten
  Edward, 67
Barbeau
  Maurice, 67
Barber
  Joel, 67
  John, 67
  Thomas, 67
  William, 68
Bardeen
  Lewis, 68
Bates
  Justus, 68
Bathrick
  Robert, 68
Baum
  John, 32, 68
Bauperland
  Francis, 68
Baxter
  Llewellyn, 32, 68
Baylis
  Richard, 68

Baywater
  John, 68
Beach
  Ansel, 68
  Valentine, 68
Beadle
  John, 68
Beaman
  Sylvanus, 68
Bear
  Adolph, 69
Beard
  James, 69
Bechold
  Antoni, 69
Becker
  Charles, 69
Beckwith
  Lester, 69
Bee
  Henry, 69
Beeby
  Henry, 52, 69
Beedle
  James, 69
Beers
  Benjamin, 69
Behur
  John, 69
Belding
  Henry, 69
Belitz
  Charles, 69
Bell
  Francis, 70
  Frank, 70
  John, 70
  Thomas, 70
Bellinger
  Samuel, 70
Beman
  Isaac, 70

Bemis
  Washington, 70
Bend
  Henry, 70
Benham
  Frank, 70
Bennett
  Arthur, 70
  Benjamin, 44, 53, 70
  Thomas, 70
Bentley
  Calvin, 32, 70
Benton
  John, 70
Berry
  James, 71
  William, 71
Best
  Samuel, 71
Betts
  Thomas, 71
Bidwell
  George, 71
Bier
  Paul, 71
Biglow
  George, 71
Bilbie
  John, 71
Bilby
  John, 71
Billings
  Floyd, 71
  Flynn, 71
  R. Flynn, 71
Billington
  Edward, 71
Birdee
  John, 71
Birdsall
  Perry, 71

Index

Bisbee
  Leroy, 71
Bisby
  Lerdy, 72
Bishop
  Joseph, 72
  Thomas, 72
Bissell
  Frederick, 72
Black
  Thomas, 72
Blakeley
  Alexander, 72
Blakesley
  Riley, 72
Bleekfield
  Richard, 72
Blell
  William, 72
Blickfelt
  Richard, 72
Bliss
  James, 32, 72
Bliven
  Milo, 72
Blooe
  John, 72
Boardman
  Theron, 72
Bodee
  John, 72, 73
Bodine
  John, 72, 73
Bogert
  Albert, 73
Bohlman
  Augustus, 32, 73
Boleau
  Daniel, 73
Bolles
  Jasper, 32, 73
Bond
  James, 73

Booth
  Martin, 73
Bopp
  Frederick, 32, 73
Borden
  Warum, 73
Bowden
  Robert, 73
Bowen
  E. J., 73
  Leroy, 73
Bowers
  Thomas, 73
  William, 74
Bowles
  William, 74
Bowman
  Jacob, 74
Boyd
  William, 74
Boyden
  Bruce, 74
Boyer
  Joseph, 74
Boyle
  Peter, 74
  William, 74
Boylin
  Bernard, 74
Bracken
  John, 74
Bradigan
  Charles, 74
Bradley
  George, 75
  Robert, 75
Bradstreet
  Mayor, 3
Brady
  Alexander, 75
  Thomas, 75
Bragg
  Lewis, 75

Brambly
  John, 75
Branard
  Mitchell, 75
Brand
  George, 44, 75
Branden
  Alexander, 75
Brant
  Mason, 75
Braton
  Christopher, 75
Brazer
  Charles, 75
  Edward, 76
  Freeman, 76
Breck
  Samuel, 76
Brecklay
  Austin, 76
Breen
  John, 76
Brenn
  John, 76
Brennan
  Robert, 76
Brewer
  Rowlin, 76
Briggs
  Halsey, 76
Brigman
  Charles, 76
Brinn
  Jacob, 76
Brino
  John, 76
Bristol
  Joseph, 76
Briton
  James, 76
Brockway
  Henry, 77

Index

Bronson
  Gilbert, 77
  Jacob, 77
Brooks
  Benjamin, 77
Brown
  Caleb, 12
  Charles, 22, 43, 46, 77
  David, 77
  George, 77
  Henry, 77
  J. B., 12
  Jacob, 76, 77
  Jerome, 78
  John, 78
  Johnson, 3, 43, 78
  Patrick, 78
  Robert, 78
  William, 18, 50, 55, 78
Brundage
  Addison, 78
Brush
  Joseph, 79
Bruton
  Christopher, 75, 79
  Christopher`, 22
Bryam
  William, 82
Bryan
  John, 79
  William, 79
Bryant
  James, 79
  John, 79
  Robert, 79
Buckla
  Anselm, 79
Buckler
  William, 79

Buell
  Cyrus, 79
Buller
  Henry, 79
Bump
  Charles, 79
Bundy
  Frank, 80
Bunt
  David, 80
Burch
  William, 80
Burdick
  George, 80
  Joseph, 80
  Lamont, 32, 80
  Wolford, 80
Burgess
  Andrew, 80
Burk
  Martin, 80
Burke
  Thomas, 80
Burleigh
  Willie, 80
Burne
  John, 80
Burns
  John, 80
  Thomas, 81
Burnside
  Ambrose, 4
  Gen., 5
Burr
  Charles, 81
  Nevell, 81
Burroughs
  Augutus, 81
Burton
  Christopher, 41, 49
  Ed, 81
  William, 81

Bush
  Charles, 81
  Peter, 81
Butler
  Alfred, 32, 81
  Daniel, 81
  Gen., 11
  Henry, 81
  Nathaniel, 81
  Simeon, 81
  Thomas, 82
  William, 82
Button
  Albert, 82
  John, 82
  William, 82
Byram
  William, 82

C

Cadwell
  Charles, 82
  Lucien, 47, 82
Cager
  John, 82, 90
Cahill
  John, 82
  Timothy, 82
Cahoon
  George, 82
Caldwell
  Charles, 83
  James, 83
  William, 83
Callahan
  Thomas, 83
Calm
  Arnold, 83
Cameron
  Daniel, 83
  Martin, 83
  Sgt., 38

Index

Camp
  Joel, 83
Campbell
  Chester, 83
  James, 83
  Robert, 83
  William, 84
Canavan
  Edward, 84
  James, 84
Canty
  James, 84
  Patrick, 84
Canute
  Samuel, 84
Capin
  Kellog, 84
Carey
  John, 84
  Michael, 84
  Phillip, 84
Carlton
  George, 84
  James, 84
Carmichael
  George, 85
Carpenter
  Atwood, 85
  George, 85
  James, 85
  John, 85
Carr
  Alfred, 85
  David, 85
  Henry, 85
  John, 85
Carragin
  Avery, 85
Carroll
  James, 85
  Richard, 85
  Timothy, 86
  William, 86

Carron
  Edward, 86
Carter
  George, 86
Carty
  William, 86
Carver
  Levi, 86
Case
  George, 86
  John, 86
Casey
  Robert, 86
Cassidy
  Andrew, 86
  William, 86
Casson
  Frank, 86
Caston
  John, 86
Caswell
  Augustus, 86
Cavanaugh
  John, 87, 138
Cawley
  John, 87
Chamberlain
  Frank, 87
  Isaac, 87
Chamberlin
  J. E., 87
Chambliss
  Gen., 10
Chaphe
  Elmore, 87
Chapin
  David, 87
Chapman
  Col., 10, 11
  Gen., 16
  George, 6, 7
  Orrin, 87

Chappee
  Charles, 87
Chappell
  Eugene, 87
  Sumner, 87
Charles
  John, 87
Chase
  George, 87
  Henry, 35
  James, 87
Cheeney, 39
Cheshire
  John, 88
Chester
  Jerry, 88
Chrisman
  William, 88
Christenson
  John, 88
Christman
  Henry, 88
  William, 88
Christopher
  John, 88
Chubbuck
  John, 88
Church
  Albert, 88
  Amasa, 88
Clark
  Charles, 44, 88
  Delos, 88
  Frank, 88
  George, 88, 89
  Henry, 89
  Lewis, 89
  Samuel, 89
  Seymour, 89
Clay
  Charles, 89
Clicknar
  Thomas, 89

Index

Clifford
  Charles, 89
  Louis, 89
Clump
  Theodore, 89, 141
Coates
  Philander, 89
Cocherin
  James, 89, 93
Cochrane
  John, 90
Cocklin
  James, 89
Coffin
  Reuben, 90
Cogen
  John, 82
Coger
  John, 82, 90
Cohn
  Max, 90
Coldgrove
  Albert, 90
Cole
  Uriah, 90
Colegrove
  Albert, 90
Coleman
  Joshua, 90
Collier
  Frederick, 90
Collins
  James, 90
  Patrick, 90
  William, 90, 91
Collister
  Frank, 91
  Franklin, 49, 50, 91
  John, 91
Colwell
  Charles, 91

Combs
  Edward, 91
Commisky
  David, 91
Comstock
  Albert, 91
Condon
  Andrew, 91
  Thomas, 32, 91
Congers
  George, 91
Conine
  Lorenzo, 92
Conlon
  John, 92
Connell
  Edward, 92
  Patrick, 92
  William, 92
Conner
  John, 92
  Michael, 92
Conners
  Richard, 92
Connors
  John, 92
  Timothy, 92
Conover
  William, 49, 58, 92
Convers
  William, 92
Conway
  John, 93
Coon
  Francis, 93
  Milo, 93
Cooney
  Michael, 93
  William, 93
Coons
  Simon, 93, 141

Cooper
  Nicholas, 32, 93
Copeland
  George, 93
Corbin
  James, 93
Corcoran
  James, 93
  John, 90
Corkery
  Daniel, 93
Corkins
  George, 48, 94
Cormant
  Carlos, 94
Cornes
  James, 57, 94
Cornish
  Frank, 94
Cornwell
  John, 94
Corrigan
  Thomas, 94
Countryman
  Martin, 94
Courtwright
  Jacob, 94
Covell
  John, 94
Covert
  Alonzo, 94
Coyle
  Edward, 94
Cradock
  Martin, 95
Craft
  William, 95, 96
Crain
  Henry, 95
Cram
  George, 95
  John, 95

Index

Crane
  Peter, 95
Cranson
  Frederick, 95
Cranston
  Joseph, 95
Crants
  Cornelius, 95
  Henry, 95
Craunce
  Delevan, 95
Crawford
  Edward, 32, 96
Crawley
  William, 96
Cray
  William, 95
Cristal
  John, 96
Crofoot
  Samuel, 96
Croft
  William, 95, 96
Cronen
  John, 96
Cront
  Henry, 96
Crooks
  Col., 4, 6
  Samuel, 1, 3, 12, 29, 43, 95, 96
Crosby
  Alpheus, 96
Crosset
  Jerome, 96
Crother
  George, 96
Crouse
  Charles, 96
Crowe
  John, 96

Crowley
  Daniel, 97
  Michael, 22, 41, 97
Croyford
  George, 97
Crumb
  De Witt, 97
Cuddeback
  Albert, 97
Cudney
  Harman, 97
Cullen
  James, 97
  John, 97
Cummings
  Birdsall, 32, 97
Curry
  Michael, 97
Custer
  Gen., 21, 26, 27
  George, 16, 17

D

Dailey
  James, 97
Daily
  John, 97
  Richard, 97
Dakins
  Jonah, 33, 98
Dalton
  Samuel, 32, 98
Daniels
  Charles, 98
  William, 98
Darby
  William, 98
David
  Elias, 98
Davidson
  Duncan, 98
  John, 98

Davis
  Alson, 98
  George, 98
  Henry, 98
  John, 99
  Lucian, 99
  Patrick, 99
  Thomas, 99
  William, 99
Day
  Julius, 99
  Morgan, 99
Dayton
  Edwin, 99
De Boe
  John, 100
De Clercq
  William, 100
De Graff
  Jacob, 100
  William, 100
De Kay
  Alanson, 100
De La Kevordina
  Nicholas, 100
De Votie
  James, 100, 101
Deal
  William, 99
Dean
  Charles, 99
DeClercq
  William, 33
Deegan
  William, 100
Deery
  James, 100
Deiotie
  James, 100, 101
Delaney
  Edward, 100
Delany
  John, 100

Index

Delevan
  Charles, 100
Denney
  James, 100
Denning
  James, 100
Denois
  Henry, 101
Depew
  Ira, 101
Depluntz
  Albert, 106
Desbrow
  Thomas, 101
Deuel
  Abram, 101
Devane
  Henry, 101
Devine
  Daniel, 101
Devlin
  James, 101
Devoe
  Isaac, 101
Dewer
  Thomas, 32, 101
Dexter
  James, 101
Dibble
  Charles, 101
Dickinson
  David, 101
Dikeman
  David, 33, 102
Dildin
  Zenas, 102
Dildine
  Zachariah, 102
Dillingham
  Richard, 102
Dime
  Frederick, 102

Dimmond
  Benjamin, 102
Doag
  James, 102
Dobbin
  Samuel, 102
Dobbs
  Dewitt, 102
Dodd
  Edmond, 102
  Edward, 102
  John, 102
Doherty
  John, 103
Doland
  Frank, 103
  John, 103
Dolph
  Francis, 103
  John, 103
Donahue
  William, 103
Donahugh
  John, 103
Donaldson
  John, 103
  Robert, 103
Donk
  Charles, 103
Donnelly
  James, 103
Dora
  Alfred, 103
  Cornelius, 104
Doras
  Cornelius, 104
Dormer
  John, 104
Dorn
  Alfred, 103, 104
Doty
  Elisha, 104

Douglass
  George, 104
  John, 104
  Walter, 104
Downey
  Thomas, 104
Downs
  Peter, 104
Doyle
  Edward, 104
  Owen, 104
Drake
  Walter, 104
Drew
  William, 105
Drost
  Andrew, 105
Droun
  Henry, 105
Drown
  Henry, 105
Du Planty
  Albert, 106
Ducan
  Antoine, 105
Ducars
  Antoine, 105
Duchring
  Max, 105, 106
Duffee
  Gen., 36
Duffey
  Lawrence, 105
Dumas
  Edward, 105
  George, 105
Dumont
  Maxine, 105
Duncan
  John, 105
Dunham
  Benijah, 105

Index

Dunn
 Edward, 105
 John, 105
Dunning
 Herman, 55, 106, 199
Dupee
 Peter, 106
Duper
 Peter, 106
Duran
 Hiram, 106
During
 Max, 105, 106
Durkee
 Shubuel, 106
Durning
 Owen, 106
Duryea
 James, 106
Duval
 Robert, 106
Dwyer
 James, 106
 Thomas, 106

E

Earl
 Robert, 106
Early
 Gen., 15, 18, 19, 21, 22
 Jubal, 13, 17, 41
Eastman
 Neil, 106
Eater
 Anthony, 107
Eaton
 John, 107
Eaves
 Frederick, 31, 107

Eberly
 John, 107
Ebz
 Charles, 107
Edgecomb
 Robert, 107
Edgerton
 Harris, 107
Edha
 John, 107, 108
Edmond
 Truman, 107
Edmonson
 Thomas, 107
Edmundson
 Thomas, 107
Edson
 Henry, 107
Edward
 Truman, 107
Edwards
 Franklin, 48, 107
 Truman, 107, 203
 William, 107
Ehde
 John, 108
Ehinger
 Charles, 108
Ehrensberger
 Frederick, 108, 109
Eichorn
 Henry, 108
Eickelbuery
 Henry, 108
Eickelburg
 Henry, 108
Eldridge
 Milo, 31
Eldrige
 Milo, 108

Elide
 John, 107
Eliven
 Milo, 108
Elkins
 George, 108
Ellerbeck
 Robert, 56, 58, 108
Elliott
 Robert, 108
Ellis
 Addison, 108
 Daniel, 108
 Jacob, 109
 James, 109
 John, 109
Emerson
 Ansel, 109
 John, 109
Emery
 William, 109
Emmet
 Oran, 53
Emmett
 Oran, 46, 48, 109
Engles
 William, 109
English
 John, 109
Ennist
 George, 109
Errinberger
 Frederick, 108, 109
Erwin
 Dennis, 109, 135
Estes
 Joseph, 109
Evans
 Clem, 109
 King, 109
 Luke, 110

Index

Evans
  Richard, 110
Evens
  Richard, 110
Everett
  Isaac, 110
Everson
  John, 110

F

Fahl
  Charles, 110
Fairchild
  Henry, 110
  Martin, 110
Falconer
  Alexander, 110
Fant
  David, 110
Farley
  Terrence, 110
  William, 110
Farrell
  James, 110
  John, 110
  Patrick, 111
Fatter
  John, 111
Faust
  William, 111
Fauth
  William, 111
Feager
  Frank, 111
Featherson
  Thomas, 111
Feenander
  Michael, 111
Feger
  Frank, 111
Fellows
  Milton, 111

Fenton
  Frederick, 111
Ferris
  Isaac, 111
  Sgt., 35, 38, 39
Field
  Nelson, 111
  Romanzo, 111
Fiester
  John, 112
Finch
  David, 112
  Henry, 33, 112
  James, 112
  Jonas, 33, 112
  Samuel, 112
  William, 112
Fingleton
  James, 112
Finimore
  John, 112
Finn
  Michael, 112
Finnemore
  John, 112
Fisher
  Adolphus, 112
  Jacob, 50, 53, 56, 58, 93, 112
Fitzgerald
  Charles, 113
  John, 113
  Michael, 113
Fitzpatrick
  John, 113
Fitzsimmons
  Bartholomew, 113
Flanders
  Orville, 33, 113
Fleming
  James, 113
  Peter, 33, 128

Flemming
  Peter, 113
Fletcher
  Douglass, 113
Flinn
  Thomas, 113
Flynn
  Edward, 33, 113
  William, 113
Foley
  Patrick, 114
Foose
  George, 114
Foote
  Charles, 114
Forbes
  Isaac, 114
  Isaiah, 114
Force
  Jacob, 114
Ford
  Isaac, 114
Forsyth
  John, 114
Forward
  John, 114
Fosdick
  Charles, 114
Foster
  Albert, 114
  Franklin, 114
Fostick
  Charles, 114
Fowler
  Aldice, 114
  John, 115
Fox
  Nicholas, 115
  Reuben, 48, 78, 92, 115
Francis
  Charles, 115

237

Index

Frank
  Gilbert, 115
  William, 115
Franka
  George, 115
Franklin
  Albert, 115
  Ira, 33, 115
Freeman
  Alderman, 115
  Milton, 31, 115
Freer
  James, 115
French
  George, 44, 47, 112, 115
  James, 116
Fridly
  David, 116
Frisch
  Lawrence, 116
Frost
  Amasa, 116
Fuffon
  Isiah, 116
Fufford
  Isiah, 204
Fuller
  Heber, 116
Fulter
  John, 116
Furzes
  William, 116

G

Gahan
  Patrick, 116
Galarman
  Edward, 116
Galivon
  Samuel, 116
Gallagher
  Francis, 116

  Jeremiah, 116
  John, 116
Gallawa
  Samuel, 117
Galliwa
  Samuel, 117
Gams
  John, 117
Garber
  Christian, 117
Gardiner
  William, 117
Gardner
  John, 117
  Joseph, 117
Garrad
  Joseph, 117
Garretty
  William, 117
Gartsee
  Henry, 32, 117
Gasper
  Peter, 117
Gates
  Atlp., 117
  Charles, 117
  Henry, 117
  Squire, 117
Gault
  Francis, 118
Gavitt
  Charles, 118
Gelennan
  Patrick, 222
George
  Henry, 118
Gerald
  James, 118
Gerber
  Christian, 118
Gere
  Byron, 118

Gerrold
  James, 118
Getty
  Joseph, 118
Gibbs
  Myron, 118
Gibson
  Harvey, 118
Gidding
  Albert, 118
Gilbert
  Charles, 33, 118
  Henry, 118
  Nathan, 118
Gillett
  John, 119
  Nathaniel, 119, 136
Gilling
  John, 119
Glavey
  James, 119
Gleason
  Edwin, 119
  Harrison, 119
Glennan
  Patrick, 31, 50, 119
Goff
  Wiliam, 119
Goit
  Henry, 119
Golding
  William, 119
Golliger
  Ananias, 119
Goode
  Thomas, 119
Goodenough
  Calvin, 120
Goodrich
  Hiram, 31, 120

Index

Goodsell
  Charles, 120
  Franklin, 120
Goodwin
  Charles, 120
  Phillip, 120
Gordon
  Charles, 120
  John, 120
  Richard, 120
Gorman
  Martin, 120
Gorzette
  Peter, 120, 121
Gosnell
  James, 120
Gott
  Alexander, 121
  Daniel, 121
Goyt
  Peter, 120, 121
Graham
  David, 121
  John, 121
Grahan
  Charles, 121
Grant, 5
  Gen., 9, 23
  General, 222
Graven
  Garritt, 121
Gray
  Lewis, 121
Greek
  William, 121
Green
  Daniel, 121
  George, 121
  Gilbert, 121
  John, 121
  Seely, 122
Greenfield
  John, 122

Greenwood
  Joshway, 122
Gregory
  John, 122
Grey
  John, 122
Gridley
  George, 122
Griffin
  Michael, 122
Griffith
  Richard, 122
Grimm
  George, 122
Griswold
  John, 122
  Samuel, 122
Grover
  Abner, 122
Guest
  Joseph, 122
Guild
  Ely, 122
Gulfayla
  Patrick, 123
Gulich
  Charles, 123
Gunsulas
  Martin, 123
Gurnee
  Samuel, 123
Gustin
  Frank, 33, 123
Gyurkonwits
  Carl Von, 123

H

Hacker
  John, 123
Hadley
  John, 123
Hager
  Henry, 123, 130

Hale
  Simeon, 123
Haley
  Dennis, 123
Hall
  Emma, 35
  Harvey, 36, 123
  Isaac, 123
  S. M., 39
  Seth, 33, 35, 123
  Sidney, 124
Halleck
  Henry, 4
Halliday
  Merville, 124
Hallock
  Ira, 124
Halpin
  William, 124
Ham
  Joseph, 124
Hamilton
  Benjamin, 124
  Williby, 124
Hammond
  Bernard, 124
  Col., 6
  Henry, 124
Hampton
  Wade, 11
Hanavan
  James, 124
Hancock
  Winfield, 6
Hand
  George, 124
  Thorne, 124
Hanlon
  Bernard, 124
Hannah
  Charles, 125
Hannon
  Dominick, 125

Index

Hanyon
  Adam, 125
  John, 20, 125
  Peter, 125
Harden
  James, 125
Hare
  John, 125
Harford
  George, 125
Harmon
  Francis, 125
  William, 125
Harrall
  Henry, 125
Harrington
  Allen, 125
  James, 125, 126
  Ransom, 126
  Silas, 126
Harris
  John, 126
  Thomas, 126
Harrison
  John, 126
Hart
  Alonzo, 126
  John, 126
  Romaine, 126
  Theodore, 126
Hartman
  Ernest, 126
Harvey
  Harry, 22, 41, 126
  Wiliam, 127
Haskin
  John, 127
Haskins
  John, 127
Haughton
  William, 127, 131

Havens
  Alonozo, 127
  George, 127
Hawkings
  Ferdinand, 33, 127
Hawkins
  Ferdinand., 127
  George, 33, 127
Hawks
  James, 127
Hayden
  Robert, 127
Hayes
  John, 127
  Patrick, 127
  Thomas, 127
Hayward
  Alfred, 128
Hazelton
  Dwight, 47, 51, 54, 59
Hazleton
  Dwight, 99, 128
Hearld
  James, 128
Hearty
  Peter, 128
Hecker
  William, 128
Hecox
  Charles, 128
  Franklin, 128
Heimer
  Augustus, 128
Helleck, 5
Hemanway
  James, 128
Hemingway
  James, 128
Hemming
  Frederick, 128

Hemminway
  James, 128
Hennessey
  Michael, 128
Henning
  Frederick, 128
  Peter, 128
  Henry
  William, 128
Herald
  Elizabeth, 222
  James, 222
  Mary, 222
Herman
  Herman, 129
Hess
  Frederick, 129
Hewlet
  William, 129, 133
H.Gibbs
  Myron, 33
Hickey
  William, 129
Hicks
  Alford, 129
Higgins
  John, 129
Highland
  Patrick, 129
Hikock
  Ashur, 129
Hilan
  Patrick, 129
Hille
  Louis, 129
Hindman
  Friend, 38
Hines
  Adolphus, 129
Hinman
  James, 129

Index

Hinning
  William, 129, 140
Hitchcock
  Richard, 129
  Samuel, 130
Hitt
  William, 130
Hocknill
  Richard, 130
Hodge
  Jacob, 33, 130
  Miles, 130
Hodges
  Henry, 123, 130
Hoffman
  Bruno, 130
Hoghkerk
  Charles, 130
Holden
  Levi, 130
Holland
  Thomas, 130
Holmes
  Robert, 130
Hoober
  Joseph, 130
Hood
  James, 130
  William, 131
Hooper
  John, 32
Hoosi
  Alexander, 131
Hopkins
  John, 131
  William, 131
Hopper
  John, 131
Horton
  William, 33, 131
Hosford
  Hiram, 131

Houghson
  William, 131, 133
Houghton
  William, 127, 131
Houser
  George, 131
  James, 131
Howard
  James, 132
  William, 132
Howe
  Elmer, 132
Howes
  Zalmon, 132
Hoyt
  Myron, 33, 132
  Samuel, 33, 132
Hubbard
  Luke, 132
Hubbardston
  Mich., 222
Huber
  John, 132
Hudgins
  David, 132
  William, 132
Hudson
  Thomas, 132
  William, 132
Hues
  Adelbert, 33, 132
Huff
  Nelson, 133
Hughes
  Edward, 133
Hughs
  Michael, 133
Hughson
  William, 131, 133

Hulbert
  Frederick, 133, 134
  John, 32, 133
Hulet
  William, 33, 129, 133
Hull
  Birney, 133
Hullt
  W., 33
Hummel
  Lewis, 133
Humphrey
  Edwin, 133
Humphreys
  Edwin, 205
Hunington
  Frank, 134
Hunt
  Alvin, 133
Hunter
  Robert, 133
Huntington
  Charles, 134
Huntly
  Arcelus, 134
Hurd
  John, 134
Hurlbert
  Frederick, 134
Hurlbutt
  Wellington, 134
Huson
  George, 134
Huston
  John, 134
Hutchinson
  Amasa, 134
  Sanford, 134

Index

I

Ingraham
  Alexander, 134
  Dunham, 134
  Isaac, 134
Irish
  Henry, 135
Irwin
  Dennis, 109, 135
Iselin
  Soloman, 135

J

Jackson
  Charles, 135
  David, 135
  William, 135
Jacobs
  Benjamin, 135
  Clark, 135
Jacobus
  Samuel, 135
James
  William, 135
Janner
  Charles, 136
Jeager
  Urban, 135, 221
Jerome
  Helom, 136
  Henry, 136
Jetty
  Joseph, 136
Jewett
  Joseph, 136
Jillett
  Nathaniel, 119, 136
Jochemsen
  Fritz, 136
Johnson
  David, 33, 136
  Dennis, 136
  Freeman, 136
  George, 136
  Gilbert, 136
  John, 136
  Milton, 137
  Robert, 137
  William, 137
Johnston
  Robert, 86, 137
Joice
  Thomas, 33, 137
Jones
  Alonzo, 137
  David, 137
  Frank, 137
  Fred, 137
  George, 137
  Gilbert, 137
  Henry, 138
  James, 31, 32, 45, 138
  John, 138
  William, 138
Jordan
  John, 138
Judd
  Hamilton, 138
Justice
  John, 138

K

Kahler
  Jacob, 138
Kane
  Peter, 138
Karney
  W. E., 139
  William, 138
Kavanagh
  John, 138
Keane
  William, 139
Kearney
  William, 139
Kearns
  John, 139
Keeton
  John, 139
Keller
  Jacob, 139
  Nicholas, 139
Kellerboore
  Conrad, 139
Kelley
  John, 139
Kelly
  James, 139
  John, 139
  Michael, 139
  Thomas, 139
Kemp
  Walter, 140
Kennedy
  John, 140
  William, 140
Kenning
  William, 129, 140
Kent
  George, 140
Kenyon
  Erwin, 140
  Francis, 140
Keyes
  George, 140
  James, 140
Kimberly
  Curtis, 140
King
  Ezra, 140
  Nathan, 141
  William, 141
Kingman
  George, 141

Index

Kipp
  Henry, 141
Kline
  Joseph, 141
Klumpp
  Theodore, 89,
    141, 171
Knapp
  John, 141
Knight
  John, 141
  William, 141
Knollier
  Theodore, 141
Koleman
  John, 141
Kruchten
  John, 141
Krutzen
  John, 141
Kunce
  Simon, 141
Kuntz
  Simon, 93, 141

L

Labrash
  James, 142
Lackey
  James, 142
Lacy
  John, 142
Ladd
  Alanson, 33, 142
  George, 22, 41,
    142
Lake
  Henry, 142
  James, 142
Lamb
  Warren, 56, 99,
    142

Lambert
  Henry, 142
Lamott
  Francis, 142
Lamper
  Cornelius, 142
Lamphier
  Cornelius, 142
Landon
  Albert, 142
Lane
  Harry, 143
Laning
  John, 143
Lanning
  Benjamin, 143
Lape
  John, 143
Larcom
  William, 31, 143
Laregan
  Edward, 143
Larkham
  William, 143
Larkin
  Andrew, 143
Larkir
  James, 143
Latham
  Charles, 143
Law
  Rufus, 143
Lawles
  James, 143
Lawless
  Samuel, 143
Lawrence
  David, 143
Lawson
  Lewis, 143
Layton
  Daniel, 31, 53,
    144

Leach
  James, 144
Leak
  James, 144
Leake
  Frederick, 59,
    144
Leard
  George, 144
Leary
  Alvah, 144
Leavy
  Alvah, 144
Lee
  Dwight, 45, 144
  Fitzhugh, 9
  Gen., 11, 23
  John, 144
  Robert E., 9
  W. H. F., 15
Lehner
  George, 144
Leibenthal
  Herman, 144
Leonard
  Isaac, 144
  John, 144
  Peter, 144
Leoser
  Christopher, 144,
    146
Lerroy
  William, 147
Lettis
  James, 144
Levine
  Paul, 145
Levory
  Lenny, 145
Lewis
  Charles, 145
  Milo, 145

Index

Lewrry
  Antoine, 145
Limbacher
  John, 145
Lina
  Ralph, 145
Lindsey
  Darius, 145
Lines
  John, 145
Livingston
  Frank, 145
  John, 145
Lloyd
  Edwin, 145
  Harlan, 46, 145, 167
Lockwood
  Daniel, 145
  George, 145
  Lebbens, 146
  William, 146
Loftus
  Patrick, 146
Lohman
  Albert, 146
Loomis
  Edwin, 146
Looser
  Christopher, 144, 146
Lord
  Herbert, 55, 56, 146
Losey
  Jesse, 45, 146
Loucks
  Morris, 146
Louis
  Arthur, 145, 146
Low
  Charles, 146
Lowe
  John, 146
Lowery
  George, 146
Lowry
  William, 147
Lozear
  Alfred, 147
Luke
  Henry, 147
Lusk
  Lycurgus, 21, 54, 55, 147, 205
Lutz
  Christian, 147
Lynch
  Lawrence, 147

M

Mack
  Edward, 147
  James, 147
  John, 147
Mackey
  Martin, 147, 153
Mahoney
  Michael, 147
Main
  Nelson, 32, 147
Maker
  Hiram, 148
Maley
  James, 148
Mallory
  Charles, 148
Maloy
  Michael, 148
Manchester
  Joseph, 148
  Martin, 148
Mandeville
  Lucius, 148
  Newton, 148
Manshardt
  Michael, 148
Manzer
  Herman, 148, 154
March
  George, 148
  Hamilton, 148
Marsh
  Isaac, 149
  Jerome, 33, 149
  Lewis, 149
Martin
  Artemus, 149
  George, 149
  Hiram, 149
  John, 149
  Keron, 149
  William, 149
Mason
  Jean, 149
  William, 149
Mater
  Jacob, 149
Mathews
  Andrew, 149
  Anthony, 149
Maxwell
  Henry, 149
  John, 150
May
  Robert, 150
Mayhew
  Martin, 150
Mcarthur
  Henry, 150
McCabe
  John, 150
  Michael, 150
McCarrack
  John, 150
McCarthy
  Florence, 31, 150

Index

John, 150
Patrick, 150
McCasnell
  Charles, 150, 151
McCauley
  James, 150
  John, 150
McCausey
  James, 151
McCay
  Joseph, 151
  William, 151, 153
McChessney
  William, 151
McCollum
  Frank, 151
McConey
  Philander, 151
McConnell
  Charles, 150, 151
McCormick
  Albert, 151
  Richard, 151
McCoy
  Donald, 151
  John, 151
McCuen
  Ambrose, 151
  Miles, 151
  Robert, 154
McCullough
  Samuel, 151
McDermott
  James, 152
  John, 152
  Patrick, 152
  Thomas, 152
McDonald
  Angus, 29
  John, 152
  Kenneth, 152

McDonough
  James, 152
McGibbon
  Alexander, 152
McGinnis
  Robert, 152
McGovern
  Charles, 152
McGowan
  Patrick, 152
McGrath
  William, 152
McGraw
  Daniel, 152
  James, 152
  William, 153
McGuire
  George, 153
  James, 153
  John, 153
  Peter, 153
McIntosh
  John, 10, 11
Mcintyre
  Thomas, 153
McKay
  Joseph, 151, 153
  Martin, 147
  Robert, 153
McKee
  Robert, 153
McKey
  Martin, 153
McKinley
  John, 153
McKinnon
  Donald, 153
Mclarren
  Andrew, 153
McLennan
  Andrew, 33, 153
  Major, 9, 12

Peter, 3, 6, 43, 153
McManey
  Patrick, 154
McMannis
  John, 154
Mcmullen
  James, 154
McMullen
  Michael, 50
Mcmullen
  Michael, 154
Mcnany
  Patrick, 154
Mcninch
  Robert, 154
McQueen
  Miles, 151, 154
McShane
  Patrick, 45, 154
Mcsorley
  Charles, 154
Meachem
  Nelson, 154
Mead
  Volney, 154
Meade
  Gen., 5, 6
  George, 29
Mecham
  Nelson, 154
Meilike
  Carl, 154, 155
  Charles, 154
Melay
  Owen, 154
Mencer
  Herman, 148, 154
Mercer
  Richard, 154
Mergawick
  Cyrack, 155

Index

Merlike
  Charles, 155
Mernin
  Patrick, 155
Merriam
  Irving, 32, 155
Merrill
  Edmond, 155
  Sylvester, 155
Merritt
  Wesley, 16
Merville
  Edward, 155
Metcalf
  Benjamin, 155
Meyer
  Morris, 155
Meyers
  Joseph, 155
  Peter, 155
Milboryne
  Joseph, 155
Milbyere
  Joseph, 155
Miles
  Theodore, 155
Millboryne
  Joseph, 162
Miller
  George, 156
  Gottlier, 156
  Hiram, 156
  John, 156
  Moses, 156
Milliman
  Gardiner, 32
Millman
  Gardiner, 156
Mills
  John, 156
  Ricewick, 156
Minoch
  William, 156

Minot
  Bartlett, 156
Mirch
  Hiram, 156
Mitchell
  Thomas, 156
  William, 156
Moat
  William, 157
Monahan
  Thomas, 157
Monckton
  William, 157
Monk
  Edward, 157
Monroe
  Andrew, 157
  Cornelius, 157
Montgomery
  Frank, 157
Moochler
  John, 32, 157, 160
Moody
  John, 157
Moon
  Jacob, 157
  Seth, 157
Moora
  Henry, 157
Moore
  Abner, 158
  Abram, 158
  Ara, 32, 158
  Bradley, 158
  Caleb, 16, 26
  Clinton, 158
  Henry, 158
  Jason, 33, 158
  John, 158
  Lewis, 47, 158
  Maj., 17
  Oliver, 158

  O.O.G., 158
  Thomas, 158
Moores
  Henry, 159
  Jeremiah, 159
Moorse
  Frank, 159
Moran
  Edward, 159
Morgan
  James, 159
  Michael, 159
Morgenweck
  Cyriack, 159
Morhe
  Phillip, 159
Morian
  Charles, 159
Morrison
  Henry, 159
  Hiram, 159
  Ira, 33, 159
Morse
  Garrett, 159
Mosby, 36
Moses
  Mark, 160
Mosher
  Amos, 160
Mosier
  Amos, 160
Mouck
  Matthew, 160
Mowers
  David, 160
  Jeremiah, 160
  John, 160
Mowry
  John, 160
Moxcey
  George, 58, 160
Moyne
  James, 160

Index

Muchner
  John, 157, 160
Mudford
  William, 160
Muler
  Jacob, 160
Mullaney
  Francis, 160
Mullen
  James, 160
Mulloney
  John, 161
Mulloy
  John, 161
Munson
  John, 161
Murch
  George, 148, 161
Murphy
  Charles, 161
  James, 161
  John, 161
  Michael, 161
  Samuel, 161
Murray
  Charles, 161
  John, 161
  Thomas, 162
Mybbyre
  Joseph, 162
Myers
  Lewis, 162
Myner
  Charles, 162

N

Narry
  James, 162
Nash
  Peter, 162
Needham
  Henry, 162

Neil
  Henry, 162
Nellis
  Clark, 162
  James, 45, 142, 162
  John, 162
Nelms
  Samuel, 162
Nelson
  Charles, 162
Newell
  Alexander, 162
  Andrew, 163
  George, 163
Newman
  Chappell, 163
  Edward, 49, 163
  George, 51, 54, 163
  William, 163
Nichelson
  Edward, 163
Nichols
  George, 163
  Washington, 163
Nicholsen
  George, 163
Nisbet
  Robert, 163
Nix
  Angevine, 163
Noble
  Henry, 163, iv
  John, 163
Nolan
  Joseph, 164
  Thomas, 164
Noonan
  Michael, 164
Norris
  Joseph, 164

Northrup
  Porter, 33, 164
  Samuel, 164
Norton
  John, 164
Nye
  Charles, 164

O

Oberle
  Antone, 164
Oberly
  Antoine, 164
Obernauer
  Valentine, 164
O'Brien
  James, 164
  John, 164
  Michael, 165
  Patrick, 165
  Terrence, 165
O'Connor
  Hugh, 165
Odell
  Jothan, 165
Odle
  Demetrius, 165
Ogden
  Frank, 165
Olcott
  George, 62, 165
Olmstead
  Henry, 33, 165
Olton
  George, 165
O'Malley
  James, 165
O'Neal
  William, 165
O'Neil
  James, 165
  Patrick, 32, 166
  Richard, 166

247

Index

Ormond
  Thomas, 166
O'Rourke
  John, 166
Orr
  John, 166
Osborn
  Robert, 32, 166
Ostrander
  Edward, 166
Ostranger
  Clinton, 166
Otto
  Howard, 166
Overhiser
  Joseph, 166

P

Packard
  Hart, 166
Palmer
  George, 166
Palmeter
  Jason, 167
Pangburn
  Myron, 167
Pardie
  James, 167
Pardy
  James, 167
Parker
  John, 167
  Thomas, 167
  William, 167
Parkhurst
  Henry, 167
Parmelee
  Stephen, 167
Parmley
  Stephen, 167
Parrot
  James, 167

Patrick
  C. W., 167
  Charles, 47
Patten
  George, 167
Patterson
  William, 167
Payne
  Arthur, 168
Payton
  James, 168
Peachey
  Noah, 168
Peachy
  Charles, 168
Peacock
  Edwin, 168
Pease
  George, 168
Peck
  Herbert, 48, 51, 55, 168
  James, 32, 168
  J.G., 33
  William, 31, 146, 168
Peckham
  Henry, 168
Peer
  Stephen, 168
Pendelton
  William, 168
Pennefether
  Richard, 168
Penny
  Sanford, 169
Perkins
  Franklin, 51, 169
  Richard, 169
Perry
  Franklin, 169
Persons
  Matthew, 169

Pew
  Thomas, 169
Phein
  Frederick, 170
Phelga
  Hiram, 169
Phelteplace
  Francis, 169
Philips
  Edson, 169
  Ethan, 169
Phillips
  Albert, 169
  George, 169
  Leonard, 169
  Martin, 170
  Norman, 170
  William, 170
Pierce
  Achibald, 170
  Daniel, 170
  Frank, 170
  Jans, 170
  John, 170
Pilaty
  Joseph, 170
Pitcher
  David, 170
Platt
  Horatio, 170
  John, 170
Player
  Charles, 170
Ploss
  Samuel, 171
Ployer
  Henry, 171
Plumb
  Ben, 171
  Theodore, 141, 171
Pomroy
  A. C., 171

Index

Porter
  Henry, 171
  William, 171
Portsmouth
  William, 171
Potter
  Charles, 171
  James, 171
Pratt, 38
  Charles, 171
  John, 171
  William, 171
Preston
  Byron, 172
  David, 172
  Wallace, 31, 172
Price
  David, 172
  Robert, 172
Primmer
  George, 172
Prinz
  Ewald, 172
Prosser
  Mathew, 172
Provost
  Isadore, 52, 172
Pugh
  Thomas, 172
Putman
  William, 172
Putnam
  Edward, 172

Q

Quackenbush
  Myron, 172
Quinlan
  John, 173
  Michael, 173
Quinlin
  Patrick, 173

R

Rabon
  Augustus, 173
Radenback
  Jacob, 173
Radner
  Jacob, 173, 178
Radway
  Bert, 173
Raleg
  James, 173
Raleigh
  N.C., 198
Randall
  Oliver, 173
Ranney
  Robert, 173
Ray
  Horace, 173
  James, 173
  Luke, 173
Raymond
  William, 174
Rea
  John, 174
Read
  Jay, 174
Reading, 37
Reagan
  Daniel, 174
  David, 174
Reddington
  Charles, 57
Reding
  George, 174
Redington
  Charles, 174
Reed
  Celey, 174
  Col., 23
  H. B. (Mrs.), 2
  Horatio, 18, 24, 25, 26, 43, 174
  John, 174
  Robert, 33, 174
Reeding
  James, 174
Reiley
  Thomas, 174
  William, 174
Reilmyer
  Adolph, 175
Reinwall
  Michael, 175
Remington
  Darius, 175
  Napoleon, 175
Reynolds
  George, 175
  Ochland, 175
  Thomas, 175
Rhiles
  George, 175
Rhodes
  Edward, 175
  Gen., 13
  Samuel, 175
Rhyon
  James, 175
Rice
  Thomas, 175
  William, 175
Rich
  Benjamin, 175
  William, 176
Richard
  Joachim, 176
Richards
  James, 176
  Luke, 176
  Victor, 176

Index

Richardson
  David, 176
  Egbert, 176
Richmaier
  Adolph, 176
Richmond
  William, 176
Riddle
  George, 176
  Thomas, 176
Ridgway
  John, 176
Right
  John, 176
Rignor
  William, 33, 177
Riley
  John, 177
  Patrick, 177
Ritter
  Myron, 177
  William, 177
Rivest
  Joseph, 177
Roach
  Edward, 177
  Martin, 177
  Michael, 177
Roaney
  Jacob, 173
Robbins
  Lyman, 178
Roberts
  Hiram, 177
  Theodore, 177
  Thomas, 177
  Timothy, 178
Robertson
  Jackson, 178
  James, 178
Robins
  Elisha, 178

Robinson
  Charles, 178
  Delos, 178
  William, 32, 178
Rodgers
  James, 178
Rodner
  Jacob, 178
Rogers
  Owen, 178
Rolston
  Robert, 178
Ronan
  James, 178
Rooney
  William, 179
Root
  Lawrence, 179
  Rubin, 179
Rorke
  John, 179
Rose
  Henry, 33, 179
  Millard, 179
  Noah, 179
  William, 179
Rosegrant
  Hiram, 179
Rosser
  Gen., 11, 19, 22, 23
  Thomas, 16, 17
Rourke
  Michael, 179
Rousseau
  John, 179
Roussou
  Frank, 179
Rowe
  William, 179
Rowley
  Andrew, 180

Royk
  Warren, 180
Rundell
  George, 180
Runkin
  Peter, 180
Russ
  George, 180
  John, 33, 180
Russell
  William, 180
Ryan
  Andrew, 180
  Francis, 180
  Frank, 180
  George, 180
  James, 33, 175, 180, 181
  Jeremiah, 175
  John, 175
  Martin, 175
  Michael, 175
  Peter, 175
  Thomas, 175
  William, 175

S

Safford
  Manley, 175
  William, 175
Sager
  William, 33, 175
Saiers
  Robert, 175
Salisbury
  Charles, 182
Sampson
  Simeon, 182
Sanderson
  William, 182
Sanford
  Willard, 182

Index

Sargeant
  James, 186
Sartchfield
  James, 182
Sartwell
  John, 182
Saur
  Henry, 182
Sawdey
  James, 182
Sawyer
  Elmer, 33, 182
  Henry, 182
Saxton
  Ransom, 182
Sayles
  Albert, 33, 182
  Amos, 182
Sayrusch
  James, 183
Scantlin
  John, 183
Scharet
  William, 183
Scheib
  William, 183
Schenck
  Valentine, 183
Schenish
  James, 183
Schepmus
  Nelson, 183
Schermerhorn
  David, 183
Schlick
  Theodore, 15, 31, 44, 183
Schlout
  George, 183
Schmith
  Jacob, 183

Scholl
  Frederick, 183
  William, 33, 183
Schorn
  Jacob, 183
Schrader
  Henry, 184
Schuh
  John, 184
Schuppert
  Charles, 184
Schurer
  William, 183, 184
Schuyler
  Charles, 184
Schwartz
  Carl, 184
Schwenberger
  Leonhard, 184, 188
Scott
  Charles, 184
  Harry, 184
  Henry, 184
  Jay, 184
  Thomas, 184
  William, 184
Scoville
  Frank, 185
Scribner
  J. D. P., 185
Scullin
  Paul, 185
Seary
  Alvah, 185
Sedgwick
  John, 6
Seedore
  William, 185
Seelen
  Frederick, 185

Seely
  Lucean, 185
Seger
  Adam, 185
Sehner
  George, 144, 185
Seiver
  Lorenzo, 144
Seize
  George, 144
Sems
  John, 144
Serenson
  William, 144
Sergeant
  Ira, 186
Seymour
  Governor, 4
Shadders
  Henry, 186
Shaefer
  Charles, 186
Shaffer
  Carl, 186
  Peter, 186
Shalows
  Joseph, 186
Shannon
  Edward, 186
  John, 186
Shareff
  Frank, 186
Shattuck
  Harrison, 186
Shaver
  Benjamin, 33, 186
  Eli, 186
Shaw
  Bernard, 186
  Lewis, 187
  William, 187

Index

Shear
  John, 187
Sheldon
  Charles, 187
  Frank, 187
Shepard
  Miller, 187
Shepardson
  Lorenzo, 32, 187
Shephard
  Charles, 187
Shepherd
  William, 187
Sherff
  Frank, 186, 187
Sheridan
  Edward, 187
  Gen., 15, 17, 36
Sherman
  Gen., 39
Sherwood
  George, 187
  Marvin, 52, 57, 58, 187
Shiels
  Edmond, 187
Shipp
  Henry, 188
Shoals
  William, 188
Shoat
  Charles, 188
Shonberger
  Leonhard, 184, 188
Shults
  Eli, 188
Shweikert
  Charles, 188
Silvernah
  David, 188
Simmons
  Aaron, 188

  Myron, 188
Simpson
  Zachariah, 188
Sims
  Lewis, 188
Sinclair
  Charles, 188
Single
  Joseph, 188
Sinzer
  James, 188
Sissen
  Terry, 189
Sisson
  Perry, 32, 189
Skeel
  Albert, 189
Skellion
  Charles, 189
Skinner
  James, 31, 189
Slater
  Truman, 189
Slavin
  Francis, 189
Sleeper
  Charles, 189
Sloan
  George, 189
Slocum
  Elisha, 189
Slout
  George, 189
Slover
  Henry, 189
Smaltz
  Carl, 189
Smith
  Adelbert, 189
  Alexander, 190
  Benjamin, 190
  Charles, 190
  Emerson, 190

  Francis, 190
  Frederick, 190
  George, 190
  J. Montryson, 191
  James, 190, 191
  John, 191
  Judson, 191
  Laura, 35
  Montresson, 192
  Nathaniel, 191
  Richard, 191
  Samuel, 191
  Theodore, 34, 191
  Thomas, 191
  Van De Mark, 192
  Wallace, 192
  William, 35
Smyth
  James, 58
  Montresson, 192
Snow
  Thomas, 192
Snyder
  Asa, 192
  John, 192
  Miles, 192
Sodus
  William, 186
Soggs
  Edward, 192
  William, 192
Somers
  James, 192
Southworth
  Robert, 32, 192
Spafford
  Henry, 192
Spaulding
  James, 192

Index

Spencer
  George, 193
Sperry
  George, 46, 49,
    52, 57, 98,
    193
  James, 193
Spindler
  Jacob, 193
Spoon
  Addison, 193
Spooner
  John, 193
Spoore
  Addison, 193
Spreadbury
  John, 50, 193
Spring
  Charles, 193
Squain
  Elexander, 193
Staff
  Henry, 52
Stallman
  Frederick, 193
Stansel
  John, 193
Stanton
  Hiram, 34, 193
  Ruben, 194
  Rubert, 194
  Sylvester, 194
Stapleton
  John, 194
Starks
  William, 194
Starr
  Henry, 3, 46, 57,
    194
Steamburg
  Hiram, 194
Steele
  Frank, 194
  James, 194
Steemburgh
  William, 194
Steenburgh
  Hiram, 194
Stein
  Frederick, 194
Stellrecht
  David, 34, 194
Stephens
  John, 195
Sterling
  Adam, 195
Stetson
  Richard, 195
Stevens
  Charles, 34, 195
  E. B., 195
  John, 195
  Warren, 195
  William, 195
Stewart
  Alexander, 195
  Ivory, 195
  Thomas, 195
Stiefvater
  Nichol, 195
Stoddard
  John, 195
Stodder
  Henry, 196
Stokes
  Jonathan, 196
Stone
  Hedding, 196
  John, 196
  Lawrence, 196
  Omer, 196
  Thomas, 196
  William, 196
Stormont
  William, 31, 196
Stratton
  Isaac, 196
Strong
  Monson, 196
Studer
  Frederick, 196
Stuffer
  Christopher, 197
Suggett
  Joseph, 44, 197
Suits
  John, 197
Sullivan
  Franklin, 197
  James, 197
  Michael, 197
  William, 197
Summers
  James, 197
Sumner
  Jeremiah, 197
Sutherland
  Mason, 35
Sutphin
  Benjamin, 197
Swan
  Henry, 197
  Thomas, 197
Swartz
  John, 197
Sweeney
  Michael, 198
Sweet
  Crosby, 198
Sweezy
  George, 198
  Nathan, 198
Swift
  Eber, 198
  Thomas, 198
Swires
  Robert, 198

Index

Sylvanus
  John, 198
Sylvester
  Albert, 198
  Charles, 198
Syphers
  Gilbert, 198

T

Tack
  Jacob, 198
Talbot
  Joseph, 198
Tallman
  Byron, 59, 198
  George, 199
  Henry, 199
  William, 199
Tappan
  Frank, 199
Tarbel
  Samuel, 199
Tarbox
  Robert, 199
Taylor
  Adelbert, 199
  Albert, 199
  Calvin, 199
  Fayette, 199
  Gayne, 199
  Henry, 199
  Israel, 31, 53, 199
  John, 200
  Orville, 200
  Robert, 200
Terril
  William, 200
Terrill
  Miles, 34, 200
Terwilliger
  Ira, 200

Thanvette
  David, 200, 201
Thayer
  Richard, 200
Thetga
  Hiram, 200
Thomas
  Hugh, 200
Thompson
  Andrew, 201
  Byron, 201
  James, 201
  John, 22, 201
  Milton, 201
  Samuel, 201
  W. P., 23
  Wellington, 201
Thonvett
  David, 200, 201
Thorns
  William, 201
Thorvitt
  David, 201
Thurnston
  Theodore, 201
Tifft
  George, 201
Tift
  George, 201
Tileston
  Arthur, 57, 202
Tindall
  Edward, 202, 221
Tobin
  John, 202
  Thomas, 202
Todd
  Robert, 202
Tombridge
  John, 202
Tomlinson
  Wilbur, 202

Topham
  Thomas, 202
Topping
  Martin, 202
Tower
  Anson, 202
Townsend
  Edward, 29
  James, 202
  Luther, 203
Tracy
  Daniel, 203
  George, 203
  Henry, 203
Trask
  Dexter, 203
Trass
  Harvey, 203
Trible
  Frederick, 203
Trifford
  Isiah, 203
Trimble
  John, 203
Tripp
  Robert, 203
Trost
  Andrew, 203
Truman
  Charles, 203
  Edwards, 203
Trumble
  Daniel, 204
  Frederick, 204
  John, 204
  Rueben, 203, 204
Trumpp
  Ernest, 34, 204
Tubbs
  James, 204
Tucker
  Almond, 204
  John, 204

Index

Tucker
  Leroy, 204
Tufford
  Isiah, 204
Turnbell
  Joseph, 204
Turnbridge
  John, 204
Turnbull
  Joseph, 204
Turner
  Henry, 204
  James, 204
  John, 34, 204, 205
  Levi, 205
Turney
  Addison, 205
Tuthill
  Charles, 205
Tutt
  William, 205
Tweed
  Samuel, 205
Tyndall
  Edward, 205

U

Umphrey
  Edwin, 133, 205

V

Valker
  John, 205
Vallance
  James, 205
Van Alstyne
  Frank, 205
Van Auker
  John, 205
Van Cortland
  James, 205

Van Cortlandt
  James, 51
Van Gelder
  John, 206
  Tobit, 206
Van Marter
  James, 54, 206
Van Rensaeler
  Frank, 206
Van Slyck
  David, 45, 206
Van Steenburgh
  William, 206
Van Vranken
  George, 206
Vandenberg
  Jans, 206
Vandermark
  Smith, 206
Varner
  Robert, 206
Vasser
  Mathew, 206
Vaughan
  Henry, 57, 207
Vibbori
  George, 34, 207
Vice
  George, 31
Vidwell
  George, 207
Vogt
  John, 207
Von Gyurkowitz
  Carlos, 207

W

Waddle
  Frank, 207
Wade
  Frederick, 207
  Iky, 36
  Isaac, 207

  William, 207
Waffles
  George, 207
Wagner
  Rant, 207
Wahl
  Franz, 207
Wailman
  Thomas, 207
Walker
  Charles, 208
  Ebenezer, 208
  George, 208
  Timothy, 208
  William, 32, 208
Wallace
  Caleb, 208
  Henry, 208
Walsh
  Luke, 208
  Michael, 208
Walter
  Audrey, 209
Walters
  George, 209
Walworth
  Walter, 209
Ward
  Henry, 209
  Israel, 31, 209
Warden
  William, 209
Wardwell
  Myron, 209
Warner
  Joshua, 209
  Stewart, 209
  William, 209, 210
Warren
  Alfred, 210
  George, 210

Index

William, 209, 210
Washburn
  George, 210
Wastens
  Endrer, 210
Waterman
  John, 210
Waters
  Edwin, 210
Watson
  Frederick, 210
  John, 210
  Thomas, 210
Watters
  Charles, 210
Weaver
  Caleb, 210
  Charles, 211
  Martin, 211
Webb
  Charles, 211
  Henry, 211
  Orson, 211
  Samuel, 211
  William, 211
Weber
  Henry, 211
  Martin, 211
Webster
  Hank, 36
  Henry, 32, 211
  Jerome, 211
Weeden
  James, 211
Weekes
  Frank, 211
Weeks
  James, 59, 212
Welch
  John, 212
  William, 212

Welchim
  Adam, 212
Well
  Henry, 212
Wellman
  Edward, 31, 212
  Frank, 212
  Thomas, 212
Wells
  Charles, 212
  Lyman, 212
  William, 16, 212
Wendenberger
  Frank, 212
Wenkilmann
  Henry, 212, 218
Wescott
  Decalyus, 34, 213
Weston
  George, 213
Wever
  Spencer, 213
Weyman
  Frederick, 213
Whalan
  John, 213
Whalen
  Larry, 213
  Peter, 213, 214
Wheaton
  Wellington, 213
Whedon
  Charles, 213
  Henry, 213
Wheeler
  Amos, 213
  Charles, 214
  George, 214
  Henry, 214
  Hubert, 214
  Ruden, 214

Wheelock
  Noel, 214
Whelan
  Peter, 213, 214
Whipple
  Emmett, 214
  Marvin, 214
White
  Alonzo, 214
  C. J., 214
  Cornelius, 214
  David, 215
  George, 34, 215
  Napoleon, 215
  Ossian, 215
  Peter, 215
  William, 215
Whitfield
  Eben, 56, 78, 215
Whiting
  William, 215
Whitman
  William, 215
Whitmore
  Alonzo, 215
  Ansel, 215
Whitney
  George, 216
  John, 216
Wicks
  Frank, 211, 216
Wightman
  Charles, 216
Wilber
  Horace, 216
Wilbert
  William, 216
Wilbur
  George, 216
Wilcox
  Eli, 216
  Henry, 216
  Siloam, 216

Index

Wilhelm
  Adam, 216
Wilkins
  Terrence, 216
Will
  Paul, 216
  Reinhold, 216
Willard
  G., 36
  George, 217
Willett
  John, 217
William
  Henry, 217
Williams
  A. J., 217
  Charles, 217
  George, 217
  Hanson, 217
  Henry, 128, 217
  Jim, 39
  John, 217
  Lorenzo, 217
  William, 217
Williamson
  Alanson, 217
  William, 218
Willis
  George, 218
Willitts
  Ingraham, 218
  Lotts, 218
Willmot
  Henry, 218
Willoughby
  Thomas, 218
Wilmington
  N.C., 141, 177
Wilson
  Conrad, 218
  Gen., 13, 16
  Henry, 218

James, 7, 9, 10, 222
John, 218
Winkleman
  H., 218
Winn
  James, 218
Winters
  Urnest, 218
Wise
  Sidney, 218
Wisner
  Oscar, 55, 167, 218
Wolff
  John, 219
Wood
  Edgar, 219
  George, 219
  Henry, 219
  John, 219
Woodard
  George, 219
Wooden
  William, 219
Wooderson
  Charles, 219
Woodruff
  Samuel, 219
Woodward
  George, 53, 219
Woolfer
  William, 219
Worden
  Vernon, 219
  William, 219
Worth
  John, 220
Wrenn
  John, 46, 219
Wright
  Adelbert, 220
  Gen., 13

George, 220
Henry, 220
John, 220
Silas, 220
Walter, 220
Wurth
  John, 220
Wygant
  William, 220

Y

Yachunson
  Flitz, 221
Yager
  Eugene, 220
Yates
  Squire, 31, 56, 69, 117, 220
Yaw
  Elijah, 221
Yeager
  Reuben, 135
  Rueben, 221
Yendal
  Edward, 202
Yendall
  Edward, 221
York
  Fayette, 32, 221
Young
  Benjamin, 221
  Christopher, 221
  Col., 13
  Robert, 221
  William, 221
Youngs
  George, 221
  Joseph, 221

Z

Zacher
  Victor, 221

Index

Zacker
 Victor, 221
Zepfel
 Robert, 221
Ziffle
 Robert, 221

www.ingramcontent.com/pod-product-compliance
Lightning Source LLC
Chambersburg PA
CBHW050134170426
43197CB00011B/1834